ANTIAIRCRAFT
ARTILLERY
ACTIVITIES
IN THE
PACIFIC
WAR

Published by Books Express Publishing
Copyright © Books Express, 2011
ISBN 978-1-78039-900-3

Books Express publications are available from all good retail and online booksellers. For publishing proposals and direct ordering please contact us at: info@books-express.com

GENERAL HEADQUARTERS
UNITED STATES ARMY FORCES, PACIFIC
APO 500

DISTRIBUTION LIST

"Antiaircraft Artillery Activities
in the Pacific War"

The Adjutant General, War Dept	2
Director of Personnel and Administration, WDGS	2
Director of Intelligence, WDGS	2
Director of Organization and Training, WDGS	2
Director of Service, Supply and Procurement, WDGS	2
Director of Plans and Operations, WDGS	5
Director of Research and Development, WDGS	2
Public Relations Division, WDSS	2
National Guard Bureau, WDSS	2
Executive for Reserve and ROTC Affairs, WDSS	2
Historical Division, WDSS	2
C of Ordnance	2
C of Engineers	2
C Signal O	2
Hq AGF	10
Hq AAF	10
Special Asst for AA, Office CG, AAF	20*
C of Naval Opns	5
Comdt USMC	5
USMA	5
USNA	5
National War College	5
Naval War College	5
Industrial College	5
Armed Forces Staff College	5
Command and Staff College	5
AAA & Guided Missiles Branch, Arty School	25
Seacoast Branch, Arty School	5
Field Arty Branch, Arty School	2
Inf School	2
Armd School	2
AGF Board No. 4	5
Coast Arty Board	2
Coast Arty Association	1
CINCPAC	5
CINCAL	5

*For distribution to Air Force units and agencies not otherwise listed.

Caribbean Defense Command	5
Panama Coast Arty Command	3
Hq PHILRYCOM	5
Hq Philippine Ground Force Command	2
32d AAA Brigade	1
42d AAA Brigade (PS)	1
70th AAA Group	1
512th AAA Gun Bn (PS)	1
536th AAA Gun Bn (PS)	1
81st AAA Group (PS)	1
94th AAA Group	1
539th AAA AW Bn (PS)	1
544th AAA AW Bn (PS)	1
570th AAA AW Bn (PS)	1
54th AAA SL Btry (PS)	1
47th AAA Opns Det (PS)	1
Hq Okinawa Base Command	2
136th AAA Group	1
87th AAA Group (PS)	1
63rd AAA Gun Bn	1
532d AAA Gun Bn (PS)	1
586th AAA AW Bn	1
511th AAA AW Bn (PS)	1
Btry A, 541 AAA SL Bn (PS)	1
46th AAA Opns Det (PS)	1
70th AAA Gun Bn	1
743rd AAA Gun Bn	1
Hq AGFPAC	5
Hawaiian Arty Command	3
Hq Eighth Army	5
138th AAA Group	1
753rd AAA Gun Bn	1
209th AAA AW Bn	1
933rd AAA AW Bn	1
162d AAA Opns Det	1
538th AAA SL Btry	1
11th A/B Div (152d AAA Bn)	1
Hq MARBO	5
69th AAA Group	1
864th AAA AW Bn	1
752d AAA Gun Bn	1
725th AAA SL Btry	1
163rd AAA Opns Det	1
Hq USAFIK	2
865th AAA AW Bn	1
Hq FEAF	2
Air Defense O, A-3	1
5th AF	1
1st Air Div	1
13th AF	1
20th AF	1
CO, HD Puget Sound	1
CO, HD Columbia	1

CO, HD SF	1
CO, HD LA	1
CO, HD S Diego	1
CO, HD Delaware	1
CO, HD Charleston	1
CO, HD Portsmouth	1
CO, HD New York	1
CO, HD Galveston	1
CO, HD Pensacola	1
CO, HD Key West	1
CO, HD Chesapeake Bay	1
CO, HD Narragansett Bay & New Bedford	1
CO, HD Boston	1
CO, HD LI Sound	1
CO, HD Portland	1
GHQ, FEC and SCAP	
CG, BCOF	1
G-1	1
G-2	1
G-3	1
G-4	1
Chief Eng	1
ESS	1
Chief Ord O	1
Chief Sig O	1
5250 Tech Intell Co	1
COMNAVFE	1
SCAJAP	1
AA Section	80

PREFACE

    This report has been compiled under the supervision of the Antiaircraft Officer, General Headquarters, United States Army Forces, Pacific. Such portions of the text as deal with operations taking place under command of General Douglas MacArthur have been reviewed by the Historical Section, G-3, General Headquarters, United States Army Forces, Pacific. Authority for publication: 1st Indorsement, Historical Division, WDSS, dated 18 October 1946, on letter, General Headquarters, United States Army Forces, Pacific, file AG 314.7 (24 Sep 46)AA, dated 24 September 1946, subject, "Report of Antiaircraft Artillery Activities in the Pacific War."

    All dates pertaining to local events are Eastern Hemisphere dates.

ANTIAIRCRAFT ARTILLERY ACTIVITIES IN THE PACIFIC

			Paragraphs	Pages
Chapter 1.	General		1	1-4
Chapter 2.	Operations			
Section	I	General	2	5-8
Section	II	Philippine Defense	3-6	9-16
		General	3	9
		Luzon	4	10
		Bataan	5	14
		Corregidor	6	14
Section	III	Central Pacific	7-10	17-20
		General	7	17
		Baker Island	8	19
		Makin	9	19
		Apamama	10	20
Section	IV	East Indies Campaign	11-15	21-27
		General	11	21
		Organization	12	24
		Darwin	13	24
		Townsville and Cape York	14	25
		Port Moresby	15	26
Section	V	Papuan Campaign	16-24	28-37
		General	16	28
		AAA Units and Organization	17	31
		Townsville	18	32
		Northern Queensland	19	33

TABLE OF CONTENTS (Continued)

Section			Paragraphs	Pages
Section	V	(Continued)		
		Darwin	20	33
		Port Moresby	21	34
		Milne Bay	22	35
		Merauke	23	36
		Buna	24	36
Section	VI	Guadalcanal Campaign	25-30	38-43
		General	25	38
		New Caledonia	26	38
		Society Islands	27	40
		Fiji Islands	28	40
		Guadalcanal	29	40
		New Hebrides	30	41
Section	VII	New Guinea Campaign	31-55	44-73
		General	31	44
		Organization of AA	32	48
		Port Moresby	33	52
		Milne Bay	34	52
		Oro Bay	35	53
		Dobodura	36	55
		Goodenough Island	37	56
		Kiriwina	38	57
		Woodlark	39	57
		Morobe, Nassau and Tambu Bay	40	58
		Bulolo, Wau and Tsili Tsili	41	58
		Bena Bena	42	59
		Nadzab	43	59
		Lae	44	60
		Kaiapit	45	60
		Gusap	46	60
		Finschhafen	47	61
		Saidor	48	62
		Hollandia	49	63
		Aitape	50	64
		Wakde Island	51	64
		Biak	52	65
		Noemfoor	53	68
		Sansapor	54	69
		Morotai	55	70
Section	VIII	Northern Solomons Campaign	56-60	74-77
		General	56	74
		Russell Islands	57	76
		New Georgia Group	58	76
		Treasury Islands	59	77
		Bougainville	60	77

TABLE OF CONTENTS (Continued)

			Paragraphs	Pages
Section	IX	Eastern Mandates Campaign	61-63	78-81
		General	61	78
		Kwajalein	62	80
		Eniwetok and Engebi	63	80
Section	X	Bismarck Archipelago Campaign	64-69	82-88
		General	64	82
		Arawe	65	85
		Cape Gloucester	66	86
		Admiralty Islands	67	86
		Green Island	68	88
		Emirau Island	69	88
Section	XI	Western Pacific Campaign	70-76	89-95
		General	70	89
		Saipan	71	89
		Guam	72	93
		Tinian	73	93
		Palau Group	74	93
		Ulithi	75	94
		Iwo Jima	76	94
Section	XII	Southern Philippines Campaign	77-84	96-106
		General	77	96
		Leyte - Samar	78	100
		Mindoro	79	104
		Palawan	80	105
		Zamboanga	81	105
		Panay	82	105
		Cebu - Negros	83	105
		Cotabato	84	106
Section	XIII	Luzon Campaign	85-90	107-114
		General	85	107
		Lingayen Landing	86	107
		Lingayen to Manila	87	110
		Subic Bay, Corregidor and Nasugbu	88	111
		Advance on Manila	89	112
		Later Activities	90	112
Section	XIV	Ryukyus Campaign	91-99	115-128
		General	91	115
		Organization	92	117
		Initial Phase	93	119
		Corps Control	94	121
		Army Control	95	122
		Ie Shima	96	124
		Kerama Retto	97	126
		Aguni, Iheya, Kume and Hedo Misaki	98	126
		Summary of AA Action	99	126

TABLE OF CONTENTS (Continued)

			Paragraphs	Pages
Section	XV	AAA Intelligence	100-108	129-136
		General	100	129
		AAOR	101	129
		Joint Operations	102	131
		Fire Direction	103	131
		New Guinea	104	132
		Middle Pacific	105	133
		Leyte	106	134
		Luzon	107	134
		Ryukyus	108	135
Chapter 3.		AAA in Other Roles		
Section	I	General	109	137-138
Section	II	Terrestrial Fire	110-111	139-148
		Automatic Weapons	110	139
		Guns	111	143
Section	III	Off-Shore Defenses	112-113	149-151
		General	112	149
		Morotai	113	149
Section	IV	Infantry Action	114-120	152-154
		General	114	152
		Bougainville	115	152
		Wakde	116	152
		Cebu	117	152
		Mindanao	118	153
		Luzon	119	154
		Okinawa	120	154
Section	V	Special Searchlight Operations	121-124	155-157
		Battlefield Illumination	121	155
		Cooperation with the Air Force	122	156
		Shore Illumination from Surface Craft	123	156
		Illumination for Construction	124	157
Section	VI	Non-Combat Functions	125-129	158-162
		General	125	158
		Dock Details	126	158
		Military Police	127	158
		Other Service Functions	128	158
		Manus Island	129	160
Chapter 4.		Administration, Training and Supply		
Section	I	General	130	163-165
Section	II	Organization	131-134	166-171
		General	131	166
		Pacific Ocean Area	132	166
		South Pacific Area	133	167
		Southwest Pacific Area	134	168

TABLE OF CONTENTS (Continued)

			Paragraphs	Pages
Section	III	Training	135-137	172-179
		General	135	172
		Training Prior to 15 Nov 1943	136	172
		Training Subsequent to 15 Nov 1943	137	176
Section	IV	Supply	138-141	180-192
		General	138	180
		Pacific Ocean Area	139	180
		South Pacific Area	140	183
		Southwest Pacific Area	141	183
Chapter 5.	Research and Development			
Section	I	General	142	193-195
Section	II	Air Transportation of AAA	143-145	196-199
		Automatic Weapons	143	196
		Guns	144	198
		Searchlights	145	198
Section	III	Flakintel	146	200-202
Section	IV	Searchlight-Fighter Team	147-149	203-205
		General	147	203
		Guadalcanal	148	203
		Morotai	149	203
Section	V	Evasive Action Studies	150	206-207
Section	VI	Ground Target Location and Survey by Gun Radar-Liaison Plane Team	151	208-211
Section	VII	Moving Target Indicator	152	212
Section	VIII	Radar Mortar Locator	153	213-214
Chapter 6.	Statistical Summaries			
Section	I	Operations	154-161	215-250
		General	154	215
		Effect of AAA Fire on Planes Engaged	155	215
		AAA Action by Campaigns	156	217
		AAA Action by Units	157	220
		Relative Standing from Combat Records of AAA Units	158	235
		Ammunition Expenditures	159	237
		Altitude of Attacks	160	241
		Terrestrial Fire	161	248
Section	II	Personnel	162-165	251-264
		General	162	251
		Personnel Strength	163	252
		Units by Type in the Pacific	164	256
		AAA Casualties in the Pacific	165	260

TABLE OF CONTENTS (Continued)

		Paragraphs	Pages
Bibliography and Annexes			265-313
Bibliography			265
Annex A	Reorganization and Redesignation of AAA Units		269
Annex B	Unit Commendations and Citations		283
Annex C	Geographical Station List of AAA Units in the Pacific 7 Dec 1941 - 15 Aug 1945		289
Annex D	AAA Units Entitled to Bronze Arrowhead Award for Assault Wave Landing Operations		311

LIST OF CHARTS OF AAA ACTION

			Page
Fig	1.	Results of Antiaircraft Fire in the Pacific	2
	2.	Philippine Defense	12
	3.	Philippine Defense (Continued)	13
	4.	Makin Atoll	20
	5.	East Indies Campaign	23
	6.	Darwin (E.I.)	25
	7.	Moresby (E.I.)	27
	8.	Papuan Campaign	30
	9.	Darwin (P.C.)	34
	10.	Port Moresby (P.C.)	35
	11.	Milne Bay (P.C.)	36
	12.	Guadalcanal Campaign	43
	13.	New Guinea Campaign	46
	14.	New Guinea Campaign (Continued)	47
	15.	Oro Bay	54
	16.	Dobadura	56
	17.	Kiriwina	57
	18.	Nadzab	59
	19.	Saidor	62
	20.	Wakde	65
	21.	Biak	67
	22.	Noemfor	68
	23.	Sansapor	70
	24.	Morotai	72
	25.	Bismarck Archipelago Campaign	84
	26.	Arawe	85
	27.	Western Pacific Campaign	91
	28.	Saipan	92
	29.	Southern Philippines Campaign	98
	30.	Leyte	101
	31.	Mindoro	104
	32.	Luzon	114
	33.	Ryukyus Campaign	120
	34.	Ie Shima	125
	35.	Okinawa	127

LIST OF MAPS

			Page
Map	1	Philippine Defense	11
	2	Bataan and Manila Bay	15
	3	Central Pacific	18
	4	East Indies	22
	5	Papuan Campaign	29
	6	Guadalcanal	39
	7	New Guinea Campaign	45
	8	New Guinea	50
	9	Eastern New Guinea	51
	10	Northern Solomons	75
	11	Eastern Mandates	79
	12	Bismarck Archipelago	83
	13	Western Pacific	90
	14	Southern Philippines	97
	15	Luzon	108
	16	Ryukyus	116
	17	Nansei Shoto	118

CHAPTER 1

GENERAL

1. **General.** a. This report of antiaircraft artillery activity in the Pacific is a summary of the participation of United States Army antiaircraft artillery in the campaigns of the Pacific theater, exclusive of Alaska and the China - Burma - India areas. The factual information has been prepared from the official records, or where these were lacking, from information obtained from accredited sources.

b. United States antiaircraft units were in active combat from the hour of the attack on Pearl Harbor on the morning of 7 Dec 1941 until the surrender of the Japanese in Aug 1945. The first warning of the approach of the enemy planes at Pearl Harbor was given by the personnel of a Signal Corps air warning radar. The first combat engagement with the enemy was made by antiaircraft elements. On the other end of the long struggle antiaircraft artillerymen on Ie Shima shot down the last attacking planes on 6 Aug, while other antiaircraft units were engaged in the support of the infantry in the mountains of northern Luzon where they continued to round up the enemy until the end of Sept 1945.

c. Because the enemy's first and most far reaching wave of attack was his air force, antiaircraft units were the principal ground force components of the earliest convoys to Australia and the South Pacific islands. In the nearly four years of the war, the antiaircraft artillery in the Pacific grew from two regiments stationed in Hawaii and two in the Philippine Islands to a force of over 90,000 officers and men scattered through the many locations where American troops were engaging

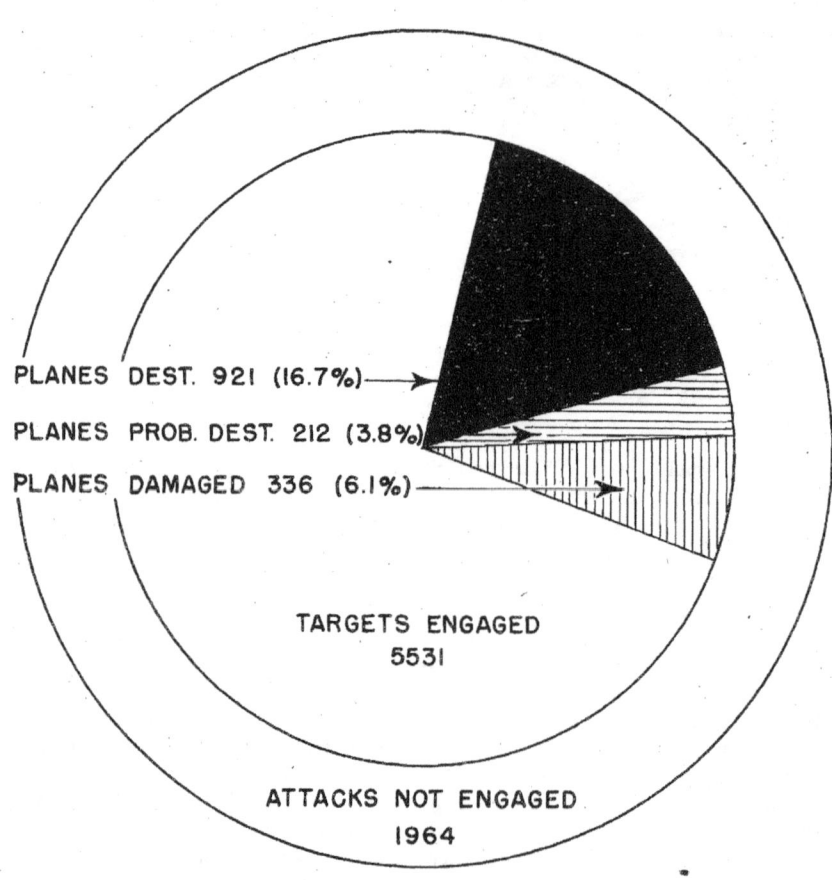

Fig. 1

the enemy or protecting harbors and beaches, supply points and airfields. Out of 7495 enemy aircraft attacking positions defended by American antiaircraft artillery during the war in the Pacific, 5531 were engaged by our guns, and 1469 (27%) were destroyed, damaged or probably destroyed by antiaircraft fire. Even more vital was the protection afforded American airfields, and supply bases and ground troops by the antiaircraft artillery in turning away enemy raiders or in keeping them at altitudes from which their bombs could do little or no damage. In addition to carrying out their primary mission, antiaircraft troops supported infantry and performed all manner of service functions.

2. OPERATIONS

SECTION	I	General
SECTION	II	Philippine Defense Campaign
SECTION	III	Central Pacific Campaign
SECTION	IV	East Indies Campaign
SECTION	V	Papuan Campaign
SECTION	VI	Guadalcanal Campaign
SECTION	VII	New Guinea Campaign
SECTION	VIII	Northern Solomons Campaign
SECTION	IX	Eastern Mandates Campaign
SECTION	X	Bismarck Archipelago Campaign
SECTION	XI	Western Pacific Campaign
SECTION	XII	Southern Philippines Campaign
SECTION	XIII	Luzon Campaign
SECTION	XIV	Ryukyus Campaign
SECTION	XV	AAA Intelligence

Section I

General

2. **General.** a. The employment of antiaircraft artillery in the war against the Japanese followed the conventional pattern laid down in our military texts. In its primary role, antiaircraft artillery is essentially a defensive weapon and the quantity required tends to be inversely proportional to the potency of the friendly air force. In the opening stages of a campaign when the opposing air forces are equal, or when the enemy is superior, the strength of friendly antiaircraft must be at a high level. As the friendly air force gains superiority the need for antiaircraft artillery becomes progressively less except for the early phases of each offensive. The charts in Chapter 2 illustrate this trend as it was experienced in the various operations.

b. The tactics of the hostile air force affect the disposition of the available antiaircraft artillery. The Japanese Air Forces generally did not employ the massed attack by large numbers of planes against point objectives that is so much a part of the tactics of the American Air Forces. Area bombing by relatively few planes was the general procedure except when the enemy was attacking areas he hoped to seize. Often the attacks seemed to be made without a definite prearranged plan, and high explosive, fragmentation, and phosphorous bombs were used indiscriminately.

c. Hostile air operations against ground targets prior to 1944 may be classed as area bombing, precision bombing, glide bombing, swing bombing, and strafing. Area bombing was normally employed against defended installations. The average Japanese aviator showed a healthy respect for antiaircraft artillery and when brought under fire usually took immediate and violent evasive action. In some cases warning that they were under radar surveillance, by firing of alert guns, served to prevent their entering the defended area. Precision bombing usually was employed against undefended objectives only and normally from an altitude of six to eight thousand feet. In swing bombing the Japanese pilot approached until just within range of the antiaircraft artillery and then banked sharply, at the same time releasing his bombs. Centrifugal force was relied on to yield the extra push needed to land the bombs in the target area. This method naturally was very inaccurate.

d. There were several standard methods of approach used by the Japanese:

   (1) Seven or eight planes orbited outside the defended areas, then split into separate flights and approached at spaced intervals. The leading plane often dropped "window" to screen following planes. One variation was for planes to approach from several directions simultaneously. In the

very early stages of the war successive waves of nine bombers each often were used.

    (2) Planes worked in pairs. One acted as a decoy and circled outside the area with running lights on. At the same time the other plane made a low altitude attack. A variation was to coordinate strafing at tree top height with a high altitude attack.

    (3) In low altitude sneak raids planes attempted to come in at such altitudes over the water or natural obstructions that radar pick-up was improbable. A variation occasionally used was to approach at very low altitudes until within 10 to 15 miles, then climb rapidly to 15,000 to 20,000 feet and attack from a steep glide. This obviously required a lightly loaded high performance aircraft.

    (4) Single planes joined a friendly flight and approached with running lights on.

    (5) Aircraft approached at high altitude, and dived and took other evasive action when engaged by antiaircraft artillery.

    (6) Pathfinder planes dropped "window" and then flares to mark the target.

    e. The violent evasive action tactics and disregard of conventional precision bombing procedures made it necessary to increase the gun density to secure sufficient volume of fire to counteract these tactics. In one case, eight batteries of 90-mm guns were emplaced on a 14,000 yard line along an approach to a vital airfield.

    f. In the fall of 1944, at Leyte, the Japanese introduced their large scale suicide attacks by the so-called Kamikaze Corps. Single planes attempted to crash-dive large ships, and in some cases, vessels as small as PT boats and even bombers. In addition to the planned Kamikaze attacks, many crippled Japanese planes attempted to crash-dive some target within reach. A modification of these suicide tactics was the use of the Baka bomb, a rocket-assisted suicide glider launched from a parent plane and having high speed but limited range and maneuverability.

    g. The types of attack varied with the defenses encountered, and shifts were usually made quickly when a weak spot in the defense was found; however, at times the enemy continued to use a previously undefended avenue of approach even after heavy antiaircraft defenses had been installed. This occurred early in the Leyte campaign when an all-around defense of the Tacloban airstrip was not installed initially because of swampy ground. The Japanese discovered the weakness almost immediately and thereafter approached from that direction. Within a few days emplacements were constructed and guns installed to fill the gap in the defense. The enemy, however, persisted in using this route for several more days although he sustained very heavy losses.

    h. Other than the suicide or Kamikaze tactics, the Japanese methods of attack against ground targets remained unchanged throughout the war. The times of attack changed, however, from many daylight raids at the start of the war to almost 100 percent night raids at the close. The favorite times were between 2100 to 2300 or 0200 to 0400, and attacks occurred most often on moonlight nights.

    i. Throughout the war the possession of adequate airfields was vital to our success. Landing strips therefore were a primary defense objective and, except in the first part of 1942, received top priority for allotment of available antiaircraft artillery. As the Allied powers assumed the offensive, supply dumps, rear area installations and shipping were profitable targets for small scale raids. Beachheads required heavy concentrations of antiaircraft artillery as did the new airfields that constantly were being established.

    j. The part played by antiaircraft artillery in countering the Japanese Air Force in the Pacific War is discussed in detail, by campaigns, in the following sections.

II. PHILIPPINE Defense

3. **General.** a. The Philippine Defense Campaign began on 8 Dec 1941 and was officially closed on 6 May 1942.

b. At the outbreak of the war the antiaircraft defenses of the Philippines consisted of the following:[1]

```
Clark Field - 200th CA (AA)
Corregidor - 60th CA (AA) less units on Bataan
Bataan - Btry G, 60th CA (AA), 3" guns
       - Btry H, 60th CA (AA), 3" guns
       - Det, Btry E, 60th CA (AA), two searchlights
Manila - Btry M, 60th CA (AA), machine guns
Fort Hughes - Btry I, 59th CA (HD), 3" guns
Fort Drum - Btry E, 59th CA (HD), two fixed 3" guns
Fort Wint - Btry C, 91st CA (HD) (PS), 3" guns
Fort Frank - Btry E, 91st CA (HD) (PS), 3" guns
Cavite - Navy, nine 3" guns
```

c. The gun batteries of both antiaircraft regiments were armed with 3-inch materiel. The automatic weapons batteries were generally equipped with twelve cal .50 antiaircraft machine guns each, except in the 200th Regiment, which had three batteries with eight 37 mm and eight machine guns.

d. Although there were 50,000 rounds of 3-inch with powder train fuze, there were only 1,600 rounds of the mechanical fuzed 3-inch which

---

[1] Memorandum to Assistant Chief of Staff, G-1, USAFFE, from CG, Philippine Coast Defense Command. 8 Sept 1941

was needed for high altitude accuracy. For automatic weapons, 36,000 rounds of 37-mm and an unlimited amount of Cal .50 ammunition were available.

4. Luzon. a. The Japanese opened their campaign to capture the Philippines with the bombing of the city of Baguio, in northern Luzon, shortly before 0900 on 8 Dec 1941 (2000 7 Dec, Eastern Standard Time). At 1230 about eighty planes struck Fort Stotsenburg, adjacent to Clark Field, in a raid that lasted 14 minutes. Nielson Field at Manila and the fighter base at Iba were attacked at the same time. Our plane losses were heavy and irreplaceable and serious damage was done to the buildings, hangars and other installations. Naval installations at Davao, Mindanao, also were hit on the 8th.

b. Five hundred officers and men from the 200th Regiment were sent to Manila on the night of 8 Dec to organize an antiaircraft regiment for the defense of the city. This regiment was designated the 515th CA (AA). Thirty-six hours after they arrived in Manila the new organization had:

    (1) Been brought to a strength of 1000 officers and men, using Philippine Army reservists.
    (2) Uncrated, assembled, and serviced from materiel available at the Philippine Ordnance Depot, equipment for three 3-inch gun batteries, one searchlight battery, and three 37-mm gun batteries.
    (3) Emplaced the gun batteries at Paranaque, Paco, and Nielson Airport, and one 37-mm battery each at Nichols Field, Nielson Airport, and the Intramuros.
    (4) Fired at enemy planes.

Although the fire was erratic it was sufficient to keep the bombers at altitudes in excess of 20,000 feet.

c. Japanese army units landed at Aparri in northern Luzon on 10 Dec. That date saw a succession of disasters for the Allies in the Pacific. Cavite Naval Yard, near Manila, was bombed into uselessness by more than 50 twin-engined bombers that leisurely dropped their bombs from altitudes beyond the range of the navy guns that provided the antiaircraft defense of the base.

d. On 12 Dec the Japanese landed on southern Luzon, and on the 20th a landing was made on Mindanao. On 22 Dec a force of 80 transports entered Lingayen Gulf, forced a landing at Agoo, and the troops that streamed ashore soon were joined by the column from Aparri.

e. The 200th CA (AA), weakened by the cadre taken for the 515th CA (AA), remained at Clark Field from 8 to 24 Dec and was then ordered

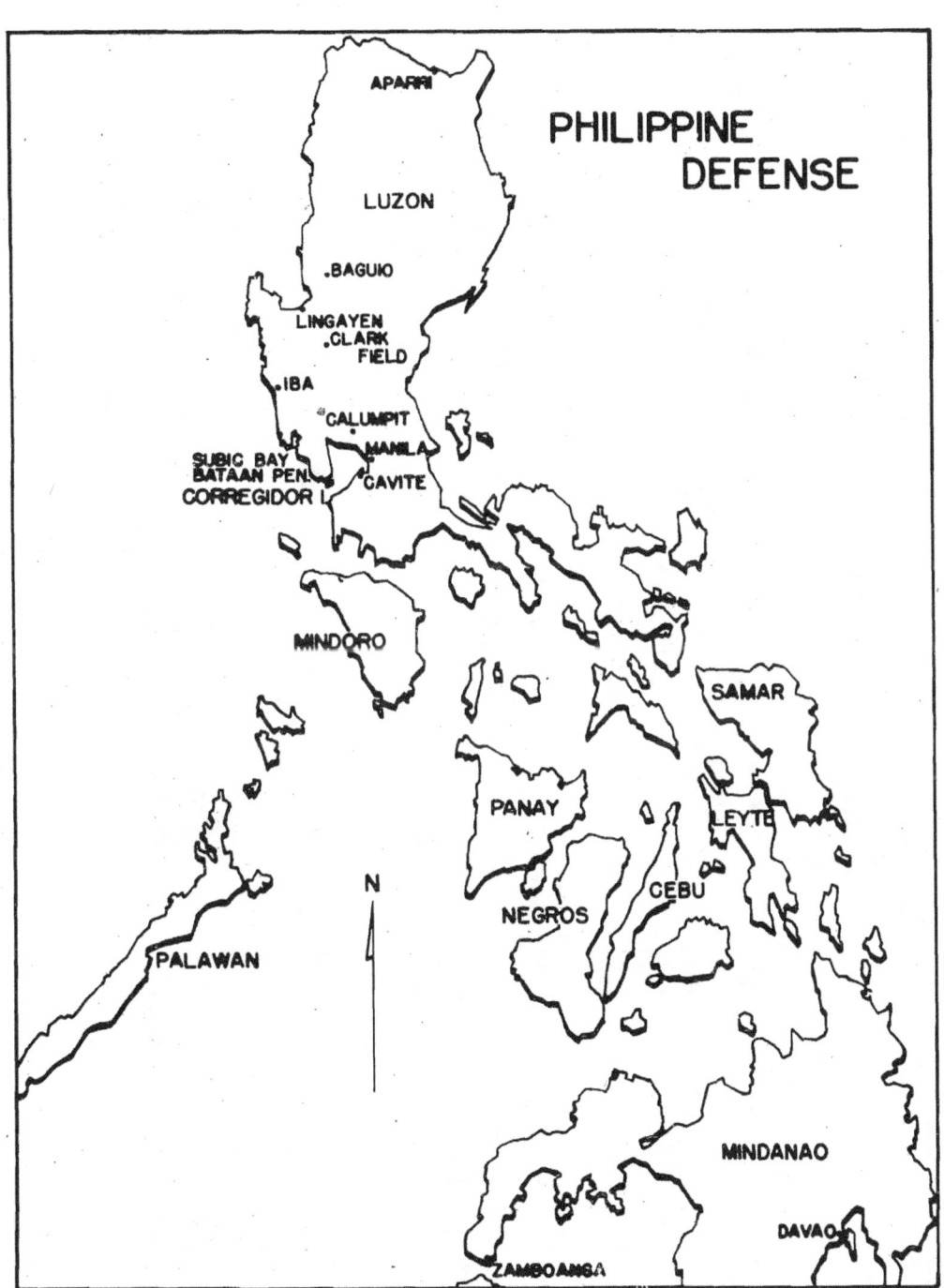

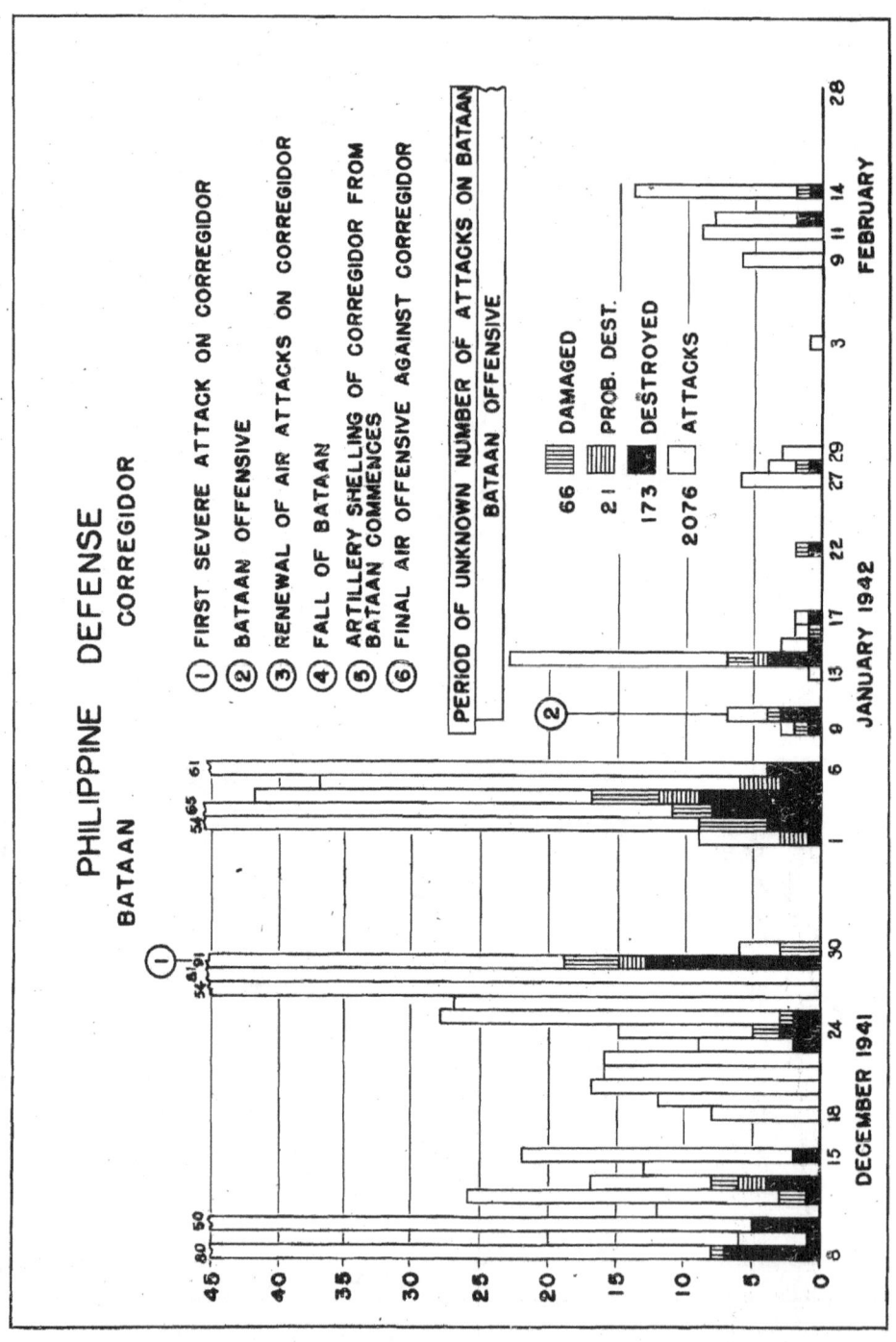

Fig. 2

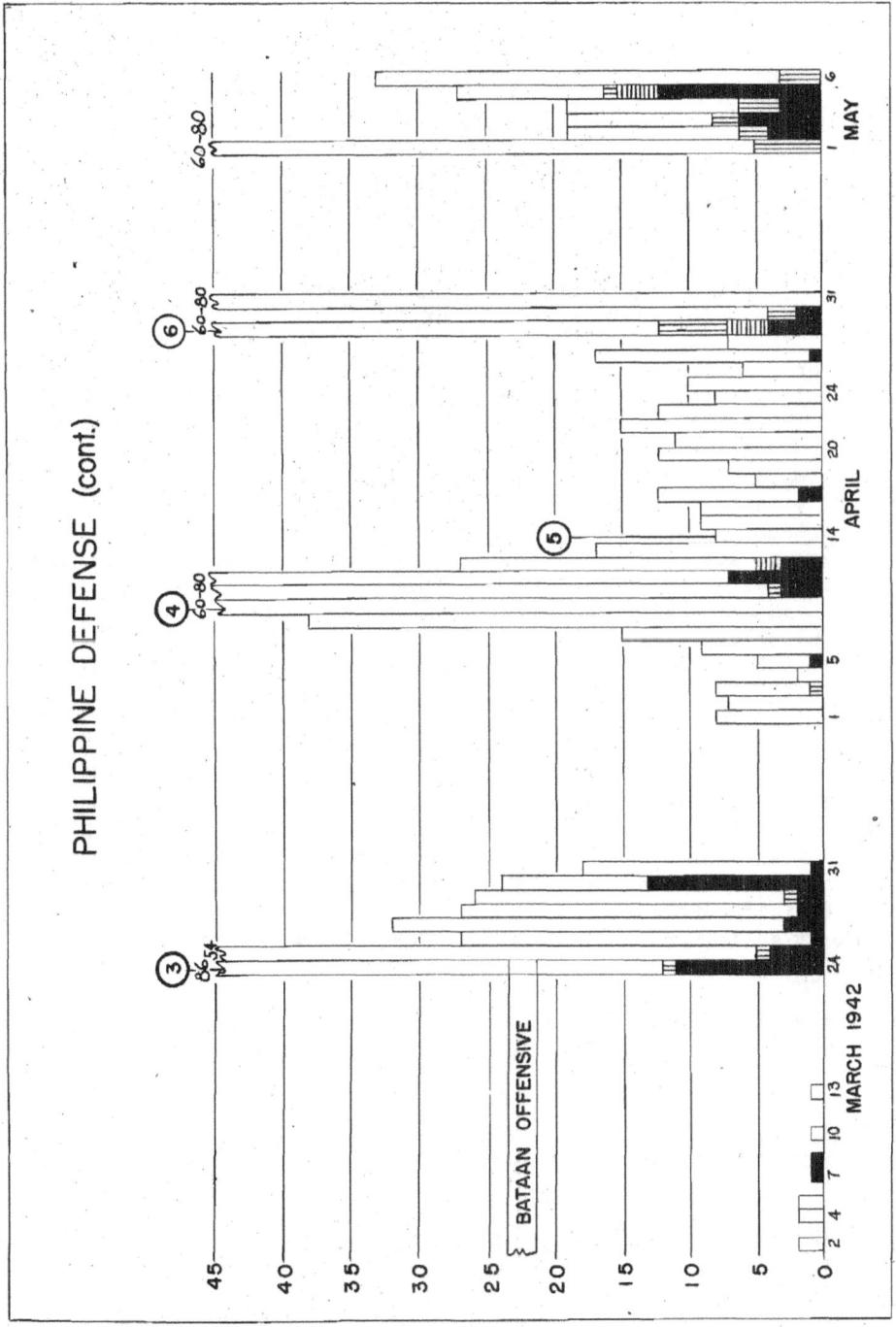

Fig. 3

to provide antiaircraft protection at Lyae Junction for the movement of troops from southern Luzon to Bataan. Manila had been declared an open city on 26 Dec.[1] The newly formed 515th CA (AA) moved at the same time to the Calumpit Bridge area where it remained until 26 Dec, guarding the vital passage through the marsh area for the forces withdrawing to Bataan. On 27 Dec two gun batteries of the 200th CA (AA) were ordered to the Calumpit Bridge area where they remained until 31 Dec.

5. <u>Bataan</u>. At the same time the 515th CA (AA) moved to the defense of the airfield near Pilar on Bataan, and subsequently shifted to augment the Cabcaben Field Defenses. On 2 Jan General MacArthur's forces completed the withdrawal to Bataan. On the night of 4 and 5 Jan the 200th CA (AA) moved to Bataan Field and set up defenses. On 1 Feb one 37-mm battery was assigned to Sisyan Point on the west coast of Bataan. Finally, on 8 to 9 Apr, the remnants of the two regiments formed an infantry defense line on the ridges south of Cabacaben Field where they were still holding firm when, on 9 Apr, the forces on Bataan reached the limit of their endurance and surrendered.[2]

6. <u>Corregidor</u>. a. On 29 Dec Corregidor received its first severe bombing, and attacks thereafter were received daily until 7 Jan. Fifty-four twin-engined bombers and an unknown number of fighters were used in the initial attack. Although the bombers flew at between 18,000 and 23,000 feet, 15 were destroyed. Ten were downed on the second day and the attackers suffered similar heavy daily losses until only eight came over on the ninth day of bombing. Yet there was no change in the altitude or method of attack until the last day when the eight planes attacked at different altitudes and from several directions instead of in the V-formation at constant altitude previously used.

b. Air activity from 8 Jan to 23 Mar was limited to occasional dive-bombing of outlying forts and shipping. No attempts were made to bomb Corregidor. During this period efforts were made to use the 12-inch mortar as an antiaircraft gun by computing data for several points within the critical zone and modifying 670-pound anti-personnel shells to take an antiaircraft fuze. Unfortunately, neither the powder train, the mechanical antiaircraft fuze, or the 155-mm shrapnel fuze would cause the 12-inch shell to burst.

c. The main effort of the enemy during the period 24 Mar to 9 Apr was in the air, with the attacking planes flying at altitudes of 27,000

---

[1] <u>Report of Performance of Coast Artillery Personnel and Equipment in the Philippine Campaign</u> -- General MacArthur -- AG 384.7, 27 May 1942 Par 32, P. 2.

[2] All antiaircraft units in the Philippine Defense Campaign received the Presidential Unit Citation with two oak leaf clusters in accordance with WD General Order Numbers 14, 21, and 22, 1942.

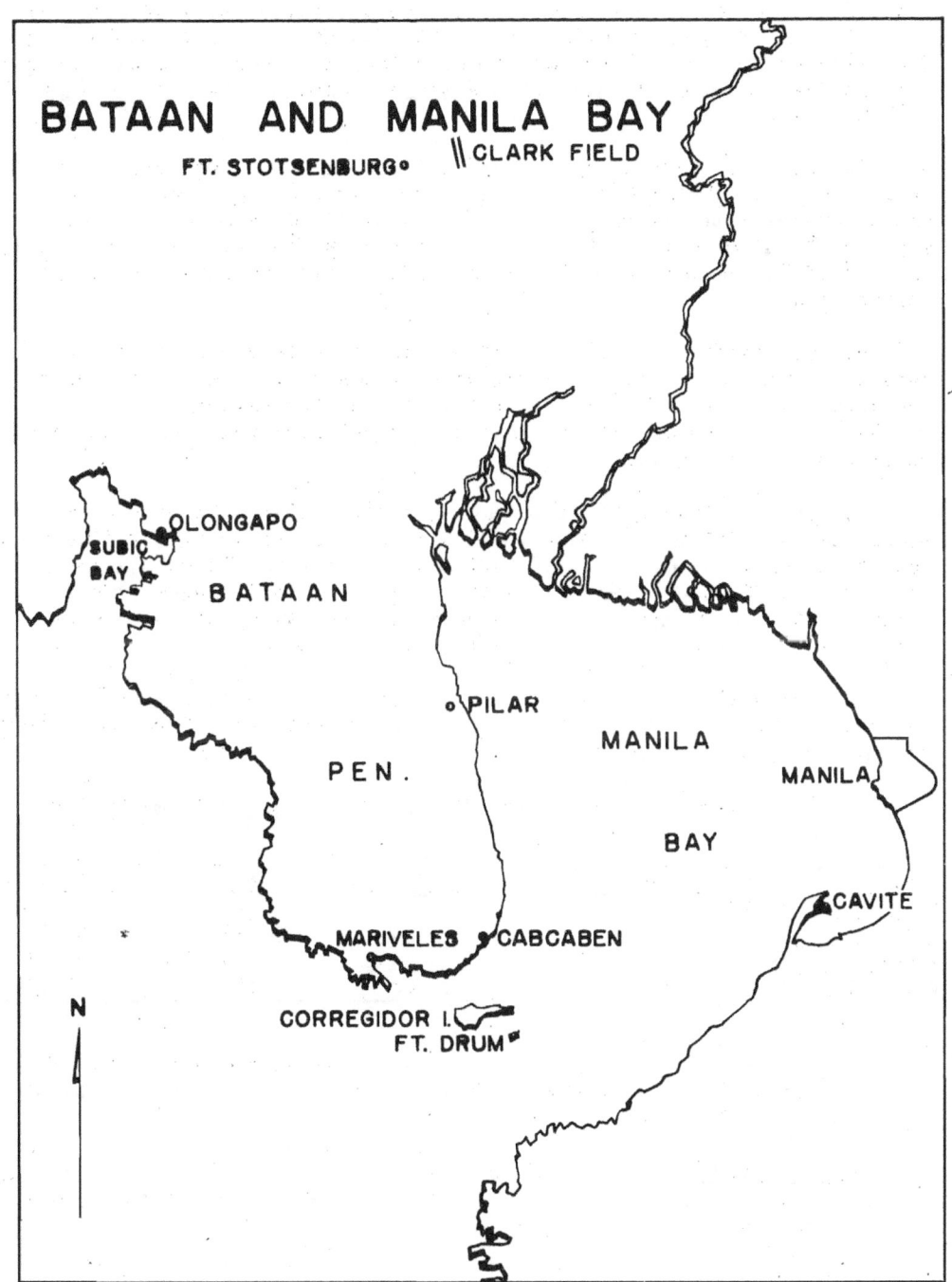

to 31,000 feet. The first night raid on Corregidor occurred on 24 Mar and there were 24 such raids during the next week, usually by only one to three planes. The bombing was very inaccurate and most of the bombs fell into the water. Returning to day raids on 29 Mar the enemy changed his tactics and came over in flights of three to six planes, still at very high altitudes.

d. Although some mechanical time fuzes had been received by submarine late in Feb there were still only enough to supply two antiaircraft batteries, and they were limited to 24 rounds expenditure per engagement. Powder train fuzes were useless at the very high altitudes, and 30% of the powder train fuzed ammunition that was fired developed malfunctions.

e. The remaining personnel of the three antiaircraft batteries sent to Bataan just before the war were evacuated to Corregidor before the surrender. Most of the materiel of one 3-inch battery was also evacuated.[1] The personnel manned the salvaged equipment and some seacoast guns on Corregidor.

f. After Bataan fell the attacks on Corregidor reached such a tempo that the "all clear" was seldom heard, and the artillery fire from Bataan and Cavite was soon intensified until on 4 May it was estimated that over 16,000 shells landed on the island within 24 hours. The effect of this bombardment was tremendous. One day's shelling is reported as doing more damage than all of the bombings.[2]

g. Corregidor capitulated on 6 May 1942 and the surrender of General Wainwright to General Homma brough a temporary end to organized resistance in the Philippines.

h. The following is a record of ammunition expenditures during the period 8 Dec 1941 to 11 Mar 1942:

Type Ammo	By: Harbor Defenses	200th CA	515th CA	Total
3-inch	6658	3824	3098	13580
37-mm	0	5236	7773	13009
Cal .50	19217	21863	2052	43132

[1] Conduct of Operations - 8 Dec 1941-6 May 1942 - The Antiaircraft Defense Command - Harbor Defenses of Manila Bay - Major General George F. Moore.

[2] AA in the Philippines 20 Sept 1943 Lt. Col. S.M. Mellnik File No. 314.7 Military Intelligence Division WOGS, Special Report Philippine Islands, P.6.

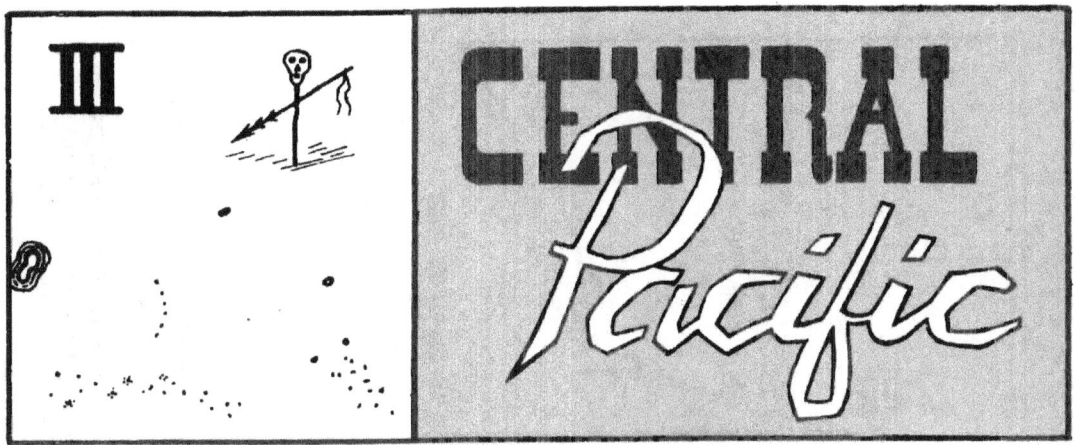

III. CENTRAL Pacific

7. **General.** a. The Central Pacific Campaign opened on 7 Dec 1941 with the Japanese air and submarine attack on Pearl Harbor and closed on 7 Dec 1943 with our seizure of the Gilbert Islands.

b. (1) The assault on Pearl Harbor found the defenses alerted only against sabotage and the damages to the Pacific Fleet and the air installations and equipment proved nearly disastrous.

(2) The Army antiaircraft defense of Pearl Harbor, Hickam, Wheeler, and Bellows Fields, and the harbor defenses on the island of Oahu was the responsibility of the 53d CA Brigade (AA). The brigade included at this time the following units:

    64th CA (AA)
    97th CA (AA) less Btries B, C, D. E, and the 3d Bn
    98th CA (AA) less Btry E and the 3d Bn
    251st CA (AA) less one gun battalion

In addition there were two antiaircraft detachments with both the 15th CA (HD) and the 55th CA (155-mm).

(3) Only the fixed batteries of the seacoast regiment were in position when the first attack came. Many of the others were not even located near their designated war positions. The joint Army-Navy exercises that had been held on Sunday morning for weeks preceding were not scheduled on 7 Dec.

(4) The enemy air attacks commenced a few minutes before 0800 and were over by 1000. Few antiaircraft batteries were able to get into action against the enemy with their major armament during the course of

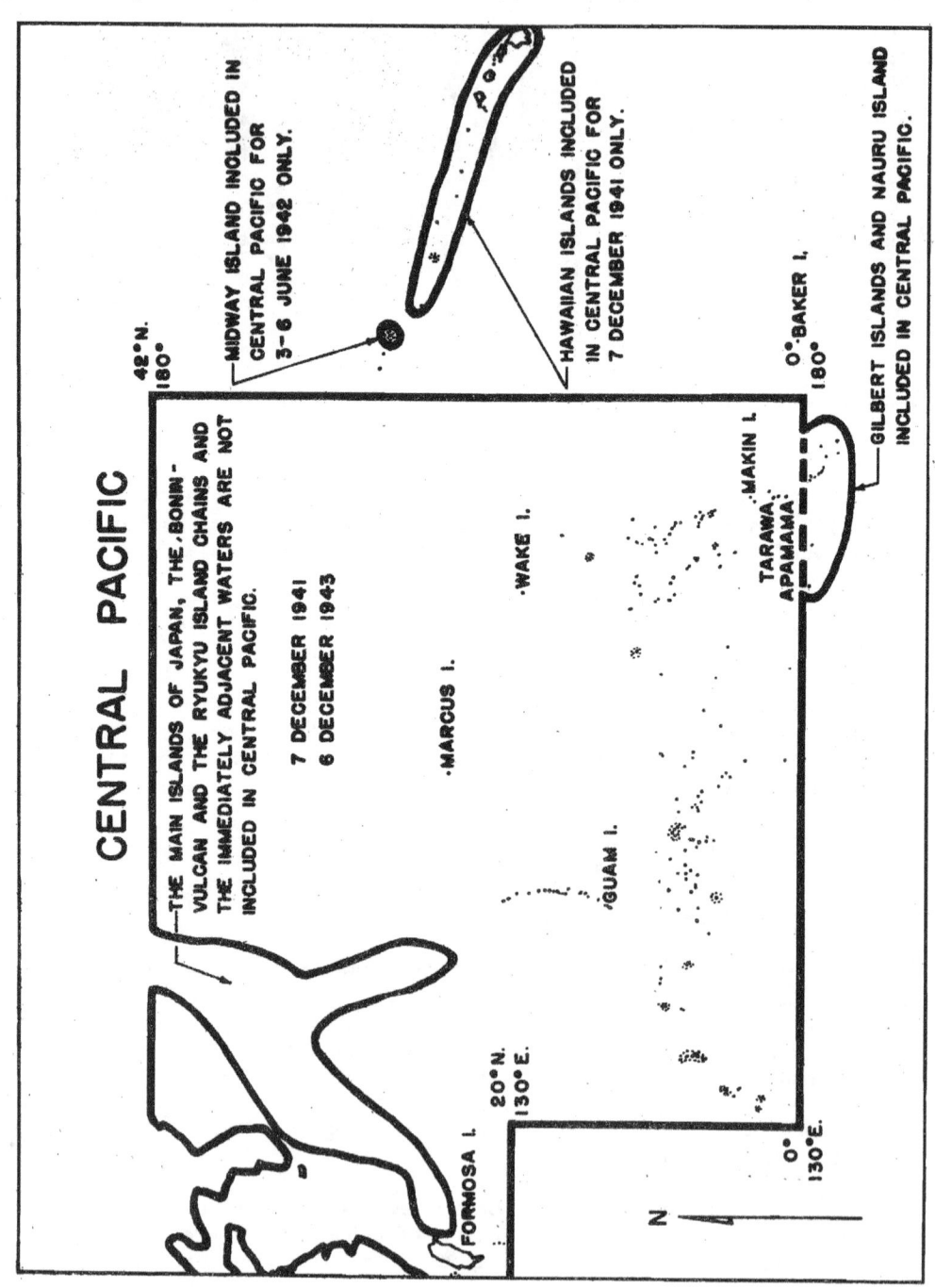

the attacks. The antiaircraft detachment of Btry F, 55th CA (155-mm) was credited with the two planes destroyed at 0815 at a cost of only 89 rounds of 3-inch ammunition. Hq 2d Bn, 97th CA (AA), engaged with small arms an enemy plane at 0815 and Btry F of the battalion fired 27 3-inch rounds at 0900. In general, however, the antiaircraft opposition to the attack was substantially ineffective.

       (5) The antiaircraft defenses of the Hawaiian islands were strengthened in early Jan by the arrival of the 95th CA (AA) (less one Bn), and by the 96th CA (AA) in Mar, and the 93d CA (AA) in May. Eventually Hawaii became a training area for many antiaircraft units en route to the Pacific war.

    c. During the months immediately after the Hawaiian attack the Japanese advanced unchecked, harassed only by minor "hit and run" raids by small naval and air forces. The Gilbert Islands were occupied by the enemy immediately after Pearl Harbor, and airfields were built there, while the air and naval bases in the mandated Marshall Islands were strengthened. This eastward progress was halted by the battle off Midway Island on 3 to 6 Jun 1942 when a large enemy naval force was decisively beaten by land and carrier based aircraft. For the next year there was little combat activity in the Central Pacific. The counter-offensive opened with the bombing of Wake Island on 5 May 1943, and similar, though infrequent, bombings of enemy-held islands continued until mid-November when the intensive bombing of the Gilbert and Marshall Islands began.

    8. <u>Baker Island</u>. a. An airfield close enough to permit support of the invasion of the Gilbert and Marshall Islands with land-based aviation was needed. Baker Island, southeast of those groups, was suitably located. On 1 Sept 1943 it was occupied by Army units, including a provisional Battalion Headquarters, Btry F, 64th CA (AA), Btries K and M, 98th CA (AA), and the 1st Plat, Btry A, 97th CA (AA).

    b. Although there was no enemy opposition to this landing it provided experience for future operations. The antiaircraft units remained on the island as garrison troops, but there were no air raids.

    9. <u>Makin</u>. a. The assault on Makin Island on 20 Nov 1943 was made by a regiment from the 27th Div. On the same day the Marines began the attack on Tarawa. The 1st Bn, 98th CA (AA) and Btries K and L, 93d CA (AA) participated in the occupation of Makin Island.

    b. By noon on D-day Btries K and L were emplaced for the antiaircraft defense of Red Beach. By noon the next day Btry K had displaced to Yellow Beach, and the gun battalion had landed and was disposed south of that beach. No enemy air activity was encountered during the assault phase of the operations, and no ground missions were fired by these units.

    c. The headquarters of the antiaircraft battalion operated as provisional Ground Defense Headquarters until the Seventh Army Garrison Force took over the responsibility for the island on 24 Nov.

d. On 3 Dec the enemy started a series of air raids terminating on 16 Jan 1944. In this period there were 36 air raids by 53 planes. Most of these raids were at night and almost all were out of range of automatic weapons. Gun batteries were equipped with SCR-268 radars for gun laying. Only two aircraft were credited as probably destroyed by unseen fire.

e. For the first time in the Pacific the enemy used window as a radar countermeasure. Initially it was effective and many rounds were fired into it. Soon crews became familiar with its appearance on the oscilloscopes and learned to track through it.[1]

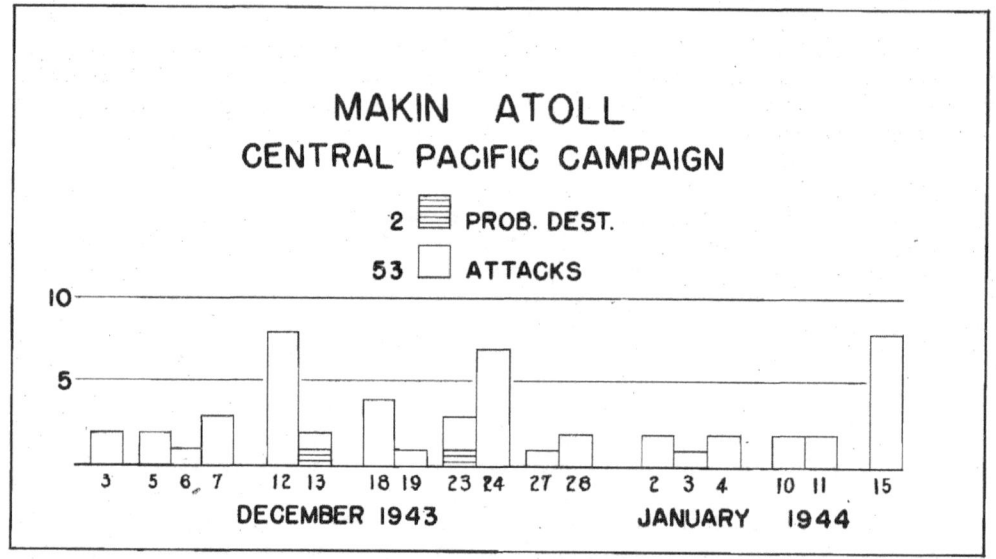

Fig. 4

10. *Apamama*. On 13 Jan 1944 the Eighth Army Garrison Force was established to take over from the Navy the ground defense of Apamama Atoll. This force was under the operational control of the naval atoll commander, and included Btry A, 93d AAA Gun Bn, Btry B, 294th AAA SL Bn, (less one Plat), Btry C, 753d AAA Gun Bn, and Btry C, 869th AAA AW Bn. Hq 296th AAA SL Bn was the Eighth Army Defense Battalion Headquarters. The only raids on this atoll occurred before this force arrived.

---

[1] Seacoast and Antiaircraft Artillery Operations in the Pacific. AFMIDPAC Sec I Par H P 4.

IV. East Indies

11. **General**. a. The East Indies Campaign opened on 1 Jan 1942 and was officially closed on 22 Jul 1942.

b. The Japanese attacks at Pearl Harbor and Luzon together with the rapid advance through the South Seas had placed the continent of Australia at the mercy of Japanese bombers. The war had caught the Allied defenses incomplete and, as the enemy progressed steadily southward, his bombing was virtually unopposed by ground defenses. In order to keep some of the continent for an Allied base American forces were dispatched to Australia with the greatest possible speed. Initial defenses were planned to run along a line stretching inland from Brisbane. However, in the Battle of the Coral Sea, fought from the 7th to the 9th of May, land and sea planes decisively defeated the Japanese task force whose mission was to seize Port Moresby and establish bases on the Cape York peninsula. The invasion of the continent was forestalled, and preparation of forces and bases for our eventual offensive could be increased

c. As a result of this change in the situation the Allied bomb line could be moved forward and in June the American antiaircraft troops were withdrawn from the defenses of the Brisbane area and redisposed in northern Queensland. It had already been decided to send some American antiaircraft artillery to Port Moresby where almost daily bombings were taking place and an invasion threatened. In July the Allies were planning a task force to seize and hold Buna Mission and Dobodura on the north coast of Papua in order to permit the establishment of airdromes there. Unfortunately the Japanese were at the same time concentrating men, planes, and ships at Rabaul and Talasea in New Britain and on 24 July it was the enemy that landed at Buna Mission.

d. This action canceled the projected allied operation and transferred the main scene of combat to Papua. It was this new attack that

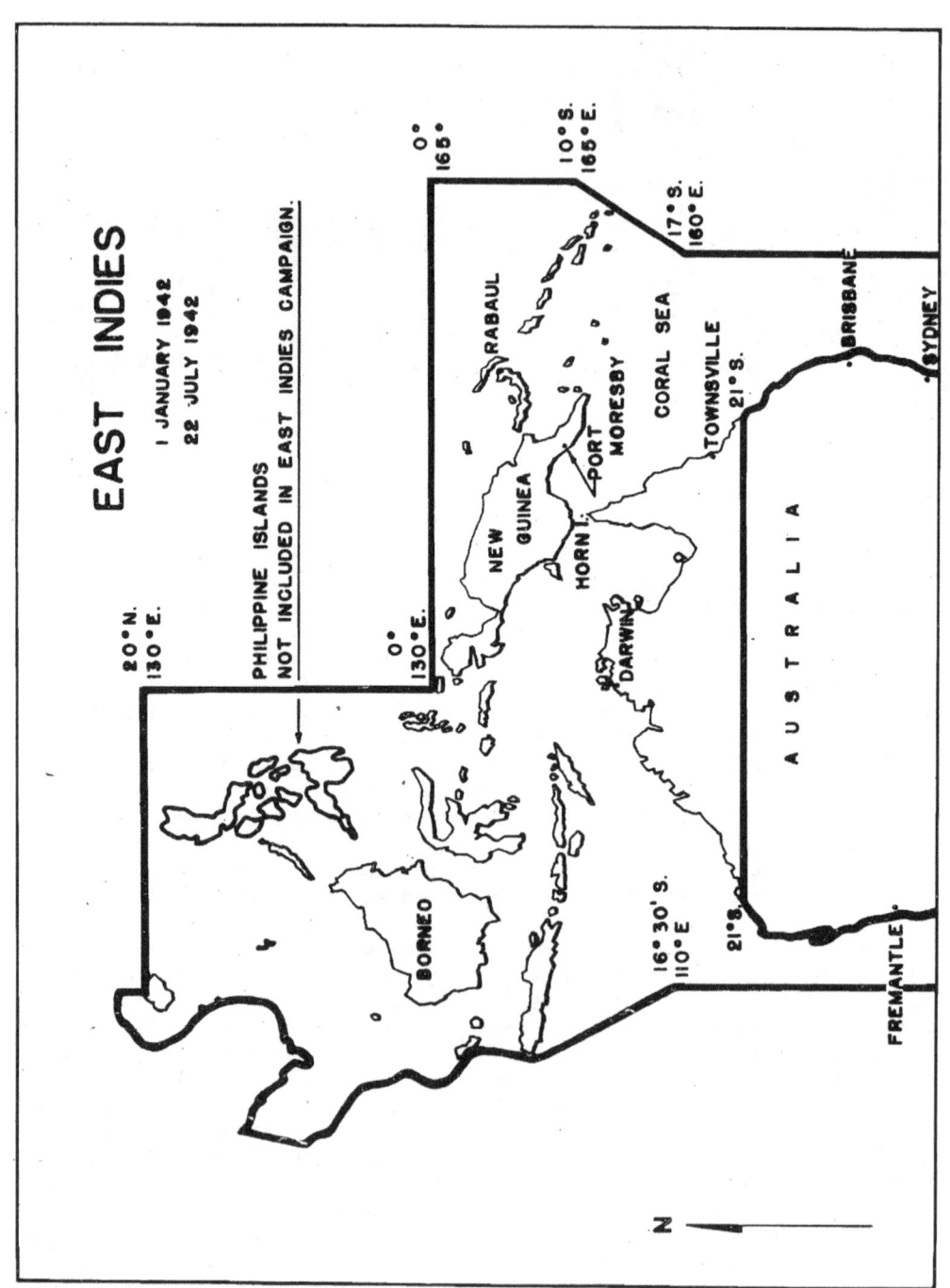

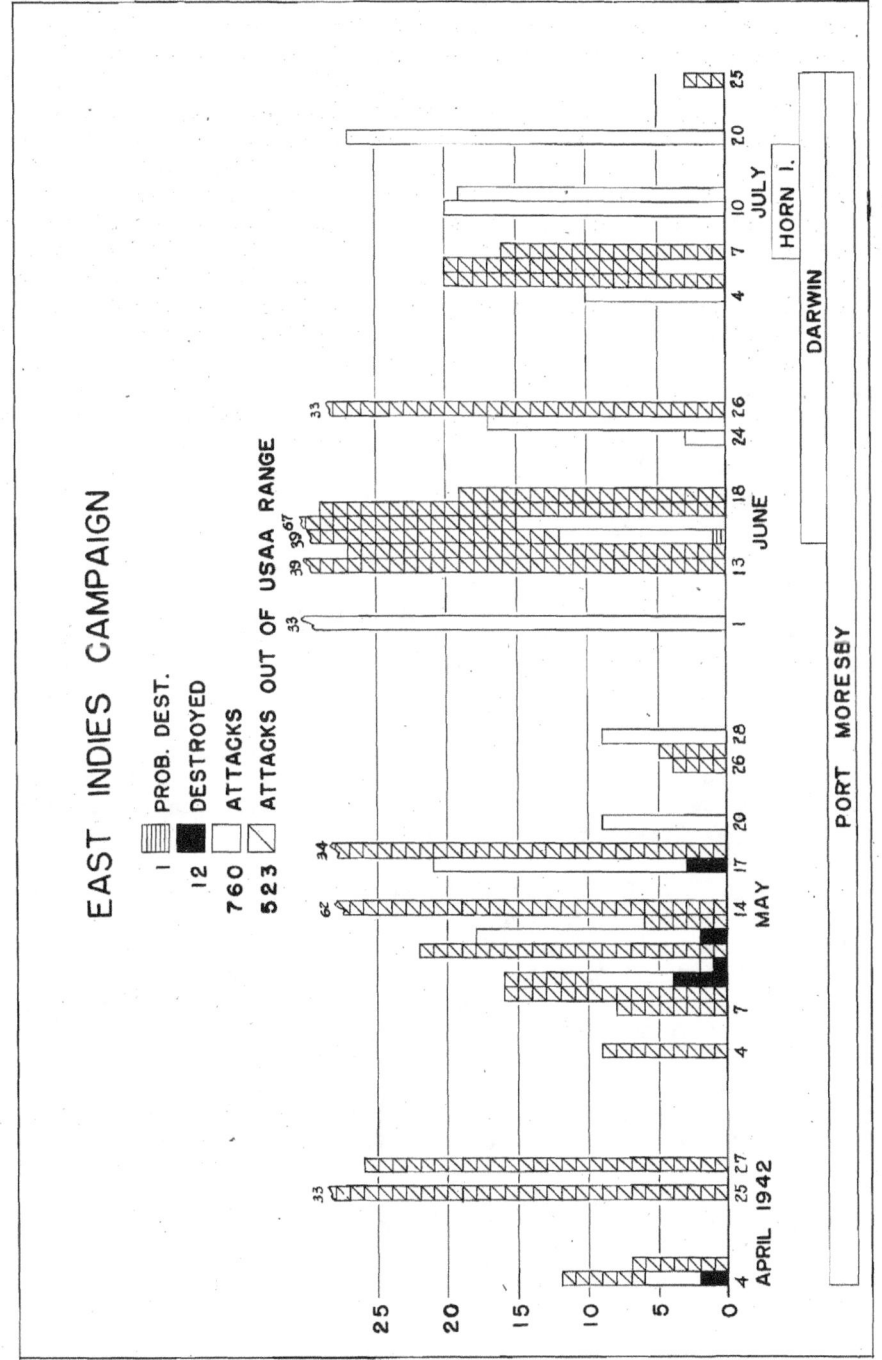

Fig. 5

- 23 -

began the Papuan Campaign and officially ended the East Indies Campaign. The threat of invasion for the Australian continent was over, and the American and Australian forces were gathering strength for the coming operations that eventually would lead them to the Japanese homeland.

12. Organization. a. The first American antiaircraft troops arrived in Australia in Mar 1942. The 40th CA Brigade (AA) arrived at Sydney Harbor on 28 Mar, and the 41st CA Brigade (AA) arrived at Brisbane on 8 Mar. The 41st CA Brigade (AA) was rendered inactive upon arrival. The Commanding General went to Melbourne to serve as Chief of Staff of the United States Army Forces in Australia, and the Headquarters furnished personnel to the Headquarters, USAFIA. Of the brigade's attached organizations, the 208th CA (AA)[1] was sent to participate in the antiaircraft defense of Townsville, the 197th CA (AA)[1] went to Fremantle, and the 102d CA Bn (AA)[2] went by air and truck convoy to Darwin.

b. Upon the arrival of the 40th CA Brigade (AA) at Brisbane the following units were attached to it:

        94th CA (AA)[1]
        208th CA (AA)
        101st CA Bn (AA)[2]
        104th CA Bn (AA)[2]

c. The Commanding General, 40th CA Brigade (AA), was designated as Commander of the Northeastern Command which unified the operational control of Australian and American antiaircraft troops from Brisbane north.

d. The 94th CA (AA) with the 101st and 104th CA Bns (AA) and several Australian units, was disposed to protect the vitally important wharf and warehouse areas and the Archer, Eagle Farm, and Lowood airdromes in and near Brisbane.

13. Darwin. a. On 19 Feb 1942 airports, docks, warehouses and nearly all ships in Darwin Harbor were destroyed or badly damaged by enemy air attack. The city was strafed and set afire; there was no resistance from the ground and the enemy bombers attacked at their leisure. The raid began without warning and eliminated Darwin as a possible port of entry for reinforcements for Australia.

b. In Mar the 102d CA Bn (AA) was sent by air transport and truck convoy to Darwin to bolster the Australian defenses then in that area. This was the first large-scale American airborne operation of the war

---

[1] A semi-mobile Regt with one gun and one AW Bn.

[2] A semi-mobile separate AW Bn armed with cal .50 AA machine guns only.

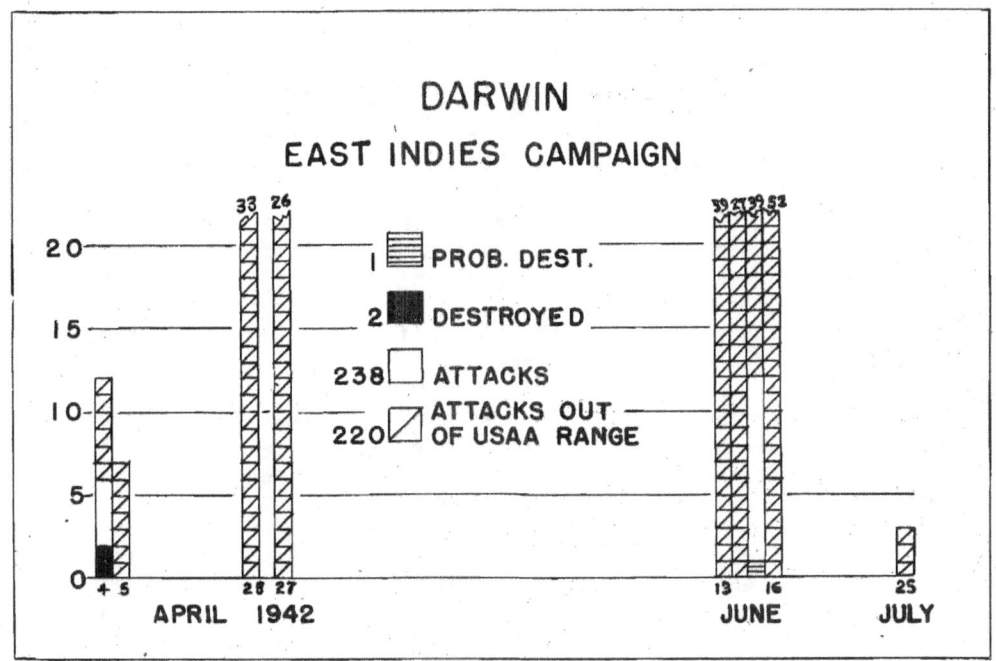

Fig. 6

and every conceivable type of aircraft was used, from obsolete transports to flying boats. The motor convoy in Apr covered 2400 miles in 13 days over roads that were so bad that in many places repairs were made while the convoy waited to get through. From Apr until the middle of June there were 10 raids. Most of the planes came over at high altitudes and were out of range of the battalion's machine guns, but on 4 Apr, in a low-level raid, the battalion shot down its first two planes.[1] Again on 15 June an additional plane was probably destroyed.

14. <u>Townsville and Cape York</u>. a. In June Regimental Headquarters with Hq 2d Bn, Btries E (less one Plat), F and G of the 94th CA (AA), and with the Australian 32d Light AA Btry, and 64th AA Co, RAE, attached, established a defense of the airstrips and repair facilities at Charters Towers, southeast of Townsville. Hq 3d Bn, with Btries D, H, L, M, and one Plat each from Btries A and E of the 94th CA (AA) defended the airstrips at Reid River and Woodstock, also southeast of Townsville. Hq 1st Bn, with Btries A (less one Plat), B, C, I, and K of the same regiment, and the Australian 33d Light AA Btry defended the airstrips at

---

[1] Entry from Btry C, 102d CA (AA) Bn and statements from five witnesses. 102d CA Bn (AA) History Australia '42 Section VIII.

Mareeba, northwest of Townsville.

    b. Hq and Btry D, 104th CA Bn (AA) furnished protection for the airstrip at Cooktown, north of Cairns, while Btry C of the same battalion covered an airstrip at Coen, still further up the Cape York Peninsula. Btries A and B were used to defend the airstrips on Horn Island at the tip of the Peninsula.

    c. On 15 May 1942 the Commanding General of the 40th CA Brigade (AA) was appointed technical representative on the staff of the Commander, Allied Air Forces, on matters pertaining to operational control of antiaircraft units under the Allied Air Forces. At the same time all antiaircraft units in the Southwest Pacific Area were assigned to Allied Air Forces for operational control.

    d. On 15 June the 707th, 708th, and 709th CA (AA) Btries, trained and equipped for airborne operations, arrived in Australia. A provisional battalion was formed to administer and to train these units in tropical operations.

    e. The original dispositions in northern Queensland were slightly changed on 23 June when Btry H and one Plat of Btry A, 94th CA (AA), were moved from Woodstock to Horn Island. On 7 July Horn Island was raided by 16 medium bombers. Btries A and B, 104th CA (AA) did not go into action as the planes were flying at approximately 20,000 feet, and were thus out of range of the Cal .50 machine guns which were the primary weapons of these batteries at that time. Although about 200 antipersonnel bombs were dropped in this raid, no casualties were sustained by our forces.

    f. On 16 Jul 1942 the 41st CA Brigade (AA), which had been inactive at Melbourne, was reactivated and assigned to the defense of Darwin and Townsville, while northern Queensland and New Guinea became the responsibility of the 40th CA Brigade (AA). The Northeastern AA Command was inactivated at that time.

    15. <u>Port Moresby</u>. a. This advance harbor in Papua was being bombed almost daily in Apr 1942 and was momentarily expecting an invasion. An automatic weapons defense was needed to counter the low-level attacks which were particularly harassing. The defenses of Brisbane were readjusted to release the 101st CA Bn (AA) and on 3 May it arrived at Port Moresby.

    b. A few days later the Japanese made five low-level attacks during which 12 enemy planes were shot down and 18 damaged. Ten of the planes destroyed were credited to the 101st CA Bn (AA). From then on, all low-level attacks ceased, although from 4 May to 22 Jul 1942, 32 Japanese raids were made on the Port Moresby area. Heavy fire from the antiaircraft units, in combination with our fighter defense, kept the

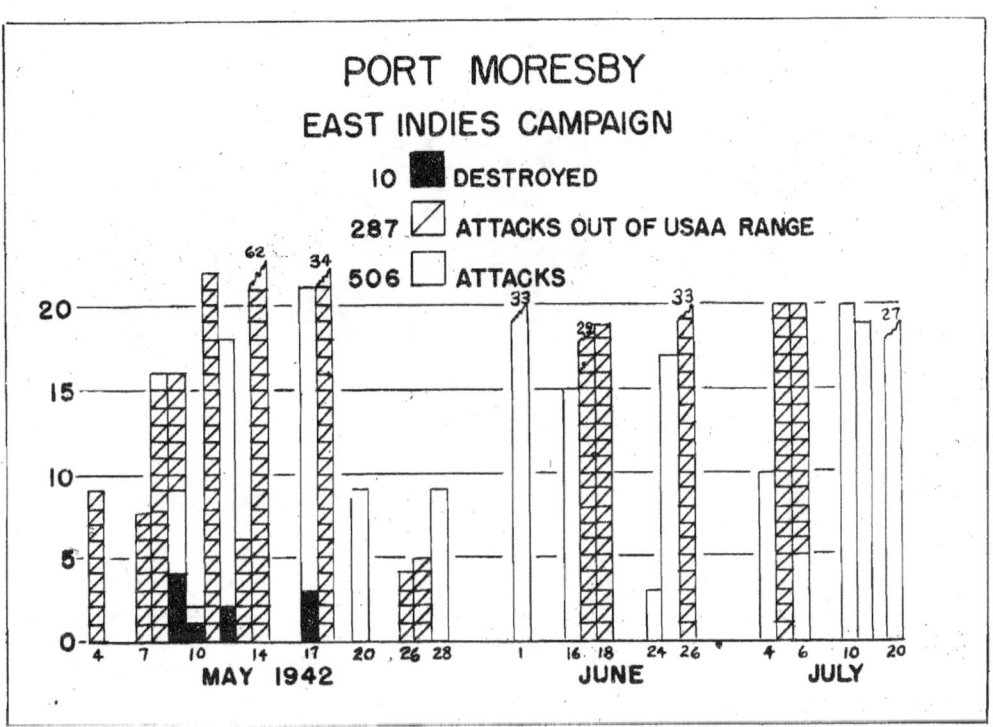

Fig. 7

enemy planes from causing other than minor damage to ground installations and personnel.

    c. In July 1942 a task force was organized and plans initiated to seize and hold Buna Mission and Dobodura, across the Owen Stanley mountains from Port Moresby. The Commanding General, 40th CA Brigade (AA) was designated commander of the antiaircraft component which consisted of three batteries from the 208th CA (AA).

    d. The Japanese landing at Buna on 24 July caused the abandonment of this plan and terminated the East Indies Campaign.

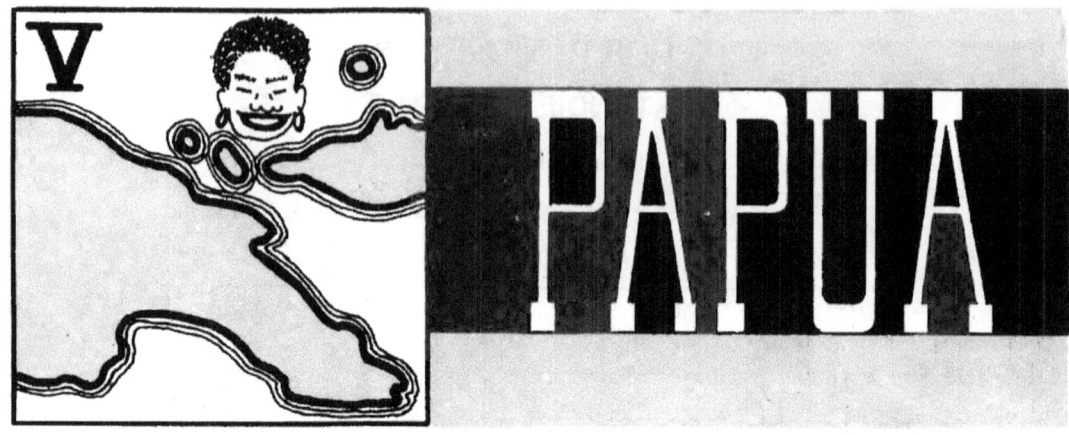

16. **General.** a. The Papuan Campaign officially opened on 23 Jul 1942 and closed on 23 Jan 1943.

b. After the failure of the Japanese expansionary operations at Midway Island and the Aleutians, the enemy returned to make another attempt to seize Papua. Instead of a wholly seaborne attack such as had been disastrously smashed in the Coral Sea in May they planned an overland drive on Port Moresby from the north, a possible reinforcing seaborne blow from the south, and the occupation of Milne Bay.

c. The initial Japanese landing on Papua took place at Gona on 21 and 22 Jul. The enemy began to do what had long been considered virtually impossible, namely to press southwards in force over the lofty barrier of the Owen Stanley Range. Some of the hardest fighting in the war took place as the small garrisons of Australian troops were pushed southward.

d. On 26 Aug the Japanese landed east of the settlements at the head of Milne Bay. They were apparently misinformed as to the strength of the defenders, and within two weeks the attack had been stopped and the invaders cleared from the area.[1]

e. Before the enemy could return in greater strength American Marines had landed at Guadalcanal and the Japanese were forced to focus their efforts on an attempt to eliminate the Allied toehold in the Solomons.

f. In Sept 1942 the enemy began to withdraw after having pushed within 20 air miles of Port Moresby. Their lines of communications extended over a mountain range passable only on foot or by air; American

---

[1] See Chap 3, Sec II, Par 110.

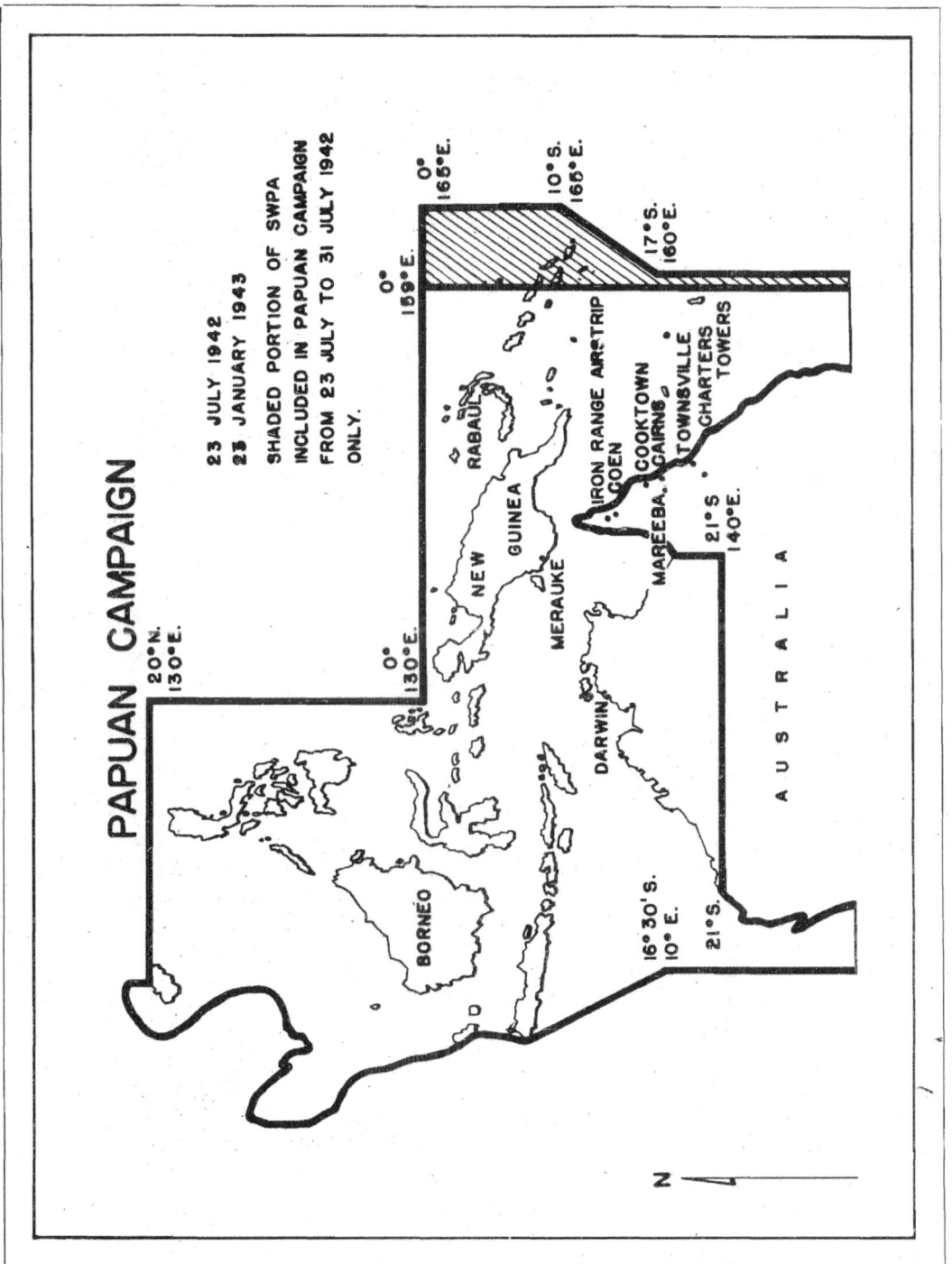

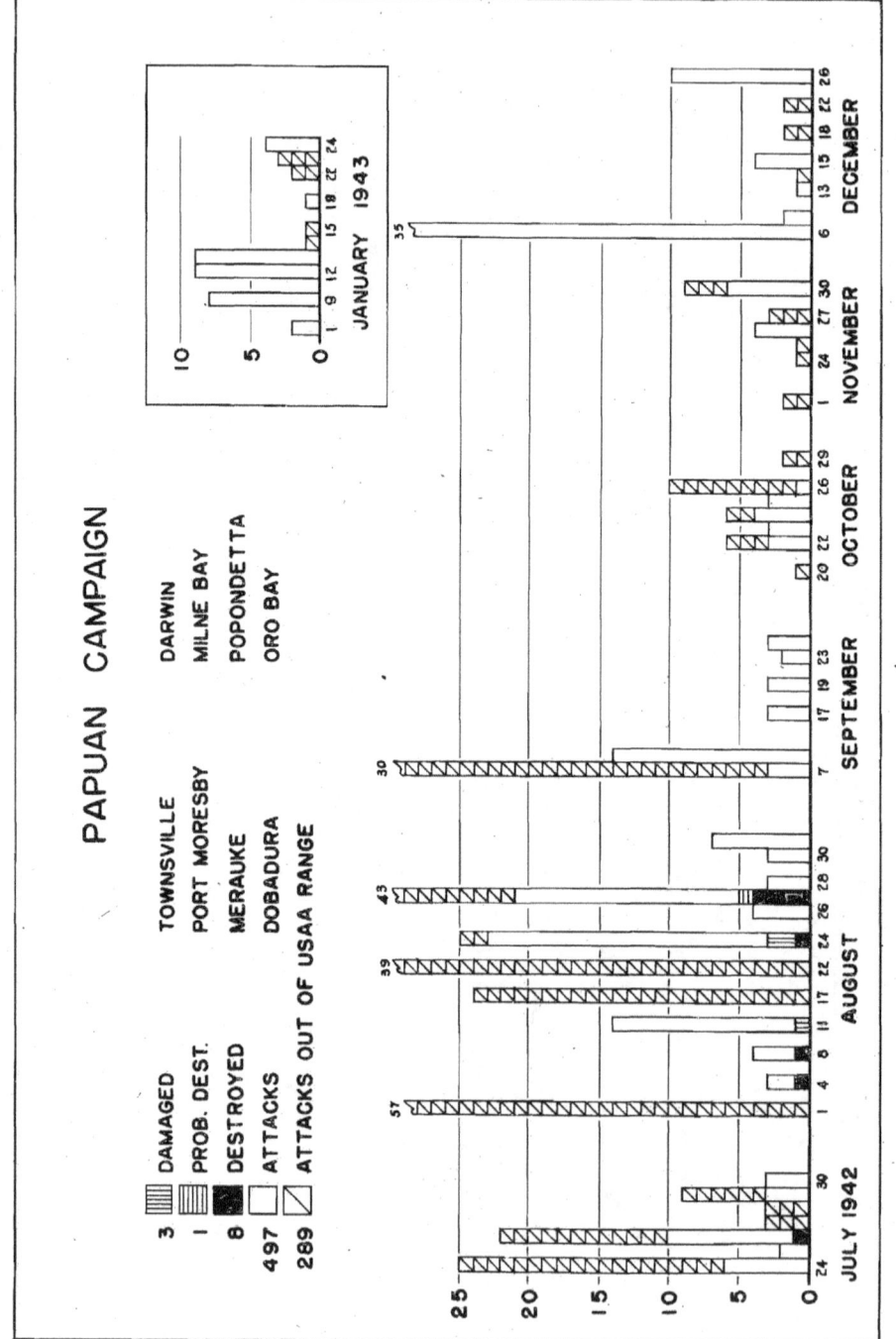
Fig. 8

and Australian planes strafed and bombed constantly; malaria and dysentery took their toll; and the Australians fought relentlessly. When the retreat was ordered the Japanese discovered that their rear was threatened. The Allies had pushed two columns across the Owen Stanley Range, the Australians having advanced against stiff Japanese resistance and the 126th US Infantry opening a new trail east of the Kokoda trail. American airfields were constructed in northern Papua at Wanigela and Pongari, and later at Popondetta and Dobodura. In Nov and Dec, American antiaircraft units flew into these airstrips with other ground troops. The enemy then concentrated their forces along the northern Papua shore between Gona and Buna. In Dec 1942 and Jan 1943, as a result of Allied siege operations, these bases were captured and the Papuan Campaign ended. Thus ended also the enemy's southward expansion.

g. Antiaircraft artillery played an important role in the Papuan Campaign. Its units were among the most forward elements and in their activity in northern New Guinea they were involved in an operation that enveloped the enemy's rear. The campaign was marked by close cooperation and coordination between the American and Australian antiaircraft units. Operations were carried on under difficult conditions of supply that were not duplicated later in the war, and could not have been overcome without the tireless efforts of the troop carrier squadrons. The Japanese changed their air tactics from low level attacks to an almost exclusive use of high altitude bombing raids as soon as the presence of our automatic weapons was discovered.

h. All American antiaircraft units participating in the Papuan Campaign received the Presidential Unit Citation.

17. <u>Antiaircraft Units and Organization</u>. a. Townsville was the main supply point for the Papuan operations. The airstrips and repair facilities in that area and on the Cape York Peninsula were the main bases of operation against the enemy in New Guinea and his supporting forces in New Britain. The portion of Australia east of longitude 145° E was excluded from the Papuan Campaign boundaries. However, since American antiaircraft units were active in that area and their service is included in no other authorized campaign, it will be described in this discussion of the Papuan Campaign.

b. All American antiaircraft units in the campaign were attached to either the 40th or the 41st CA Brigades (AA) and were under the operational control of the Allied Air Forces. The 41st Brigade had the mission of defending Townsville and Darwin. The defense of Queensland north of Townsville, and of New Guinea, was the responsibility of the 40th CA Brigade (AA). Actual control of the Townsville defenses, however, remained in the hands of the 208th CA (AA) until mid-September when the Commanding General, 41st CA Brigade (AA), assumed control.

c. The following units were under the control of the brigades at the beginning of the campaign:

> 40th CA Brigade (AA):
> 94th CA (AA)
> 208th CA (AA)
> 101st CA Bn (AA)
> 104th CA Bn (AA)
>
> 41st CA Brigade (AA):
> 197th CA (AA)
> 102d CA Bn (AA)
> 707th, 708th, and 709th CA (AA) Btries

A reorganization of the three regiments in the theater was effected on 13 Aug 1942 to conform with the latest Tables of Organization. Details are given in Annex A.

    d. On 3 Oct 1942, the 101st CA Bn (AA) was transferred from the 40th to the 41st CA Brigade (AA). At the same time the New Guinea Provisional AA Groupment was established and the following units were attached to it for operational control:

> 101st CA Bn (AA)
> 1st Bn Hq, 208th CA (AA)
> Btries A, B, C, H, and I, 208th CA (AA)
> Btry C, 104th CA Bn (AA)

The new groupment was a United States Army command functioning under the Headquarters, Composite AA Defenses, New Guinea, which was the antiaircraft command of the Allied New Guinea Force.

    18. **Townsville.** a. The 208th CA (AA) initially was in command of the combined antiaircraft defenses of the Townsville area. On 25, 28, and 29 Jul the regiment experienced its first air raids, the first at Townsville. In each case the attacks were made by flying boats at night. The first saw searchlights in action, but due to a cirrus cloud layer the planes were not illuminated. A string of bombs was dropped in the water about 600 yards south of the dock area. On 28 Jul, one plane jettisoned bombs on the Many Peaks ridge northwest of Townsville. On 29 Jul one bomber came in early in the morning at 19,500 feet. The plane was held in steady illumination by American searchlights for nine minutes while Australian fighters engaged it as it crossed over the city. Some shells were seen to strike the plane but did not disable it. The bombing was completely ineffective, all but one bomb landing several miles off shore. This was the first time on record that the fighter-searchlight team was employed in the Southwest Pacific.

    b. The 208th CA (AA) remained in tactical position at Townsville until 16 Sept 1942 when some units were withdrawn and departed for Port

Moresby on 15 Oct. Its responsibilities were taken over progressively by the 197th CA (AA). Units of the 102d and 104th CA Bns (AA) subsequently occupied tactical positions at Townsville for short periods. There was no further enemy action.

19. <u>Northern Queensland</u>. a. On 5 Jun 1942 the 94th CA (AA) and the 104th CA Bn (AA) were moved from Brisbane to take over defense of airstrips in North Queensland.[1] The reorganizations of 13 Aug[2] stripped the Charters Towers defenses of their armament, so the Regimental Headquarters and the newly activated 3d Bn Hq were moved to Cairns on 21 Sept. Btries D and C[3] later went to Port Moresby, arriving in Dec. The other units of the 94th CA (AA) remained in Queensland until Jun 1943. No raids occurred at these points during this period.

b. In Oct 1942, airstrips having been developed at Iron Range, high up on Cape York Peninsula, the 2d Bn Hq, 197th CA (AA), with Btries A, B, E, F, and I moved there and established the antiaircraft defense.

c. At the end of 1942 the need for antiaircraft defenses at Cooktown had ceased to exist, and Australian antiaircraft units had taken over the Horn Island responsibilities. As a result, Btry A[4] and one Plat of Btry K[4] of the 94th CA (AA) and all of the 104th CA Bn (AA) except Btry D at Merauke were released from tactical positions and went into staging areas at Townsville.

20. <u>Darwin</u>. At the beginning of the Papuan Campaign units of the 102d CA Bn (AA) were in position at the RAAF airdrome at Darwin, and at the 28, 34, and 65 Mile airdromes and Batchelor Field, all south of Darwin. Heavy air raids were encountered on the 25th, 26th, 29th, and 30th of Jul. A raid took place on the 23d of Aug and the last raids of the campaign in this area occurred on 23 and 24 Oct 1942. No great damage resulted from these high altitude raids and the battalion had no action. In early Nov the battalion was moved to Townsville and its role in the Papuan Campaign was ended.

---

1 See Par 14a.

2 See Par 18c.

3 Btry L prior to the Aug reorganization.

4 Btries H and A respectively prior to Aug reorganization.

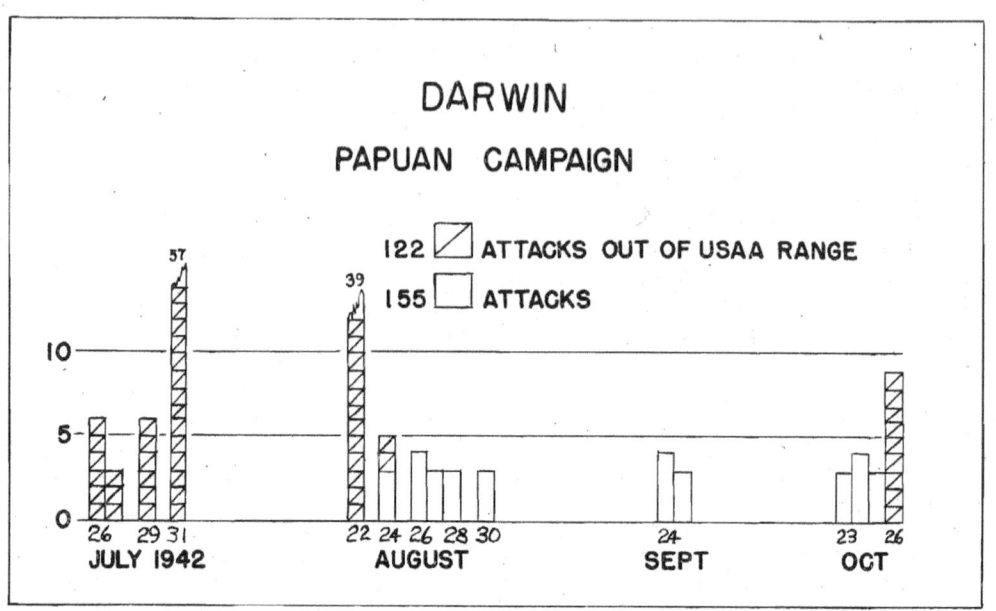

Fig. 9

21. <u>Port Moresby</u>. a. The 101st CA Bn (AA) arrived at Port Moresby on 3 May 1942 and occupied positions there and at Milne Bay throughout the Papuan Campaign. It was reinforced by Australian light antiaircraft in the protection of the several strips then in use.

b. On 24 Jul the first raid of the campaign occurred at Port Moresby. No damage was done either to our installations or to the enemy planes. Two days later, 26 Jul, there was a low-altitude strafing attack and one Zeke was shot down by the battalion. Four additional planes were destroyed in Aug. Most of these raids were at high altitudes (10,000 to 27,000 feet), outside the range of automatic weapons fire.

c. Elements of the 208th CA (AA) began to reach New Guinea in Oct. Hq 1st Bn arrived at Port Moresby 19 Oct with Btry A. Btries B, G, H, and I followed shortly thereafter.

d. The 708th CA Btry (AA) was flown to Port Moresby on 27 Sept 1942 and remained there until 23 Oct when it was sent temporarily to guard the strip at Rorona, about 20 miles west, against possible enemy use. While at Port Moresby, in Oct, the unit underwent two high-altitude raids which could not be engaged.

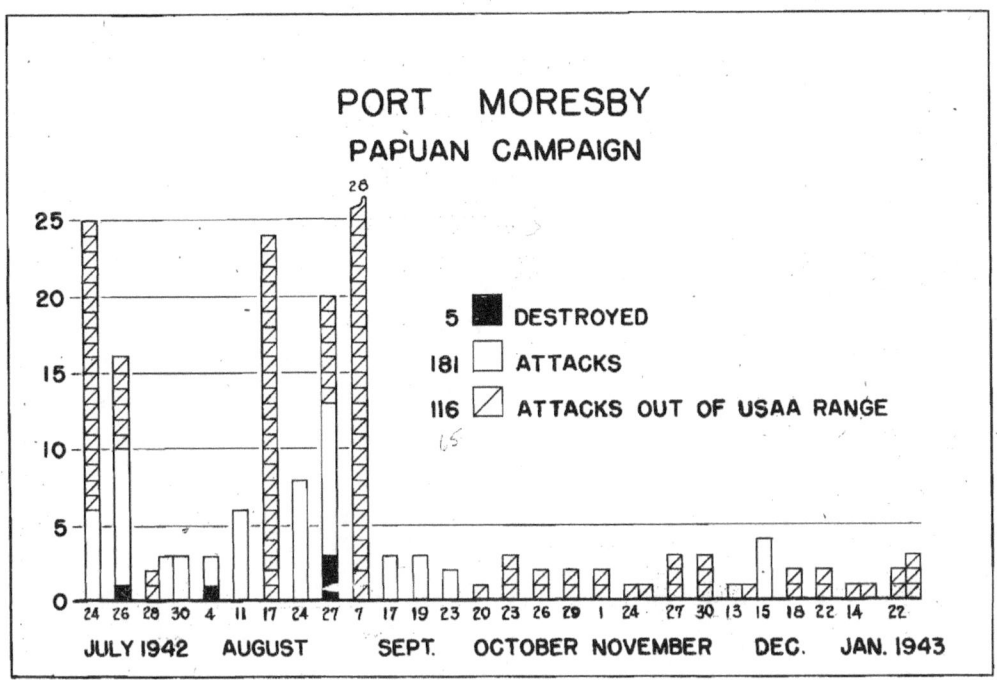

Fig. 10

e. Btries D and G, 94th CA (AA), arrived at Port Moresby in mid-December 1942 to strengthen the defenses there. Btry C, 208th CA (AA), was in position at Port Moresby from mid-December to early Jan while pausing enroute to Oro Bay.

22. <u>Milne Bay</u>. a. A detachment of 2 officers and 46 enlisted men of the 101st CA Bn (AA), equipped with antiaircraft machine guns, went to Milne Bay on 3 May 1942 where they remained until early in Dec. Btry C, 104th CA Bn (AA), arrived in Milne Bay on 30 Jul and was the first American antiaircraft unit in this theater to use the 40-mm guns against the Japanese. The 709th CA (AA) Btry was flown into Milne Bay on 19 Aug in a conglomeration of B-24's, B-17's, Sunderlands, and Hudsons.

b. Raids on 8, 11, 25, and 28 Aug by a total of 36 fighters and dive-bombers provided diving and strafing targets. The 101st claimed two planes destroyed, one probably destroyed, and three damaged, while Btry C, 104th CA Bn (AA), was credited with one plane damaged.

c. The part played by antiaircraft units in the ground action when the enemy launched a drive against Milne Bay is set forth in Chap 3, Sec II, Par 110.

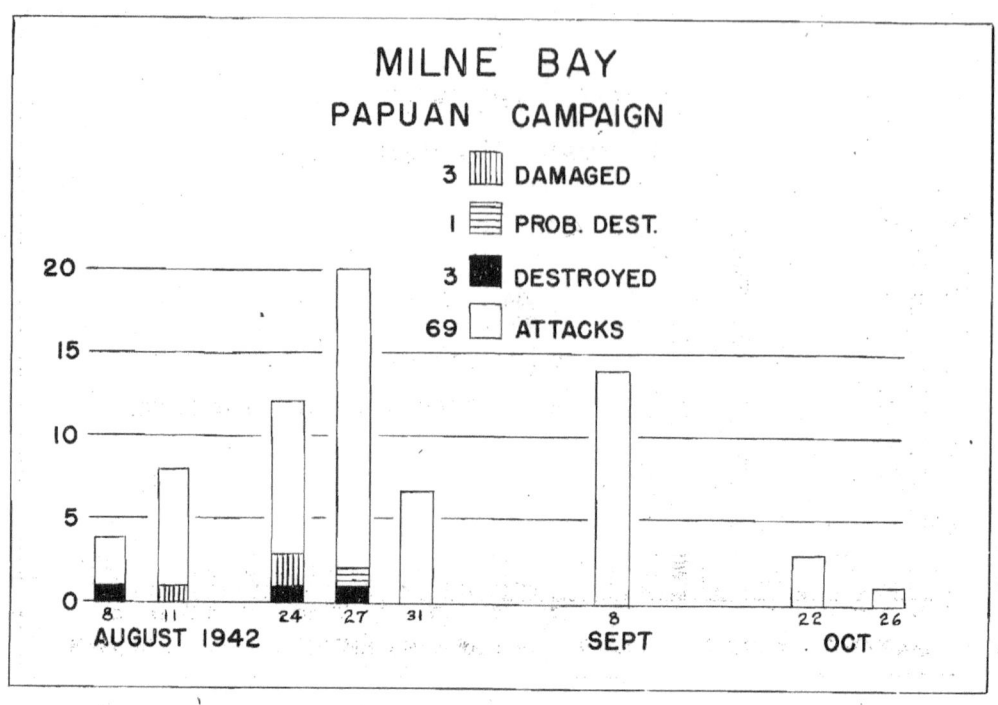

Fig. 11

23. **Merauke**. Btry D of the 104th CA Bn (AA) moved from Coen, Queensland, to Merauke, Dutch New Guinea, completing the journey on 15 Aug 1942. Since the place was well within range for a Japanese attack in force along the southern shore of New Guinea from the west, this was regarded as a possible suicide mission. Fortunately, the enemy never moved against Merauke and there were no air raids there until Dec 1942. The raids continued sporadically until May 1943 and inflicted negligible damage to military facilities. After the first few visits the enemy kept out of range of the antiaircraft guns emplaced to defend the airstrip.

24. **Buna**. a. To clear the enemy from the Buna-Gona area was the final goal of the Papuan Campaign. Advance airstrips were constructed to facilitate tactical air support of the ground assault troops. On 6 Oct 1942 the 707th CA (AA) Btry was flown to Wanigela to defend the strips there. On Thanksgiving Day, 26 Nov it was flown to Dobodura. Three raids, on 26 Nov, 30 Nov, and 7 Dec, resulted in claims of two planes damaged in each raid. At 1105 on 26 Dec nine fighters came in at low altitudes and the battery scored hits and claimed one plane destroyed and two probables.

b. The 708th CA (AA) Btry was flown from Rorona to Popondetta in Dec.

Both moves were made in C-47 transports. The battery underwent a medium altitude raid at Popondetta on 6 Dec. There was no antiaircraft action.

    c. Btries C and E of the 208th CA (AA) and one Plat of Btry K, 94th CA (AA), were organized in Nov into the 1st Provisional AA Group under the 40th CA Brigade (AA). Btry E landed at Oro Bay on 1 Dec 1942 and Btry C on 6 Jan 1943. The Japanese launched heavy raids on shipping in the bay. On 9 Jan 1943 at 1400, six enemy planes, fighters and bombers, raided Oro Bay in a low-level attack. One plane was believed to have been damaged by machine-gun fire. The many subsequent attacks were a part of the New Guinea Campaign.

GUADALCANAL
VI

25. **General.** The first offensive action by Allied forces in the South Pacific Area occurred on 7 Aug 1942 when American Marines landed on Guadalcanal and Tulagi Islands in the southern Solomons, officially opening the Guadalcanal Campaign. However, for some months prior to that time American troops had been arriving for the defense of the islands south and east of the Solomons group. As the operations in that area were not included within any of the officially designated campaigns the details of the tactical utilization of the antiaircraft units in the defenses of New Caledonia, the Society, Fiji, and New Hebrides Islands is included in this section on the Guadalcanal Campaign.

26. **New Caledonia.** a. The possibility of a thrust by the Japanese against the Free French island of New Caledonia was met by sending the task force from the United States which landed at Noumea on 12 Mar 1942. The expedition, elements of which later formed the Americal Division, included the 70th CA (AA). Its batteries were placed to provide protection for the principal airfields and dock areas on the island, from Noumea to Plaines des Gaiacs, 165 miles away. In Nov the 214th CA (AA) arrived from New Zealand and temporarily occupied tactical positions while completing preparations for its later move to Guadalcanal where it arrived on 30 Jan 1943.

b. The 1st Marine Barrage Balloon Group and four batteries of the 14th Marine Defense Battalion, two Navy antiaircraft units, and the 203d Heavy Antiaircraft Battery of the New Zealand Army had in the meantime joined the defenses of the island. The 70th CA (AA), less Btry I, departed in June to participate in the Northern Solomons operations and left the antiaircraft responsibility to the remaining units.

c. In Sept 1943 Hq 117th AAA Group arrived and was designated the

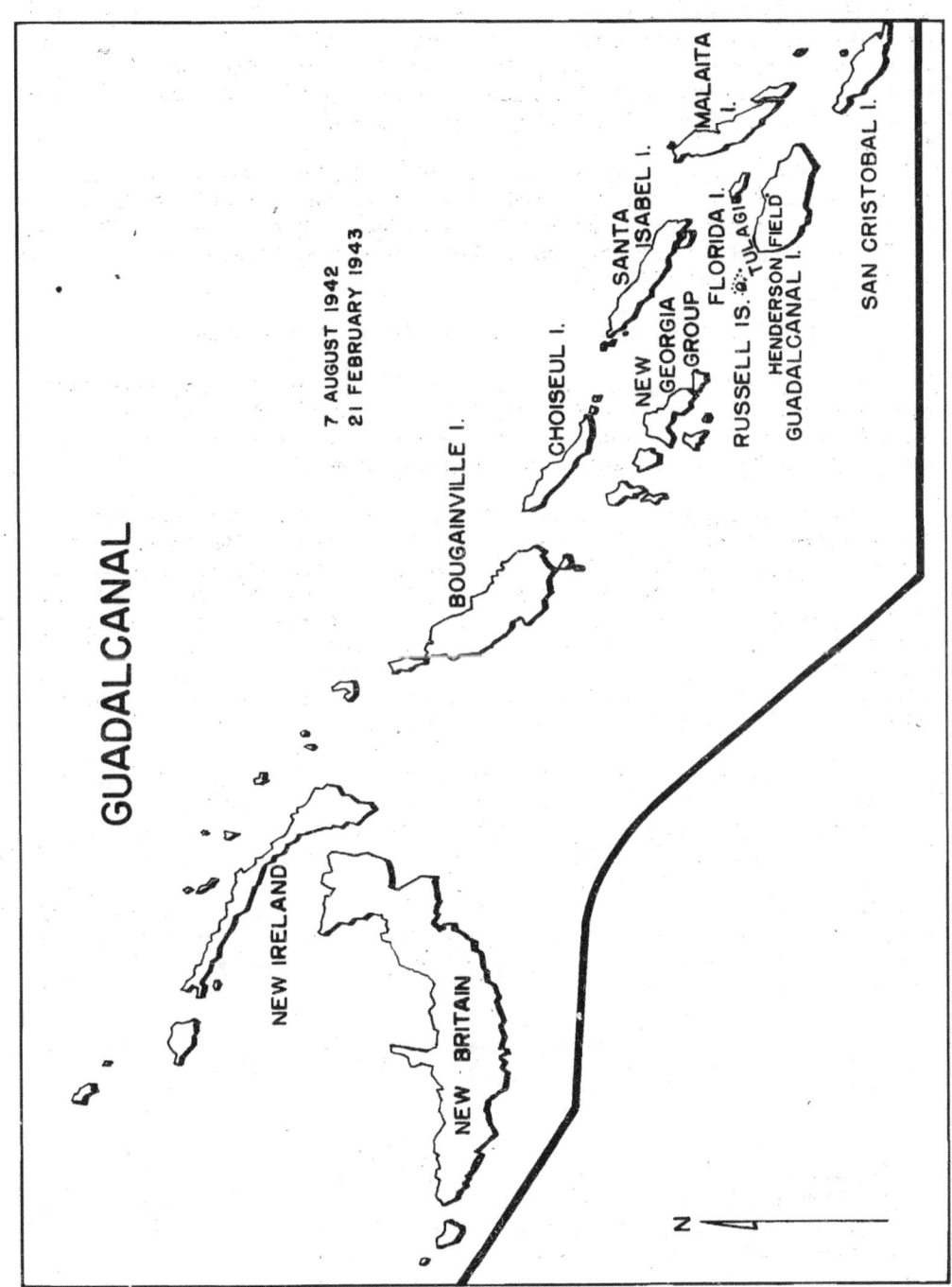

AA Command of the Island Command. Its functions included the coordination of the defenses, exercise of operational control, and supervision of training of all antiaircraft units on the island, as well as serving as Noumea Regional AA Command. On 27 Nov the Group Headquarters was relieved as AA Command of the Island Command by the 14th Marine Defense Battalion, all other units having been relieved.

d. The 518th AAA Gun Bn, activated on 12 Nov, was cadred from units in the Solomon Islands, and filled with replacements in Dec. It started its training with materiel discarded by Marine units. The battalion continued in training until Nov 1944, when it departed to participate in the Luzon Campaign.

e. There were no raids on New Caledonia at any time.

27. <u>Society Islands</u>. Another possible target for Japanese expansion early in 1942 was the Society Islands group. The 198th CA (AA) landed at Bora Bora in Feb 1942 and remained in position there for almost a year, but saw no action against the enemy.

28. <u>Fiji Islands</u>. Control of the Fiji Islands was essential to the security of our supply lines to Australia. The 77th CA (AA) was moved to Tongatabu in May 1942 while the 251st CA (AA) was sent to Lautoka in June, where they occupied positions without any combat action. In Sept and Oct the 739th AAA Gun Bn, the 205th AAA AW Bn, and the 233d AAA SL Bn arrived here, where they occupied defensive positions for a year. The 77th CA (AA), less the gun battalion, left in Apr 1943 for Efate. The gun battalion moved to Espiritu Santo in Jan 1943, and the 251st CA (AA) left Fiji in Nov for Bougainville.

29. <u>Guadalcanal</u>. a. Although the initial landing by the Marine forces on 7 Aug 1942 was not seriously opposed, the Japanese later resisted vigorously and the struggle for domination of Guadalcanal was bitterly contested for several months. On 10 Jan 1943 the American forces started their final offensive which eliminated organized enemy resistance and brought official closing of the campaign on 21 Feb 1943. Enemy air activity against the airfields continued in diminishing frequency into Nov, and the mopping up of scattered enemy groups continued for some time.

b. On the first day of the invasion the Marines landed their own antiaircraft artillery in the form of units of two Marine Defense Battalions.[1]

---

[1] The normal Marine Defense Bn was composed of a heavy group with three gun Btries and one SL Btry, and AW group of two Btries, one armed with eight 40-mm guns, and a seacoast group with two Btries equipped with four 155-mm guns each.

g. After 18 June the gun batteries of the 70th CA (AA) were engaged against Japanese bombers attacking Carney Field and shipping. Most of these attacks came on moonlight nights and were made by single planes or small flights of planes, at altitudes of 22,000 to 27,000 feet, over cloud cover, thus necessitating the use of radar data. The results of the firing are unknown. The automatic weapons batteries saw very little action and none in the daytime. During this period a total of five men were wounded by enemy action.

h. The defense of Henderson Field area resulted in the destruction of 14 enemy planes, in the probable destruction of eight, and in damage to six others by Army antiaircraft action. Due to the small size of the defended area and the close-in perimeter, use of the normal fighter-searchlight technique was impracticable. A plan was put into operation in mid-May for using day fighters orbitting overhead to attack illuminated enemy planes after bomb release. The cooperation and fine work of both searchlights and pilots resulted in the destruction of five two-engined bombers on one night.

i. In the fall of 1943 the two antiaircraft regiments represented at Guadalcanal were reorganized into group headquarters and separate battalions.[1] Hq, 70th AAA Group thereafter set up an antiaircraft training center under direction of Hq, 68th AAA Brigade. Hq, 214th AAA Group, and attached battalions were relieved on 22 Dec by the 117th AAA Group and returned to New Zealand.

j. The 117th AAA Group, in addition to its Hq, consisted of:

    497th and 967th AAA Gun Bns
    199th AAA AW Bn, less Btry D, with Btry D, 925th AAA AW Bn
    475th AAA AW Bn, less Btry D
    362d AAA SL Bn, less Btry C

The 356th AAA SL Bn was later attached. This group remained on Guadalcanal until mid-December of 1944 but there were no further enemy air attacks.

30. <u>New Hebrides</u>. a. While the hotly contested struggle for Guadalcanal was in progress the New Hebrides were occupied by Allied forces. The 76th CA (AA) arrived at Espiritu Santo on 2 Sept 1942 and immediately set up antiaircraft defense of the air field and the surrounding supply installations. The bay area was shelled twice by unidentified seacraft in October. The first enemy air activity took place in Jan 1943, when there were three night raids, with two additional in Feb and occasional raids until Oct 1943. Almost no damage was caused by these raids and there were no claims on enemy aircraft.

---

[1] See Annex A, Par 3C.

The Japanese airstrip was speedily occupied and renamed Henderson Field. During its development and operation it was defended ably by the 3d Marine Defense Battalion until the Marine antiaircraft artillery was relieved by the 214th CA (AA) units that arrived progressively up to 31 Jan 1943.

c. As fighter strips were completed on each side of Henderson Field the antiaircraft artillery had to protect an area approximately 6,000 by 15,000 feet, in which three strips, the dispersal and repair areas were concentrated. To provide adequate heavy gun strength the 214th CA (AA) augmented its own organization by utilizing two provisional gun batteries that had been organized on New Caledonia, using cadres from its other gun batteries supplemented with men from headquarters and searchlight batteries. The materiel used had been left by the 3d Marine Defense Battalion. This gave the regiment six gun batteries.

d. In June the 9th Marine Defense Battalion was relieved of the defense of Carney Field, a newer landing area approximately 15 miles west of Henderson Field on the northern shore of Guadalcanal. This defense was then taken over by the Guadalcanal Groupment[1] of the 70th CA (AA). Other elements of this regiment were at the same time engaged in operations in the Northern Solomons.

e. In July 1943, in order to provide additional heavy gun firepower as Carney Field was extended, Btry H, an automatic weapons battery, was converted to a 90-mm gun unit. On 5 Aug Btry C and Btry K (less one Plat) were moved to reinforce the defenses of Segi Point, New Georgia. The 2d Plat of Btry K joined its parent organization in early Oct. Hq and Btry G, 70th CA (AA), left on 13 and 14 Oct, leaving only the Hq of the 1st and 3d Bns and Btry H at Carney Field.

f. The defended airfield was subjected to 29 hostile raids in 31 days. Two hundred and twenty planes were involved in these raids, of which 120 participated in the daylight raid of 16 Jun 1943. Due to restrictions on fire only 16 planes in this raid became targets for the fire of the 214th CA (AA). The Japanese respect for our antiaircraft artillery at Guadalcanal is reflected in the fact that of the 111 planes that came within antiaircraft gun range 65 delivered their attacks from 20,000 feet altitude or above.[2] The low percentage of automatic weapons targets was probably due to the expensive lessons the 3d Marine Defense Battalion had given the Japanese during the early months of the campaign.

[1] Regtl Hq, Hq 1st and 3d Bns, and Btries C, D, G, and H.

[2] <u>Unit History</u> - 214th AAA Group, 8 Sept 1945, Par 1, P. 2 and 3.

b. In Feb 1943 the 198th CA (AA) arrived at Efate, New Hebrides, to protect the two airstrips on the island. There is no record of any raids there; the unit left in Nov for operations in the Northern Solomons.

c. In Apr and May 1943 the gun battalion of the 77th CA (AA) occupied positions at Espiritu Santo to reinforce the defenses already established by the 76th CA (AA). The units formed in the reorganizations[1] of the 76th and 77th CA (AA) moved out from Espiritu Santo during the mid-winter (1943-44). Their tactical positions were taken over by the 466th AAA AW Bn and the 742d AAA Gun Bn which had arrived in Oct 1943. The antiaircraft defenses of Espiritu Santo remained under control of Hq 76th AAA Group until June 1944, by which time the 466th AAA AW Bn and the 742d AAA Gun Bn had already departed for Cape Gloucester.

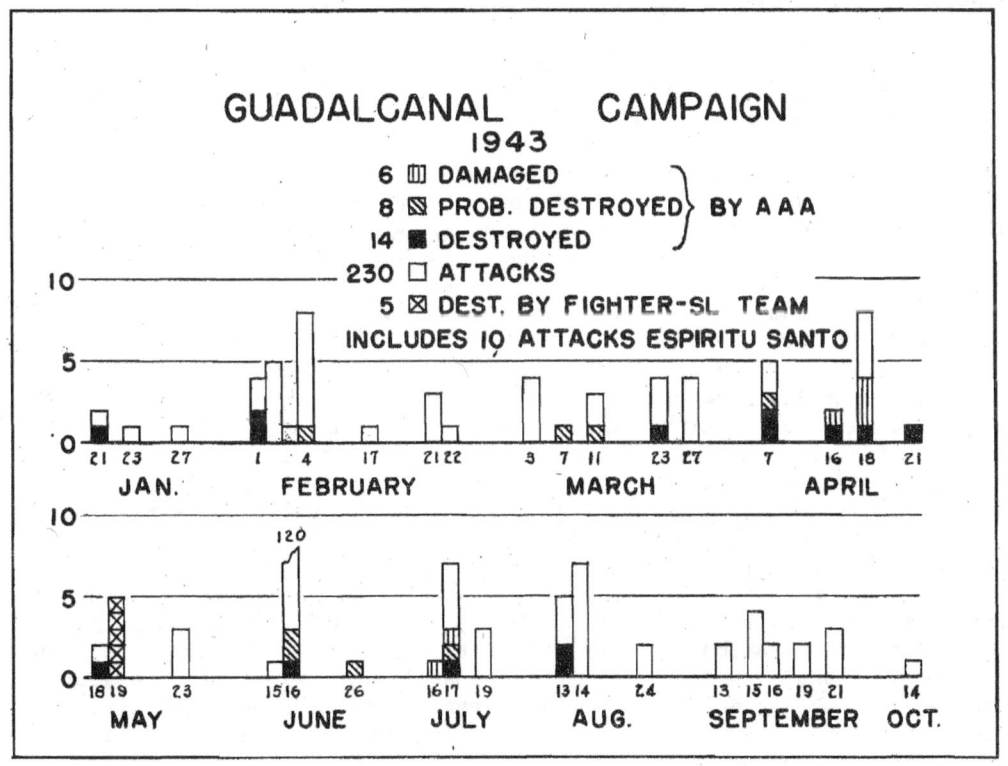

Fig. 12

[1] See Annex A, Par 3 B.

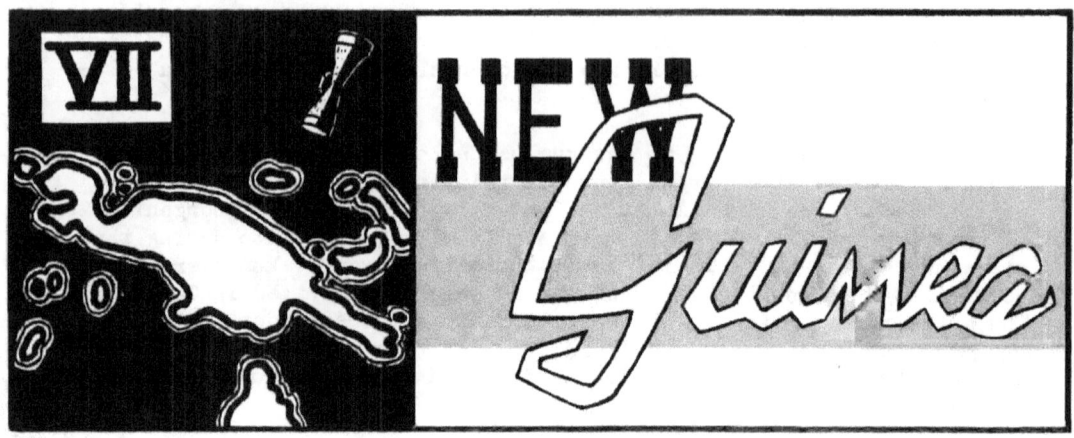

VII. NEW GUINEA

31. **General.** a. The New Guinea Campaign officially opened on 24 Jan 1943 and closed on 31 Dec 1944.

b. With the wiping out of the Japanese defenses of the Buna area at the end of Jan 1943 the initial moves began in the drive to clear the enemy from New Guinea. The Japanese tried desperately to hold their air superiority and during the spring of 1943 their aircraft repeatedly raided Darwin, Port Moresby, and the Allied outposts in northeastern New Guinea without serious damage to our installations but at appreciable cost to their air strength.

c. Tactical air support and shipping were becoming available for amphibious advances against Japanese areas. In Jun 1943 the Allies launched two simultaneous drives, one aimed at Munda in the Solomons and one towards Salamaua and Lae, the nearest enemy strongholds to Buna. At the same time they obtained fighter strips from which to harrass the enemy by seizing Kiriwina and Woodlark Islands, north of eastern Papua.

d. The push on Lae and Salamaua by Australian and American troops, supported by antiaircraft of both armies, was a hard fought battle up the coast from Buna and the fighting carried deep into the lower reaches of the Owen Stanley Range. The two seacoast strongholds fell, in Sept, to troops which struck on all sides, arriving by land, sea, and air. The Australian Ninth Div then pushed north along the coast and Finschhafen was captured on 2 Oct.

e. While this drive up the coast was in progress the Australian Seventh Div moved up the Markham River Valley to outflank the enemy on the north side of the Finisterre Range. The Japanese attempts to get behind the Allied positions by building a road across the mountains from Bogadjim were effectively countered. This push was supported almost

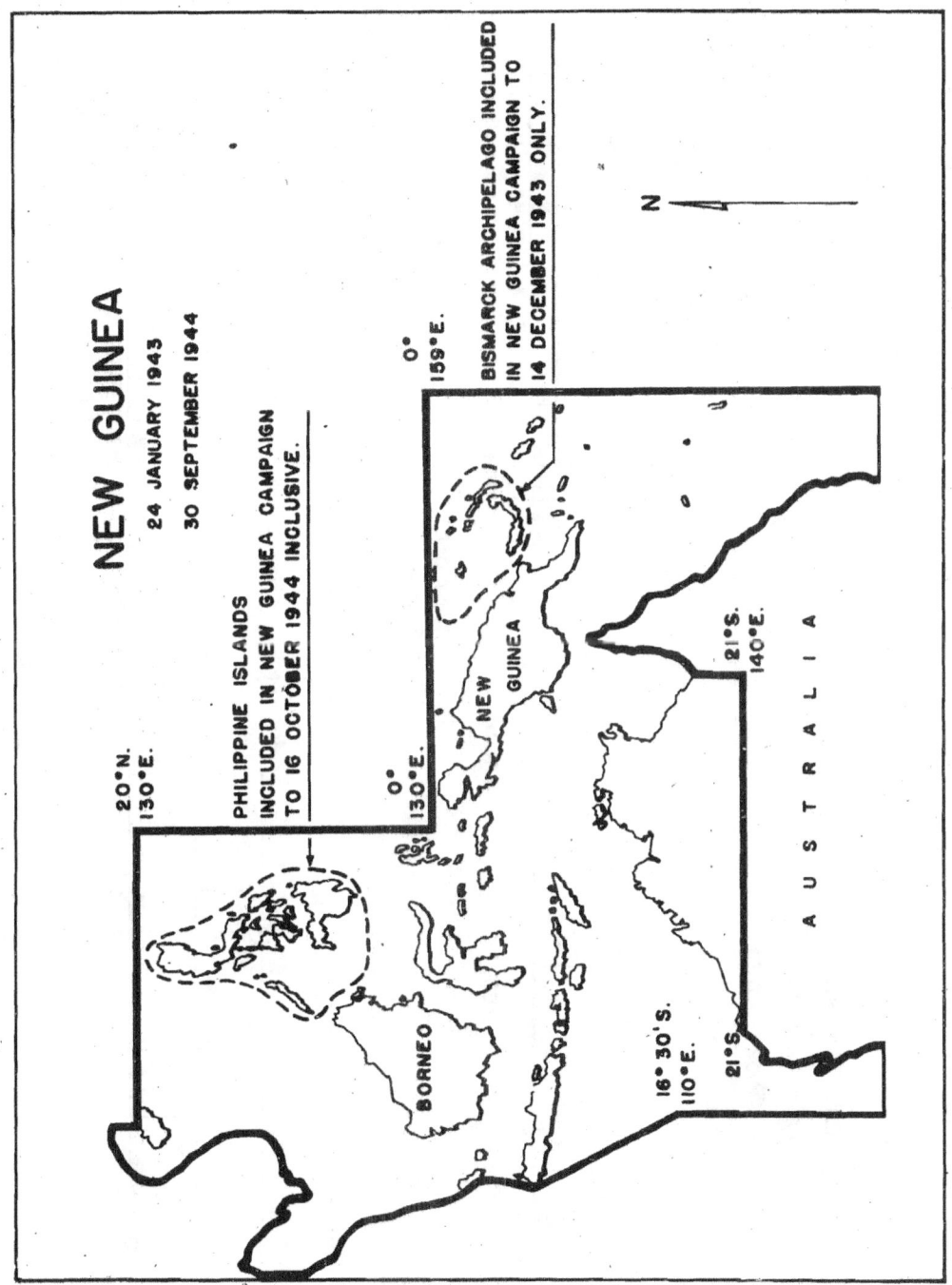

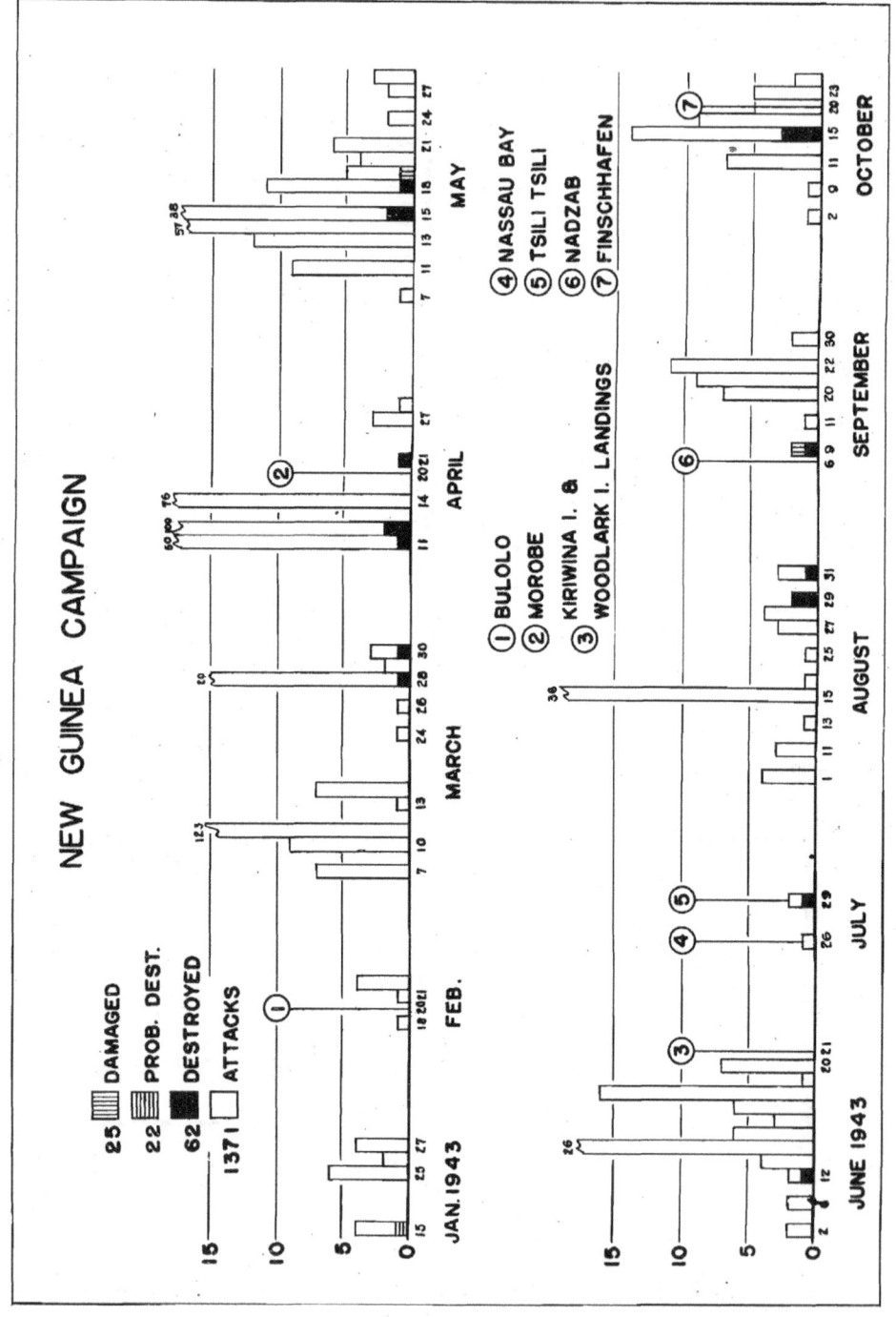

Fig. 13

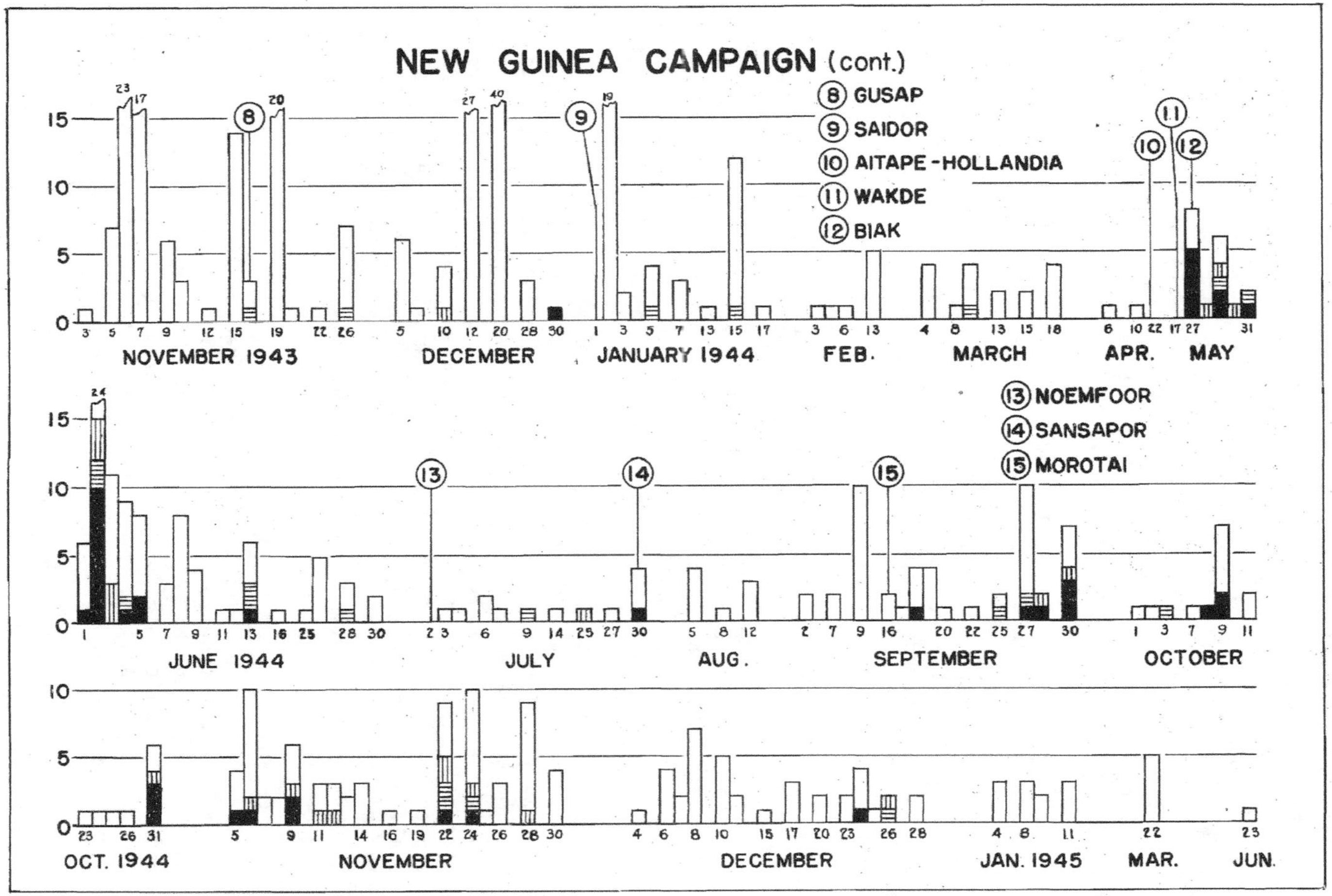
NEW GUINEA CAMPAIGN (cont.)
8 GUSAP
9 SAIDOR
10 AITAPE-HOLLANDIA
11 WAKDE
12 BIAK
13 NOEMFOOR
14 SANSAPOR
15 MOROTAI
NOVEMBER 1943
DECEMBER
JANUARY 1944
FEB.
MARCH
APR.
MAY
JUNE 1944
JULY
AUG.
SEPTEMBER
OCTOBER
OCT. 1944
NOVEMBER
DECEMBER
JAN. 1945
MAR.
JUN.

Fig. 14

entirely by air power and in addition troops were transported by air to small unsurfaced strips at Kaiapit, Bena Bena, and Dumpu.

   f. In Jan 1944 United States troops, by an amphibious landing, took Saidor, beyond Finschhafen. This cut off over 100 miles of coastline from reinforcement from Madang and opened up another advanced air strip. American landings at Aitape, Hollandia, and Tanahmerah Bay on 22 Apr cut off the big Japanese base at Wewak and isolated large bodies of enemy troops. The Australian push up the coast resulted in the capture of Madang and Alexishafen later that month. All of these attacks were preceded by heavy aerial bombing.

   g. In May 1944 the American forces jumped forward to Wakde and Biak Islands, both north of Dutch New Guinea and west of Hollandia, the latter island only 900 miles from the Philippines. The Noemfoor operation of 2 Jul, the landings at Sansapor later that month and at Morotai on 15 Sept brought the New Guinea Campaign to a close. As a result of this campaign the Allies had gained a series of large air bases, within operating range of the Philippines and Borneo.

   h. In the first six months of this campaign the enemy was still capable of assembling large numbers of airplanes on airdromes within range of the Allied strong points in eastern New Guinea. His failure to make more frequent and heavier attacks on the growing bases at Oro Bay, Dobodura, and Milne Bay was not understood. The few that he did make are indicated in the charts accompanying this section. Most of the large raids were made at altitudes that limited the time and volume of heavy antiaircraft gun fire and provided no automatic weapons targets.

   i. Except for occasional raids, the Japanese pilots selected altitudes of attack above the most effective ranges of the defending weapons. They also resorted promptly to evasive action tactics once fire was opened on them or they had dropped their bombs. The effect of re-equipping our units with 90-mm guns and SCR-584 radar appears in the increased percentage of attacks over ten and twenty thousand feet experienced in the later operations of the campaign. It was especially noticeable at Morotai where, after the second gun battalion got into position at the end of Oct, approximately 40% of the attacks were made at altitudes of over 20,000 feet and 32% at between 15,000 and 20,000 feet. Night-time raids became the rule.

   32. *Organization of the Antiaircraft Artillery*. a. All antiaircraft units in tactical positions in New Guinea on 10 Feb 1943 were either assigned or attached for tactical control to the 40th CA Brigade (AA) which, on 16 Jan, had been assigned to the Sixth Army and further assigned to the Allied Air Forces for operational control. The 94th CA (AA), the 208th CA (AA), the 104th CA Bn (AA), and the 707th, 708th, and 709th CA Btries were then assigned to the brigade and the 101st

CA Bn (AA) was attached for tactical control.[1]

b. The units in New Guinea at the beginning of the campaign were located as follows:

    Port Moresby: Hq 1st Bn, and Btries A, B, G, H, and I
                      208th CA (AA)
                      101st CA Bn (AA)
                      Btries D and G, 94th CA (AA)

    Milne Bay: Btry C, 104th CA Bn (AA)

    Poppondetta: 708th CA (AA) Btry

    Dobodura: 707th CA (AA) Btry
                709th CA (AA) Btry

    Oro Bay: Btries C and E, 208th CA (AA)
             One Plat of Btry K, 94th CA (AA)

c. On 15 May 1943 the antiaircraft regiments in the Southwest Pacific area were reorganized into separate group headquarters and battalions.[2] In Jun 1944 the 40th CA Brigade (AA) headquarters and the gun and automatic weapons battalions which had retained their designation as coast artillery (AA) were redesignated as antiaircraft artillery units, and they will be so named hereafter.

d. The period from Apr to Oct of 1943 provided less combat activity than had Feb and Mar and was utilized mainly in training for future operations.

e. On 14 Oct Hq 32d AAA Brigade landed at Milne Bay in New Guinea, thereafter moving forward with Hq Sixth Army to which it was attached. On 18 Oct the following units in tactical positions were attached to the Sixth Army for training and operational control:

    Hq 94th AAA Group
    163d and 743d AAA Gun Bns
    104th, 209th, 469th, and 470th AAA AW Bns
    236th AAA SL Bn

f. The 40th AAA Brigade maintained operational and administrative control of all antiaircraft units in New Guinea that were assigned to the Allied Air Forces. The 32d AAA Brigade had only administrative

---

[1] 40th AAA Brigade Unit Histroy, 2 Oct 45, p 17.

[2] See Annex A, Par 2B.

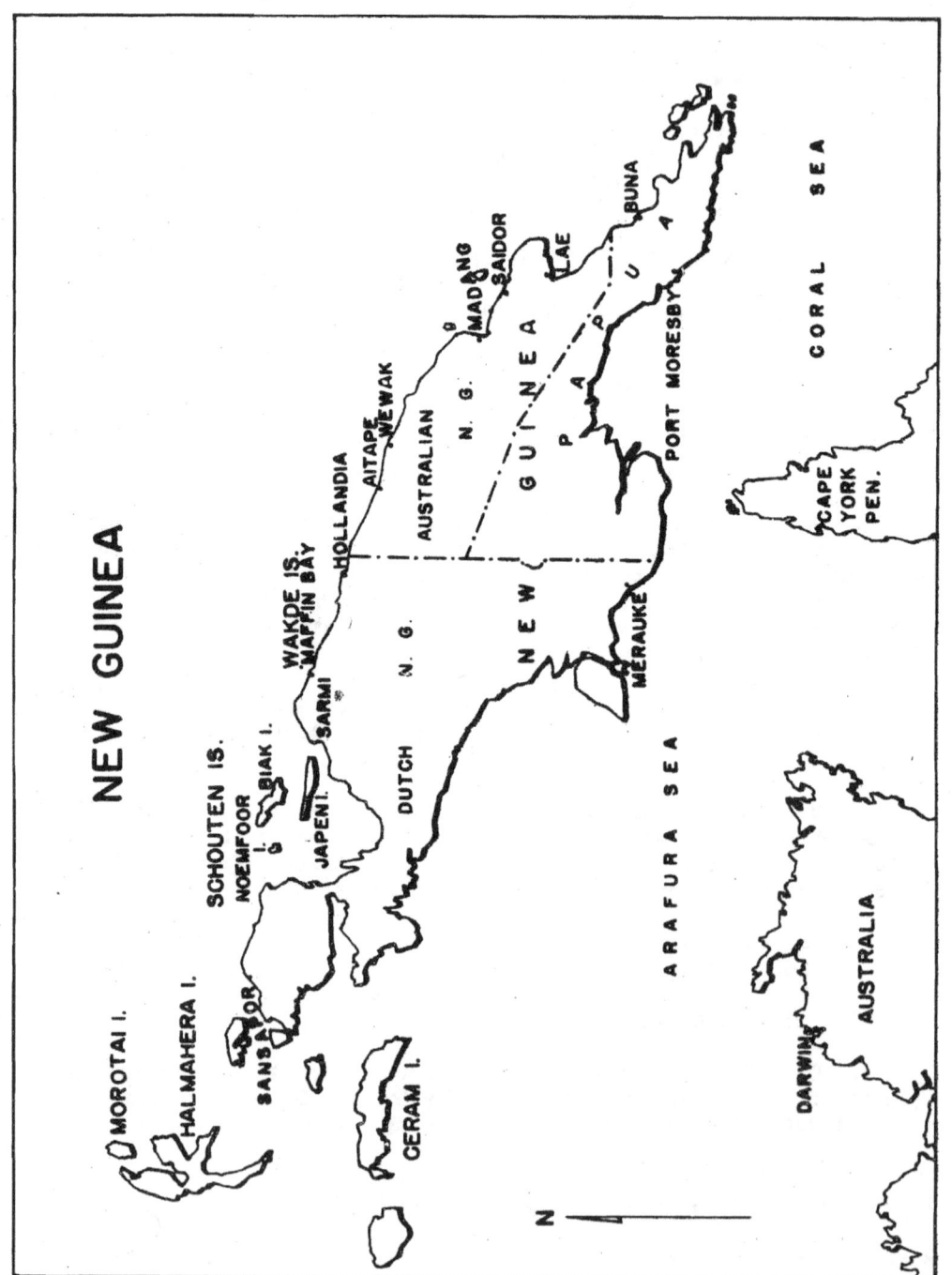

control of those units assigned to the Sixth Army which were engaged in tactical operations, they being attached for operational control to the task force concerned.

g. On 15 Nov 1943 all antiaircraft units in the Southwest Pacific areas were assigned to the 14th AA Command and thereafter were attached to other major commands for tactical uses as required. In general, the command organization followed a cycle. As units were committed to an operation they were attached to the Sixth Army, with specific re-attachments to corps and divisions, and often in the final stages of the campaign, as at Morotai, to the Eighth Army. Later, as the air activities at the locality became predominant they were attached to the air forces, usually through the 40th AAA Brigade, and finally, when no longer needed tactically at the location, and if time permitted, they reverted to the 14th AA Command for refitting and training prior to another operation.

33. <u>Port Moresby</u>. a. The American antiaircraft forces in the defense of Port Moresby at the beginning of this campaign are listed above.[1] This defense was supplemented by the Australian antiaircraft units, which manned eight 3.7" guns and some 36" searchlights.

b. During the period of the New Guinea Campaign there were 11 high altitude raids on Port Moresby. Three of these took place in Jan and caused considerable damage. On 12 Apr 40 medium bombers and 50 fighters attacked the airfields and shipping at Port Moresby from high altitudes. The combined Australian and American antiaircraft claimed two planes destroyed and four probably destroyed in this raid. Allied fighter planes completed the destruction of a large portion of the attacking force. Credit for destroying two planes was awarded jointly to Btries A and B, 208th CA (AA). Credit was given to Btry D, 743d AAA Gun Bn, for destroying two planes in a night raid on 15 May 1943.

c. During the following months there were three additional high-altitude night raids, by flights of up to three aircraft. The last raid took place on 17 Jun 1943 and shortly thereafter the movement of US antiaircraft units from Port Moresby to more advanced locations commenced.

34. <u>Milne Bay</u>. a. The bulk of the antiaircraft defense of Milne Bay was Australian, but Btry C, 104th AAA AW Bn, continued to defend one airstrip at the beginning of the New Guinea Campaign.

b. On 14 Apr 1943, 36 medium bombers, 10 dive bombers, and 30 fighters attacked airdromes and shipping, damaging three vessels. Australian antiaircraft units claimed four planes destroyed and one probably destroyed and the defending fighters caused the enemy

---

1 See Par 32b.

considerable additional losses.

c. This was the last large-scale Japanese air activity at Milne Bay, although intermittent but less intense air raids occurred during Apr, May, Jun, and Jul. The Allied Air Forces kept the Japanese bases neutralized from then on, and destroyed so many planes that the enemy was unable to recover the initiative in the eastern New Guinea area. Early in Jun Btry C, 104th AAA AW Bn, moved forward to Dobodura.

d. Between Aug and Oct the 744th AAA Gun Bn and Btry B of the 237th AAA SL Bn arrived and took up tactical positions at Milne Bay. These were the last of the 41st AAA Brigade units to leave Australia.

e. Although there was little enemy air activity there after the summer of 1943, antiaircraft defenses were maintained for more than a year longer. Milne Bay was a highly important supply base and staging area during this entire period. Additional antiaircraft units continued to arrive and to share in the defense for a time. The 741st AAA Gun Bn arrived on 14 Oct. When the Hq 6th AAA Group arrived on 1 Nov they became responsible to the base for the antiaircraft defenses. In Dec two batteries of the 207th AAA AW Bn were added to the defenses and Btries A and D of the 741st AAA Gun Bn moved out. The 210th AAA AW Bn, which had arrived in May, was replaced by the remaining batteries of the 207th battalion in early 1944. Other changes of assignment, including the replacement of the 207th AAA AW Bn by the 208th AAA AW Bn, occurred during the period prior to the departure of the 6th AAA Group in May 1944.

f. During the whole period Nov 1943 to May 1944 there were only six alerts and only once was an enemy aircraft seen. Upon the departure of the 6th AAA Group, Hq 741st AAA Gun Bn assumed control of the tactical defenses of Milne Bay, using Btries B and C of that battalion, the 208th AAA AW Bn, and Btry A, 238th AAA SL Bn. These units provided the antiaircraft defense of Milne Bay until 30 Oct 1944.

35. <u>Oro Bay</u>. a. Oro Bay was a vital link in the supply line for the forces engaging the Japanese at Buna and along the New Guinea coast, and for the growing air bases at Dobodura. It was defended by frequently changing units of American and Australian antiaircraft artillery.

b. Btry E, 208th CA (AA), came to Oro Bay in Dec 1942. Some of its sections were among the first of the task force troops on the beach, and the battery remained there until Sept 1943. It received credit for shooting down two Japanese dive-bombers while still armed with single mount cal .50 machine guns. Btry C, 208th CA (AA), arrived in Jan 1943 and was in position until relieved by Australian heavies in Jun. It, too, is credited with two enemy planes shot down. Btry C, 102d AAA AW Bn, was in position at Oro Bay from Jul to Nov 1943 but had no action except a few rounds fired by one section at an out-of-range target in the raid of 15 Oct.

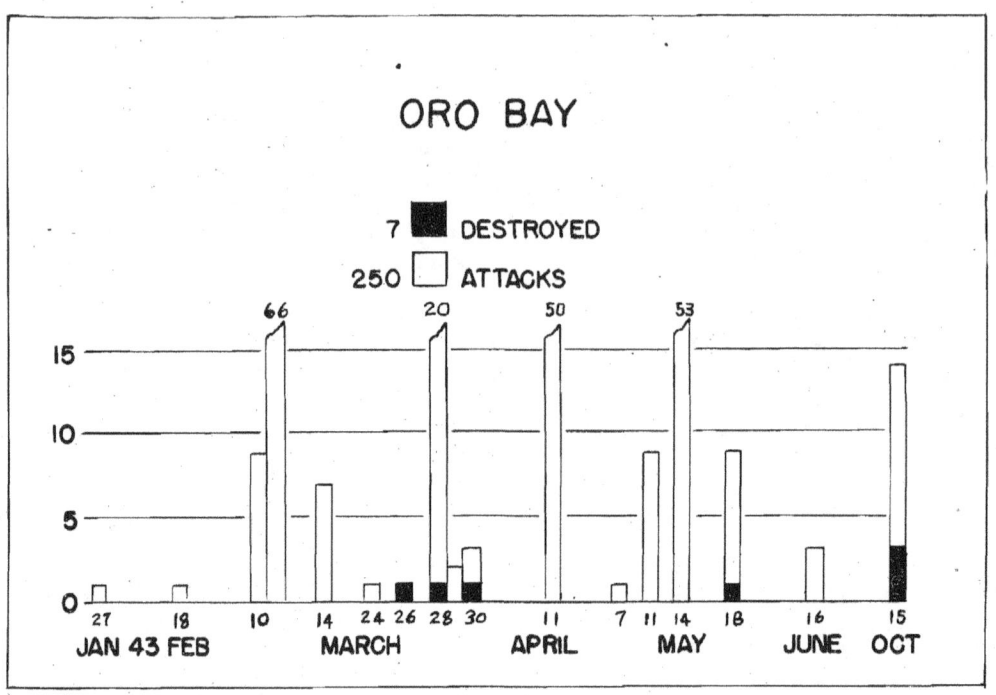

Fig. 15

c. Btry B, 477th AAA AW Bn, relieved Australian troops in Feb 1944 and remained in tactical location until Nov. There was no action during that period.

d. The Japanese made a heavy raid with 40 to 50 planes on 11 Apr 1943 in an attempt to cripple our shipping. Relatively little damage resulted. The combined Australian and American antiaircraft units claimed four planes destroyed. Our fighters engaged and destroyed a large part of the attacking force. In a small raid on 18 May one enemy bomber was destroyed. Other raids in May and Jun resulted in no enemy losses and little damage to Allied property.

e. In a dramatic raid on the morning of 15 Oct eight enemy planes dive-bombed the ship on which Btry B, 102d AAA AW Bn, was loaded enroute to Finschhafen. Some of its guns were emplaced on the deck of the LST. Three of the bombers were destroyed by the battery's weapons and two others were destroyed by the naval antiaircraft guns, while the other three were believed to have been damaged by the combined antiaircraft fire. United States fighters intercepted the remaining dive-bombers and escorting fighters, and the air force claimed that only one returned to the enemy bases in New Britain.

36. **Dobodura.** a. The development of the Dobodura air base, home of the First Air Task Force, from one grass strip at the beginning of the campaign to seven surfaced and one grass strip in Oct called for increasing amounts of antiaircraft artillery. The two airborne machine gun batteries which furnished the initial antiaircraft defense were reinforced by automatic weapons and gun batteries as the area was opened up and the units could be transported in. Btry F, 208th CA (AA), arrived on 19 Mar from Townsville and was followed by Btry D, 745th AAA Gun Bn on 16 May. Btry C of the same battalion and elements of Btry B, 236th AAA SL Bn, arrived from Oro Bay on 5 Jun. Btry C, 104th AAA AW, arrived on 11 Jun. A provisional headquarters staffed with personnel from the headquarters of the 208th AAA Group and the 211th AAA AW Bn controlled the defenses here and at Oro Bay until Jul.

b. At the peak of the defense the following units were in position around the strips, the two airborne machine gun batteries having moved out in Jun and Aug as the reinforcements moved in:[1]

       Hq 208th AAA Group
       745th AAA Gun Bn
       211th AAA AW Bn (less Btry C)
       Btry C, 104th AAA AW Bn
       102d AAA AW Bn (less Btry C)
       238th AAA SL Bn (less Btries A and C)

c. The 477th AAA AW Bn, arriving in Jan 1944, replaced the 102d Bn which had moved forward in Oct. Btries C and D, 744th AAA Gun Bn, were temporarily in positions in Sept while staging in the area. In the early months of 1944, as the use of the air strips diminished, the defenses were weakened by movement of units to other operations.

d. Hq 197th AAA Group was given command of the combined Australian and American antiaircraft defenses of the entire Buna-Oro Bay-Dobodura area from its arrival in mid-July until its departure for Nadzab in early Sept. At this time the joint command passed to the 208th AAA Group which had been responsible for the Dobodura defenses since its arrival early in Jul.

e. Almost all of the raids during the period were at high altitudes. In Oct the Dobodura defenders went into action a number of times against enemy planes crossing the area after attacking Buna or Oro Bay, as well as on several raiding planes striking at the air strip area. One plane was destroyed and one damaged by the fire of the 745th AAA Gun Bn, while the 211th CA Bn (AA) received credit for destroying one plane. The 211th Bn lost one man killed and had several wounded when two bombs landed in its headquarters bivouac.

---

[1] Unit designations used are those after reorganization of 15 May 1943 see Annex A.

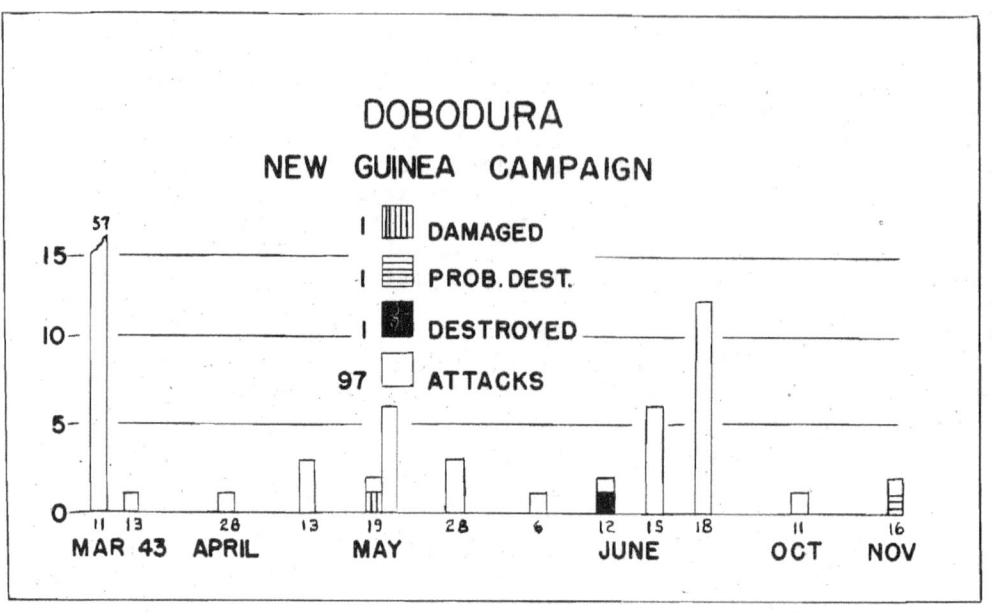

Fig. 16

37. <u>Goodenough Island</u>. a. Late in Oct 1942 a single Australian battalion occupied this strategic island to deny its use to the Japanese in the struggle for the northern Papuan coast. In May of 1943 American units began to move on to the island to develop it as a staging area. In the fall it became the headquarters for the Sixth Army.

b. The first antiaircraft units to arrive were Btries A and B of the 104th AAA AW Bn, and Btry A, 236th AAA SL Bn. On 6 Aug the 94th AAA Group Hq, which had directed the antiaircraft defense of the Sixth Army Hq at Milne Bay, landed at Goodenough. From there it exercised tactical command of the antiaircraft defenses of Goodenough, Kiriwina, and Woodlark Islands. With it came Btries A and D of the 743d AAA Gun Bn and the 209th AAA AW Bn (less Btry C).

c. In Nov Hq 32d AAA Brigade took over the command of the area antiaircraft defenses. Later in the month, Btries B and C of the 163d AAA Gun Bn arrived and went into tactical positions. Btry C, 209th AAA AW Bn, also was moved in from New Guinea to join its parent battalion after a year of independent action.

d. Up to this time there had been no enemy air activity against Goodenough. However, a night raid by 28 enemy bombers took place on 20 Dec. Although there were some Allied airplanes destroyed, antiaircraft fire and searchlights successfully prevented damage to the airstrip and to the Sixth Army installations. There were several low-altitude sneak raids later but the Dec raid was the only heavy air attack on the island.

e. During the month Goodenough was the staging area for the offensive operations against Arawe and Saidor. The 32d AAA Brigade Hq moved to Finschhafen with the Headquarters Sixth Army at the end of Feb 1944, and the importance of Goodenough rapidly diminished as the Allies successfully gained new positions to the northwest along the New Guinea coast. The antiaircraft units progressively left as they were needed for new operations.

38. <u>Kiriwina</u>. a. A surprise landing was made on Kiriwina Island by the 158th RCT on 22 Jun 1943 to secure the strategic airstrip there. Hq and Btries B and C, 743d AAA Gun Bn, Btries A, B, and D, 209th AAA AW Bn, and the 1st Plat, Btry A, 236th AAA SL Bn, were attached to the task force. These units had staged at Milne Bay and participated in the landing. Between 3 Aug and the end of Oct there were ten air raids by the enemy, all of them small and most of them at night. Antiaircraft fire rendered these raids ineffective. Credit for one plane probably destroyed was given to the 743d AAA Gun Bn.

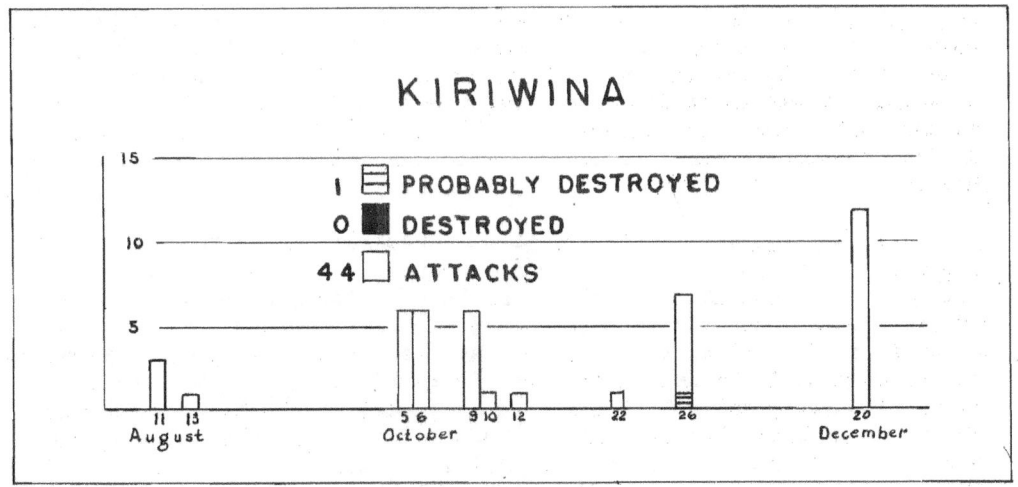

Fig. 17

b. Hq 116th AAA Group arrived in Dec with Btry D of the 741st AAA Gun Bn. Hq 743d AAA Gun Bn departed with Btries B and D of the 209th AAA AW Bn for Saidor on 25 Dec 1943. The other units remained at Kiriwina until the spring of 1944. There was no further antiaircraft action.

39. <u>Woodlark</u>. a. On the same day, 22 Jun 1943, that Kiriwina was occupied the 112th Cav Regt landed on Woodlark Island. The antiaircraft defense was provided by the 12th Marine Defense Battalion which

- 57 -

remained in position until Nov.

b. In that month Hq and Btries A and B, 470th AAA AW Bn, Btries A and D of the 163d AAA Gun Bn, and the 1st Plat, Btry B of the 236th AAA SL Bn replaced the 12th Marine Defense Battalion. The defenses were under control of Hq, 470th AAA AW Bn.

c. There was only one bomber sneak raid over the island but, due to the hill masks, warning was ineffective and no antiaircraft weapons fired at the enemy targets. In Mar 1944 all units left, the island having been abandoned as an airbase.

40. <u>Morobe, Nassau and Tambu Bays</u>. a. Following the capture of the Buna-Gona defenses Australian and American forces pushed northwestward along the coast after the retreating remnants of the enemy. Our antiaircraft went along wherever it could be used. When Morobe was reached Btry C, 209th AAA AW Bn, moved in from Port Moresby on 20 Apr 1943 for antiaircraft defense of the stores and harbor. Australian heavy antiaircraft guns were subsequently emplaced.

b. After Nassau Bay was occupied on 30 Jun part of the battery was moved forward. This process was repeated in Aug when Tambu Bay came into Allied use; eventually the whole battery was in advanced posts. It was while based here that several 40-mm sections of Btry C made it possible for the infantry to cross the hitherto impassable Roosevelt Ridge[1] to assist in the capture of Salamaua. In these operations Btry C had relatively few air engagements, but received credit for destruction of three planes at Tambu Bay and a float plane at Morobe.

41. <u>Bulolo, Wau, Tsili-Tsili</u>. a. Progress along the coast as represented by these operations was concurrent with an airborne advance inland. The 708th AAA MG Btry, an airborne unit, was transported on 19 Feb from Poppondetta to Bulolo, a strip only a few miles from the airstrip at Wau which, with Bulolo, was used to supply by air Australian troops engaged in harassing the enemy's rear and denying him the use of the Wau strip and gold mines. In July part of the battery took up positions at Wau. The sections at Bulolo had a number of engagements with enemy aircraft returning from raids on Wau.

b. In Jul 1943 Btry C, 211th AAA AW Bn, was employed in an airborne operation into the Markham Valley. It occupied positions on an uncompleted strip at Tsili-Tsili to provide a defense for the fighter escorts that made possible the destructive Aug raids on Wewak. After the Japanese located the strip that month 33 raids were experienced. Btry C claimed three planes probably destroyed and was instrumental in

---

1 See Chap 3, Sec II, Par 110.

driving off the others. The 709th AAA MG Btry also went to Tsili-Tsili by air in July. In a raid on 15 Aug 1943 that battery claimed the destruction of one Jap fighter, and several other fighters were believed to have been damaged.

42. **Bena Bena (Garoke Field).** A detachment of one officer and thirteen enlisted men from Btry C, 211th AAA AW Bn, was moved to Bena Bena to protect the strip on 12 Jun 1943, remaining there until 12 Oct. As a result of one 24 plane raid on 14 Jun the battery claimed one aircraft destroyed.

43. **Nadzab.** a. The need for a more advanced base than Dobodura after the fall of Salamaua and Lae led to the parachutist seizure on 5 Sept 1943 of the broad fields at Nadzab, 25 miles up the Markham Valley from Lae. The 707th AAA MG Btry moved in by air the next day. The 708th AAA MG Btry followed by air ten days after the airborne attack. On 29 Sept the headquarters of the 197th AAA Group arrived and exercised control of the antiaircraft defenses at Nadzab, Finschhafen, and Gusap, until Mar 1944.

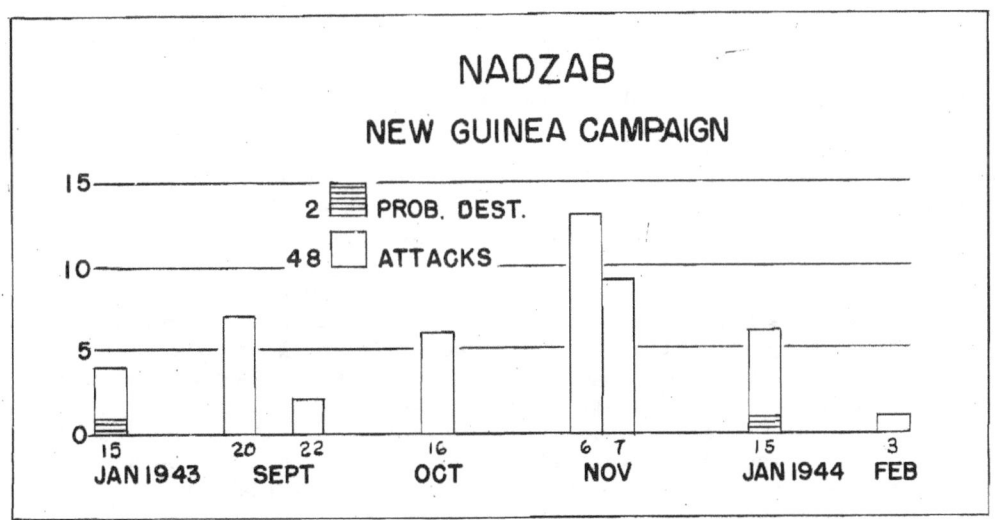

Fig. 18

b. Early in Oct personnel of Btries B and C, 744th AAA Gun Bn, were flown in to prepare positions for their guns which were to be moved as soon as a passable road could be completed from Lae. Btry A, 102d AAA AW Bn, and Btry C, 211th AAA AW Bn, came by C-47 planes in Oct with all of their armament, again emphasizing the value of the study of the air transportation of standard 40-mm guns detailed in Chap 5, Sec II, Par 142 of this report.

c. In Dec 1943 Hq 12th AB AAA Bn, the 665th and 670th AAA MG Btries, and the 472d AAA AW Bn arrived to reinforce the Nadzab defenses. The 101st AAA AW Bn reached Lae by water from Port Moresby on 12 Dec and moved into Nadzab about a week later. The 161st AAA Gun Bn arrived in Jan 1944. In Mar, when the 197th AAA Group moved forward to Gusap, the 10th AAA Group took over command of the area antiaircraft defenses.

d. During Dec and Jan there were seven enemy air raids, on only one of which the planes came within reach of the emplaced weapons. This occurred on 15 Jan, when six dive-bombers strafed the airstrips, and the 101st AAA AW Bn claimed credit for hits on four planes. The 707th and 708th AAA MG Btries each received credit for one probable destruction in the same raid.

e. The weapons for the 744th AAA Gun Bn units did not arrive until after these raids. Except for a single plane raid in Feb there was no further enemy air action at Nadzab.

44. <u>Lae</u>. Btry D, 102d AAA AW Bn, landed at Lae on 19 Sept 1943 shortly after the Australians had taken the area. Their mission was to protect the air strip then being repaired for Allied use. Hostile air action was limited to two daylight raids, on 21 and 22 Sept, at medium altitudes. The battery engaged on both occasions with unknown results. In Dec the battery moved to Gusap.

45. <u>Kaiapit</u>. After its stay at Tsili Tsili the 709th AAA MG Btry moved by air on 23 Sept 1943 to Kaiapit, where for three weeks it provided both antiaircraft and ground defenses for the airstrip. No action took place before the 709th left for Gusap.

46. <u>Gusap</u>. a. In order to strike deeper into the enemy areas, to beat down his air force at its bases, and to harass his supply lines along the coast, the Fifth Air Force decided to build strips at Gusap, 75 miles further up the Markham Valley. These strips were to be used for advanced bases for fighter planes escorting the bombers that took off from Nadzab. The distance and the terrain conditions were such that it was impracticable to build a supply road. All the personnel, equipment, and supplies to build and operate the five strips, as well as the antiaircraft and other ground troops to defend the area, had to be transported by air.

b. Btry A, 102d AAA AW Bn, was flown to Gusap on 7 and 10 Nov 1943, followed by Btry C a week later and by Btry D in mid-December. During the same period, the 662d, 663d, 671st, 672d, and 709th AAA MG Btries arrived. Hq 9th AB AAA Bn arrived on 2 Dec and became the antiaircraft defense command for Gusap in Jan.

c. On 15 Feb Hq 3d AB AAA Bn arrived to take over the tactical control of four of the machine gun batteries. Hq 197th AAA Group moved up from Nadzab in Mar and commanded the defenses at Gusap until Jun. At that time Hq 3d AB AAA Bn, together with the batteries under its control, was withdrawn to Nadzab; the 9th AB AAA Bn followed in Jul to train for future operations.

    d. There were two raids on Gusap in Dec 1943. Four planes strafed the area on the tenth and 27 planes made a raid two days later. On 15 Jan 1944 Btry C, 102d AAA AW Bn, received credit for one plane damaged, and on 4 Mar Btry D of the same battalion claimed to have shot down two planes, scored two probables and one damaged. In a raid on 29 Mar there were no results.

    e. Early warning was not effective in this locality. The proximity of the mountains surrounding the strips interferred with the operation of the lightweight early warning radar and the difficult terrain made it impossible to maintain enough observation posts for an effective AAAIS.

47. Finschhafen. a. As soon as the fall of Lae was certain the Australians started their drive along the coast to capture Finschhafen. The Allied plans called for the establishment there of airstrips and a sub-base with harbor installations capable of handling Liberty ships.

    b. The task of making an amphibious landing to coordinate with the coastal push was assigned to the Australian 20th Brigade, supported by the United States 532d Boat and Shore Regiment. The landings at Scarlet Beach, five miles north of Finschhafen, began on 22 Sept 1943. Against stiff Japanese resistance the Australians drove south and Finschhafen was cleared on 2 Oct. The Japanese, however, withdrew into the hills and in the following weeks launched several strong counter-attacks. It was not until 5 Nov that the Japanese were finally cleared from Satelberg Hill, a short distance northwest of Finschhafen.

    c. The initial antiaircraft support was provided by Australian units, but Btries A and B, 744th AAA Gun Bn, landed on 20 Oct and Hq and Btry B, 102d AAA AW Bn, arrived two days later. The commander of the 102d Bn assumed control of the American antiaircraft which was concentrated for the defense of the air strip being constructed south of Finschhafen, and the adjoining harbor and shore facilities. There were frequent raids during Oct and Nov. Most of these came at night, usually made by a single plane characteristically known as "Sewing Machine Charley". The enemy usually was fired upon, using SCR-268 data, but with no known results.

    d. When Hq and Btry A, 237th AAA SL Bn, and the 664th AAA MG Btry arrived early in Nov the Bn Hq relieved Hq 102d AAA AW Bn of area command of American antiaircraft and set up an antiaircraft operations center. Raids continued but most of them centered on the northern part of the area which was protected by Australian antiaircraft. Hq 102d AAA AW Bn shortly went to Gusap.

e. In Feb the 166th AAA Gun Bn and the 478th AAA AW Bn joined the Finschhafen area defenses, and Hq 120th AAA Group arrived in Mar to assume command. In the succeeding months Finschhafen became the principal staging and training area for antiaircraft units in the Southwest Pacific[1] and a large number of the units in the theater spent some time there.

48. Saidor. a. After the successful Allied operations at Lae, Salamaua, and Finschhafen, followed by advances up the Markham and Ramu Valleys, a landing without losses was made by units of the 23d Div at Saidor on 2 Jan 1944. This move was intended to cut off reinforcements for the enemy from Madang and to make available an advanced fighter base from which to protect our bombers and harass the enemy's troops and shipping. The antiaircraft units attached to this Sixth Army task force were staged at Goodenough Island and included Hq and Btries A and D, 743d AAA Gun Bn, Btries B and D of the 209th AAA AW Bn, and the 2d Plat, Btry A, of the 236th AAA SL Bn.

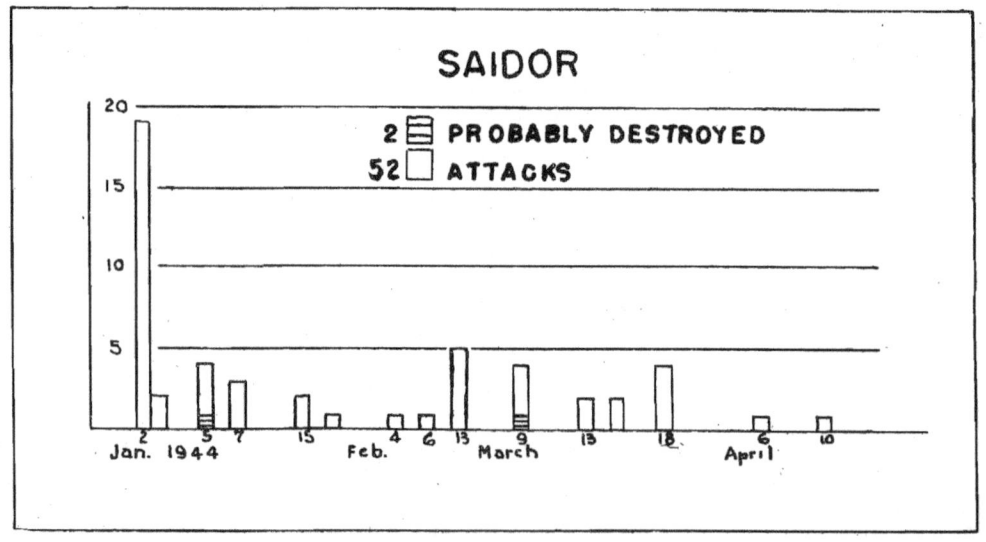

Fig. 19

b. During the period from 2 Jan to 10 Apr 1944 there were 18 raids. Antiaircraft weapons engaged 46 enemy planes with a score of two planes probably destroyed for the 209th AAA AW Bn. Some of the raids caused considerable damage, especially on 15 Mar when twelve bombs dropped by two enemy planes destroyed a gasoline dump.

c. All the units remained in position until 9 Nov 1944 when Btries B and D of the 209th AAA AW Bn were moved to Finschhafen. The 743d AAA Gun Bn departed from Saidor on 11 May 1945.

---

[1] See Chap 4 Sec III Par 137 a (7).

49. **Hollandia.** a. The landings to take Hollandia on 22 Apr 1944 were simultaneous with the landing at Aitape. With I Corps directing the operations, the 41st Div (less the 163d RCT) came ashore at Humboldt Bay while the 24th Div (less the 34th RCT, I Corps reserve) debarked at Tanahmerah Bay, about 30 miles to the west, and converged on the airstrip areas adjacent to Sentani Lake, inland between the two bays.

b. For this operation the 116th AAA Group was attached to the 41st Div and landed with them at Humboldt Bay. The 469th AAA AW Bn, the 165th AAA Gun Bn, Btries A and C of the 163d AAA Gun Bn, and Btry B of the 227th AAA SL Bn were attached.

c. At the same time Hq 94th AAA Group landed at Tanahmerah Bay with Hq and Btries B and D of the 163d AAA Gun Bn, the 104th AAA AW Bn, and Btry A of the 227th AAA SL Bn as attached units. The Group, less Btry A, 104th AAA AW Bn, was subsequently ordered into position adjacent to the airdromes. The overland route from Tanahmerah to the air strip area was blocked by mountains, so the antiaircraft units moved down the shore by LCT and cut through 12 miles of jungle after landing at Hollandia. Btry A, 469th AAA AW Bn, joined the Group in the initial airdrome defense.

d. The mission of the antiaircraft units was the defense of the landing areas and docks, with provision for the defense of the airstrips as it became necessary. The first air attack came the day after the landing, when one low-flying plane approached without warning and started a fire in a captured enemy dump. The fire later spread to Allied ammunition and ration stores and as a result of this calamity, troops fighting at Hollandia were on half rations for several weeks after the raid.

e. Although during the first three weeks air raid alerts were sounded six to eight times each night, on only three occasions did enemy bombers appear. The last raid was made without dropping bombs, due to the intense fire of antiaircraft units.

f. Although the 32d AAA Brigade did not officially enter the operations, a Provisional Groupment Headquarters was formed under the acting Brigade Commander and exercised operational control over the antiaircraft units engaged.

g. On 6 May the 673d, 707th, and 708th AAA MG Btries were flown in and took up defensive positions at the airdromes.

h. Btries B and C of the 166th AAA Gun Bn arrived at Hollandia on 13 May 1944 and added to the defense of the expanding air facilities. Btry C, 163d AAA Gun Bn, took position along Hollandia Bay while Btry A of the same battalion moved to Tami airstrip, which the Japanese had been constructing but had not completed. At the end of June Btry A of the 163d AAA Gun Bn took over the positions of Btry B, 163d AAA Gun

Bn, which with Btry C of the same battalion, departed from Hollandia on 7 Jul.

 i. The last enemy air raid at Hollandia was made on 27 May 1944 but no bombs were dropped. The antiaircraft units settled down to a static defense of the airstrips, ground installations and shipping in the bay.

 j. The Hollandia operation was officially ended on 6 Jun 1944. On 20 Jun Hq 116th AAA Group was relieved from tactical assignment and departed from Hollandia, and at that time the Provisional Groupment Headquarters was abolished. On 26 Sept 1944 Hq 94th AAA Group departed to stage for another operation.

 50. <u>Aitape</u>. a. At the same time that the Allied forces made the jump past the enemy stronghold at Wewak to Hollandia, a landing was made at Aitape by the 163d RCT, supported by the 383d AAA AW Bn, to which were attached Btries B and C, 743d AAA Gun Bn, and the 1st Plat, Btry C, 227th AAA SL Bn.

 b. Antiaircraft guns were on the beach ready for action within 45 minutes of the initial landing and by nightfall a large part of the force, with radar and searchlights, was prepared for action. Enemy ground opposition was relatively light. Our assault forces moved inland quickly, leaving numerous Japanese snipers to be mopped up, some by antiaircraft troops.

 c. The only enemy air attack occurred on the night of 27 - 29 Apr, during a thunderstorm, when an enemy plane made a successful low altitude attack on a Liberty ship in the anchorage. One aircraft was observed but not identified as it flew over the beach at extremely low altitude prior to its attack, but the antiaircraft artillery did not engage as there were friendly aircraft in the area.

 d. In early May the antiaircraft units moved to permanent tactical positions. The gun batteries were placed under the field artillery fire direction center for terrestrial fire missions. As the new positions were occupied the antiaircraft situation became static and the units devoted most of their time to training for future operations and experimenting on various methods of employing antiaircraft materiel to assist in ground combat.

 e. On 10 Sept 1944, with offensive operations at an end at Aitape, the 383d AAA AW Bn departed to participate in the landing at Morotai. The other antiaircraft units remained several months more.

 51. <u>Wakde Island</u>. a. Having moved our ground operations forward to Hollandia, even more advanced bases were desired. The next landing of the campaign was made on Wakde, a small coral island just off the Dutch New Guinea coast, about 120 miles west of the Hollandia base. It offered very favorable terrain for a large airstrip.

b. Hq and Btries A and D of the 166th AAA Gun Bn, Btries B and C of the 202d AAA AW Bn, and Btry B, 236th AAA SL Bn, were attached to the Sixth Army task force whose main components were the 158th and 163d RCTs. This force landed on Wakde Island on 17 May 1944 and soon spread over the shore facing the island, from Arara to the Tor River. Btries A and D of the 202d AAA AW Bn joined the force on 24 May.

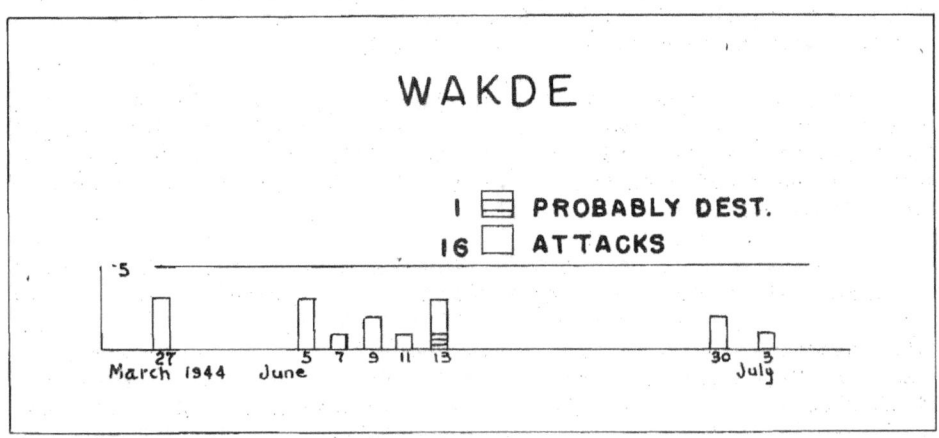

Fig. 20

c. During the operation at Wakde there were eight raids by 16 planes, mostly taking place at night. The first raid came on 26 May, a heavy attack engaged by guns, automatic weapons and searchlights. Only one plane probably destroyed was confirmed in the whole period, credit going to Btry D, 166th AAA Gun Bn. No visible targets for automatic weapons were presented in any of the raids, but on two occasions barrage fire by the 202d AAA AW Bn drove off the enemy planes.

d. On no occasion did enemy raiders penetrate the defended area or bomb any installation when antiaircraft artillery was released to fire, but, unfortunately, release normally came only after the bombs had been dropped.

e. The extension of the operation to the New Guinea shore gave the gun battalion opportunities for long-range terrestrial fire,[1] as the Maffin Bay area was cleared for a future staging area.

52. **Biak**. a. The landing on Biak Island followed closely after the taking of Wakde. When the 41st Div, reinforced, landed on 25 May 1944 it was supported by a strong antiaircraft force which included:

---

[1] See Chap 3 Sec II Par 111 i.

- 65 -

Hq 208th AAA Group
165th AAA Gun Bn
476th AAA AW Bn
Btry C, 236th AAA SL Bn
674th and 675th AAA MG Btries

b. Last minute changes limited the planning phase to ten days. The first antiaircraft troops to land were the machine gun batteries which were ready to fire five minutes after landing.

c. Btry B, 165th AAA Gun Bn, and Btries A and B, 476th AAA AW Bn, as well as Btry C, 236th AAA SL Bn, all were emplaced on Z-day. Btry A of the 165th AAA Gun Bn, and Btry C of the 476th AAA AW Bn, arrived to augment the beach defenses the next day. All the antiaircraft units in the task force had landed by 31 May.[1]

d. The Japanese air reaction to this landing was more prompt and active than against the preceding assaults. There were 36 raids by 124 aircraft resulting in a confirmed total of 24 planes destroyed, 7 planes probably destroyed and 10 damaged. Nine of the raids were made during daylight and 27 at night. Seven of the first 12 raids were between dawn and dusk whereas only two of the last 24 were daylight raids. Both of these were made at dawn and at a very low altitude, and arrived with no radar warning.

e. The daylight raids were made mostly by fighters which strafed and dive-bombed the beachhead during the early phases of the operation. The night raids generally were medium-altitude attacks, except in the first ten days of the operation, when several were low-altitude attacks.

f. Most of the daylight targets came in very low, parallel to the shore line, and made excellent targets for the automatic weapons emplaced on the beach. The fire of the multiple-mount (M-51) cal .50 antiaircraft machine guns was especially effective against this type of target. The night raids in many cases were driven off by the 90-mm guns and the damage resulting from the raids was comparatively light. The searchlights were used to advantage in illuminating both low and high flying targets.

g. Of the 24 planes destroyed, 16 were credited to the 476th AAA AW Bn, which unit received a Presidential Citation for its efforts in this operation.

h. The Biak operation marked the beginning of planned efforts by the enemy in the Southwest Pacific area to set up radar interference. There had been indications in 1943 of experiments with radar countermeasures and these were experienced frequently in the Makin Island

---

1 Final Combat Reports 165th AAA Gun Bn, 476th AAA AW Bn.

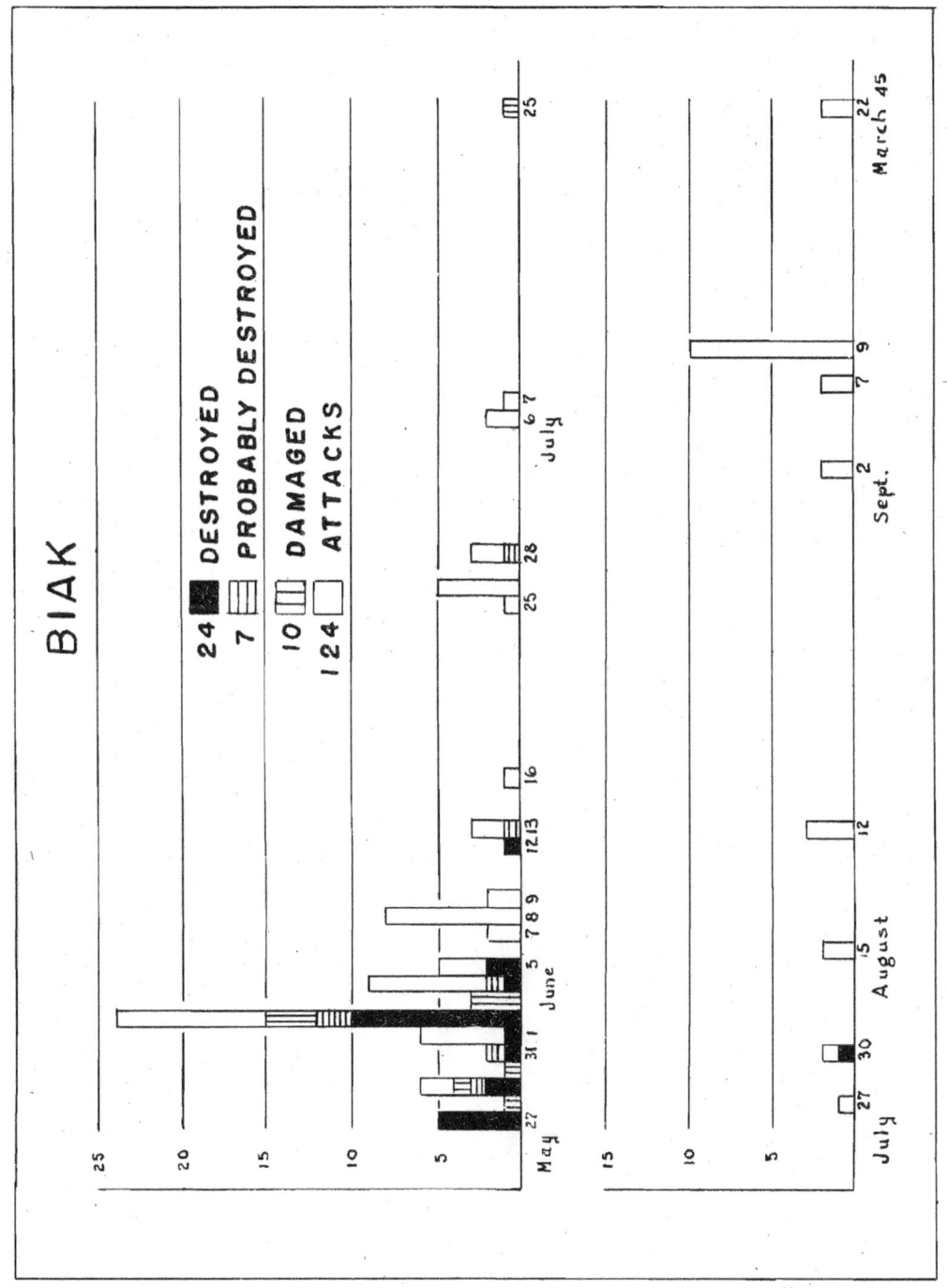

Fig. 21

- 67 -

battle.[1] There was practically no jamming during the early stages of the operation but more and more instances were noted during the later high-altitude night raids. The SCR-268's were able to track through this interference with little difficulty and the SCR-584's were not hampered. The interference was often caused by foil reflectors dropped in the area by decoy planes.

    i. During the operation, which was officially declared ended on 20 Aug, the antiaircraft units participated in almost all types of ground firing, the 90-mm guns in counter-battery, the automatic weapons in field artillery support, and personnel in patrol action and perimeter defense.

    53. <u>Noemfoor</u>. a. The next Allied move to isolate garrisons in Dutch New Guinea and provide advanced fighter bases involved the taking of Noemfoor Island which, with Biak, controls the entrance to Goelvink Bay.

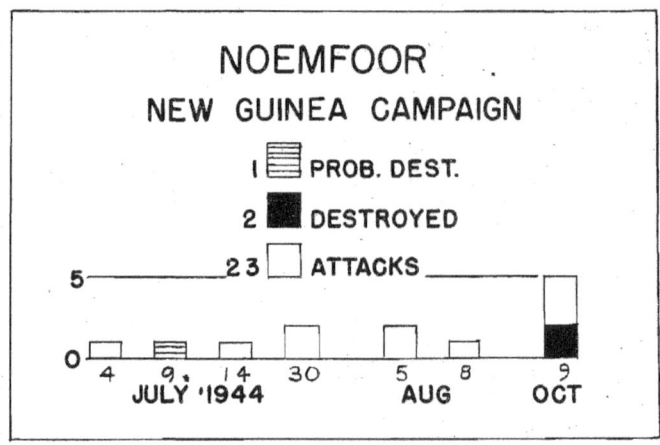

Fig. 22

    b. The landing on 2 Jul 1944 was by a Sixth Army task force, consisting principally of the 158th RCT. The antiaircraft units in the operation were led by Hq, 116th AAA Group, and included the 487th AAA AW Bn, 745th AAA Gun Bn, Btry A of the 222d AAA SL Bn, and the 707th and 708th AAA MG Btries. Btries B and D of the 745th AAA Gun Bn, 11 sections of the 487th AAA AW Bn, and both of the machine-gun batteries were landed with the assault forces and were in position ready to fire that day. The remaining units came in later.

1 See Par 9 e.

c. Japanese air reaction consisted of seven intermittent raids by 13 aircraft during Jul and Aug. The 487th AAA AW Bn received credit for one plane probably destroyed on 9 Jul. After a lull of more than a month four enemy planes, one at low altitude, attacked on 9 Oct in the last raid. The 487th AAA AW Bn destroyed one, and a twin-engine bomber was credited to the 745th AAA Gun Bn.

d. After the first four days the 707th and 708th AAA MG Btries were relieved from their antiaircraft mission and assigned to perimeter defense and counter-intelligence patrolling. Btry A, 222d AAA SL Bn, was used for illuminating the bomber strips at Noemfoor and while thus employed developed new techniques[1] in cooperating with the air forces on the ground.

e. All air attacks came at night, or just prior to dawn, generally at low altitude in cooperation with a high-altitude diversionary aircraft. At all times when antiaircraft fire was not restricted the results were effective in limiting damage. Hits were scored on 23% of the attackers.

f. All of the antiaircraft units remained at Noemfoor after the campaign had officially ended on 31 Aug 1944, until moved to stage for other operations.

54. Sansapor. a. Jumping to the western end of New Guinea on 30 Jul 1944, a Sixth Army task force landed at Sansapor and in the succeeding days enlarged their control of the area to include nearby Middelburg and Amsterdam Islands, where two airstrips were constructed. The task force was composed principally of the 6th Div. Hq 33d AAA Group was attached in order to coordinate the antiaircraft defense provided by the 496th AAA Gun Bn, 198th AAA AW Bn, 674th and 675th AAA MG Btries, and Btry B, 222d AAA SL Bn.

b. The landings took place with almost no enemy opposition. Btry D of the gun battalion, Btry D of the automatic weapons battalion, and the 674th AAA MG Btry, as well as elements of the searchlight battery landed on D-day to provide antiaircraft protection for the beachhead. The remaining units landed soon afterwards and within ten days all units were in position at Sansapor, or on Amsterdam and Middelburg Islands.

c. During the whole period of the Sansapor occupation there were 15 air raids by 23 planes. Japanese tactics were at first fairly successful in minimizing the effectiveness of the antiaircraft artillery defenses. Decoy planes approached from the sea to occupy the attention of the radars while the main attack force came in over the mountains to escape detection. They were often able to drop bombs before the gun

---

[1] See Chap 3, Sec IV, Par 122 a.

batteries could shift to the real target. By more careful attention to primary and secondary defense sectors, with the mainland batteries covering the mountain approaches, the enemy planes were thereafter engaged before they reached their bomb release lines. The last anti-aircraft action took place on 30 Dec 1944 when an enemy reconnaissance plane was shot down by the 496th AAA Gun Bn at a time when the harbor and channel were filled with supply ships for the Luzon operation.

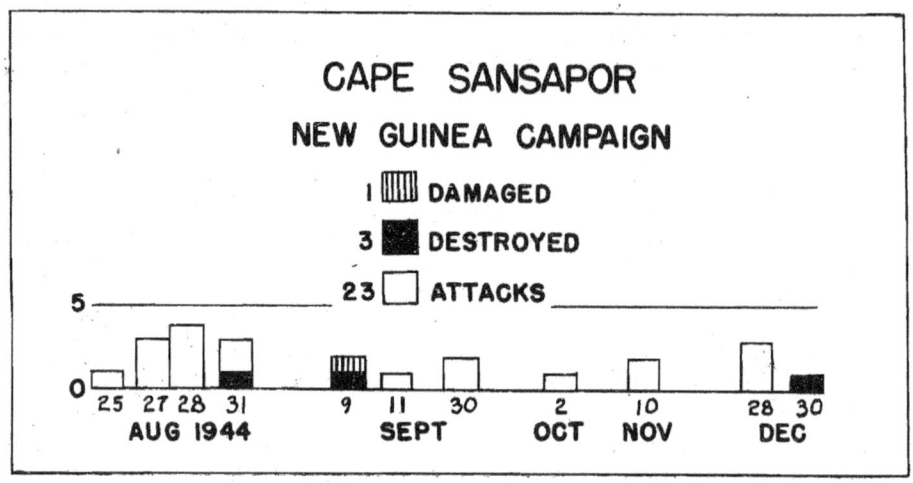

Fig. 23

d. The only enemy losses were credited to the 496th AAA Gun Bn, a total of three planes destroyed and one damaged.

e. While at Sansapor Btry B of the 222d AAA SL Bn effectively illuminated 18 planes, 13 of which were flicked originally on SCR-268 data at ranges from 35,000 to 56,000 yards. They also provided illumination for construction work on the two air strips.

f. Sansapor was evacuated in Apr 1944 and the antiaircraft units were moved to staging areas.

55. <u>Morotai</u>. a. The Morotai operation was directed by the XI Corps under the Sixth Army, the assault being made by the 31st Div reinforced by the 126th RCT. This landing put the Southwest Pacific forces north of the equator and in the very midst of Japanese strong points. Within 20 miles to the west lay the well-garrisoned Halmaheras. The airdromes of Davao, 400 miles northward; the fields of the Celebes, 225 miles due west; and Ceram, 400 miles to the south, presented powerful threats. The nearest Allied base, lightly held Sansapor, was over 300 miles distant. As a result more antiaircraft units than had been

used in any operation up to that date were committed:

    Hq 214th AAA Group
    528th and 744th AAA Gun Bns
    383d, 389th, and 785th AAA AW Bns
    229th AAA SL Bn (less Btry B)

    b. The landings on 15 Sept 1944 were preceded by naval shelling and air bombing, and the assault forces went ashore without meeting enemy fire. Many of the larger landing craft grounded 100 feet or more off shore, making it necessary for the troops to wade into the landing beaches, and many vehicles were stalled for hours in holes in the coral shelf.

    c. Detachments of Hq 214th AAA Group, 744th AAA Gun Bn, and the 229th AAA SL Bn landed on D-day with Btries B and D of the gun battalion all of the 383d AAA AW Bn, and one searchlight section. The other units followed at intervals planned to meet the growing needs as the captured area was cleared and developed. One searchlight, without radar, the automatic weapons, and one battery of 90-mm guns were in firing position by dusk, and a temporary Group AAOR was functioning.

    d. The initial mission of the antiaircraft artillery on Morotai was the defense of the landing beaches and surface craft within range, with a subsequent mission of protecting the airdrome, beachheads, and dock and service areas. With the arrival of the 13th Air Force in strength in Oct the airdrome defense became paramount, and coverage of the other areas was incidental, but actually remained as complete as before due to the quantity of antiaircraft units available and the small size of the occupied area. Late in Nov offshore defense also became an assigned responsibility of the group commander, using antiaircraft weapons with support from the field artillery.[1]

    e. No enemy planes appeared in the air at Morotai until the morning after the landing when a single plane dropped two bombs. With the exception of Port Moresby, enemy air attacks against Morotai continued longer than anywhere in the Southwest Pacific. The peak came in late Nov when the operations of the 13th Air Force crowded the concentrated strip area with planes and repair facilities. The attack of 11 Jan marked the close of the enemy's active efforts to disrupt the air base. Single plane attacks in Mar and Jun 1945 were merely nuisance raids. In all the enemy made 80 raids with 179 planes. Two hostile planes were turned back when the alert gun was fired; antiaircraft action against 13 others was withheld by order of the Fighter Sector Controller. For his efforts, the enemy had 17 planes destroyed, 7 probably destroyed, and 12 damaged by antiaircraft fire. In addition four planes were destroyed and two probably destroyed by the fighter-

---

[1] See Chap 3, Sec III, Par 113.

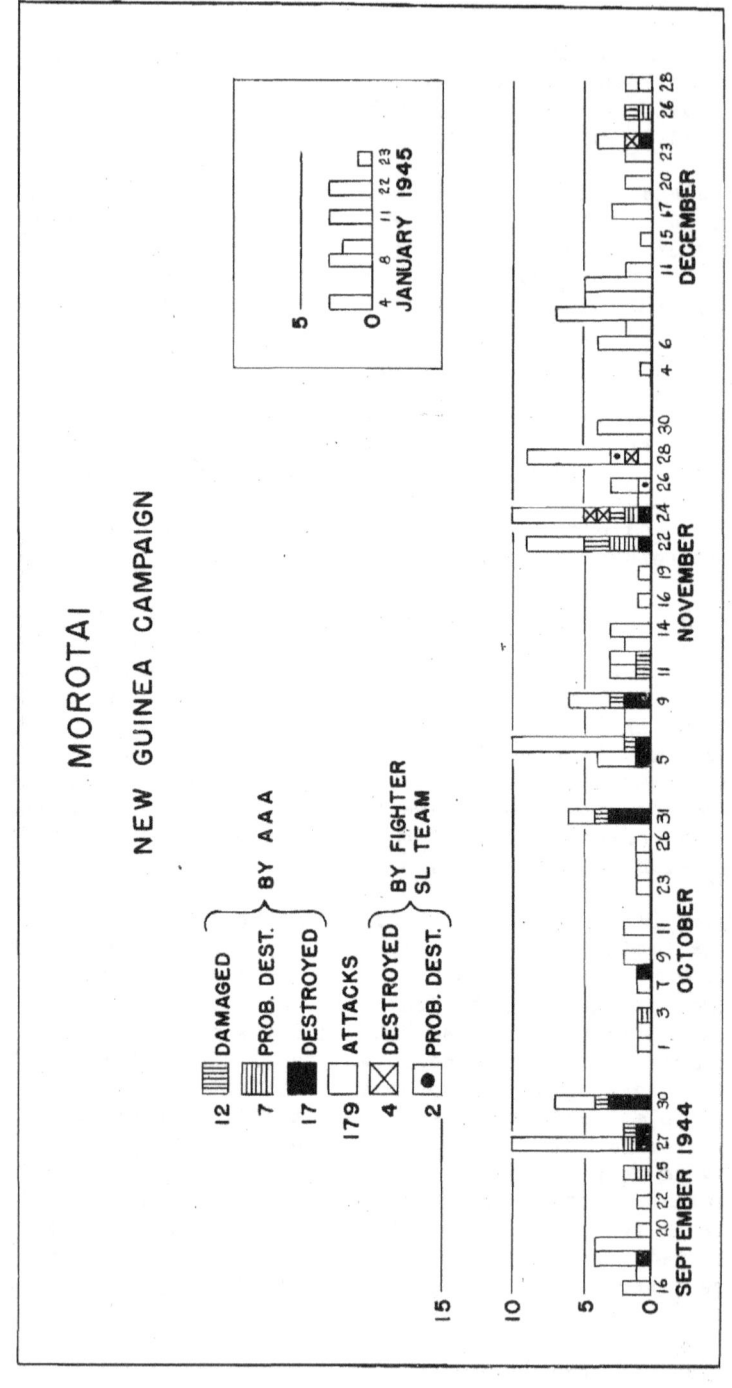

Fig. 24

searchlight team.

f. Antiaircraft artillery permitted only 19 enemy sorties out of 179 attacking the area to place bombs in the vital strip area. Three of these occurred when "hold fire" status prevented action, and two others were by planes sneaking in at low altitudes from the mountains without warning. Antiaircraft fire pushed the enemy to very high altitudes, and on 75 occasions caused him definitely to turn away outside the bomb release line, jettisoning his bombs. Sixty-seven were turned away by 90-mm fire. This indicates that much more damage was inflicted by heavy gun fire than could be confirmed.[1]

g. New techniques in the use of the searchlight-fighter team, originated by the 214th AAA Group at Guadalcanal, were utilized at Morotai and resulted in four enemy planes destroyed and two probably destroyed. Experiments using the gun-laying radar and the field artillery liaison plane produced methods for target and other position locating which were later used to excellent advantage in the Philippines and Okinawa. These subjects are treated in more detail in Chap 5, Sec VI, Par 151.

h. The operation was declared officially terminated on 4 Oct 1944. However, attacks on the perimeter continued until the end of the year and the last enemy air raid came nine months after that closing date.

i. On 1 Apr 1945 the 383d AAA AW Bn was released from attachment to the 214th AAA Group and attached to the 31st Div for the Mindanao operation. The 389th AAA AW Bn departed on 13 Jul, the 528th AAA Gun Bn on 30 Jul, and the 744th AAA Gun Bn on 16 Aug, to prepare for the invasion of Japan.

---

[1] <u>Antiaircraft Artillery at Morotai, NEI</u> 214th AAA Group, 24 Jan 1945.

VIII. NORTHERN SOLOMONS

56. <u>General</u>. a. The Northern Solomons Campaign began on 22 Feb 1943 and was officially closed on 30 Sept 1944, except for Bougainville Island, where it was continued until 21 Nov 1944.

b. By early Feb 1943 American infantry had pocketed the last Japanese forces on Guadalcanal near Cape Esperanza. Enemy attempts to land supplies by warship convoys had been thwarted, and his constant air attacks on Henderson Field from Munda on New Georgia had been countered by strong air and antiaircraft defenses. The heavy air attacks of 29 Jan and 1 Feb on an American reinforcement convoy for Guadalcanal marked the last determined attempt of the Japanese to prevent consolidation of the American foothold in the Solomons.

c. Late in Feb American troops moved on to the Russell Islands, about one third the distance to New Georgia, and found them evacuated, but enemy air raids continued against Guadalcanal from Rabaul and Northern Solomons bases. By midsummer a coordinated ground, air, and naval offensive to clear the enemy from the northern islands was in progress. Landings were made on Rendova and New Georgia on 30 June, with the Japanese base at Munda as their goal. Munda was captured on 5 Aug and a landing on Vella LaVella followed ten days later. On 26 Oct New Zealand troops with American antiaircraft artillery invaded the Treasury Islands. On 1 Nov the initial landing on Bougainville took place at Empress Augusta Bay, and fighting continued there at varying intensity until the close of the campaign a year later.

d. All the Army antiaircraft units participating in the Northern Solomons Campaign were assigned to the 68th AAA Brigade by USAFISPA on 2 Oct 1943. In the subsequent operations they were attached to the attacking task forces for varying periods. These attachments involved

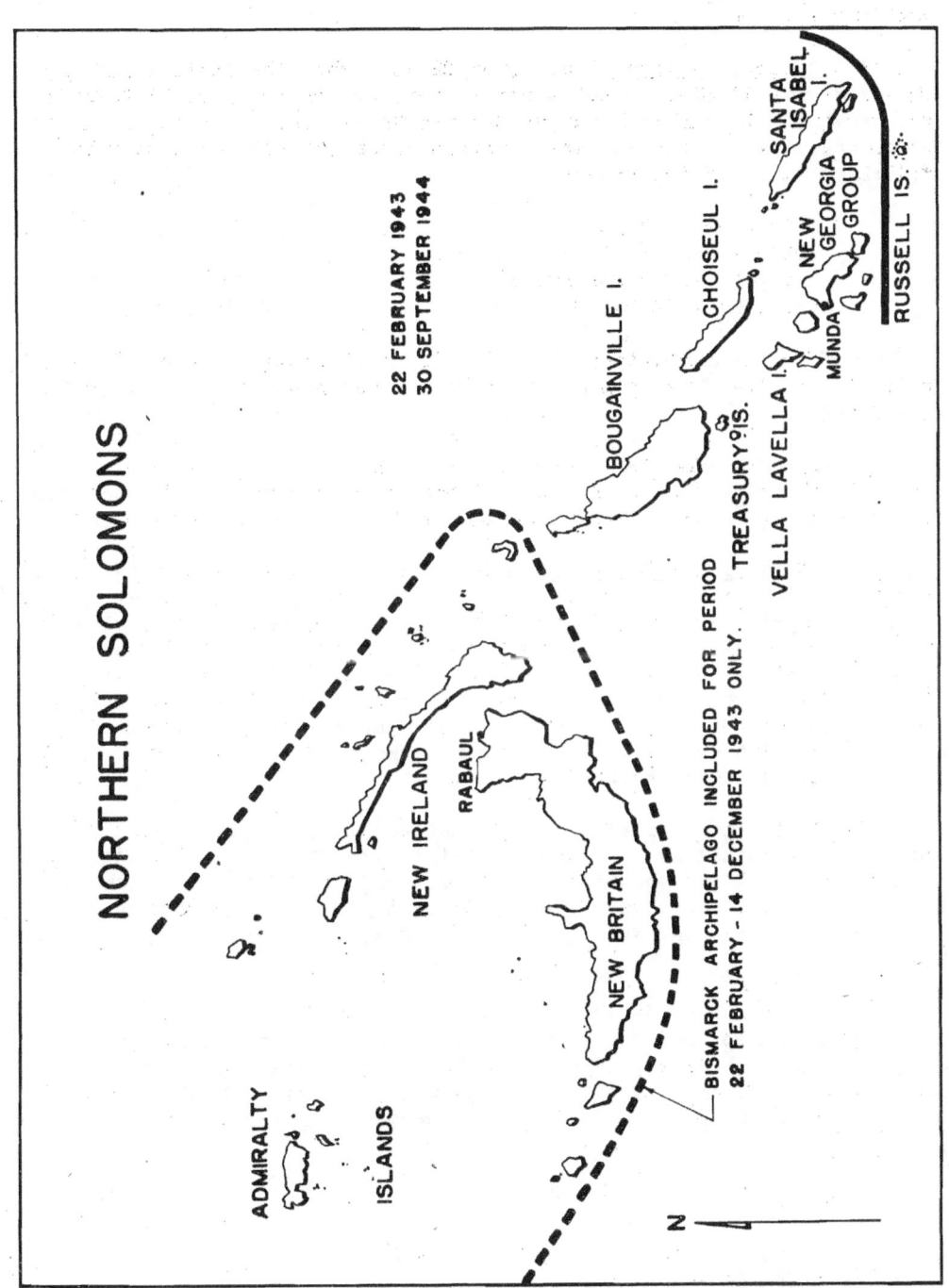

operations with XIV Corps, the 3d New Zealand Division, and I Marine Amphibious Corps.

57. <u>Russell Islands</u>. a. From 22 Feb, when the initial landings were made, until Nov, the antiaircraft defenses on the Russell Islands were provided by the 10th Marine Defense Battalion. When the 13th AAA Group arrived on 9 Nov the antiaircraft defenses were taken over by the following units of the group:

      164th AAA Gun Bn
      933d AAA AW Bn
      Btry D, 199th AAA AW Bn
      725th AAA SL Bn (Sep)

b. The only antiaircraft action in the Russells came on the night of 13-14 Jan 1944 when one Japanese bomber was shot down by the 164th AAA Gun Bn.

c. Hq 76th AAA Group arrived on 10 June to take over the tactical control of the battalions on the islands, and remained until the close of the campaign. There was no antiaircraft activity during this period.

58. <u>New Georgia Group</u>. a. On 30 Jun 1943 the XIV Corps invaded New Georgia. A provisional battalion of the 70th CA (AA) consisting of 2d Bn Hq and Btries A, B, E, and F had staged on Guadalcanal and landed with the attacking forces at Viru Harbor and Segi Point on New Georgia, and at Oleana Bay on Vanguna Island. In Sept Btry B moved to Vella LaVella where it provided antiaircraft gun protection for a barge unloading point. In the course of several dive-bombing attacks the battery was credited with one plane destroyed and one probably destroyed. Btry E moved to Rendova in October.

b. In Nov the regiment was reorganized[1] into a group headquarters and separate battalions. Group Hq, Btries A and C of the 70th AAA Gun Bn, Btries B and C of the 925th AAA AW Bn, and Btry C of the 250th AAA SL Bn were all in position at Segi Point; Btry B, 70th AAA Gun Bn was still on Vella LaVella, and Btry A, 925th AAA AW Bn was in position at Rendova.

c. Early in Dec the 77th AAA Gun Bn, the 938th AAA AW Bn, and Btry A, 374th AAA SL Bn, arrived with the principal mission of defending the Munda air field. Shortly afterwards the Hq, 77th AAA Group arrived to coordinate the antiaircraft defenses at Munda. During their stay on New Georgia, the 70th and the 77th AAA Gun Bns were each credited with one enemy plane destroyed, and one probably destroyed.

---

[1] See Annex A, Par 4.

59. **Treasury Islands.** a. On 26 Oct 1943 the 198th CA (AA) went ashore with the initial landing force of the 3d New Zealand Division. The first wave of infantry troops met no opposition, but by-passed enemy troops in concealed pillboxes and foxholes met the antiaircraft artillerymen on the second wave with considerable sniper, machine gun, and mortar fire. One 90-mm gun was destroyed when one of the landing craft was hit.

b. The 198th CA (AA) was reorganized[1] while in the Treasury Islands into the 198th AAA Group Hq, the 736th AAA Gun Bn, the 945th AAA AW Bn, and Btry A of the 373d AAA SL Bn.

c. During the period 27 Oct 1943 to 15 Feb 1944 there were 145 air attacks on the area defended by the regiment and it received credit for eight planes destroyed and four probably destroyed. Antiaircraft fire prevented practically any damage from these raids.

60. **Bougainville.** a. The first Army antiaircraft unit to go into Bougainville was Btry D, 70th CA (AA), which, attached to the 3d Marine Defense Battalion, went ashore at Empress Augusta Bay on 8 Nov 1943 with I Marine Amphibious Corps. The 251st CA (AA)[1] landed on 1 Dec with the mission of defending the Torokina area. Although enemy aircraft were engaged on numerous occasions there are no reports of planes destroyed or damaged by the 251st CA (AA). The 90-mm guns were used extensively for terrestrial fire[2], and the searchlights for battlefield illumination[3], with excellent results. The 199th AAA AW Bn arrived on 15 Jan 1944 to reinforce the antiaircraft defenses of the area along the coast, north of the Torokina air strip, and on Peruata Island. On 25 Jan one plane was shot down by the battalion's fire and some units engaged in terrestrial action with the enemy.[2]

b. The remainder of the 70th AAA Gun Bn arrived on Bougainville in June 1944 and furnished antiaircraft protection for the airstrips at Empress August Bay until the battalion left in Nov and Dec to stage for the Luzon operation.[4] The 70th AAA Gun Bn destroyed three planes, shared in the destruction of an additional plane, probably destroyed four, and damaged one. The units of the 251st AAA Group moved out in Nov and the 199th AAA AW Bn left in Jan 1945.

---

[1] See Annex A, Par 3 d.

[2] Chap 3, Sec II, Par 111.

[3] Chap 3, Sec IV, Par 110.

[4] *Unit History.* 70th AAA Gun Bn, 21 Aug 1945, P. 4.

61. **General.** a. The Eastern Mandates Campaign officially began on 31 Jan 1944 and ended on 14 Jun 1944.

b. After the costly seizure of bases in the Gilberts the next objectives in the central Pacific lay in the Marshall Islands, the so-called "Eastern Mandates" of Japan. Located in the approximate center of the Marshall group, Kwajalein Atoll surrounds a sixty-mile long lagoon providing an excellent sheltered anchorage for an almost unlimited amount of shipping.

c. Following an unprecedented preliminary bombing and shelling the southern islands at Kwajalein were invaded by the 7th Div on 31 Jan 1944. At the same time Roi and Namur Islands in the northern part of the atoll were captured by the 4th Marine Division, to dominate the spacious lagoon. Simultaneously, Majuro Atoll, about 300 miles southeast of Kwajalein, was occupied without opposition by the 2d Bn, 106th Inf of the 27th Div. No antiaircraft troops were involved in that landing. From Kwajalein a naval task force carrying the 22d Marine Regiment and the 106th Inf went northwest over 400 miles in mid-February to secure Eniwetok Atoll.

d. These captures opened new sea areas for American activities and made possible large-scale air and sea operations much closer to the main bases of Japanese strength. The raid on Truk, on 16 Feb, which resulted in the destruction of 201 enemy planes and 23 ships, and the blow at Saipan, with similar success five days later, followed closely upon the operations in the Marshall Islands. Other enemy bases were rendered useless by being isolated, and their garrisons were left to starve. The naval strikes continued until they reached a peak in June when the bombings began that culminated in the invasion of Saipan.

e. The antiaircraft units that participated in the operations of this campaign were combined into Army Defense Battalions to provide the garrisons for the atolls after their seizure.

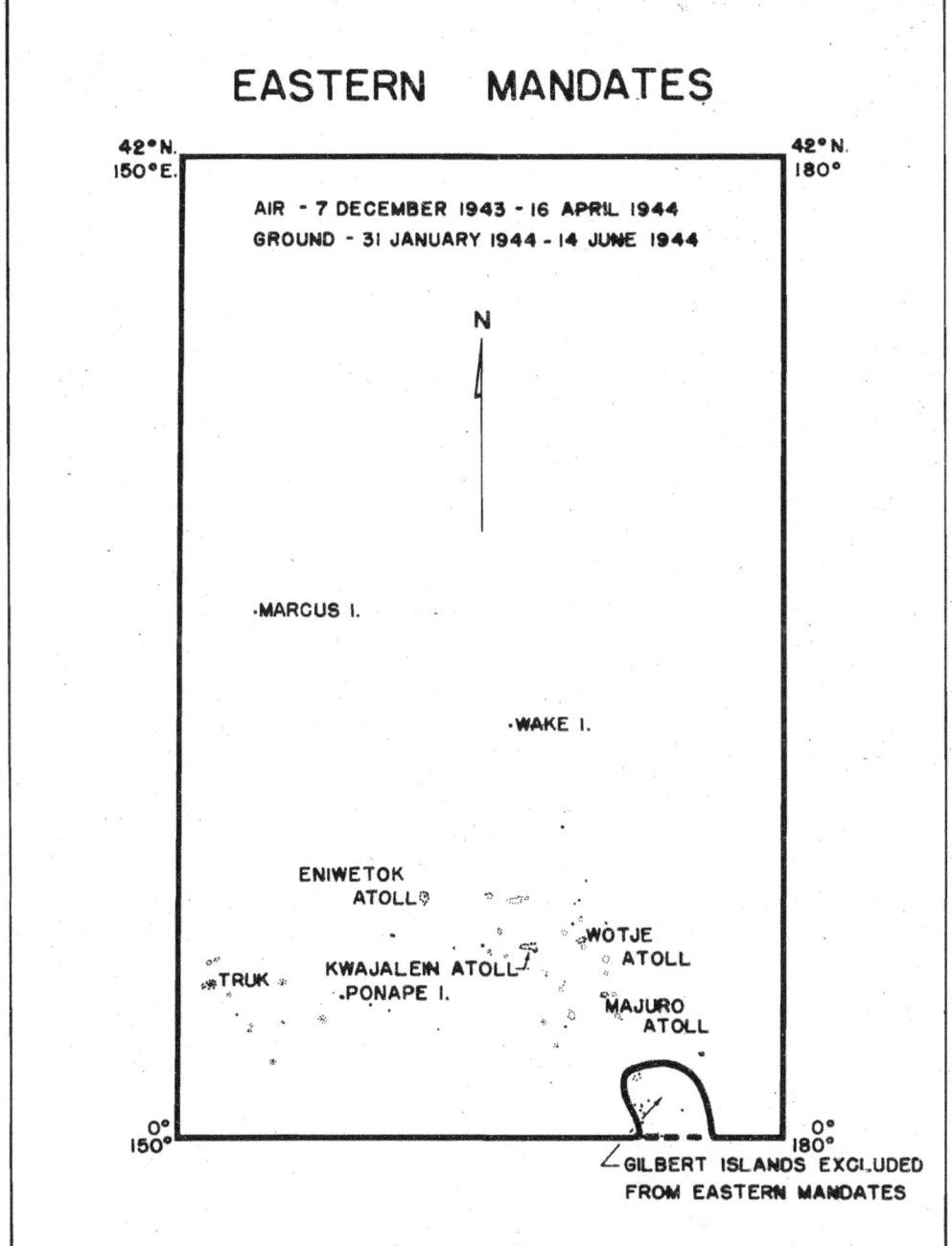

62. **Kwajalein.** a. The antiaircraft artillery at Kwajalein was organized into the 4th Army Defense Battalion which had a three-fold mission: to provide antiaircraft protection for the assault troops, to provide antiaircraft and ground defense for the atoll when it became an advanced base, and finally, to carry out the necessary rehabilitation of the area after its capture. The battalion initially included the following antiaircraft units:

    Hq, 139th AAA Group
    96th AAA Gun Bn
    Btries A and C, 98th AAA Gun Bn
    Btries A and B, 753d AAA Gun Bn
    Btries A and D, 867th AAA AW Bn
    Btry A, less one Plat, 296th AAA SL Bn

b. During the assault phase the Defense Battalion was attached to the 7th Div and its subordinate units were attached to Battalion Landing Teams which occupied various islands in the atoll. The antiaircraft artillery was late in going ashore and it was not until D plus 3 that all antiaircraft elements had landed with their weapons. The delay was due to the use as infantry reinforcements of antiaircraft troops who had gone in early as shore party personnel. There were no air raids during or after the landing.

c. On 10 Apr 1944 the 1st Plat, Btry B, 230th AAA SL Bn arrived. On 1 Oct Btry A (less one Plat), 296th AAA SL Bn, and the 96th AAA Gun Bn (less Btry A), left for return to Oahu. In Feb 1945 Hq, 139th AAA Group, officially departed but its personnel remained to serve as the Island Command. On 1 July all garrison troops on the island were relieved.

d. There were no army units on Roi and Namur Islands.

63. **Eniwetok.** a. The task force attacking the Eniwetok Atoll on 17 Feb 1944 included Marine Regimental Combat Team 22, given the misson of seizing Engebi Island, and the 106th RCT of the 27th Div with the mission of capturing Eniwetok Island. The garrison force, attached as at Kwajalein, was the Third Army Defense Battalion. It included the following antiaircraft units:

    Hq and Btry A, 867th AAA AW Bn
    Btry A, 96th AAA AW Bn
    Btries A and C, 98th AAA Gun Bn
    One Plat, Btry A, 296th AAA SL Bn

Hq, 967th AAA AW Bn provided the command for the Defense Battalion.

b. Engebi was captured on schedule by the Marines with little resistance, but the island of Eniwetok proved to be a difficult objective, and the 106th RCT finally had to be reinforced by the Marines from Engebi.

c. The 3d Army Defense Battalion assumed complete control of the atoll and relieved the two combat teams on 2 Mar. On 8 Mar the Japanese made their first of two air raids. The results of the antiaircraft fire were undetermined. The night raid disrupted island communications and destroyed some stores, including an ammunition dump. The second and last raid took place on 14 Apr, a high-altitude attack in which Btry C, 98th AAA Gun Bn, was credited with one plane probably destroyed. The Defense Battalion was relieved on 12 Sept 1945 and departed in Oct.

X. Bismarck Archipelago

64. **General**. a. The campaign for the Bismarck Archipelago opened on 15 Dec 1943 and was officially closed on 27 Nov 1944. Air attacks on the islands had been carried out prior to the opening date, when the area was included in the New Guinea Campaign, but ground troops did not invade the archipelago until Dec of 1943.

b. The first landings were made at Arawe, New Britain, on 15 Dec 1943, and at Cape Gloucester on 23 Dec. While patrols were still encountering enemy resistance on New Britain, troops of the 1st Cav Div, on 29 Feb 1944 moved into Los Negros to start the conquest of the Admiralty Islands. The occupation of Emirau Island on 25 Mar and the landing on Green Island on 25 May sealed effectively the enemy strongholds at Rabaul and on New Ireland. The ring thus thrown around the islands kept supplies and reinforcements from reaching the enemy in the archipelago, and made further occupation of the group of islands by our forces unnecessary.

c. As these objectives were successively taken, enemy air activity in the area constantly diminished. Attacks by Army, Navy, and Marine planes on Rabaul and Kavieng were largely responsible for the reduction of Japanese air resistance to our landing on the islands near Rabaul. Army Air Force elimination of Japanese air strength at Wewak and Hollandia also stopped the air attacks on Cape Gloucester and Arawe. As a result few enemy raids were made against shore installations after the landings were completed and few enemy planes were destroyed by antiaircraft fire.

d. Ground action, after the initial areas were secured, was confined mainly to patrol activities, but antiaircraft units were called upon on several occasions to furnish terrestrial fire in support of infantry troops.

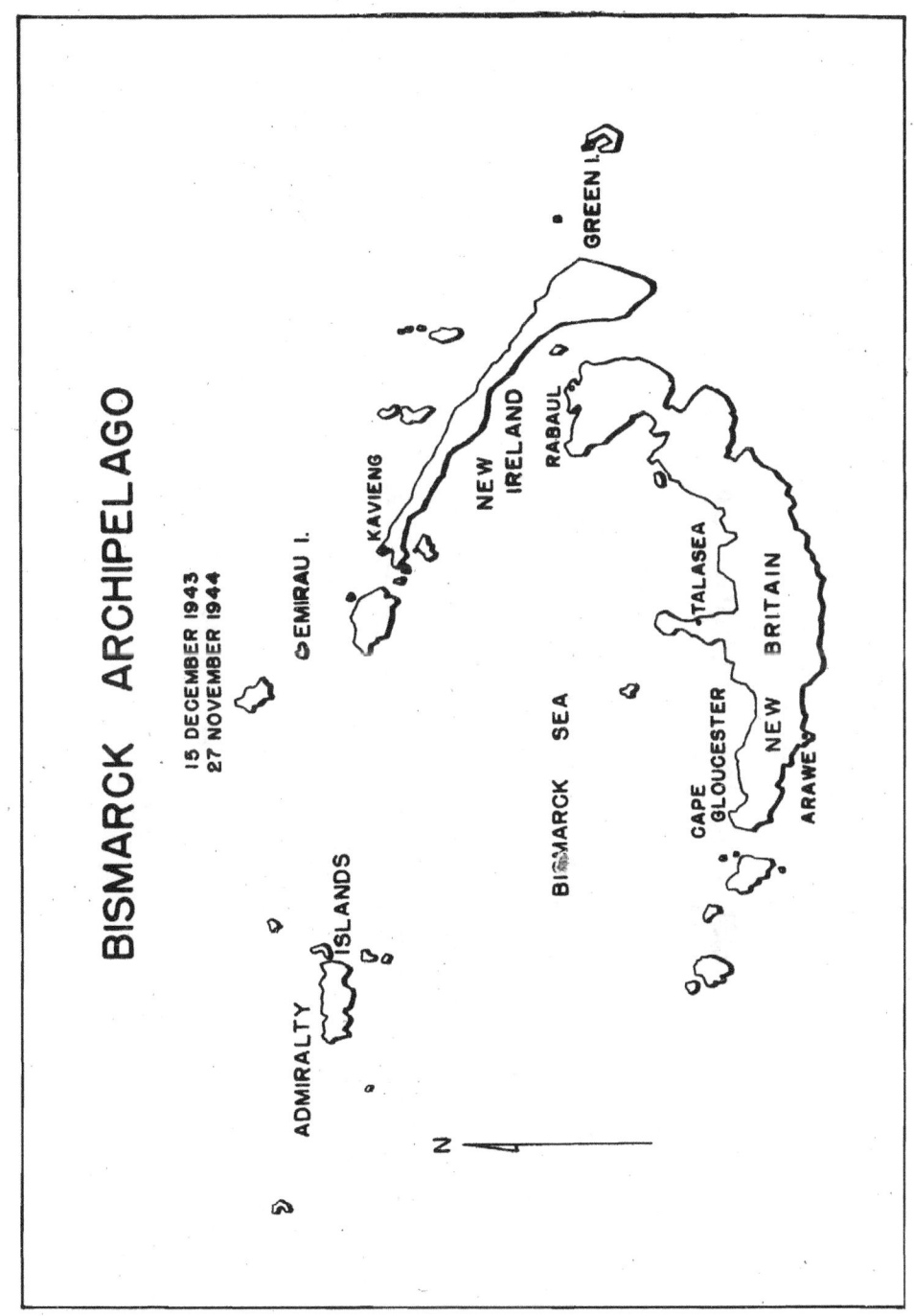

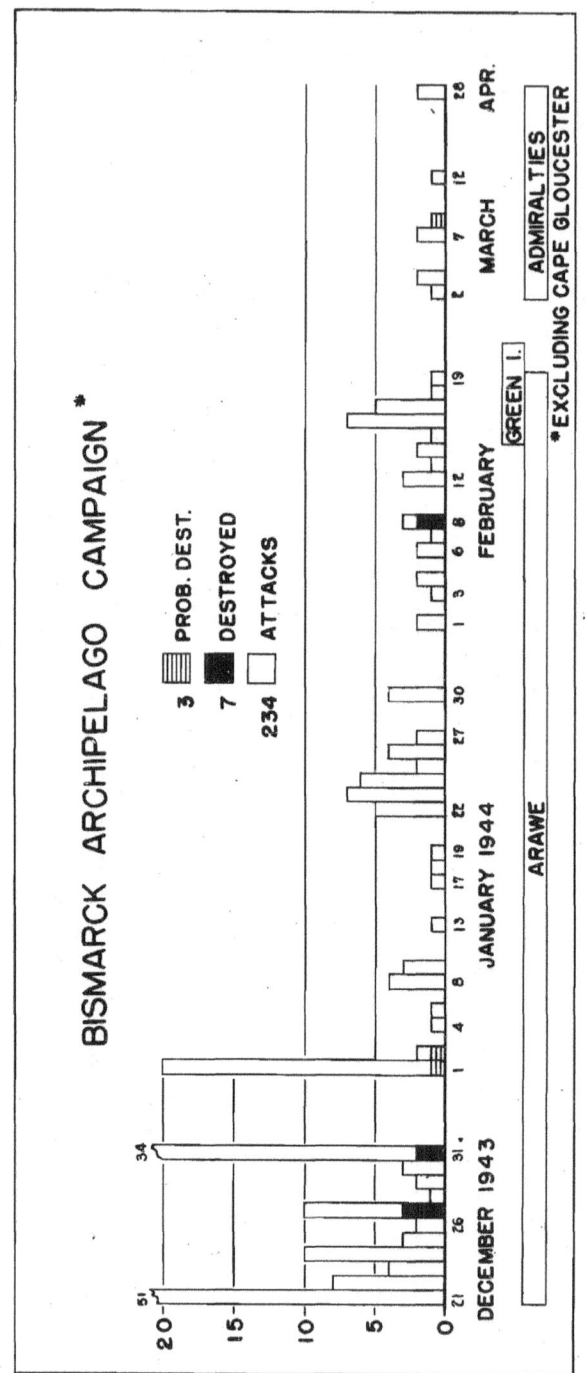

Fig. 25

e. A major portion of the time during the latter months of the campaign was utilized by antiaircraft units for training in preparation for future operations.

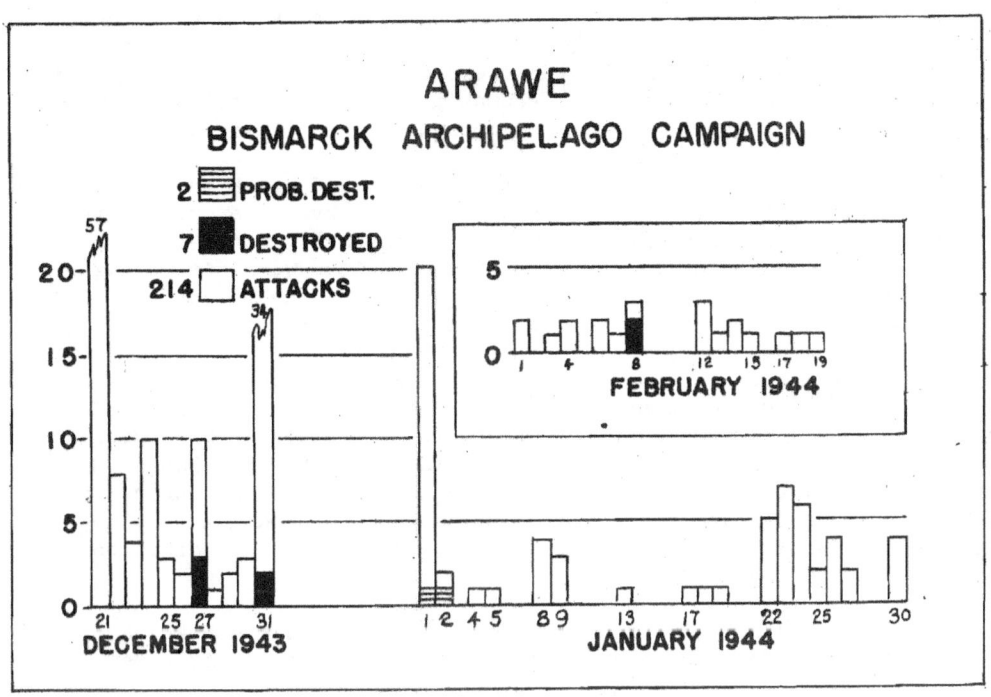

Fig. 26

65. <u>Arawe</u>. a. The strategy of the Cape Gloucester operation called for an earlier landing at Arawe, to draw and hold troops on the south shore of the island, and to prohibit Japanese reinforcements from landing there and crossing the island to help in the fighting at Cape Gloucester. For this mission a task force was built around the 126th RCT. Btries C and D of the 470th AAA AW Bn furnished the antiaircraft protection for the assault, under the direction of Hq, 236th AAA SL Bn. The antiaircraft mission was the defense of shipping and beaches, of the ground troops and supplies, and terrestrial fire in support of infantry troops.

b. The landing took place on 15 Dec 1943. The antiaircraft machine guns constituted the first antiaircraft artillery ashore. The crews of these guns were given credit for bringing down two enemy planes of the first twenty that raided the beach at 0900 that morning.

c. The beachhead was attacked daily, often several times, from D-day to 19 Feb 1944. During the first few days the enemy raiders came in at low altitudes for bombing and strafing of shipping and ground installations, but later they attacked at higher altitudes. Unfortunately the absence of 90-mm gun defenses permitted continual medium-altitude bombing by the enemy. The damage wrought by enemy bombers led to reinforcement of the defenses, late in Jan 1944, by Btry A, 741st AAA Gun Bn, followed by Btry B, 236th AAA SL Bn. During the remainder of the operation only a few raids were made against the ground installations, but the gun battery on several occasions was called upon to engage in terrestrial fire.

d. During this period 428 alerts were sounded of which 150 were for actual raids. A total of 775 bombs were dropped by the enemy, 96 in one night. This was a large effort against a very small, congested area. Btries C and D of the 470th AAA AW Bn were credited with destroying six enemy aircraft, with two probably destroyed during the operation. One destroyed plane was credited to the 741st AAA Gun Bn.

66. Cape Gloucester. a. After the successful landing at Arawe the 1st Marine Div landed at Borgen Bay, just west of Cape Gloucester, on 26 Dec 1943. No army antiaircraft units were attached for the landing, protection being furnished by the 12th Marine Defense Battalion. On 7 Jan 1944 the 469th AAA AW Bn arrived to assist in the defense of the beachhead area, and the landing strips at Cape Gloucester. On 7 Apr, with offensive operations at an end, the battalion embarked to stage for future operations.

b. Up to 21 Feb 69 red alerts were called. The 469th AAA AW Bn submitted claims for four planes destroyed, but these claims were never confirmed.

c. The 6th AAA Group with Btry C, 238th AAA SL Bn, the 466th AAA AW Bn, and the 742d AAA Gun Bn attached, arrived at Cape Gloucester late in May 1944 and took over the antiaircraft defense from the Marines. Since there was little enemy activity in this area, training to prepare the units for future operations was the major occupation. During the period 7 Jun to 14 Aug 1944 five alerts were called but no enemy aircraft were identified.

d. On 4 Dec 1944 the 6th AAA Group, with attached units, embarked to stage at Finschhafen.

67. Admiralty Islands. a. Elements of the 1st Cav Div initially were assigned the mission of a reconnaissance in force of the Admiralty Island group. Due to the success of the initial landing on Los Negros and the weak enemy defenses found, the reconnaissance was extended to include the seizure of the entire group of islands by the division.

b. The mission of the antiaircraft defense for the division was given to Hq 15th AAA Group and the following attached units:

168th AAA Gun Bn
211th AAA AW Bn
Btry C, 237th AAA SL Bn
673d AAA MG Btry (AB)

 c. The assault was set ahead of the original scheduled date with the result that many preparations had to be made very rapidly. Some of the antiaircraft units had only a day or two of staging. Equipment was borrowed from antiaircraft organizations defending the staging area in order to equip fully the units going into operation.

 d. Btry C of the gun battalion, Btry A of the automatic weapons battalion, and the machine-gun battery landed with the assault echelon at Los Negros on 29 Feb 1944. The other units arrived during the next three weeks. In the initial phase the antiaircraft artillery provided protection for the convoy and landing beaches. A defense against possible sea-borne attack was established and antiaircraft weapons were used to reinforce the field artillery units of the 1st Cav Div.

 e. The 673d AAA MG Btry was so disposed that it was a major factor in repulsing a banzai charge early in the occupation. The details of this action are given in Chapter 2 Section II.

 f. Searchlight illumination was provided for the construction of an airstrip at Los Negros.

 g. The antiaircraft defense was extended to cover the naval base headquarters and stores area on Manus Island as well as the army airstrips on Los Negros.

 h. Enemy air opposition to the occupation of the islands was negligible, and only a few enemy raids were made within range of antiaircraft weapons. The 211th AAA AW Bn received credit for the probable destruction of one plane.

 i. On 29 Apr 1945, two Japanese planes (Dinahs) from Rabaul made a surprise attack on Seadler Harbor, the Navy's anchorage near Manus Island. The planes came in for the attack below 100 feet altitude, without being detected, and hit two floating drydocks with their torpedoes.

 j. Later, when the situation had stabilized, a training program was instituted to prepare the units for future operations.

 k. On 25 May 1944, the 15th AAA Group was relieved from attachment to the Cav Div and attached to the 40th AAA Brigade. Group Hq was further attached to the Thirteenth Air Force on 28 Aug and moved away with the Air Force Headquarters shortly thereafter. The units formerly attached to the 15th AAA Group departed from the Admiralty Islands in Oct 1944, for participation in the Leyte Campaign. On 6 Dec the 933d AAA AW Bn arrived, followed by the 70th AAA Gun Bn on 21 Dec and the 76th AAA Gun Bn on 8 Jan 1945. The 77th AAA Group and the 77th AAA Gun Bn followed a month later and all occupied tactical positions.

1. The Admiralty Islands operation closed on 18 May 1944.

68. <u>Green Island</u>. a. On 15 Feb 1944, the 967th AAA Gun Bn landed on Green Island with elements of the 3d New Zealand Division. A small Japanese ground force offered stiff resistance but was quickly eliminated and the island was wholly occupied. During the first night seven enemy air raids were made but the antiaircraft units could not fire as the radars were not yet in operation and no firing data was available. Enemy raids continued for only a few nights and the results of the antiaircraft fire were undetermined. Btry A, 362d AAA SL Bn, joined the defenders on 25 Feb.

b. On 25 May the 13th AAA Group and the 925th AAA AW Bn arrived at Green Island. Upon arrival the group headquarters assumed tactical control of the antiaircraft defenses hitherto under the 3d New Zealand Division. The group headquarters also acted as a provisional Island Command from 30 May to 10 June, being relieved on the latter date by Hq, 93d Div Arty. The attached units of the 13th AAA Group were the 967th AAA Gun Bn, 925th AAA AW Bn, and Btry C, 374th AAA SL Bn. Enemy opposition was negligible and the group maintained defensive positions until 1 Oct 1944, at which time it prepared to stage for a new operation.

69. <u>Emirau Island</u>. The 14th AAA Group with the 471st AAA AW Bn, 737th AAA Gun Bn, and 725th AAA SL Btry (Sep) attached, landed on Emirau Island on 25 Mar 1944 with the 4th Marine Regiment and set up the antiaircraft defense of the airstrip without opposition. Although Emirau Island was only 90 airline miles from the enemy base at Kavieng, New Ireland, and some 240 miles from the enemy base at Rabaul, New Britain, not a single raid of any type was experienced during the entire eight month stay of the group on that island.

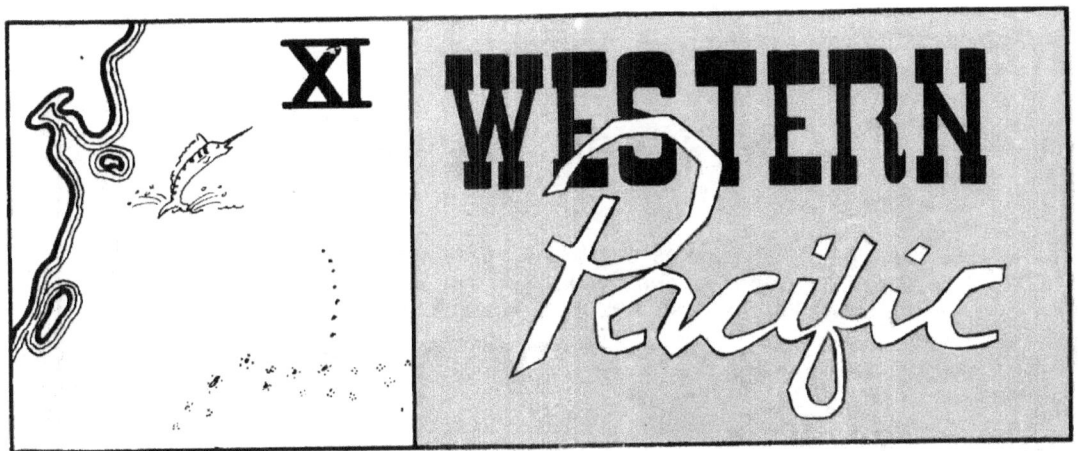

XI WESTERN Pacific

70. <u>General</u>. The Western Pacific Campaign opened on 15 Jun 1944 and was officially closed on 18 Feb 1945. It was divided into two major operations, the invasions of the Marianas and of the Western Carolines, which set the stage for seizure of Iwo Jima, within fighter escort range of Tokyo.

71. <u>Saipan</u>. a. The Marianas operation opened with the landing on Saipan on 15 June, in order to secure a base for B-29 operations against the Japanese homeland. The conquest of this island, and the subsequent engineering accomplishments, enabled the first Superfortress raid to be made on Japan from a Pacific base on 24 Nov.

b. The assault force of the V Amphibious Corps included Hq, 86th AAA Group, Btries A and B of the 751st AAA Gun Bn, the 864th AAA AW Bn, and a Prov AAA Gun Group staff.[1] Two automatic weapons batteries and a gun battery were attached to each Marine division for the assault. One section of each automatic weapons battery was equipped with an M-16 multiple machine gun half-track in place of its normal equipment. The number of personnel of the assault units was held to the minimum requirements for efficient operation.

c. Due to poor handling of antiaircraft equipment in landing and low priorities for landing boats, the antiaircraft gun defense for approximately 12 days consisted of only Btry A, 751st AAA Gun Bn. During this period several night bombings took place. The arrival of the other gun batteries in the next few days strengthened the defenses. Infrequent bombing attacks took place during the remainder of the operation.

---

[1] <u>Seacoast and Antiaircraft Artillery Operations in the Pacific Area</u>, MIDPAC, Dec 1945, Part c, P.2.

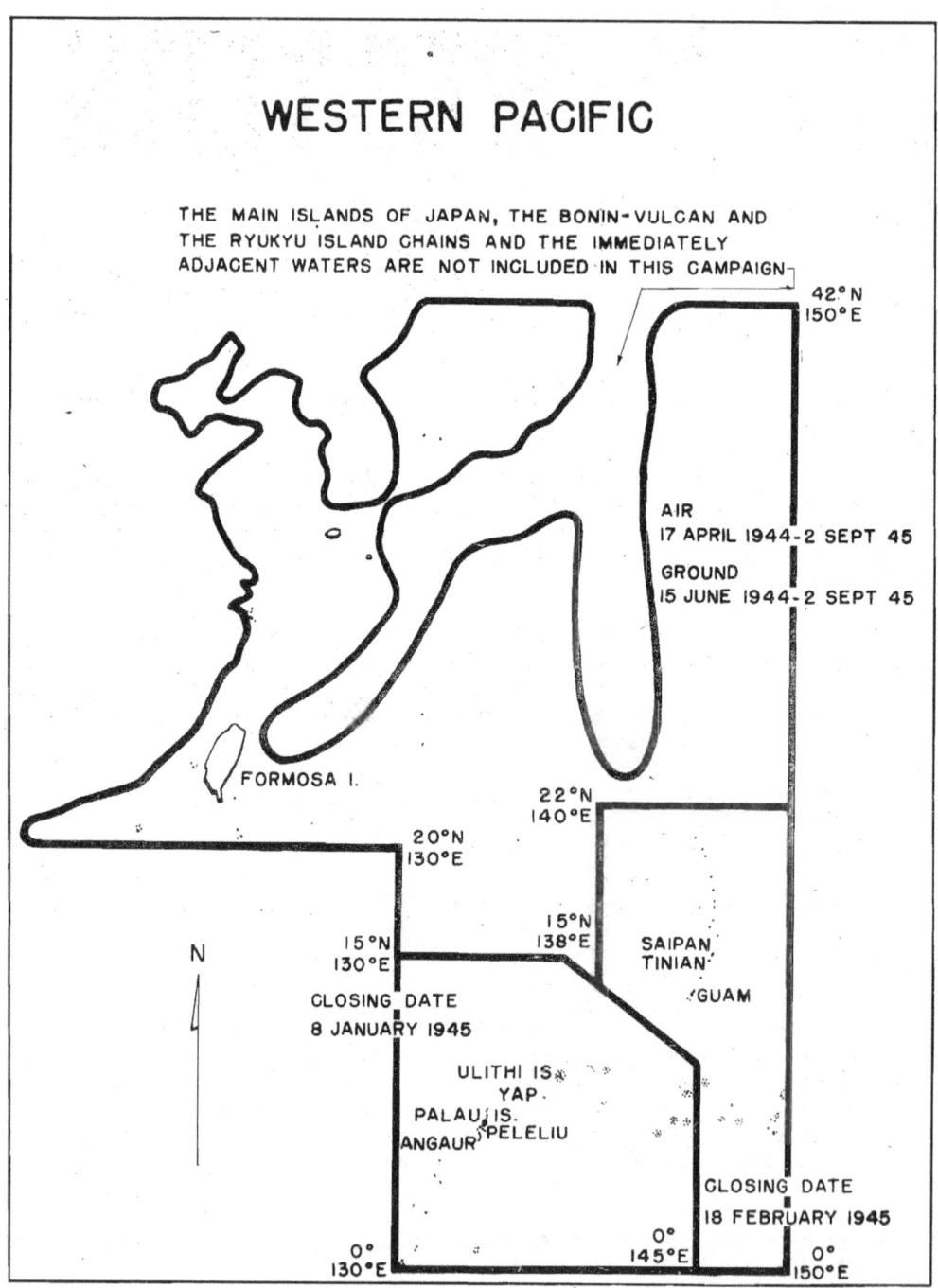

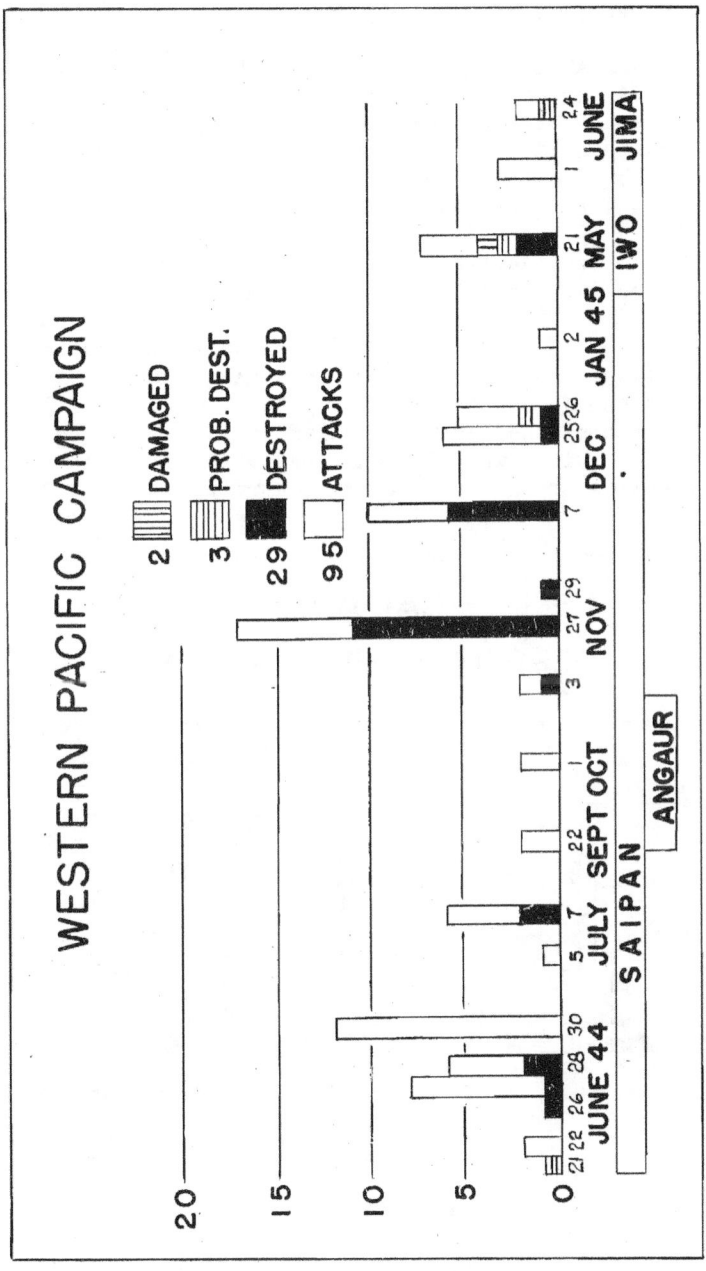

Fig. 27

d. The following antiaircraft units, assigned to the Saipan Garrison Force, formed part of the task force:

    206th AAA AW Bn (less Btries C and D)
    865th AAA AW Bn (less Btries B and C)
    501st and 738th AAA Gun Bns
    Btries B and C, 867th AAA AW Bn
    Btry B, 296th AAA SL Bn
    Btry B, (less one Plat), 230th AAA SL Bn

The nucleus of the headquarters of the Saipan Garrison Force was two officers and 80 enlisted men from Hq, 751st AAA Gun Bn.

e. On 25 June the garrison force, then under the antiaircraft commander, was assigned the defense of the southern portion of the island and the elimination of snipers. The mopping up of most of the Japanese stragglers was accomplished by antiaircraft troops. Subsequently, the other parts of the island were turned over to the garrison force until on 10 Aug the entire area was under its control.

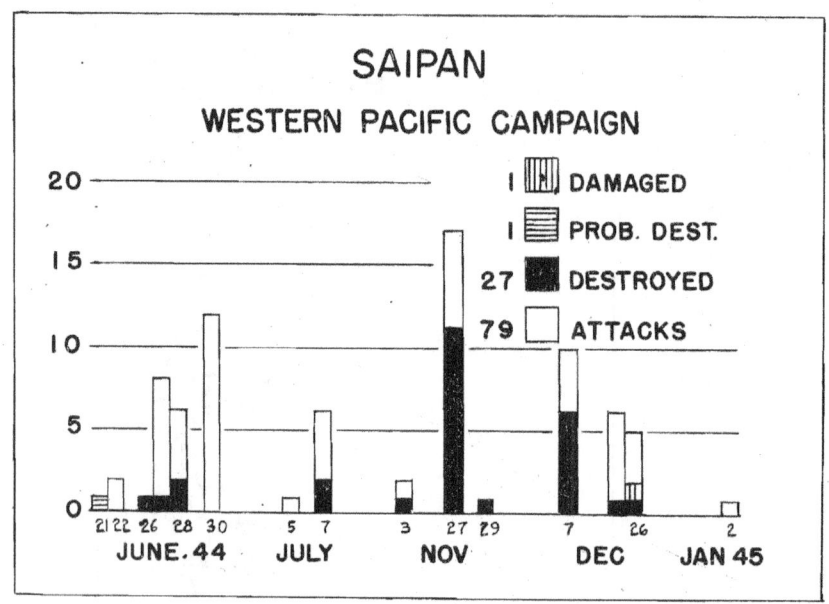

Fig. 28

f. From 15 June to 2 Jan, the date of the last raid, approximately 79 enemy sorties were flown against Saipan. Against these attacks, antiaircraft units were credited with 27 planes destroyed, one probably destroyed, and one damaged. The majority of attacking planes were heavy gun targets until immediately after the first B-29 raid on Japan when the enemy switched to strafing and bombing the airfields at low altitudes in an apparent effort to knock out our big bombers. Between 27 Nov and 7 Dec, 22 such sorties were made from which fifteen enemy planes were destroyed by antiaircraft fire. Thereafter all attacks were made at medium and high altitudes.

g. No new enemy tactics were used although single planes attempted, with considerable success, to sneak in behind the fixed echoes of Tinian Island and approach low over the water against the southwest parts of Saipan while the main flight continued at high altitude up the east coast of the island in order to engage the attention of the defenders. "Window" was dropped on almost every raid but never in sufficient quantity to saturate the radar screens.

h. In addition to their primary mission antiaircraft units fired on terrestrial targets on several occasions. Btries A and B of the 751st AAA Gun Bn were the only artillery units available to prepare for and support the ground attack which cleared the Japanese from Nafutan Point.[1]

72. **Guam**. a. Most of the antiaircraft units in the Guam landing of 21 Jul 1944 were furnished by the Marine Corps, but the 7th AAA AW Bn was attached to the 77th Div for the assault.

b. The battalion began its debarkation on 24 July. On landing, Btry A was attached to the 1st Prov Marine Brigade. All units of the battalion were ashore and in positions near the beachhead by the end of the next day. On the 30th the entire battalion was attached to the Marine Brigade and was in positions in the Apra - Orote Point region. Four days later it received the mission of defending the Agab - Dadi Beach area, protecting the south flank and patrolling. There were no enemy air attacks either during the assault or subsequently.

c. The Guam Garrison Force initially included the 64th AAA Gun Bn and the 868th AAA AW Bn (less Btries B and C); later the 771st AAA Gun Bn was added. However, the island's security was primarily a Navy responsibility.

73. **Tinian**. The Tinian landing on 24 July was the last of the Marianas operations. All of the antiaircraft defense was furnished by the Marine Corps.

74. **Palau Group**. a. The Western Carolines operation opened with landings on Peleliu and Angaur Islands in the Palau group on 17 Sept. There were no Army antiaircraft units with the reinforced 1st Marine Div

---

[1] See Chap 3, Sec II, Par 111 h.

which invaded Peleliu.

b. The 483d AAA AW Bn, attached to the 81st Div, was the only Army antiaircraft unit on Angaur. The 7th Marine AAA Bn shared the antiaircraft defense responsibility. Btry D landed on the third day of the attack and the remainder of the Army battalion landed on the next day. The battalion moved to Ulithi in Oct.

c. Four enemy air raids were made on Angaur, only one of which came within range of automatic weapons. No planes were shot down or damaged.

75. <u>Ulithi</u>. a. Ulithi Atoll was invaded on 23 Sept by the 323d RCT of the 81st Div. Btries C and D, 751st AAA Gun Bn, and Btry C (less one Plat) of 230th AAA SL Bn, furnished the initial antiaircraft defense of the islands. However, on 20 Oct the 483d AAA AW Bn moved from Angaur Island to Ulithi to provide low altitude defense for the airfield which was located on the largest island in the group.

b. The 771st AAA Gun Bn (less Btries A and B), and the 2d Plat, Btry C, 294th AAA SL Bn, were sent to Ulithi Harbor to augment the antiaircraft force, but were not employed tactically and were later sent to the garrison of Guam.

c. There was no enemy air activity at Ulithi. The only auxiliary role of the antiaircraft troops was assisting the 323d RCT in clearing a small number of Japanese from Tais, a small island of the atoll.

76. <u>Iwo Jima</u>. a. Although the bloody fighting at Iwo Jima was not included in any of the officially designated campaigns,[1] it follows logically the operations at Guam, Saipan and Tinian and is therefore reported in this section on the Western Pacific Campaign.

b. In the fall of 1944 plans were initiated for the capture of Iwo Jima, a small volcanic island eight miles square, lying in the path of the bombing run from the newly-won bases in the Marianas, to the target areas in Japan. Located in the Volcano Group of islands only 800 miles from the Japanese mainland, it proved of inestimable value as a haven for crippled B-29's and as a base for fighter escorts.

c. The assault by the V Amphibious Corps started on 19 Feb 1945. Resistance was the heaviest yet seen in the Pacific war and the struggle was fierce and costly. The island was finally secured on 14 Mar.

d. The army antiaircraft units in support of the assault were Hq 138th AAA Group, with the 506th AAA Gun Bn and the 483d AAA AW Bn at-

---

[1] Battle credit has been given to troops which served on Iwo Jima under the "Ground Combat" subsection of War Department General Order Number 33, 1945.

tached. The garrison echelon included Btries C and D, 206th AAA AW Bn, the 752d AAA Gun Bn (120-mm), the 947th AAA Gun Bn, Btry C, 295th AAA SL Bn, and the 163d Opns Det.

    e. No antiaircraft units were landed on D-day because of the unexpectedly severe resistance; thus it was not until 25 Feb (D/6) that the antiaircraft battalions of the assault force began to unload. Two gun batteries and three automatic weapons batteries were in position ready to fire by dark. The Group Commander and two radio operators were the only headquarters personnel to get ashore until D/11. A considerable part of Hq and Btry B, 483d AAA AW Bn, was still aboard their LST when it departed for Saipan on 3 Mar, insufficient time having been given in which to unload.

    f. On the third night, while all antiaircraft units were still afloat, shipping off Iwo Jima was attacked by six Zekes. Several suicide crash attacks took place. One Zeke attempted to crash dive the LST on which Btries A and B, 506th AAA Gun Bn were loaded. The enemy plane was shot down by the fire of the gun batteries' machine guns and the ship's 40-mm guns.

    g. The remaining antiaircraft units which were to comprise the garrison were all in position by 30 Apr. No enemy aircraft had closed to gun or machine gun range since the first units had landed.

    h. The only enemy raids on the island were one each on 21 May, 1 June and 24 June. In the first raid from five to seven planes came over in three flights. Two were destroyed, one probably destroyed, and one damaged. Half of the antiaircraft gun ammunition supplied for the Iwo Jima operation had been VT-fuzed and it was believed that one of the destroyed planes was shot down by VT-fuzed shells in the first salvo. No planes were destroyed in the two later raids, but one plane was probably destroyed in the 24 June raid. This made the record of the Iwo Jima antiaircraft artillery two destroyed (16.7%), two probably destroyed (16.7%) and one damaged (8.3%) out of a dozen attackers.

77. <u>General</u>. a. The Southern Philippines Campaign opened on 17 Oct 1944 and was officially closed on 1 Jul 1945, except for the island of Mindanao where it was extended to 4 Jul.

b. The landing of troops on 17 and 18 Oct 1944 on the islands of Dinagat, Suluan, and Homonhon, which covered the entrance to Leyte Gulf, marked the beginning of an operation involving large land, sea, and air forces. The objective was to split the Philippines, north from south, and to secure an operating base for air and amphibious assaults on Luzon. The initial landing on Leyte on 20 Oct was followed by the establishment of a beachhead on the adjacent island of Samar on 24 Oct. A very critical period existed when Japanese sea forces attempted to destroy our invasion fleet and sever our lines of communication with the troops already landed. The Japanese were defeated in the fierce air and naval battles on 23 and 26 Oct 1944, which largely destroyed the enemy naval striking power. The later landings in the Philippines, which took place in rapid succession, met with a minimum of interference from enemy sea forces.

c. On 7 Dec 1944 additional American forces landed on Leyte, this time at Ormoc on the northwest coast of the island. On 15 Dec the island of Mindoro was invaded, placing the western approaches to the Philippines in American hands just as possession of Leyte controlled the eastern approaches.

d. Marinduque Island was assaulted on 3 Jan 1945, and Palawan was invaded at Puerto Princesa on 28 Feb, sealing off the western entrance to the Sulu Sea. Other landings followed: on Mindanao at Zamboanga on 10 Mar, on Panay on 18 Mar, on Cebu on 26 Mar, on Negros on 29 Mar, on Jolo on 9 Apr, on Bohol on 11 Apr, on Balabak on 16 Apr, and at Cotabato

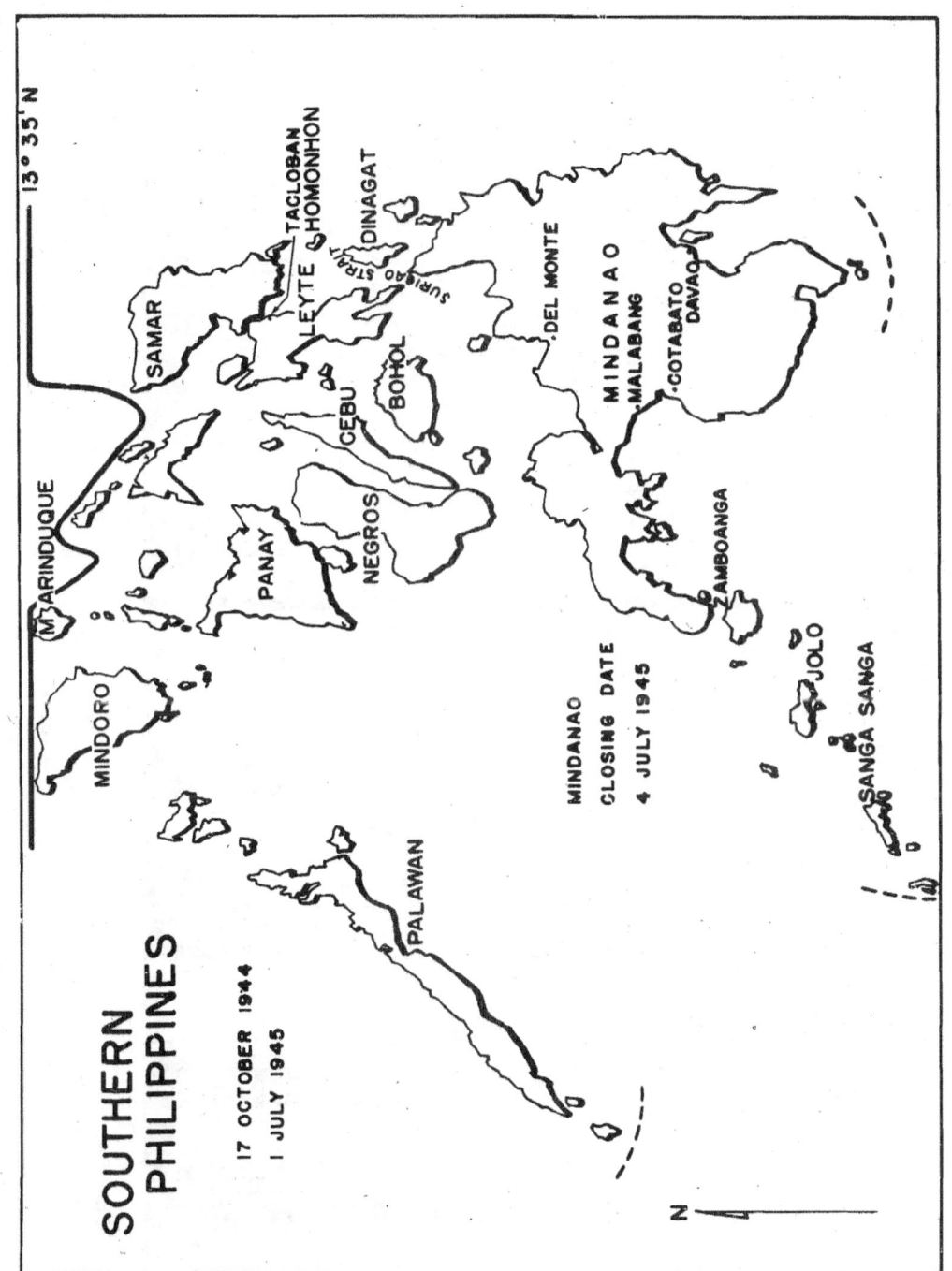

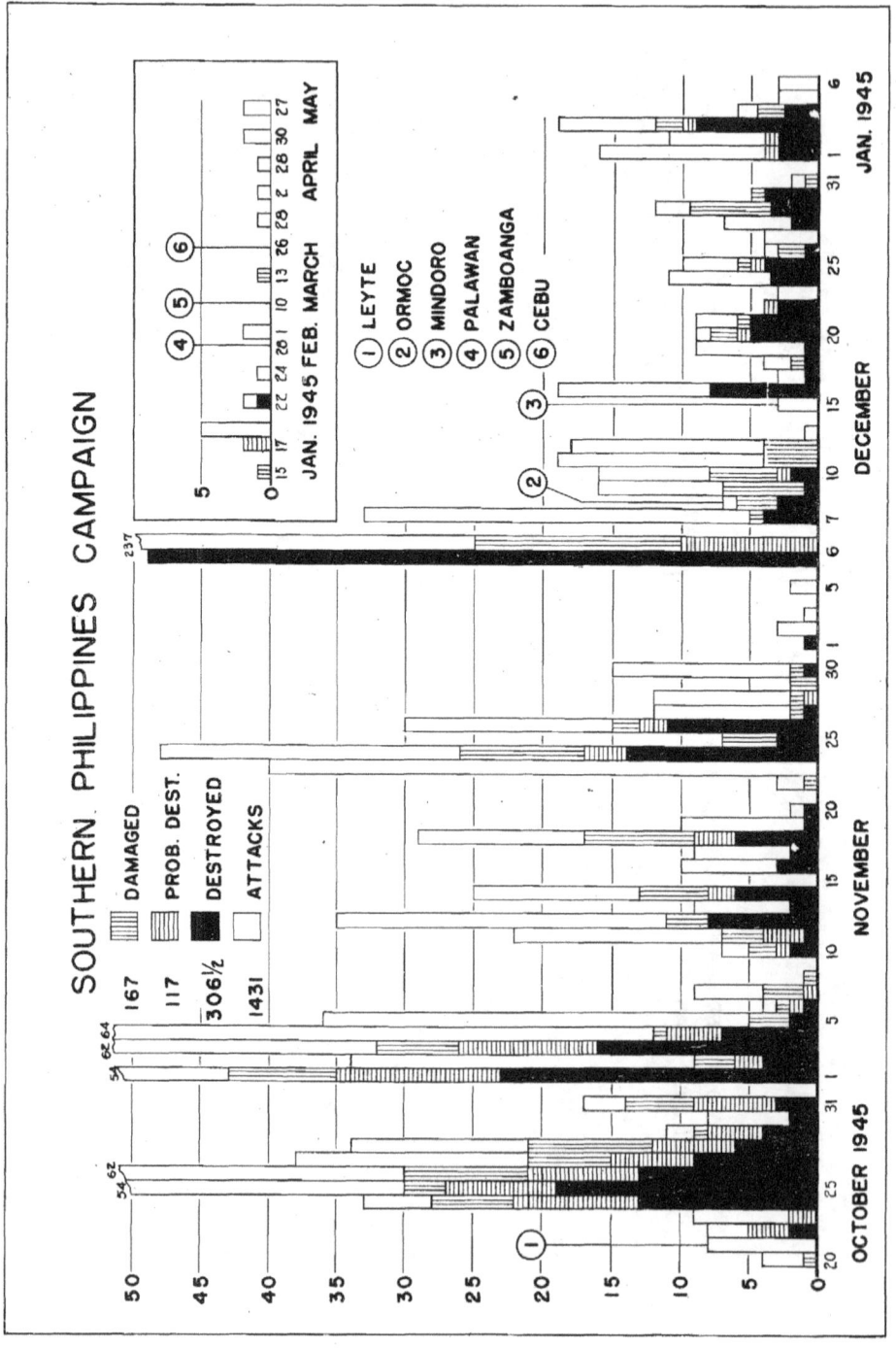

Fig. 29

on Mindanao on 17 Apr. The latter landing led to the fall of the city of Davao in the first week of May. These assaults, with the subsequent successful liberation of the islands by the ground troops, officially closed the Southern Philippines Campaign on 1 Jul 1945.

 e. The role played by antiaircraft units in this campaign was not only of great importance but varied in scope. Protection of landing operations and airfields from enemy aircraft was of primary importance, and proved essential at Leyte and Mindoro. At the other points there was little or no Japanese air activity, consequently, extensive use was made of antiaircraft units in supporting ground forces by terrestrial fire.

 f. Other special assignments given to antiaircraft units in this campaign are indicated below. On the island of Mindanao some units served actively as infantry patrols; others controlled a main road artery. On Leyte, antiaircraft troops were forced to organize a ground defense against enemy paratroopers who overran the antiaircraft position. Severe casualties were suffered before the paratroopers were wiped out. Other duties included the common use of searchlights as beacons for friendly planes and as a means of illumination for unloading facilities; the use of antiaircraft troops as dock workers, conducting schools, and serving as military police.

 g. In the campaign as a whole antiaircraft units engaged 1431 enemy aircraft, of which they shot down $306\frac{1}{2}$ (21.6%), probably destroyed 117 (8.2%), and damaged 167 (11.7%). The distribution of these attacks and the antiaircraft results in each attack are illustrated in Fig 29.

 h. This campaign saw the initial use by the Army in this theater of antiaircraft ammunition fuzed with the T-74 "proximity" fuze. Three battalions at Leyte, one at Mindoro, and two at Morotai used this fuze. Although only a limited number were fired the results appeared to be very satisfactory. Because of the meagre supply the batteries were able to fire only three to five rounds per gun per target with the T-74 fuzes, and continued their fire with M-43 fuzed rounds. For a time, because of security reasons, firing with the proximity fuze in directions where unexploded rounds might land in enemy-held territory was prohibited. Thus some batteries fired only shells with M-43 fuzes. This mixing of fuzes made certain observation of "proximity" fuze results difficult. However, on two occasions the T-74 fuze was used exclusively with notable effect. On Mindoro one plane was destroyed by the 166th AAA Gun Bn at an expenditure of 16 rounds, and on Leyte five rounds fired by Btry A of the 504th AAA Gun Bn brought down another plane.

 i. Antiaircraft artillery units in the Southern Philippines Campaign were under the Sixth Army until 26 Dec 1944 when tactical control passed to the Eighth Army. Effective 25 May 1945 the units were relieved from attachment to the Eighth Army, attached to the Far East Air Forces, and further attached to the Thirteenth Air Force. During these changes the missions of the antiaircraft artillery remained the same.

j. On 28 Aug and 1 Nov the Hq, 15th and 10th AAA Groups, were attached to the Thirteenth and Fifth Air Forces respectively and served as advisory staff sections in those air headquarters until relieved on 18 May 1945. During Oct 1944, Hq, 40th AAA Brigade, was attached to Hq, Far East Air Forces, to serve as administrative command for antiaircraft artillery units attached to the Air Forces, and as antiaircraft staff section of the air headquarters. This function was terminated on 15 Jun 1945.

k. The backbone of the Japanese air arm in the Philippines was broken during the periods of the Leyte and Mindoro operations, hastening the rapid and successful completion of the Southern Philippines Campaign.

78. <u>Leyte - Samar</u>. a. The Leyte operation originally was planned to take place in Dec after landings on the Talaud Islands and Mindanao, but the discovery of Japanese weakness in the area led to a sudden advancing of the date by two months. The mission given to the Sixth Army, supported by allied air and naval forces, included the following:

(1) To seize such objectives in the Tacloban and Dulag areas as were required to initiate and insure uninterrupted air and naval operations therefrom.
(2) To establish control over San Juanico and Panaon Straits to permit access of light naval forces into Samar, and open Surigao Strait to our light naval forces and other shipping.
(3) To prepare to initiate operations to complete the consolidation of Samar and to destroy or contain hostile garrisons in the Visayas.

b. All antiaircraft units participating in the operation on A-day, 20 Oct 1944, were attached to the Sixth Army, with further attachments as follows:

    Hq, 25th AAA Group (attached to X Corps)
      168th AAA Gun Bn
      210th, 211th, and 469th AAA AW Bns
      Btry C, 237th AAA SL Bn

    Hq, 97th AAA Group (attached to XXIV Corps)
      502d and 504th AAA Gun Bns
      485th, 801st, and 866th AAA AW Bns
      Btry A, 230th AAA SL Bn

c. Immediately upon landing on A $\neq$ 1, the 32d AAA Brigade Hq established an operations room, in the absence of any operations detachment, and in conjunction with Sixth Army personnel planned the tactical

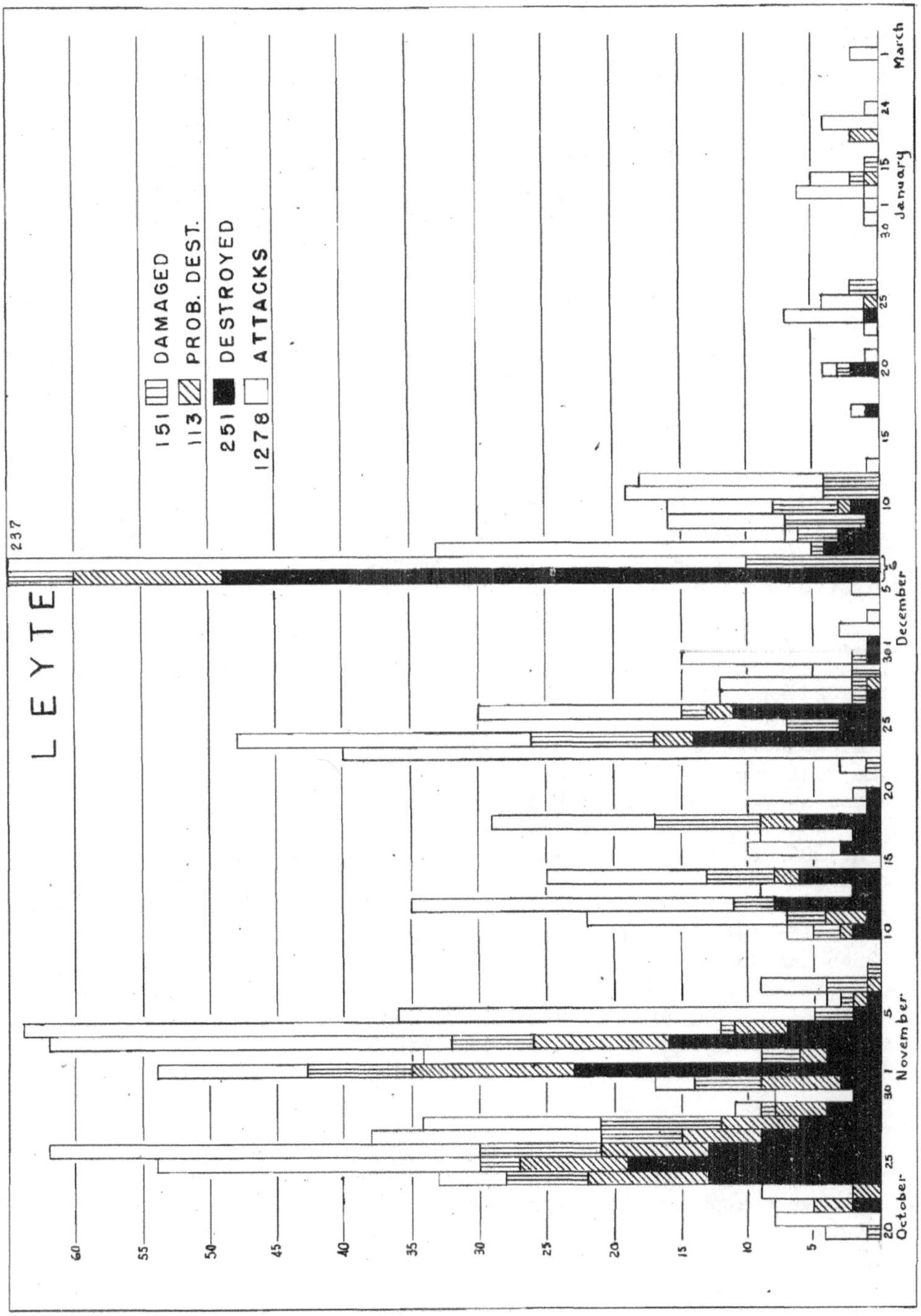
LEYTE
151 DAMAGED
113 PROB. DEST.
251 DESTROYED
1278 ATTACKS
237
60
55
50
45
40
35
30
25
20
15
10
5
October
November
December
January
March

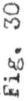

Fig. 30

disposition of all units on Leyte. On 3 Nov the 25th AAA Group, with its battalions, was attached to the brigade and shortly thereafter the brigade commander was named coordinator of antiaircraft defenses of Leyte Island. On 20 Nov all other antiaircraft units attached to the Sixth Army at this location were placed under the control of the 32d AAA Brigade.

  d. The 146th Opns Det, landing on 4 Nov, took over the operation of the AAOR under brigade supervision. Landing at the same time, Hq Det and the 3d and 4th Plats of the 57th CA Surface Warning Btry joined the defenses.

  e. (1) On 13 Nov the 94th AAA Group arrived, consisting of the following units:

    Hq, 94th AAA Group
     166th AAA Gun Bn
     202d AAA AW Bn
     Btry B, 237th AAA SL Bn
     673d AAA MG Btry

  (2) Although this group was on Leyte only 15 days staging for the operation against Mindoro its units saw action and received credit for destroying three enemy planes.

  f. Hq, 198th AAA Group, with the 102d, 199th, and 925th AAA AW Bns, and the 356th AAA SL Bn attached, landed later and were attached to the 32d AAA Brigade.

  g. The 7th AAA AW Bn arrived on Leyte on 23 Nov and was attached to the 77th Div, while the 508th AAA Gun Bn came ashore on 31 Jan but remained assigned to the 14th AA Command.

  h. Other units arrived on Leyte subsequently and staged for later operations.

  i. The antiaircraft defense of the beachhead on Samar was under the 25th AAA Group until the arrival of the 13th AAA Group on 25 Feb 1945. The 510th AAA Gun Bn, the 478th AAA AW Bn, and elements of Btry C, 356th AAA SL Bn, arrived during the campaign and played important roles in the defenses of the southwestern Samar areas. Later the zones of defense were broadened to include Guiuan on the southeastern tip of Samar.

  j. The enemy committed the majority of his Philippine aerial strength in the battle for Leyte and the disastrous effects of this decision were apparent in the remainder of the Southern Philippines Campaign.

k. Allied carrier-based aircraft provided air cover for the landing operations, and due to their neutralization of enemy air fields there was very little air opposition for the first three days of the campaign. On A plus 4, 5, and 6, the famous Battle of Leyte Gulf took place. Several of our carriers were sunk or damaged and the naval planes from these carriers used the Tacloban airstrip as a haven and operating base. This led to a concerted effort by the enemy to neutralize that strip, together with the strips and general areas around Dulag and Burauen. The intensity of the enemy attack is illustrated by the record of one antiaircraft battalion which alone engaged 73 enemy planes during the three days of the sea battle, definitely destroying 14 and damaging at least four.

l. An all-around defense of the Tacloban airstrip was not installed in the early stages of the operation because of swampy ground in one direction. This weakness was noted quickly and exploited by the Japanese. Within a short time the defense was balanced and the Japanese suffered heavy losses as they continued for several days to approach from the same direction.

m. On 6 Dec the enemy launched a combined paratroop, bombing, and ground attack in the vicinity of San Pablo. During this action antiaircraft artillery personnel distinguished themselves not only in the execution of their primary mission but also in direct combat with enemy ground troops. Total credits to Army antiaircraft fire in this phase alone were 47 planes destroyed, 11 probably destroyed, and 15 damaged, with an estimated loss to the enemy of over 400 paratroopers and air crew personnel.

n. After the first two weeks of almost continuous day and night attacks, air opposition lessened slightly but continued very active until the middle of Dec when it fell off rapidly. The extent of this decline is illustrated in the accompanying chart. (Fig   ). The extremely small number of sorties after 15 Dec was probably due to the landings occurring in rapid succession on other Philippine islands, and to the tremendous loss of planes suffered by the enemy in the first two months of the campaign.

o. The success achieved by antiaircraft units is shown by the record of 251 planes destroyed, 113 probably destroyed, and 151 damaged out of 1278 sorties. The proportion of attackers in each category is 19.8%, 9.0%, and 12.0% respectively.

p. The 168th AAA Gun Bn used a captured Japanese twin-mount 25-mm dual purpose gun and received credit for destroying two planes and damaging one with 205 rounds from this weapon.

q. The tactics employed by the Japanese in the Leyte Campaign varied but little from those employed in previous operations, except in emphasizing the suicide dive as an approved maneuver. The pilots of crippled attacking airplanes almost invariably tried to dive directly into sea targets. Some success was achieved as a number of Liberty ships and warships were sunk.

79. *Mindoro*. a. The initial landings on Mindoro took place on 15 Dec 1944. The task force included Hq, 94th AAA Group, under whose command were the 166th AAA Gun Bn, 202d AAA AW Bn, Btry B, 237th AAA SL Bn, and the 673d AAA MG Btry.

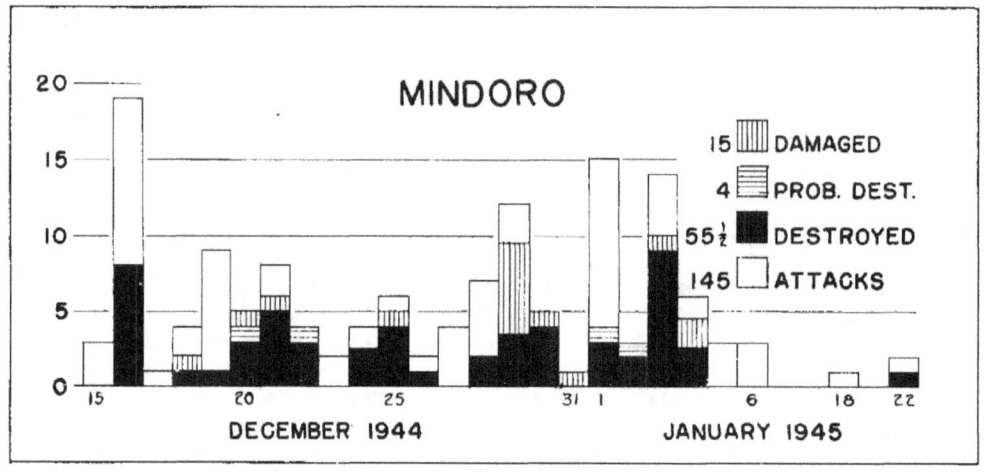

Fig. 31

b. These units subsequently were augmented by the arrival of the 102d AAA AW Bn (less Btry A), the 205th AAA AW Bn which was attached to the 24th Div, and the 487th AAA AW Bn which was attached to the X Corps.

c. During the early stages of this operation constant daily air attacks were received and from D-day through 6 Jan 1945 a total of 145 enemy targets were engaged of which $55\frac{1}{2}$ (38.3%) were destroyed, 4 (2.7%) probably destroyed, and 15 (10.3%) damaged by antiaircraft artillery fire. This record of 51% of the targets engaged being hit by antiaircraft fire is notable. The abrupt termination of air raids on Mindoro was undoubtedly traceable in large part to this costliness of attack. During the remainder of the campaign only three raids took place, with the destruction of one more plane.

d. Japanese air tactics were the same as those used in previous operations. Suicide tactics as originated at Leyte were continued at Mindoro, with some damage to our shipping. Approximately two-thirds of the enemy air raids were made at altitudes under 10,000 feet, in

- 104 -

order to avoid radar detection by coming in behind natural obstacles.

80. __Palawan__. a. The mission of antiaircraft units during the initial phases of the Palawan action was the customary assistance in antiaircraft defense of the convoy while afloat, protection of the beachhead during landing operations and assistance in the defense of the beach against enemy waterborne targets. This mission subsequently was changed to antiaircraft protection of airdromes and combat installations in the Puerto Princesa area and defense of the beaches against waterborne targets.

b. To accomplish this the 476th AAA AW Bn (less Btries C and D), Btry A, 166th AAA Gun Bn, and elements of Btry B, 237th AAA SL Bn were attached to the 186th RCT of the 41st Div. Air opposition proved to be light, consisting only of three sneak raids. The operation of radar warning instruments was hampered seriously by continuous fixed echoes from surrounding mountains, so that targets approaching at low-level were able to sneak in from some directions without detection.

c. Here, as elsewhere, the searchlights were used on numerous occasions as homing beacons for friendly planes and to provide illumination for the engineers during the night construction of air strips.

d. The antiaircraft units on Palawan moved to Zamboanga in July to train with their parent organizations.

81. __Zamboanga__. a. Troops of the 41st Div landed at Zamboanga, Mindanao on 10 Mar 1945 against mild opposition. Most of the Japanese had withdrawn into the mountains where they eventually were liquidated. The two existing airfields were quickly occupied. Antiaircraft protection for the beachhead and the airfields was provided by the 202d AAA AW Bn, the 166th AAA Gun Bn (less Btries A and B) and elements of Btry B, 237th AAA SL Bn. Air opposition was very light, consisting of only two sneak raids. One plane was damaged. The 2d Plat of Btry C, 202d AAA AW Bn, was moved to the island of Sanga Sanga, near the Borneo coast, on 31 Mar. No enemy air action took place there.

b. The units remained in tactical position until the end of July when intensive training was begun for the invasion of Japan.

82. __Panay__. In its seizure of Panay Island on 18 Mar 1945 the 160th RCT of the 40th Div had the 470th AAA AW Bn attached. There was no enemy air activity while on the water, and little opposition on the beaches. The three batteries were set up around supply dumps to provide antiaircraft defense, and remained there until the cessation of hostilities. There was no action.

83. __Cebu - Negros__. a. By the time of the landings on Cebu and

Negros Islands on 26 and 29 Mar 1945 respectively, enemy air opposition was no longer a threat. The antiaircraft units with the landing force were thus given the primary mission of furnishing fire support of ground troops. In carrying out this mission on Cebu the 746th AAA Gun Bn and the 478th AAA AW Bn (less Btries C and D) were attached to the Americal Div.

b. Plans for the Negros landing called for the initial employment of eight machine-gun sections from the 470th AAA AW Bn. The 739th AAA Gun Bn arrived on Negros on 17 Apr and was attached for artillery reinforcement purposes to the 40th Div. The 470th AAA AW Bn (less Btries C and D), moving from Panay Island on 23 Apr, also was attached to the division for the same role. Numerous ground missions were fired, which resulted in the destruction of dugouts, pillboxes, and other enemy installations.

84. <u>Cotabato</u>. a. The task force landing on 17 Apr 1945 at Cotabato, Mindanao, included Hq, 116th AAA Group, to which were attached the 487th AAA AW Bn, Btry B, 166th AAA Gun Bn, and three sections of Btry B, 237th AAA SL Bn.

b. Subsequently, the 383d AAA AW Bn, the 496th AAA Gun Bn, Btry B, 222d AAA SL Bn, and the 143d AAA Opns Det arrived and were attached to the Group Hq, which was in turn attached to the X Corps, Eighth Army.

c. By the time of this landing enemy air activity over the Philippines had been so completely reduced that no air attacks were made by the enemy. Therefore, troops of the group were used in the operation of the Malabang Area Command and the Bugo - Del Monte Area Command, being charged with security of the areas, and supply, administration, and transportation functions.[1]

---

1 See Chap 3, Sec V.

85. <u>General</u>. a. The Luzon Campaign officially opened on 9 Jan 1945 and closed on 4 Jul 1945.

b. The Sixth Army plan of attack provided that I Corps, with the 6th and 43d Divs attached, and XIV Corps with the 37th and 40th Divs attached, were to be the assault troops. In reserve were the 25th Div and the 158th RCT. The mission of the assault forces was to secure beachheads in the Lingayen - San Fabian - Rabon area, and then launch an attack to seize the central plain and the Manila area. The two corps were to land abreast, with divisions abreast, and as rapidly as possible consolidate their landings into one beachhead. At the appropriate time the XI Corps was to land in the Subic Bay area, seal off the Bataan Peninsula, and effect a juncture with the southward drive of the main American force.

c. Antiaircraft troops were assigned the mission of assisting in antiaircraft defense while afloat and, upon landing, to protect beaches, bridges, airstrips, troop concentrations, supply installations and other vital objectives.

86. <u>The Lingayen Landing</u>. a. The 68th AAA Brigade was attached to the Sixth Army as the senior antiaircraft artillery headquarters for the Luzon operation, and the brigade commander was designated as coordinator of antiaircraft defenses. The brigade headquarters closed at Bougainville 11 Dec 1944 and the advance echelon landed in the Lingayen area on S-day, 9 Jan 1945.

b. On 20 Nov 1944 all antiaircraft units committed to the operation were attached to the Sixth Army and further attached by Sixth Army for the water movement and initial landing operations, as follows:

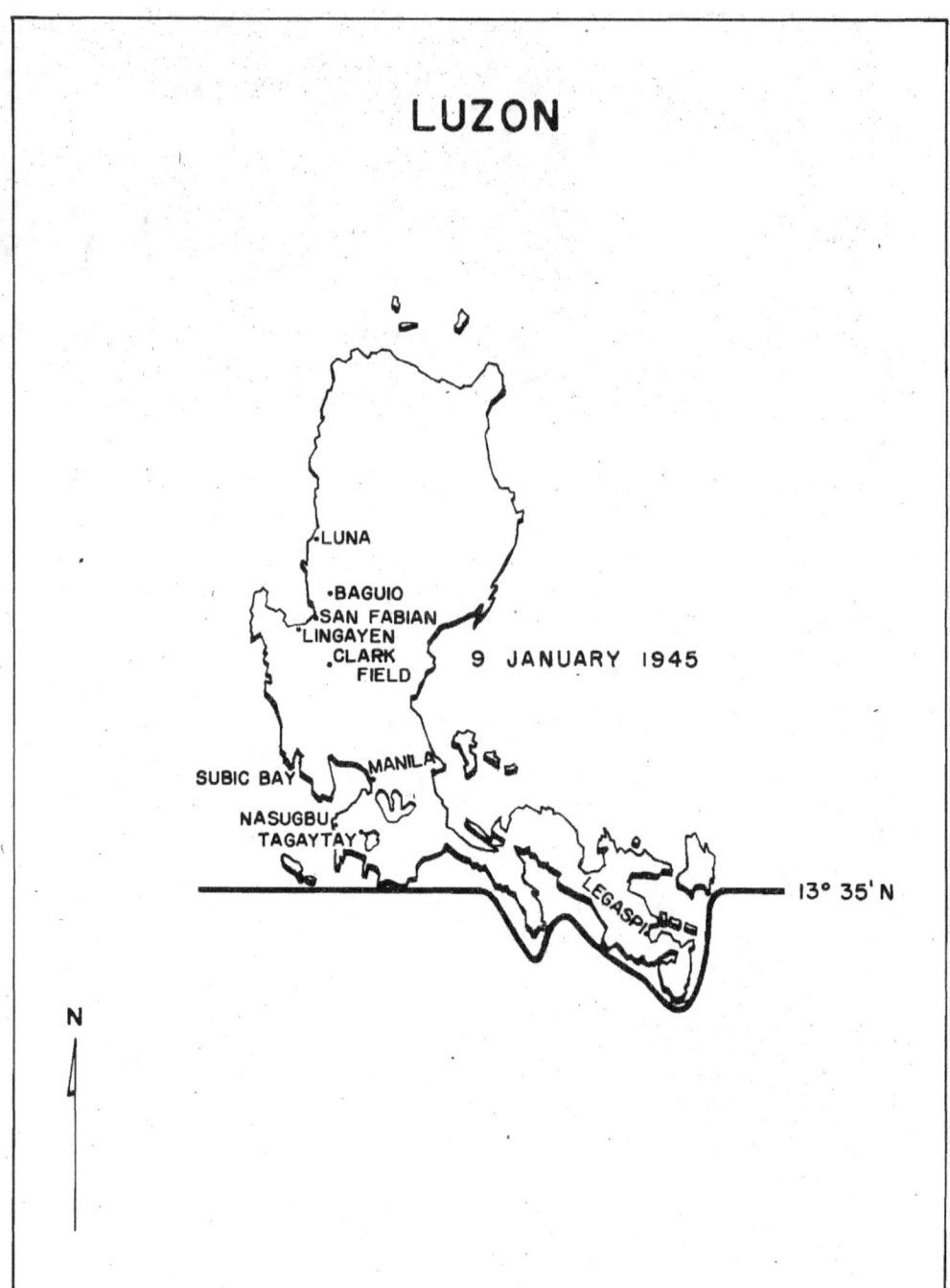

To Sixth Army:	Hq, 68th AAA Brigade, and 144th AAA Opns Det
To I Corps:	Hq, 197th AAA Group 161st AAA Gun Bn 470th AAA AW Bn 198th AAA AW Bn (less Btry A) 222d AAA SL Bn (less Btries A and B)
To XIV Corps:	Hq, 251st AAA Group 70th AAA Gun Bn 209th AAA AW Bn (SP) 951st AAA AW Bn 373d AAA SL Bn (less one Plat each of Btries B and C)
To 158th RCT:	707th and 708th AAA MG Btries Btry A, 198th AAA AW Bn

c. There was little enemy activity over the convoy enroute to the objective area until Philippine waters were entered. Automatic weapons had been emplaced on deck to supplement the ships' antiaircraft artillery. Official credit was given to the 469th and 951st AAA AW Bns for destroying one enemy plane each while enroute, and to the 198th AAA AW Bn for destroying one in Lingayen Gulf.

d. The landing on 9 Jan 1945 was practically unopposed by enemy ground forces. The greatest difficulty was encountered in landing equipment in the heavy surf and on unsuitable landing beaches. Landing craft grounded 100 or more yards from the shore-line, making it necessary for troops and equipment to go ashore through water up to five feet in depth. Waterproofing of vehicles for six-foot immersion saved most of the antiaircraft vehicles which rolled ashore under their own power. Ponton bridges used for unloading causeways were swept sideways, causing innumerable delays in getting rolling stock ashore. These difficulties persisted throughout the first few days of unloading on the western beaches and delayed the landing of much antiaircraft equipment. One 90-mm gun battery, three searchlights, and the equivalent of six automatic weapons batteries were ready for action with I Corps on the night of S-Day; two and a half automatic weapons batteries and four searchlights were in position with XIV Corps.

e. Enemy air opposition on S-day was directed at the shipping in Lingayen Gulf and consisted of several small raids (1-2 planes). Due to the character of the beaches, the amount of shipping involved, and changes in priority for unloading caused by the limited enemy air activity, the schedule for debarking antiaircraft artillery collapsed completely, early the first day. Some units could not function effectively for several days afterwards because necessary materiel, equipment, and personnel had not been unloaded. Nevertheless, the assault units were almost entirely ashore and ready for action within the first week.

f. The terrain in the Lingayen area, in general, is a vast expanse of fish ponds and rice paddies cut through with numerous rivers, creeks, and irrigation ditches, and thus was unfavorable for the tactical disposition of the antiaircraft units. Fortifications were affected by the high water table, making it necessary to employ built-up revetments in almost every case.

g. The beachhead area was congested with army personnel and equipment and the confusion was intensified by natives moving along the roads and beachheads. The great number of bridges destroyed increased the difficulties, even though ponton bridges were constructed by the engineers as rapidly as possible. Travel from one point to another involved excessive time. The wide dispersal and rapid forward displacement of antiaircraft units called for continual inspection and reconnaissance which existing road conditions rendered difficult and arduous.

h. For the first few days enemy air activity was limited to single plane daylight raids which caused no damage. Two enemy raiders were damaged by the 209th and 951st AAA AW Bns. Only five contacts were made with enemy troops during this period although units on the eastern beachhead were subjected to enemy mortar and artillery fire. Up to 19 Jan antiaircraft casualties from enemy action were two killed and eight wounded, and known casualties inflicted upon the enemy by antiaircraft artillerymen were six killed. The only non-assault antiaircraft unit to land during this period was the 469th AAA AW Bn on 16 Jan.

87. Lingayen to Manila. a. On 20 Jan all antiaircraft units on Luzon were detached from ground units and became part of the 68th AAA Brigade which was charged with providing the antiaircraft defenses for the balance of the Luzon operation. As the battle progressed southward the area requiring protection expanded to include Clark Field, the Manila area, and the network of supply routes. To accomplish the assigned mission, to which was added support for the ground forces, many redispositions were made. Hq, 251st AAA Group, with the 70th AAA Gun Bn, 469th AAA AW Bn, and the 373d AAA SL Bn attached, was assigned the antiaircraft defense of the Lingayen airstrip and bridges, and other installations in the Lingayen - Binmaley area. The 951st AAA AW Bn with Btry D, 209th AAA AW Bn (SP) attached, furnished antiaircraft defense for bridges and important installations in the XIV Corps zone of action during its advance.

b. The 197th AAA Group with the 161st AAA Gun Bn, 198th AAA AW Bn, 707th and 708th AAA MG Btries, and 222d AAA SL Bn (less Btries A and B) attached, provided antiaircraft defense for Mangaldan airstrip and the bridges, unloading beaches, supply dumps and other important installations in the Dagupan - Mangaldan - San Fabian area. The 470th AAA AW Bn with Btry B, 209th AAA AW Bn (SP) attached, was available to I Corps during its advance. The 209th AAA AW Bn (less Btries B and D) defended the 13th Armored Group. Its forward echelon was originally placed with

I Corps but owing to determined Japanese resistance in the hills north of the central Luzon plains the armor moved forward with the XIV Corps which advanced swiftly south through the central Luzon plain to Manila.

c. Due to the paucity of enemy air activity, antiaircraft defense needs were light and did not change rapidly. Antiaircraft units were used principally to guard highway bridges and a railhead located at Bayombong against both air and ground attack.

88. Subic Bay, Corregidor, and Nasugbu. a. In order to prevent the Japanese from repeating the tactics of the American forces in 1941-42 and making a prolonged resistance on the Bataan Peninsula the reinforced XI Corps was landed in southern Zambales province on 29 Jan. The initial objective after establishing a beachhead was the seizure of the airfields near San Marcelino and the naval facilities at Subic Bay.

b. The antiaircraft artillery units in this landing were:

Hq, 120th AAA Group
508th AAA Gun Bn
210th and 950th AAA AW Bns
Btry C, 227th AAA SL Bn

These units had little action as only two enemy planes appeared during the entire operation, and the antiaircraft was in "hold fire" status at that time.

c. Elements of this task force made the attack on Corregidor, and Btries A and C of the 950th AAA AW Bn participated in the recapture of the fortress. Their only actions included a terrestrial fire mission into an enemy-held ravine, and several scattered ground contacts involving small numbers of troops.[1]

d. As the drive down the central Luzon plain developed favorably, a plan was made for a thrust towards Manila from the south, by a landing at Nasugbu, the seizure of Tagaytay Ridge, and a drive north to the city. The 11th AB Div was selected for the assault. The antiaircraft units involved were the 152d AB AAA Bn, which was the organic antiaircraft battalion of the airborne division, and Btry A of the 102d AAA AW Bn.

e. The landing was made 31 Jan but not without difficulties. Though enemy resistance was negligible the beach presented a real problem. The LST's grounded with eight feet of water off the ramps and not until 16 hours after beaching were ramps built out from shore and unloading begun. Most of the equipment, while being towed ashore, moved through three or more feet of water.

[1] See Chapter 3, Section II.

f. Inasmuch as there was no air action in this operation Btry A, 102d AAA AW Bn, was utilized in a terrestrial role. Fire missions undertaken had as their targets barges and troop concentration areas.

89. <u>The Advance on Manila</u>. a. In contrast to the forces met by I Corps, the XIV Corps met comparatively minor opposition in the central Luzon plain and in two weeks time was in Manila. This rapid movement meant frequent changes in position to carry out the mission of furnishing antiaircraft defense for supply dumps and highway and railroad bridges on the route to Manila, and also increased steadily the total number of objectives requiring antiaircraft defense. The organic transportation of the semimobile automatic weapons battalions was inadequate for the many moves involved in the wide dispersion of antiaircraft units necessary to meet the Corps' antiaircraft requirements. Self-propelled units were not so handicapped and proved the value of their mobility in fast moving situations.

b. In the central Luzon plain the antiaircraft units furnished their own ground defense. There were few friendly troops in the area other than in the front line, and many of the enemy had been by-passed. During the period 20 Jan to 15 Mar the antiaircraft troops in this area had 38 ground contacts with the enemy menacing their gun positions. The infiltration patrols varied in number from one to 30 Japanese.

c. On 22 Feb the 14th AAA Group was assigned to defend Clark Field and establish and operate a group AAOR at the 51st Fighter Control Center located in Angeles. The 251st AAA Group assumed responsibility for the antiaircraft defense of the Manila area on 8 Mar 1945.

90. <u>Later Activities</u>. a. The 102d AAA Brigade arrived in Manila on 9 Mar in the first convoy to enter the harbor after its recapture. The brigade was charged with the defense of all army installations on Luzon south of a line running across the island approximately through Tarlac and Cabanatuan.

b. Units initially assigned to the Brigade were:

Hq, 6th AAA Group, with 513th AAA Gun Bn attached
Hq, 14th AAA Group, with 518th AAA Gun Bn, 471st AAA AW Bn, and 373d AAA SL Bn (less Btries A and C) attached
Hq, 120th AAA Group, with 508th AAA Gun Bn, 210th AAA AW Bn (less Btry D), 950th AAA AW Bn (less Btries A and C), and Btry C, 227th AAA SL Bn, attached
Hq, 251st AAA Group, with 507th AAA Gun Bn, 101st and 951st AAA AW Bns, Btries A and C, 950th AAA AW Bn, and Btry C 373d AAA SL Bn, attached
156th AAA Opns Det

c. Within a month the 472d AAA AW Bn arrived and was attached to the 14th AAA Group at Clark Field, and the 734th AAA Gun Bn joined the 251st AAA Group.

d. The role played by the brigade was mainly static. Its late arrival on the scene, when Japanese air attacks had ceased, limited its antiaircraft combat, but its units engaged in considerable ground fighting, killing 106, wounding 3, and capturing 23 of the enemy. Units of the brigade suffered five deaths and three wounded by enemy fire of all types.

e. On 1 Apr 1945 the 158th RCT landed on Legaspi, Luzon, with the mission of clearing the Japanese from that area and driving north to a junction with the forces moving southward. The only antiaircraft unit in this operation was Btry D, 210th AAA AW Bn. There was no enemy air activity but the battery furnished fire support for the infantry, maintained road blocks, and furnished security patrols. This mission lasted until 1 June when the battery rejoined the battalion.

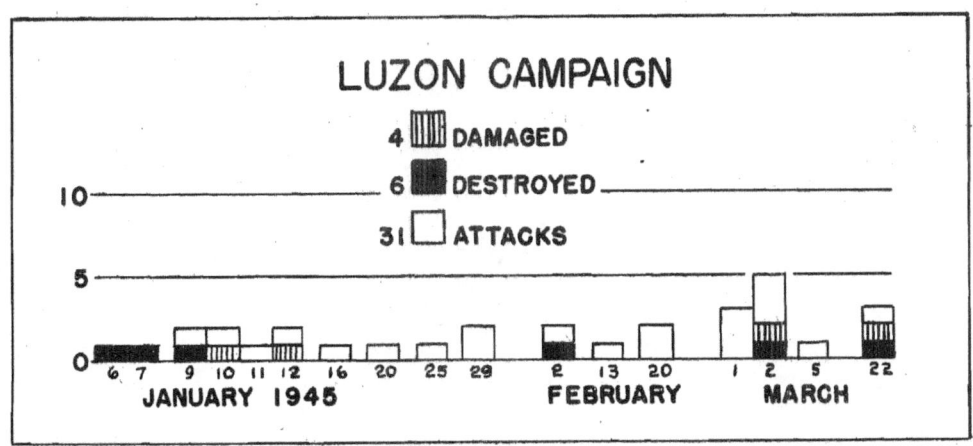

Fig. 32

f. On 24 May the 102d AAA Brigade and attached units passed to the control of the Far Eastern Air Forces, with further attachment to the V Fighter Command. At that time the 94th and 197th AAA Groups were under the brigade's control.

g. About 1 June 1945 an extensive training program was instituted by the 102d AAA Brigade under which units were removed from defensive positions for three weeks at a time. This afforded all fire units an opportunity for centralized training and recreation.

h. It was indicative of the low state of the Japanese Air Force in the Philippines that in this major operation the antiaircraft units under the 68th AAA Brigade were subjected to only 21 raids, in which but 31 enemy planes participated. Six enemy planes were destroyed and four damaged. Casualties of the brigade from all combat were 6 killed in action and 56 wounded in action. The 102d AAA Brigade units lost five killed and 12 wounded in action.

i. Terrestrial firing, as a secondary mission, was called for more frequently during the Luzon Campaign than in any previous campaign. The antiaircraft units, using organic fire-control equipment, fired on normal field artillery targets, and in some instances, against waterborne targets, in each case with excellent results. This activity is covered in detail in Chapter 3, Section II of this report.

j. On 1 July the control of offensive operations in Luzon, including 68th AAA Brigade activities, passed to the Eighth Army. Self-propelled units of the 209th AAA AW Bn and a battery of the 161st AAA Gun Bn were active in northern Luzon, but most of the troops of that brigade were collected at Luna, La Union, to prepare for the invasion of Japan. The 102d AAA Brigade continued under attachment to the Far Eastern Air Forces.

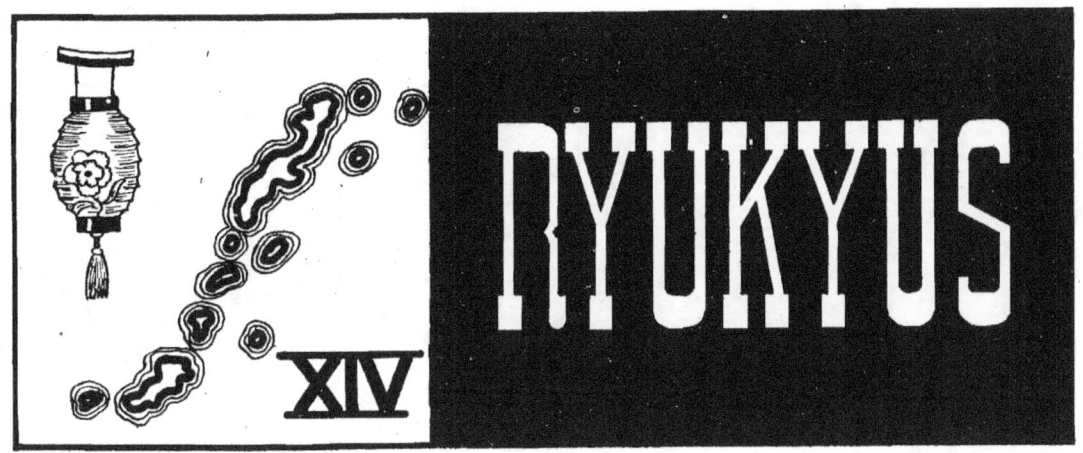

91. __General__. a. The Ryukyus Campaign opened on 26 Mar 1945 and was declared officially closed on 2 Jul 1945. Its objective was Okinawa and such surrounding islands as were necessary for security of the installations to be made on that island and of its anchorages.

b. As in the previous Pacific campaigns, the landings in the Ryukyus were preceded by carrier strikes and intense naval bombardment. Preliminary landings made by the 77th Div on the Kerama group of islands from 26 to 31 Mar resulted in securing an anchorage and seaplane base beyond the range of Japanese artillery, as well as an artillery emplacement on Keise Shima from which the landings on Okinawa could be supported.

c. The Tenth Army launched its main attack Easter Sunday, 1 Apr 1945, on the beaches north and south of Hagushi, with the Marines of the III Amphibious Corps on the left or northern flank and the infantry of the XXIV Corps on the right. The landings met with light opposition and the immediate objectives, Yontan and Kadena airfields, were captured on the first day. By the second day the island was cut in two. The Marines then turned north and, continuing to meet with light opposition, brought the whole of the northern part of Okinawa under control by 21 Apr. To the south of the original landings the XXIV Corps ran into stubborn opposition from a well-prepared series of defense lines and made slow and bloody progress.

d. It was not until late May and early June, when the four Army divisions of the XXIV Corps were reinforced by the two Marine divisions, that the final Japanese defense line from Naha to Shuri to Yonabaru was breached and the enemy opposition began to disintegrate. On 21 June organized resistance was declared over and on 2 July the campaign ended.

e. The mission of the antiaircraft units in the operation was to

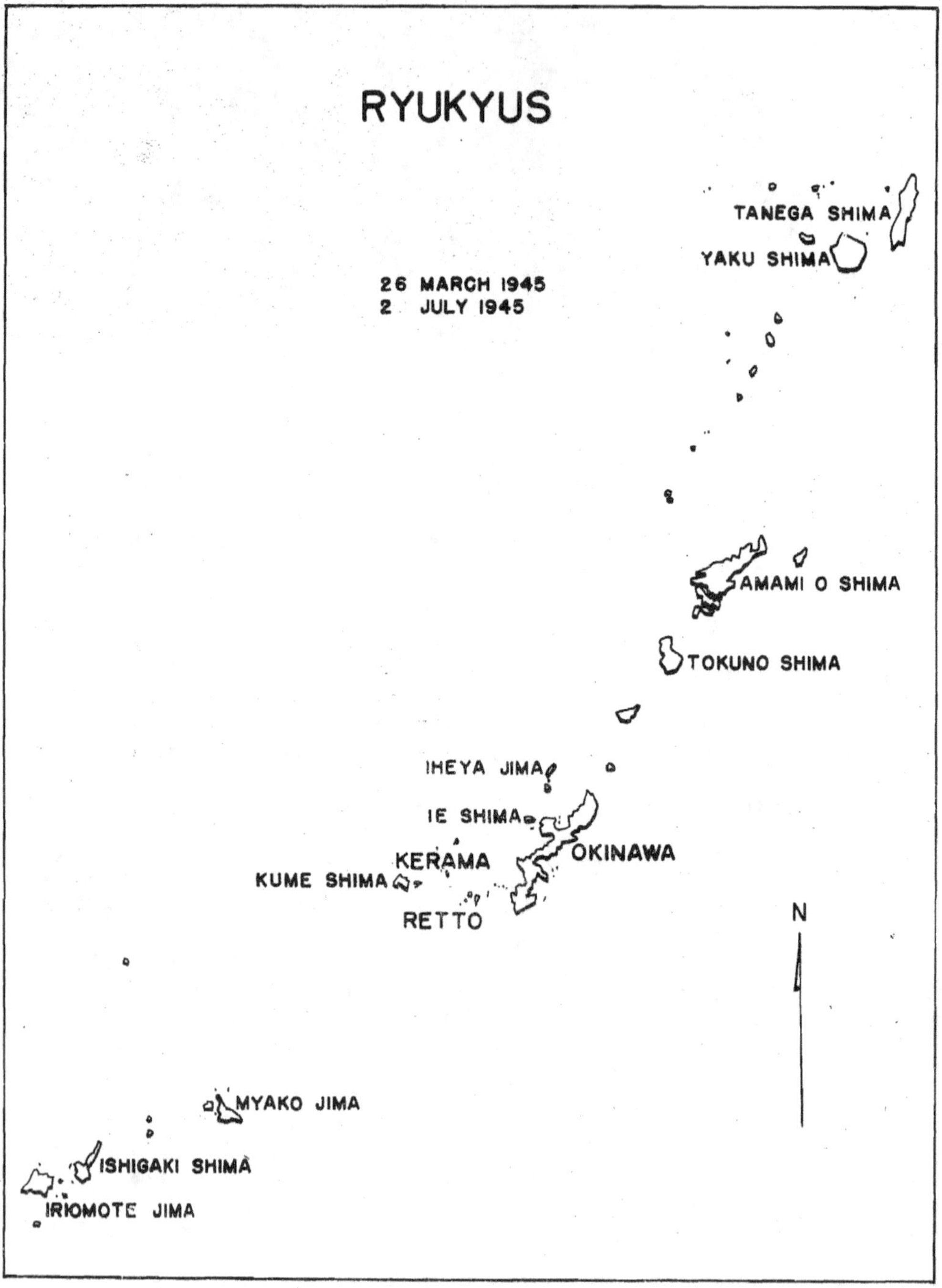

RYUKYUS

26 MARCH 1945
2 JULY 1945

TANEGA SHIMA
YAKU SHIMA

AMAMI O SHIMA

TOKUNO SHIMA

IHEYA JIMA
IE SHIMA
KERAMA   OKINAWA
KUME SHIMA
RETTO

N

MYAKO JIMA
ISHIGAKI SHIMA
IRIOMOTE JIMA

provide antiaircraft defense of the landing beaches, airfields, ports, and major military installations, to support the ground defense of the landing beaches, and to supplement the field artillery as directed.

92. Organization. a. The antiaircraft force was divided into assault and garrison echelons. The situation was unusual in that for the first time a large Marine force came under an Army antiaircraft command in an operation.

b. For the assault phase the following units were under army control:

Hq, Tenth Army AAA
Hq, 53d AAA Brigade

Other assault units were attached as follows:

To XXIV Corps
  Hq, 97th AAA Group
  Hq, 230th AAA SL Bn
To 7th Div
  502d AAA Gun Bn
  861st AAA AW Bn
  Btry C, 866th AAA AW Bn
  Btry A, 295th AAA SL Bn
To 96th Div
  504th AAA Gun Bn
  475th AAA AW Bn
  Btry C, 294th AAA SL Bn
To 77th Div
  93d AAA Gun Bn
  7th AAA AW Bn
  2d Plat, Btry A, 295th AAA SL Bn
To III Amphibious Corps
  Hq, 1st Provisional AAA Group
  2d Marine AAA Bn[1]
  16th Marine AAA Bn

c. The following units comprised the garrison echelon:

Hq, 43d, 44th, 136th, and 137th AAA Groups
63d, 98th, 369th, 503d, 504th, 514th, and 940th AAA Gun Bns
388th, 586th, 779th, 834th, 866th, and 870th AAA AW Bns
5th and 8th Marine AAA Bns

---

[1] The Marine AAA battalion is a composite unit of four gun batteries, two automatic weapons batteries (six 40-mm and six 20-mm guns per battery) and a searchlight battery. The battalion also has organic search radar equipment.

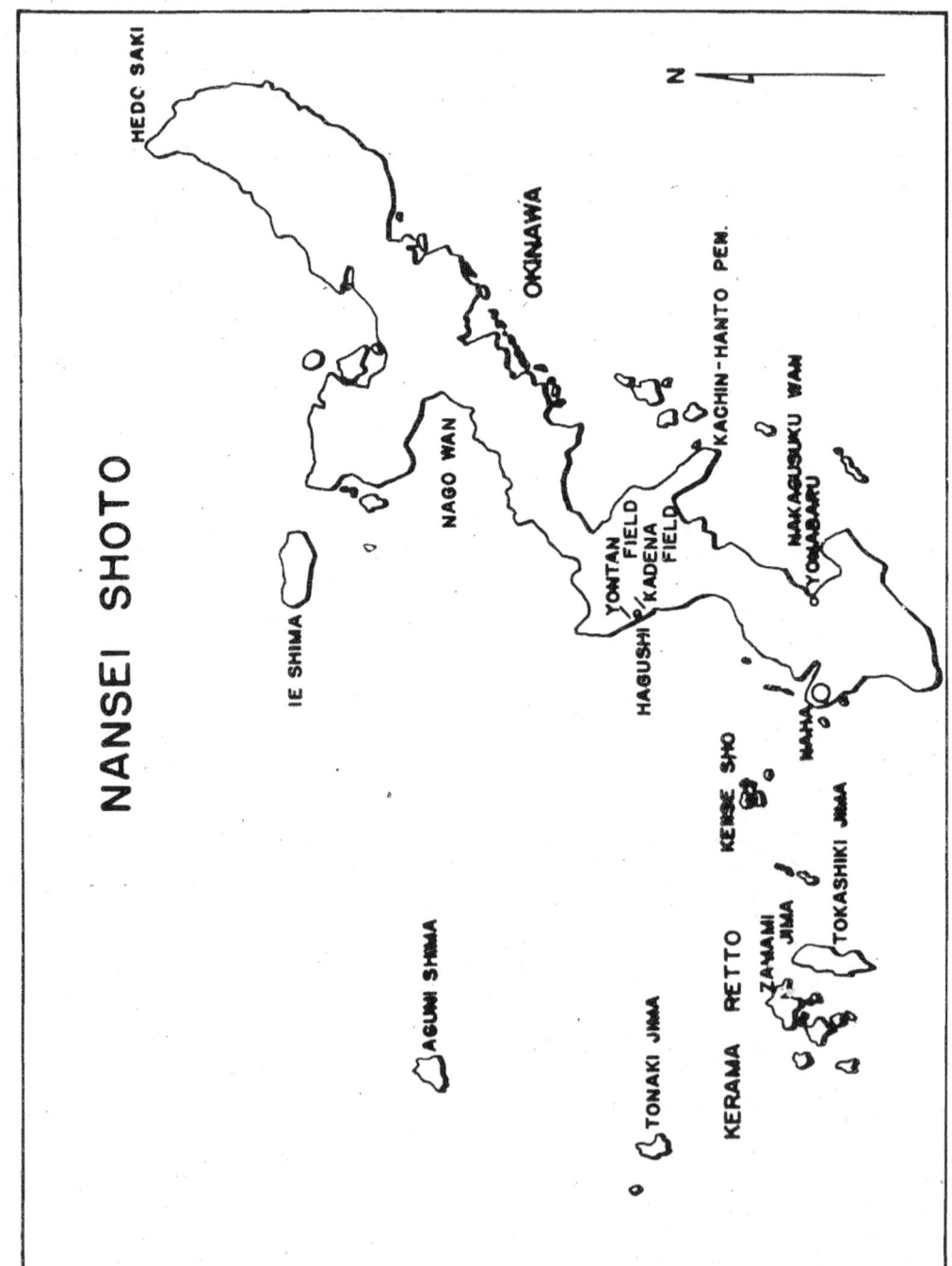

d. The indicated early attachments of assault units were changed as the assault progressed, as set forth in the paragraphs following.

e. Preparation and training of the antiaircraft units for the operation took place in three widely separated areas. The Marine 1st Provisional AAA Group with the 2d and 16th Marine AAA Battalions had engaged in an intensive training program at Kauai, T. H., from Mar 1944, and had established liaison with the Tenth Army and III Amphibious Corps before being sent, in Jan of 1945, to augment the defenses of Guam and Tinian. They embarked for Okinawa from the Marianas.

f. The 97th AAA Group and the other Army assault units had participated in the Leyte Campaign. They were relieved from their tactical assignments on Leyte in Feb and had only a month for refitting and training, which did not include target practice or amphibious rehearsals. However, ample opportunity was afforded to establish liaison with the XXIV Corps and the assault divisions.

g. The 53d AAA Brigade conducted an intensive training program at Oahu for many of the units of the garrison echelon. The program included target practices for all weapons, thorough indoctrination in local defense and field fortifications, AAAIS training, and an amphibious rehearsal. Liaison was established there with the Tenth Army Headquarters before the assault echelon sailed on 17 Feb.

h. The convoys for the Army troops of the assault echelon assembled in Leyte Gulf in Mar and engaged in extensive maneuvers before setting sail for the Ryukyus. For security reasons personnel were not allowed to leave their ships, and staff officers of the 53d AAA Brigade and the 97th AAA Group could arrange only one brief meeting to supplement the liaison previously carried on by courier.

i. There was ample opportunity, in general, to establish intimate contact between battalions and groups. The most serious deficiency in this respect was the lack of liaison between the brigade headquarters and the assault group headquarters and battalions.

j. The 7th AAA AW Bn, attached to the 77th Div, was the first antiaircraft unit to leave Leyte, sailing on 21 Mar with the Western Islands Attack Force. It participated in five separate landings in the Keramas during the six days preceding the invasion of Okinawa. Most of the battalion was withdrawn by 1 Apr and assisted the naval gunners in the division's convoy to repel Japanese suicide bombers.

k. The remainder of the Army antiaircraft artillery in the assault force left Leyte on 26 and 27 Mar with the Southern Attack Force and arrived off Okinawa on L-day, 1 Apr.

93. **Initial Phase.** The initial phase of the main assault, during which the antiaircraft units remained under divisional control, lasted

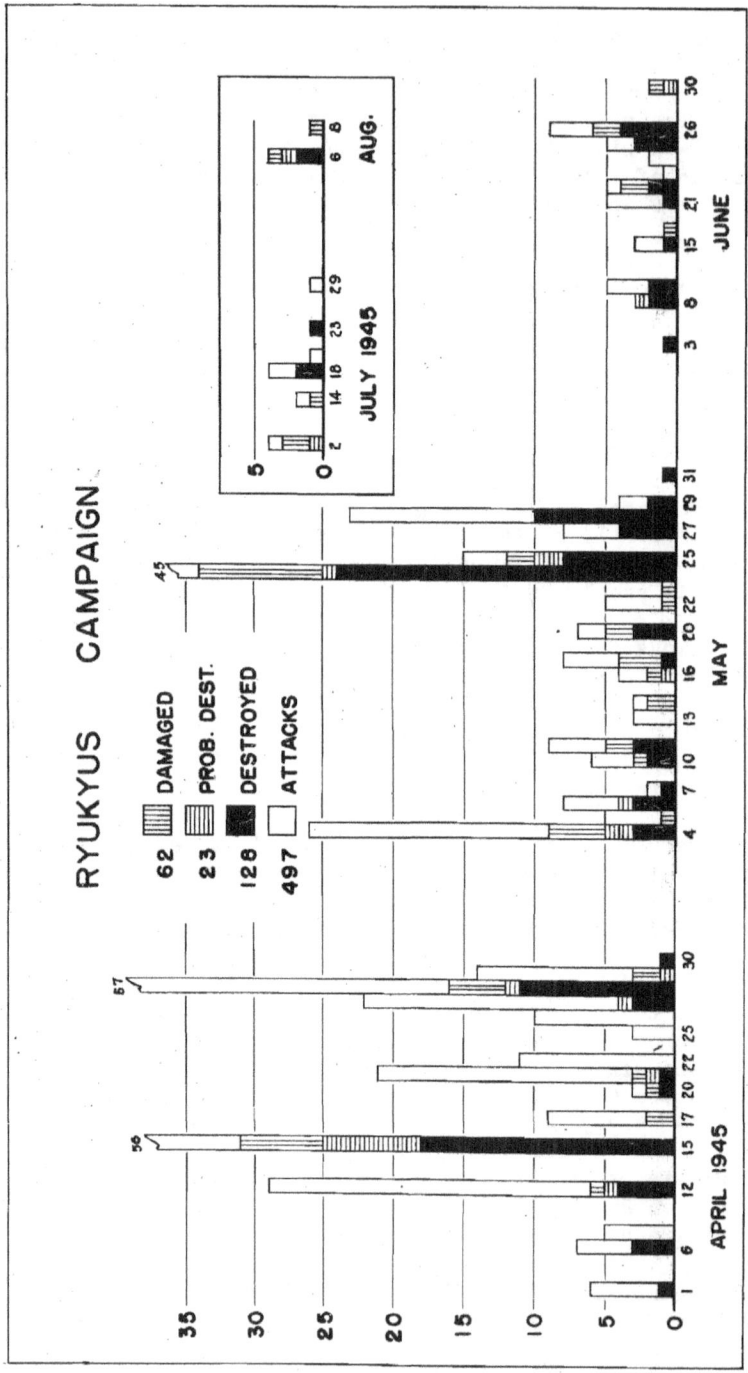

Fig. 33

four days. By nightfall of L-day elements of two batteries of the 861st and 485th AAA AW Bns were ready for action and at 1745 hours some M-51 quadruple mount machine guns of Btry D, 861st AAA AW Bn, destroyed one of a group of seven enemy fighters attacking the shipping off shore. By evening of the second day two batteries of the 502d and 504th AAA Gun Bns were in position and an advance party of Hq 97th AAA Group was coordinating the antiaircraft defense. By the third day the two automatic weapons battalions ashore had all of their weapons in operation, and Btry A of the 504th AAA Gun Bn was firing a field artillery mission for the 363d FA Bn. All antiaircraft units attached to the 7th and 96th Divs were ready for action by the time the 97th AAA Group Hq took over control at 1600 hours on 5 Apr. However, only the one enemy flight on the first day had penetrated the fighter cover and the naval antiaircraft to become a target for land-based guns.

94. _Corps Control Phase_. a. The corps control phase of the operation, during which the antiaircraft artillery was under the command of the two group headquarters, lasted from 5 through 19 Apr. The Marine 1st Provisional AAA Group, which had been unable to unload during the first days of the invasion because of poor beaches and higher priority traffic, was given priority after 5 Apr, and by 12 Apr was in position around Yontan airfield in the III Amphibious Corps' zone. The 53d AAA Brigade Hq, with the 162d Opns Det, also came ashore during that period and prepared to assume command of the antiaircraft artillery as soon as control of the air defense was relinquished by the Naval Combat Information Center afloat to the Air Defense Command ashore. The brigade's AAOR was set up by 13 Apr but was kept out of operation pending the release of control by the Navy. This change of control was effected on 20 Apr, when the brigade took over command.

b. During this phase of the campaign from 5 to 20 Apr two important developments took place. Yontan and Kadena airfields were put into operation and drew some of the enemy's attention away from shipping targets. Air raids were more frequent; in two heavy raids on the 12th and 15th of April land based antiaircraft destroyed 21, probably destroyed 8 and damaged 7 enemy planes in addition to the large number accounted for by the fighter cover.

c. The reckless and indiscriminate firing of small caliber and machine guns by other than antiaircraft artillery personnel, both afloat and ashore, was more damaging than any Japanese raid. On 6 Apr two American fighters were shot down, an ammunition dump and an oil barge destroyed, and casualties among the ground forces were estimated at 7 killed and 50 wounded, all as a result of uncontrolled fire on friendly planes. The following day another friendly flight of three planes was engaged over Yontan airfield; one plane was destroyed, another damaged, and the third crash landed. Immediate steps were taken by higher commanders to remedy the situation, and antiaircraft machine guns not in antiaircraft units were either dismantled or brought into the antiaircraft control system. However, it was ten days before the situation could be completely cleared up. Though antiaircraft units had maintained good fire discipline and were responsible for only a very small portion of the enormous volume of fire directed at the friendly planes, they were handicapped during the rest of the campaign by the reluctance of the Navy to release the antiaircraft artillery to fire while friendly planes were in the air.

d. Control of antiaircraft fire and of the entire air defense was, from the beginning, exercised by the Naval Task Force Commander from the USS El Dorado, over the Inter-Fighter Director net and the local air warning net. By monitoring these nets in the initial phases, as well as later, antiaircraft units received directly the control and alert signals and also the early warning information provided by the Navy radar picket ships that were stationed 30 to 70 miles from the defended area. This early warning service proved to be completely efficient and made the AAAIS problem immeasurably easier. As quickly as possible the gun battalions set up AAOR's for the divisional antiaircraft artillery, and during the phase of the battle under corps control, the two group headquarters opened operations rooms.

95. <u>Army Control Phase</u>. a. At 0001 hours, 20 Apr, Hq 53d AAA Brigade took control of all antiaircraft artillery then ashore, including the Marine battalions. From then on alert and control signals, as well as air warning and AAAIS information, were disseminated to the land-based antiaircraft artillery through a central AAOR operated by the 162d AAA Opns Det.

b. On the night of 20 Apr, the Japanese struck at Yontan and Kadena airfields in a series of raids with a force of more than 50 planes, only seven of which penetrated the fighter patrols and the fire of ships offshore. Those that were successful used the tactics of following American fighters in. Although antiaircraft fire was restricted through most of the raid, automatic weapons destroyed one and damaged another enemy plane. The Antiaircraft Artillery Commander conferred at once with the Commander, Combat Intelligence Center, in order to obtain freedom to fire more promptly when enemy attacks were imminent. As a result, the antiaircraft artillery was released to fire during the majority of the attacks which followed; on the first night seven of the ten planes that penetrated the defended area were destroyed and one probably destroyed, and on the second night six were destroyed, one probably destroyed, and four damaged out of a total of approximately 16 planes.

c. Raids continued with almost daily frequency, as shown on the accompanying chart (Fig 33). The biggest test of the antiaircraft defenses on Okinawa, however, occurred the night of 24-25 May, when the Japanese made eight raids on Yontan airfield and in the later attacks attempted to land suicide troops on the airfield itself. Eleven of the twenty-four planes involved were destroyed and one probably destroyed, and of the five planes attempting to land troops only the last plane succeeded in crash landing after being hit. Six to eight Japanese emerged alive and did considerable damage to airplanes on the ground before being killed. A concurrent series of 32 attacks on the airfield at Ie Shima met with a similar reception.

    d. Important changes were made in late April in the antiaircraft defenses. The automatic weapons defense had been unbalanced in favor of the XXIV Corps area because of the small number of 40-mm fire units in the Marine Defense Battalions defending the northern area. Originally there had been no opportunity to coordinate the gun defense set up by the Marine units protecting Yontan and the XXIV Corps antiaircraft gun defense of the Kadena area. A readjustment was necessary not only to integrate these defenses but also to protect installations in the eastern part of the island and to intercept raids which were showing an increasing tendency to come from the east and northeast. The 1st Provisional AAA Group was given responsibility for the automatic weapons protection of the entire Yontan-Kadena area in addition to the gun defense of Yontan. The 861st AAA AW Bn, with an attached searchlight platoon, was transferred to the Marine group, and the 866th AAA AW Bn (less one Plat), then in the process of landing, further augmented the automatic weapons defense in the area. At the same time the gun defenses in the Yontan-Kadena area were coordinated in an overall defense plan. The 97th AAA Group, in addition to providing gun defense of the Kadena area, was given the further missions of gun defense of the Katchin-Hanto region in eastern Okinawa, automatic weapons protection for the XXIV Corps field artillery zone, and support for the corps artillery in southern Okinawa.

    e. On 7 May the 1st Provisional AAA Group was given complete responsibility for the antiaircraft defense of the Yontan - Kadena area. This defense was augmented by the 8th Marine AAA Battalion, which had been in position around Nago in northern Okinawa since their arrival on 19 Apr, and by the newly arrived 5th Marine AAA Battalion. The 97th AAA Group provided the defense for the Katchin - Hanto area, the southernmost Hagushi beaches, and the XXIV Corps artillery zone. The 137th AAA Group, which landed on 3 May, was held in readiness for the antiaircraft defense of the Naha region.

    f. Rectification of the brigade defense area was completed on 31 May with the relief of the 97th AAA Group from their mission on the southern Hagushi beaches. The 1st Provisional AAA Group assumed responsibility for defense of all installations on western Okinawa and the 97th AAA Group for eastern Okinawa, which included Chimu and Awase airfields, a patrol bomber base on the Katchin Hanto peninsula, and the anchorage and landing beaches in Nakagusuku Wan, later renamed Buckner Bay.

    g. In May a radar surveillance net was established by the 230th AAA SL Bn using SCR-268s. Four sets were used on the western coastline and five on the eastern shore. Later, long range radar set up on the northern tip of Okinawa and on outlying islands relieved some Navy picket ships of their assignments.

h. On 15 June, 2d Marine Air Wing's Air Defense Control Center near Yontan airfield began taking over control of the defense from the Combat Information Center afloat for brief periods during the day. By the end of June ADCC was in complete control.

i. Anticipating the complete investment of the island the 137th AAA Group, with the 98th AAA Gun Bn, the 834th AAA AW Bn (SP) (less two batteries), and Btry A, 325th AAA SL Bn attached, was assigned the antiaircraft defense of southern Okinawa, to include the harbor and airfield at Naha, and Yonabaru Harbor. On 30 June Machinato airfield was added to the 137th AAA Group's zone, and the two remaining batteries of the 834th AAA AW Bn (SP), as well as Btry B of the 861st AAA AW Bn, were added to its command. The 97th AAA Group improved its defenses around Nakagusuku Wan by emplacing a gun battery and an automatic weapons battery on the island of Tsugen which closed the harbor on the east.

j. Several units joined the Okinawa garrison after the campaign was officially closed on 2 Jul 1945. Hq 43d AAA Group arrived on 5 July and was assigned to the defenses of the Baten Ko and Yonabaru areas. Its AAOR started operation on 10 Aug and on 17 Aug its mission was extended to include Naha and Machinato. The 586th AAA AW Bn arrived on 12 Aug and was in tactical positions at Naha, Yonabaru, and Machinato by 7 Sept.

96. Ie Shima. a. Ie Shima, a small island off the northwest coast of Okinawa, important for its two airstrips, was invaded on 16 Apr by the 77th Div. The two antiaircraft battalions and the searchlight platoon attached to the division were delayed in the occupation of positions by sniper fire on the beaches and by the large number of mines planted on the island; however, by 20 Apr all of the assault fire units were ashore and ready for action. During this phase of the operation antiaircraft personnel removed over 50 mines at a cost of one enlisted man killed and one seriously wounded. In May the 136th AAA Group Hq moved to Ie Shima from Okinawa, and on the 22d took control of the antiaircraft units on the island, the Group Commander also being designated Island Seaward Defense Commander. The following troops were attached to the Group:

   93d AAA Gun Bn
   7th and 383th AAA AW Bns
   2d Plat, Btry A, 295th AAA SL Bn

b. The 948th AAA Gun Bn and the remainder of Btry A, 295th AAA SL Bn, arrived at Ie Shima after the Group Hq had assumed command.

c. On 19 Apr the antiaircraft units on Ie Shima were assigned to the Okinawa Island Command and attached to the Ie Shima Island Command.

d. Raids on Ie Shima occurred regularly from 26 Apr to 8 Aug but were intense on only two occasions, both in conjunction with raids on Okinawa. The first was on the night of 27-28 Apr when ten planes attacked, with antiaircraft artillery destroying one and damaging two. The second was the night of 24-25 May when out of 32 attackers 18 were shot down and 7 damaged.

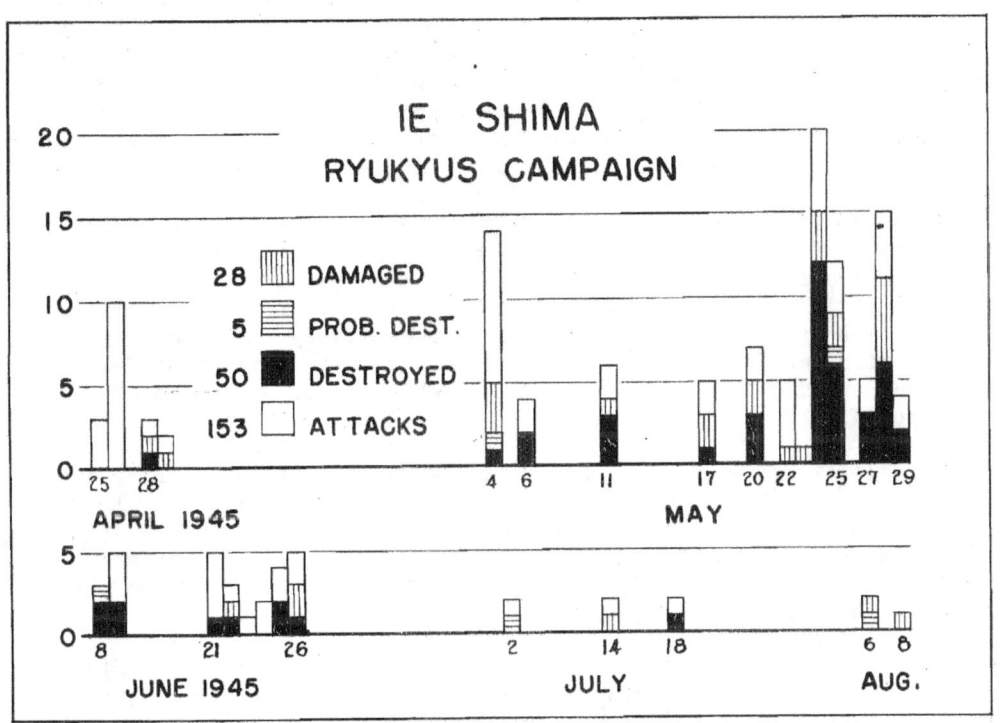

Fig. 34

e. It was on this occasion that the 93d AAA Gun Bn made its record of 15 1/3 planes destroyed in $6\frac{1}{2}$ hours with an average expenditure of 120 rounds for each plane destroyed.

f. Disaster also hit the antiaircraft artillery here. Early on the morning of 24 June, during a raid by two Japanese planes, seven bombs landed among the gun pits and one 60-kilogram navy bomb scored a direct hit on the platform of a 90-mm gun of Btry D, 93d AAA Gun Bn, killing the crew of 12 men and setting fire to the emplacement. Another hit beside the emplacement of a nearby 40-mm gun killed four and injured two men who were not in the pit. Although a third of the ammunition stored in the 90-mm gun pit was detonated by the ensuing fire, and considerable damage was sustained by the fire-control equipment during the raid, the battery cleaned up the debris and was back in action with three guns in seven hours.

97. <u>Kerama Retto</u>. a. As previously related, the 7th AAA AW Bn landed in the Keramas with the 77th Div.

b. When the division withdrew from the group of islands on 31 Mar it left behind a battalion of infantry and Btry D of the 7th AAA AW Bn on Zamami, and the 420th FA Group with a platoon of Btry B, 7th AAA AW Bn, on Keise. The latter platoon received counter-battery fire from enemy artillery on Okinawa, and helped repel a suicide force which attacked the island in amphibious tanks and small boats on the night of 9 Apr. Btry D was withdrawn on 18 Apr and the platoon of Btry B on 14 May, leaving the defense of the anchorage to naval antiaircraft artillery. However, at the request of the naval commander, the 505th AAA Gun Bn with a platoon of Btry C, 866th AAA AW Bn, was sent to the islands of Zamami, Tokashiki, and Geruma to augment the antiaircraft defenses of the anchorage. The first elements landed on 25 May. Small groups of enemy infantry still operated in the islands, but the careful organization of the positions for ground defense checked effectively the usual Japanese infiltration tactics. The battalion came under the command of Hq, 44th AAA Group on 10 June, when the group commander assumed command of all army ground forces in the Keramas.

c. Air raids were few. After the campaign officially ended on 29 July, the 505th AAA Gun Bn was credited with destroying one plane. Most of the action by both guns and automatic weapons of this battalion was in support of the 870th AAA AW Bn[1] which was acting as infantry in the islands, having on 23 May relieved the infantry battalion left by the 77th Div.

98. <u>Aguni, Theya, Kume, and Hedo Misaki</u>. In order to relieve the navy picket ships, air warning radars were installed on these three outlying islands. Antiaircraft protection was furnished by units of the 866th AAA AW Bn. At Hedo Misaki, on the northern tip of Okinawa, where another radar station was set up, Btry C (less one platoon) of the 866th AAA AW Bn was in position. The Hedo Misaki installation was the only one attacked by the Japanese; in an engagement involving a single plane the plane was destroyed.

99. <u>Summary of Antiaircraft Artillery Action</u>. a. The accompanying chart (See Fig 35) shows the day by day incidence of enemy air attacks that came within reach of the land-based antiaircraft artillery (Army and Marine) on Okinawa, and the extent of confirmed damage to the raiding planes. The increased tempo of air attacks on the ground installations after the airfields became operative is evident. The attacks on Ie Shima followed the same general pattern.

---

[1] Chap 3, Sec IV, Par 20.

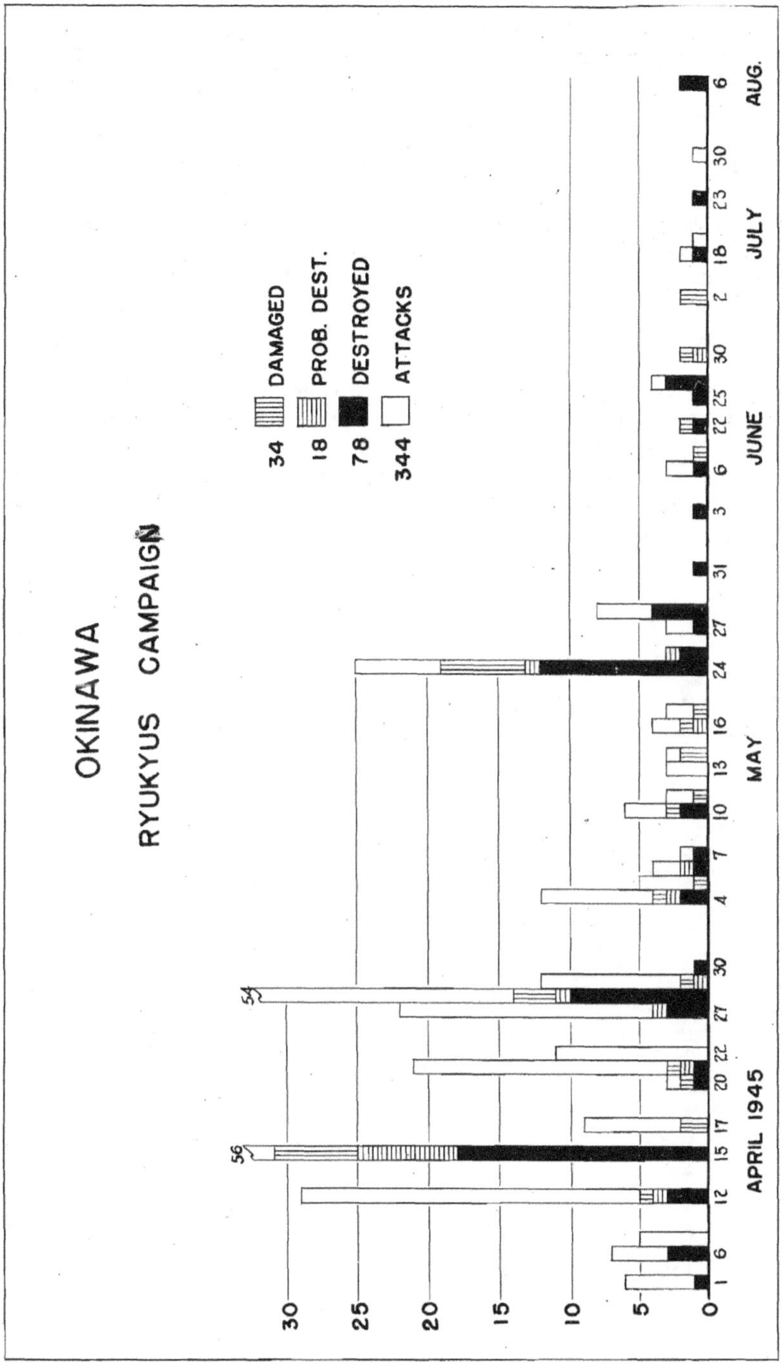
OKINAWA
RYUKYUS CAMPAIGN
34 DAMAGED
18 PROB. DEST.
78 DESTROYED
344 ATTACKS
0
5
10
15
20
25
30
56
54
1 6 12 15 17 20 22 27 30
APRIL 1945
4 7 10 13 16 24 27 31
MAY
3 6 22 25 30
JUNE
2 18 23 30
JULY
6
AUG.

Fig. 35

b. The results of antiaircraft action in this campaign were of a high order. Of the 497 enemy planes attacking, the land-based antiaircraft units destroyed 128, or 25.7%, probably destroyed 23, or 4.9%, and damaged 62, or 12.5%, despite the fact that fire was restricted during 52 of the attacks.

c. The Japanese made most of their attacks on land installations during the hours of darkness. Low-level attacks at night were a common feature during Apr. The success of the searchlight-automatic weapons team in destroying planes is indicated by abandonment of these low altitude attacks by the Japanese in May. The low-level attacks in June were directed at shipping and were for the most part out of range of land-based automatic weapons.

d. Much of the success of the air warning service in the Ryukyus operations was due to the Navy picket ships that performed their mission efficiently in spite of being under constant and violent air attacks themselves. Besides supplying distant warning of the approach of enemy air attacks, these ships directed the fighter interception within their zones.

XV. AA INTELLIGENCE

100. <u>General</u>. In the collection, evaluation and dissemination of general information of the enemy, antiaircraft intelligence in the Pacific war followed the pattern of all other combat intelligence. However, the procedures in establishing and using the AAAIS and the AA Operations Room, while following basic War Department doctrine[1], were necessarily adapted to the conditions imposed by amphibious warfare, jungle and mountain hazards to communications, and existing early warning radar facilities.

101. <u>AAOR</u>. a. The AAOR, as the control center of the antiaircraft defense, received its principal information from the AAAIS. The AAAIS incorporated all antiaircraft units in the defended area and included a network of visual observation posts, especially vital in the difficult terrain of the Southwest Pacific area, as well as radar detection installations. In addition, information might come to the AAOR from many other sources, including the Air Force Control Center, the

---

[1] Field Manual 44-8.

Navy Combat Intelligence Center (CIC) afloat, other AAOR's, and from line troops. This information came directly from its source in some installations, or was relayed from subordinate communication centers or operations rooms in others. The determining factor normally was the amount and kind of communication facilities available. The use of direct data lines from the radar to the plotter, in the AAOR, was the favored solution. Local conditions, especially in amphibious or extremely mobile situations, sometimes indicated other solutions which were practical and resulted in efficient defense.

  b. The physical location of the AAOR was determined by three factors, communications facilities, permanence of installations, and local security. Practical experience in amphibious operations proved the desirability of an AAOR installed in a vehicle which landed with the first antiaircraft troops, and which was placed where communications were most favorable. In some of the later operations the simultaneous landing and adjacent installation of the AAOR and the Fighter Control Center were planned. As the operation progressed and the target area was secured, these installations were developed and combined into a normal operations center, or abandoned for a more permanent joint installation.

  c. Except for installations in Australia and Hawaii, and on Luzon in the late spring of 1945, few elaborate operations rooms were established. It was evident from the beginning of the campaign that the island to island warfare made speed of installation paramount. The AAOR however, underwent a somewhat standard transition. In the assault phase simplicity of control and flexibility were emphasized. As the situation became more static, efficiency of operation could be stressed. Battalion operations rooms set up while communications were scarce and troops were moving rapidly, were consolidated or were subordinated to a central AAOR operated by a group or brigade, and all elements of the antiaircraft defenses were integrated into one unit.

  d. In the early days of the war few officers or enlisted men had been specially trained for work in the AAOR. Since antiaircraft tables of organization and equipment made no provision for large operations sections, personnel already assigned to other duties were used in the AAOR, and the necessary special equipment was improvised. In Aug 1944 the 146th AA Operations Detachment was organized on Bougainville Island, using personnel from Hq 68th AAA Brigade. There was little opportunity for special training and when the unit landed on Leyte in Oct it was scarcely familiar with its equipment. In that same month antiaircraft operations detachments, equipped with mobile operations rooms, began to arrive in New Guinea from the United States. These had been activated in Apr and May of that year and had undergone intensive training prior to departure for the theater. Upon arrival, they were given further training in the Antiaircraft Training Center at Finschhafen, New Guinea, where problems peculiar to the Southwest Pacific were emphasized. Of the seven detachments which arrived only two participated in amphibious landings.

102. <u>Joint Operations</u>. Direction of the air defense measures in the early phases of amphibious operations was the function of the Task Force Commander afloat. To implement it the Navy established a Combat Intelligence Center afloat which performed functions comparable to the Army Fighter Control Center and AAOR ashore. Sources of information for this CIC were radars and observers on small craft deployed so as to give all-around coverage. Upon landing, the Army antiaircraft units monitored the CIC air-warning net; battalion or group AAOR's insured that this information reached all fire units, and also disseminated information received from visual observers located with the troops on the perimeter. As soon as antiaircraft radars became operative they began furnishing data to the AAOR by radio, which the AAOR relayed to all antiaircraft units, and in some cases to the CIC. When land-based aircraft assumed the fighter cover responsibility and the Navy could withdraw the bulk of its air force it was common for the control of air defense to revert from the Navy to the Army, with the responsibility delegated normally to the senior Air Force Officer. Radio contact with the Navy CIC was maintained through a liaison net and for the exchange of intelligence.

103. <u>Fire Direction</u>. a. Basic fire direction was exercised through SOP's issued by the antiaircraft commander, which prescribed primary and secondary sectors of responsibility and general instructions to insure the maximum number of targets being engaged in multiple attacks. At times, however, the commander or his operations officer (AAOO) exercised immediate fire direction by ordering units to engage certain targets or by ordering a particular procedure required by the situation. In the more elaborate installations the AAOO frequently was assisted by gun, automatic weapons, and searchlight officers.

b. As in other theaters antiaircraft combat action was governed by joint directives of the Army, Navy, Air Force, and our Allies. The general principle that the local fighter controller could restrict the fire of the antiaircraft artillery prevailed, and under it the action of antiaircraft units in the Pacific was controlled by air officers of either the Army, the Navy, the Marines, or the Royal Australian Air Forces.

c. There were many occasions on which antiaircraft fire was unduly restricted by overly cautious or inexperienced Air Force control officers. However, as units worked together with the same Air Force personnel, team work was developed, and mutual confidence resulted in close cooperation, and a minimum of restriction.

d. Considerable difference existed between the Army and the Navy procedures and terminology in exercising operational control over the antiaircraft artillery. The Army control system originally used terms and code words based on RAAF practice. There were two controls, "Hold Fire", and "Released to Fire", and three conditions of readiness, "Red Alert", "Yellow Alert", and "All Clear". However, after the Philippines had been secured, the Army SOPs in the Pacific were revised to conform with the naval practice. This made use of two controls, "Green" and "Yellow", and, in effect, two conditions, "Red" and "Blue". A third readiness status, condition "Black", gave warning for a parachute attack.

104. <u>New Guinea</u>. a. The first American antiaircraft units came to New Guinea from Australia. The methods used in AAOR's, where permanent installations and complete wire communications facilities existed, were not always suitable for use in the mountains and jungles, cut by the rivers and bays, of Papua. It was necessary to depend almost entirely upon radio communication.

b. In most of the landings that took place in leap-frog fashion along the coasts of New Guinea the beachheads were established on long narrow strips of land between high mountains and the sea. The jungles made it impossible to position radars where they could cover the section blocked by mountains. The blind area in the AAAIS system could be overcome only by use of visual OP's. However, the mountain jungles were almost as inaccessible by foot as they were by vehicle. To obtain effective observation it was often necessary for troops to go farther inland than other patrols had penetrated; OP's were frequently established far beyond the defended perimeter.

c. One of the outstanding OP's was known as the "Golden Voice", an Australian outpost on the eastern side of the Owen Stanley mountains. In 1942, while the Japanese still held Lae and Salamaua, it furnished warning to Port Moresby whenever Japanese planes took off from their bases for a strike on the Allied advance elements.

d. During landing operations, at least for the assault waves, OPs were the only source of direct AAAIS data.

e. The effectiveness of these OPs depended not only upon their location but also upon their communications. Experiments were conducted at Finschhafen to determine the practical maximum limits of low-powered radios (SCR-284s), in the jungle. Groups were sent out with guides from the Angau constabulary. They were supplied by air and moved from one site to another to obtain the best coverage of the avenue of approach, while keeping effective communication with the net control center.

f. Decentralized control, unusual in so large a defense area, characterized the organization and functioning of the AAOR at Morotai. As a result of the large amount of antiaircraft artillery concentrated in an area already congested with other troops unusual communication difficulties were presented. The radar warning data, instead of being transmitted directly to the central AAOR, was plotted in battalion operations rooms. Only filtered plots were sent to the group AAOR's. A "voycall" (interphone) system was used to connect the group AAOR's. Nearly all control was left to the battalion commanders.

105. <u>Middle Pacific</u>. a. AAOR and AAAIS procedure in the MIDPAC area was influenced largely by the fact that operations were under Naval command.

b. At Ulithi, air defense measures for the atoll and for ships in the anchorage were coordinated in an Air Defense Control Center ashore. This ADCC was commanded and operated by the Marines, by the Navy, and by the Army, in succession. The radars of all three forces furnished early warning. Within the ADCC an AAOR was maintained by the senior antiaircraft commander.

c. At Saipan the operation of the AAOR was hampered initially by poor coordination between the Army and the Navy. The original plan called for operational control of shore-based antiaircraft artillery by the fleet air warning officer aboard the control ship, through the Army Commander ashore. Although there was hostile air action during the first four days of the landing, no control information was received ashore. The antiaircraft commander finally obtained authority from the commanding general of the assault force to exercise control over antiaircraft fire on the basis of antiaircraft radar warning. Aboard ship, fleet intelligence served antiaircraft units well but when the information was monitored by units ashore it could not be used since the location of the fleet center, on which range and bearings were based, was not known to the units on shore.

d. (1) At Iwo Jima, before the landing and until an AAOR could be set up on shore, air warning service was furnished by the Navy. Both warnings and controls would be announced to the Army antiaircraft units by the Navy. These warnings were never adequate for shore antiaircraft purposes for two reasons:

      (a) "Flash Red" was intended as a general air raid alarm and came too late to enable antiaircraft units to man equipment.

      (b) Initial plots only were given and no attempt was made to follow up and keep continuous intelligence flowing for antiaircraft units.

(2) On D / 12 an AAOR was established by Hq 138th AAA Group. Warning information was furnished by the ADCC, operated by a signal aircraft warning unit, and from gun battery radars. No battalion AAOR's were organized and information was sent from the group AAOR to the batteries by radio and later by telephone. On D / 23 an antiaircraft oper-

ations detachment took over the AAOR.

106. <u>Leyte</u>. a. As in previous operations, operational control of antiaircraft artillery was exercised by the Navy. Radar intelligence, air warnings and fire restrictions were broadcast by Commander, Support Aircraft, from the Fighter Director Ship. This information from Navy plots went from the spotting ship to the control ship, to Commander Support Aircraft, to the Corps Air Officer, and thence to the antiaircraft group.

b. When the 32d AAA Brigade's AAOR was established on A ∤ 1, the alert status and fire control instructions were still given by the naval controller. Due to atmospheric conditions and a poor location, radio transmissions from the AAOR to the units were received only intermittently and with great difficulty, but since the firing units could monitor the transmissions from the Fighter Director Ship they received the same information from this latter source with less time lag.

c. On A ∤ 7 the FCC took over direction of Army fighters and antiaircraft artillery ashore while the Fighter Director Ship still maintained control of carrier based fighters and naval antiaircraft artillery. In spite of close liaison there were occasional conflicts in the alert status.

d. The permanent FCC and AAOR were not established until 7 Dec after a month's delay caused by difficulty in building roads and installing wire. Radio, however, remained the primary means of reliable communication until the campaign closed. In an attempt to improve radio transmission, voice transmissions were replaced by CW between the brigade and the group AAOR, with some improvement noted.

107. <u>Luzon</u>. a. Initially, antiaircraft operational control was exercised by the Navy Controller afloat. All units monitored the Naval Air Warning Net. Few difficulties were experienced. The Fighter Control Center and the brigade AAOR were set up together on shore on S ∤ 2.

b. An antiaircraft operations detachment, attached to the brigade for the purpose of operating the AAOR, landed on S-day without equipment. Brigade equipment was used initially by the detachment to establish the AAOR.

c. On S ∤ 8 the FCC took over operational control from the Navy. Air warning from the AAOR was furnished ground units over a designated net. The two antiaircraft groups under brigade operated their AAORs in their own sectors, and relayed warning from brigade to their attached units by radio, supplemented by wire. Direct lines led from the brigade AAOR to the group AAORs. Information from the searchlight radars came into the FCC over direct wire lines. Gun radars (SCR-584's) were tied directly into the brigade AAAIS for air warning only. Alert warning guns, both 90-mm and 40-mm, after initial connection through subordinate units, were ultimately connected directly by wire and radio to the brigade AAOR.

  d. Throughout the operation reliance was placed principally upon radio communication. Wire communication rarely proved satisfactory.

  e. During the drive south to Manila, a mobile AAOR, operated by personnel from the operations detachment, accompanied the mobile antiaircraft units. Its primary sources of information were the brigade AAOR and the mobile Signal Corps radars with the forward elements. Radio furnished the primary means of communication.

  108. *Ryukyus*. a. During the entire period operational control was exercised through the Combat Information Center afloat. The firing and control status for ship and shore antiaircraft artillery were determined usually by the task force commander in person.

  b. Picket ships, controlled by the Force Fighter Director, were stationed in all directions from 30 to 70 miles out from the landing beaches. Each picket ship furnished early warning and also controlled fighter aviation.

  c. Aircraft plots were broadcast from the Combat Information Center in polar coordinates with a known point of origin on the island, and could be picked up by all units.

  d. The 53d AAA Brigade AAOR brought together and plotted all information from the Force Combat Information Center, the picket ships reporting on the inter-fighter net, and the battalion AAORs reporting filtered information from gun radars, the visual OP's, and the Marine Group AAOR. Eighteen SCR-268's belonging to the 230th AAA SL Bn arrived unexpectedly on 26 Apr and were used to establish a surveillance net on both sides of the island.

  e. The following tabulation indicates the effectiveness of the air warning service during the period 20 Apr - 21 Jun 1945. The long range coverage was due to the superior Naval picket ship coverage.

Range of Raid at Pickup	No of Raids	Percent
0 - 15 miles	4	13
16 - 35 miles	40	38
36 - 55 miles	34	33
56 - 75 miles	10	10
Unknown[1]	6	6

[1] (Raids approached from same general direction as other raids being tracked or under fire.)

3. IN OTHER ROLES

SECTION   I
              General

SECTION   II
              Terrestrial Fire

SECTION   III
              Offshore Defense

SECTION   IV
              Infantry Action

SECTION   V
              Special Searchlight Operations

SECTION   VI
              Non-Combat Functions

Section I

General

109. __General__. a. From the days just before the fall of Bataan until after the official closing of hostilities, antiaircraft personnel and materiel were used at many times and places in support of the ground forces. It is notable that while the use on Bataan involved the abandonment of their antiaircraft mission and equipment, the battles of Okinawa

and Northern Luzon called for the engagement of terrestrial targets as the primary mission of their antiaircraft weapons.

b. Terrestrial fire by antiaircraft guns did not become common in the Pacific theater until 1944. In the jungles of the Southwest Pacific Area, field artillery was not used extensively against the Japanese because of the difficulty of getting it into position and observing its fire. In the conquest of the atolls in the Pacific Ocean Area most of the artillery fire was furnished by the guns of supporting naval craft.

c. In some cases antiaircraft commanders failed to acquaint the task force and artillery commanders with the capabilities of antiaircraft weapons in a ground role. Where the capabilities of antiaircraft artillery in terrestrial fire were fully understood, and conditions justified this employment, efficient use was made of the antiaircraft units assigned to the tasks, and both infantry and field artillery expressed their complete satisfaction with the manner in which the missions were performed.

d. The use of antiaircraft troops in combat against the enemy on the ground increased as the war progressed. This resulted in action with primary weapons against his fortifications and shelters, and in an infantry role in repelling his attacks in patrolling, and in a few instances in offensive action. Antiaircraft troops also assisted the infantry by illuminating the battlefields.

e. The following totals of enemy casualties inflicted by antiaircraft units in ground action prior to VJ-day include only tabulated casualties known to have been inflicted by antiaircraft personnel. They do not include enemy dead and wounded resulting from antiaircraft fire used in artillery support roles, except in those rare cases when bodies could be counted. Estimates of the number killed and wounded in silencing enemy pill-boxes, strong points, and gun positions, in sealing enemy-held caves and in harassing fire are not included.

Enemy Killed in Action	Enemy Wounded in Action	Enemy Prisoners of War
1599	72	411

In addition to the above enemy losses the 475th AAA AW Bn, in carrying out a mission of collecting and processing prisoners of war in the vicinity of Bayombong, Luzon, during Sept 1945, was responsible for killing in action 11 Japanese and taking 9,806 prisoners of war.

Section II

Terrestrial Fire

110. **Automatic Weapons.** a. After the resistance by the men of the 200th CA (AA) to the Japanese in the last days of the defense of Bataan, the next recorded use of antiaircraft artillery in support of ground action in the Pacific war was at Milne Bay by the 709th CA Btry (AA). This airborne machine-gun battery was flown in from Townsville on 19 Aug 1942 in a conglomeration of bombers and flying boats. The machine guns of the battery were deployed to provide defense of the beach and of an airstrip under construction, against an expected enemy ground attack. Their mission required also that they protect the length of the strip from parachute attack. In the attack which materialized two positions on the beach had to be abandoned. The next morning a Japanese battalion in advancing along a jungle trail opening onto the airstrip, attempted to cross the clearing and ran head-on into the weapons of the antiaircraft battery and other machine guns mounted on an American engineer half-track. The fire of the cal .50 guns was a decisive factor in stopping the enemy and holding the strip. The enemy were never able to cross the strip. This point marks the farthest advance of the Japanese in the Milne Bay battle.

b. The positions of the enemy on Roosevelt Ridge, just west of Nassau Bay in New Guinea, barred the Allied advance toward Salamaua in Aug 1943. After 23 days of the bitterest kind of fighting with small arms, mortars and light artillery, the enemy still held the ridge. Btry C, 209th AAA AW Bn was called upon for assistance. Seven Bofors and 16 cal .50 machine guns were emplaced at about 1400 yards range, and after 35 minutes of fire by these weapons on 14 Aug our infantry occupied half the ridge without opposition. When strong resistance stopped our advance on the remainder of the heights the guns were relocated. After six Bofors and 15 cal .50 machine guns had fired for 20 minutes, our infantry occupied the remainder of the ridge without opposition.

c. During the battle of Soanatalu, Mono Island, Treasury Group, in Nov 1943, the guns of Btry G, 198th CA (AA), were deployed on the beach. Approximately 100 enemy troops attempted to cross it, in an effort to reach several landing craft beached near the battery. The enemy was turned back from the beach by the antiaircraft fire with a loss of about 60 killed. The battery suffered no casualties.

d. During the desperate Japanese counterattacks on Bougainville during Mar 1944, the 199th and 951st AAA AW Bns moved sections into the perimeter defense system, and, under the operational control of the 37th Div, rendered effective support to the defense.

e. In the Aitape operation in mid-1944 the 383d AAA AW Bn made extensive preparation to furnish terrestrial fire in support of the ground troops. Weapons were moved into position and fire plans coordinated with the appropriate infantry commanders. However, no attacks developed in which the weapons could be used. At Aitape, also, an M45 quadruple cal .50 mount was emplaced on a PT boat and used to strafe enemy trucks and barges up and down the coast. The volume of fire made this an ideal weapon for such a mission. Antiaircraft searchlights mounted on PT boats were used to furnish illumination during these attacks.[1]

f. On Biak Island on 9 Jan 1944 the 476th AAA AW Bn emplaced two 40-mm guns to fire into enemy-held caves north of Parai. After a few bursts of fire no enemy activity was observed.

g. On 26 Jun 1944, the 864th AAA AW Bn furnished terrestrial fire for the infantry attack on Nafutan Point, Saipan. Two 40-mm guns and one M16 multiple-gun motor carriage were sited to fire into enemy caves. The firing was at an average range of 2000 yards, yet hits were secured in cave entrances as small as three feet in diameter. Later, an enemy detachment which broke through the perimeter attacked the area from which these weapons had been fired. The guns had been withdrawn, however, prior to this attack.

h. Btry A, 102d AAA AW Bn, was attached to the 11th AB Div for the landing at Nasugubu, south of Manila, on 31 Jan 1945. As no air opposition developed the 40-mm guns were withdrawn from antiaircraft defense missions and employed to support the division artillery. The first mission was fired on 6 Feb when one platoon was employed to neutralize pillboxes and enemy personnel in defensive positions in the outskirts of Manila. The next day two 40-mm guns assisted the division artillery in the destruction of a seacoast heavy gun emplacement. During the evening of 9 Feb an enemy barge was sunk as it attempted to leave Manila Harbor; later three more waterborne targets were destroyed. On 10 Feb the last mission was fired, another heavy gun emplacement being taken under counter-battery fire.

i. On 19 Feb 1945 Btry A, 950th AAA AW Bn, participated in the landing on Corregidor. Upon landing they were immediately employed to cover possible enemy escape routes. The battery fired 88 rounds of 40-mm ammunition at a ravine in which the enemy were grouping. After the fire an infantry patrol found over 100 dead Japanese in the ravine. The credit was divided between the battery and the Air Corps which had

---

[1] See Sect V, Par 123.

bombed the area.

j. On 9 Apr 1945, four 40-mm guns from Btry D, 925th AAA AW Bn, were attached to the 1st Provisional Battery, formed to support Eighth Army operations in the Ormoc-Villaba area of Leyte. Approximately 200 targets, including huts, caves, machine-gun nests and bovouac areas, were engaged effectively with 3,743 rounds of 40-mm HE shell.

k. Btry D, 469th AAA AW Bn, was attached to the 25th Div in the Balete Pass area of Luzon on 7 Apr 1945, but due to the tactical situation and the difficult nature of the terrain no ground support missions were fired. However, on 14 Apr, the battery was attached to the 33d Div, and on 19 and 20 Apr the first missions were fired, one section firing on six positions believed to be camouflaged pillboxes. On another mission an enemy cave was taken under fire and with five rounds of AP and three rounds of HE ammunition the cave was cleared. This was typical of results obtained elsewhere with the 40-mm gun.

l. The 210th AAA AW Bn furnished support fire to the 158th RCT at Legaspi, on Luzon, during Mar and Apr 1945. The weapons were often emplaced under direct enemy observation, in order to give close support.

m. The 198th AAA AW Bn had all four batteries in action on Luzon as ground-support weapons in Apr and May 1945. Btry A was with the 33d and Btry C with the 37th Div at Nagiulan during Apr; Btry D was with the 43d Div at Bocaue and Btry B with the 38th Div at Marikina. Enemy caves, hillsides, and observation posts, where the presence of enemy troops was indicated or suspected, and machine gun nests were common targets. Approximately 11,000 rounds of 40-mm and 134,000 rounds of cal .50 ammunition were expended in this effort. The number of casualties inflicted on the enemy could not be determined due to the nature of the terrain and the enemy policy of removing dead and wounded. The battalion suffered two killed and eleven wounded in the series of actions.

n. The 209th AAA AW Bn (SP) was used extensively in a terrestrial role on the island of Luzon. Platoons from this battalion were in action supporting the infantry with terrestrial fire from 5 Apr to 31 Jul 1945. The customary method employed was to attach a unit from this battalion to a semi-mobile automatic weapons battery, thereby making the half-tracks available to tow the 40-mm guns. However, the first ground support mission did not follow this organizational pattern. Btry A was attached directly to the 32d Div to support it in the drive up the Villa Verde Trail. Caves, pillboxes, machine guns, and a mountain gun were destroyed by the fire of this battery. Generally, the guns worked directly with the infantry patrols, using SCR 300's for communication. Frequently, the patrols marked targets with smoke grenades and then withdrew while fire was placed on the target. From 5 Apr to 29 May 1945, the battery expended 3252 rounds of 40-mm and 30,880 rounds of cal .50 ammunition.

o. The first mission combining self-propelled and semi-mobile automatic weapons came on 26 Apr when a platoon of Btry D was attached to Btry C, 198th AA. AW Bn, and in turn, this reinforced battery was attached to the 37th Div. Support was given to the infantry in the fighting around Baguio; in all, two missions were fired. A similar combination of a platoon of Btry C, and Btry D, 198th AAA AW Bn, supported the 43d Div in the rolling hills and rice fields near San Jose and then moved to the Ipo Dam area to support the 38th Div. Here, only the 40-mm guns were fired. This mission began on 4 May and ended on 18 June. A platoon from Btry C, 209th AAA AW Bn, was combined with Btry B, 198th AAA AW Bn, and supported the 38th Div in the vicinity of Baguio from 6 May to 19 June. A total of 137,000 rounds of cal .50 ammunition was expended, mostly in preparation fire. The other platoon of Btry B was attached directly to the 6th Div. From 15 June to 30 June the sections supported many infantry patrols by firing on enemy-held ridges and caves. From 1 to 15 June the 2d Plat, Btry D, in support of the 37th Div in the Cagayan valley, strafed ravines, draws, and bamboo thickets. On 15 June the 1st Plat, Btry D, and the 2d Plat, Btry C, joined in this mission. In addition to the normal support activities these three platoons patrolled roads and convoyed supplies.

p. Btry A, meanwhile, attached to the 6th Div, also in the Cagayan Valley, took part in army patrol actions. In the above operations the 198th AAA AW Bn destroyed 11 machine guns, 2 tanks, 2 field pieces, and 28 pillboxes, killing 258 Japanese in the process. Thirty-eight casualties were sustained.

q. The 478th AAA AW Bn, less Btries C and D, landed with the assault troops on Cebu Island on D-day, 26 Mar 1945. From this time until 7 Apr the battalion served in an antiaircraft role; on that day the Americal Div called upon the battalion to support the infantry advance with direct fire against pillboxes, dugouts, and machine-gun positions in the Baskan area. Individual gun sections were attached directly to the supported infantry units. Since most of the enemy installations were located on the crest of a hill, or on the slopes facing friendly positions, 40-mm fire could be placed directly and effectively upon them. In 20 days of such missions, 19 pillboxes, 25 machine gun and mortar positions, 7 tunnels and caves, 1 supply dump and 7 observation or command posts were destroyed and 117 enemy were killed.

r. The 470th AAA AW Bn had Btries A and B in action on Negros Island with the 40th Div. In the month from 25 Apr to 25 May 1945, these batteries destroyed 20 dugouts, 4 huts, 3 machine guns, 8 20-mm guns, and 1 truck, started 7 fires or explosions and killed 36 Japanese. Probable results include 20 dugouts, caves, and pillboxes destroyed, 1 radio and power plant smashed, 1 3-inch gun and 8 20-mm guns knocked out, as well as 29 enemy killed. In firing 173 missions the two batteries expended 13,663 rounds of 40-mm ammunition while 71 quadruple mount machine-gun missions used 407,985 rounds of cal .50 ammunition.

s. In the Mindanao operation Btry D, 487th AAA AW Bn, was attached to the 24th Div on 24 Apr 1945. A road block was set up on 3 May one-half mile northwest of Teril, using the M51 mount to cover the road. The battery continued to support the infantry until 10 Aug 1945. Targets taken under fire were caves, buildings, shacks, pillboxes, and troop concentrations at ranges of from 400 to 4500 yards. Five caves, nine pillboxes, 42 buildings and shacks, and one 3-inch dual purpose gun were destroyed. The battery fired nearly 4000 rounds of 40-mm ammunition.

t. The 478th AAA AW Bn established road blocks at Cebu Island on the Sacsas-Ilihan Road and also gave ground fire support to the Americal Div with unrecorded results.

u. Early in the Okinawa Campaign the 2d Plat, Btry B, 7th AAA AW Bn, was stationed on the small island of Kiese Shima just off the coast of Okinawa. From this island a battalion of medium field artillery was engaged in shelling Japanese installations on Okinawa. On the night of 9 Apr 1945 the enemy sent a force to the island to destroy the artillery. In repelling this night attack the antiaircraft platoon destroyed a motor launch, an amphibious tank, and several canoes which were being used to transport the assault force. The platoon suffered two killed and four wounded in the engagement.

111. <u>Guns</u>. a. The first recorded use of an Army antiaircraft gun battalion in a ground support role in the Southwest Pacific Area was at Arawe, New Britain, on 12 Feb 1944, when Btry A of the 741st AAA Gun Bn fired a terrestrial mission under the direction of the Task Force Field Artillery. The target, an enemy supply dump at Tatanewati, was destroyed by this fire.

b. On 23 Feb 1944 another mission under the same fire control was fired by this battery. In this mission enemy positions at Tagiiwati were taken under fire. Observers reported the results as "good".

c. On 4 Mar 1944, at Los Negros Island in the Admiralties, Btry C, 168th AAA Gun Bn, was engaged by enemy artillery. Counter-battery fire silenced the enemy positions. Later in the day more enemy guns were sighted and destroyed by 90-mm fire. On 12 Mar, Btry B was ordered by division artillery to fire a barrage on Hauwei Island, and a total of 59 rounds was fired on this mission.

d. The next reported use of an antiaircraft gun battalion in such a mission was at Bougainville during the period 13 Mar to 4 Apr 1944. Guns of the 746th AAA Gun Bn were placed in positions on the outer perimeter of the defense zone. By direct laying on the enemy positions, they were given the mission of silencing enemy artillery that was causing heavy losses to infantry forces in the area. The emplaced guns not only destroyed the enemy artillery positions but also pillboxes and supply dumps in the vicinity. The exposed position of the 90-mm guns in the front lines, however, resulted in mortar fire being brought on one position, killing a number of the gun crew.

 e. During the attack on the Hollandia airdromes, the 163d AAA Gun Bn fired ground missions on 25 and 26 Apr in support of the advancing infantry.

 f. In June 1944, the 165th AAA Gun Bn, at the request of the Task Force Artillery, engaged a Japanese naval gun position during the Biak Island operation. Btry B fired 197 rounds of point-detonating ammunition and the enemy battery was silenced.

 g. On Saipan an antiaircraft gun battalion fired several ground missions. The first terrestrial fire of the 751st AAA Gun Bn was against five targets in the area north of Magicienne Bay on 21 Jun 1944. Eighty rounds of 90-mm ammunition were expended. On 22 June the battalion fired a counter-battery mission against guns located on the island of Tinian. In both cases observation was poor and the results doubtful.

 h. After registering the previous day, Btries A and B, 751st AAA Gun Bn fired a half-hour of preparation fire on 26 Jun 1944, using a total of 1300 rounds. Air bursts were employed with the rounds bursting at tree top level. After the area was captured by the infantry approximately 800 enemy dead were counted, of which it is estimated that between two and three hundred were killed by the artillery fire. It was noted that the guns fired more effectively when directed by field artillery methods than by director control.

 i. In the Wakde Island operation, Btry A, 166th AAA Gun Bn, effectively assisted the field artillery in direct support of the infantry attack on Lonetree Hill. On 10 July, Btry B arrived at Toem on the nearby New Guinea shore and neutralized enemy strong points in the vicinity of Sarmi, west of Maffin Bay. This battery continued to fire terrestrial missions until mid-September.

 j. On Morotai the 528th AAA Gun Bn in the period Oct to Dec 1944 supported the field artillery with 90-mm fire on numerous instances. Targets were located by use of maps or by the gun radar-liaison plane method developed at that station.[1] The targets usually engaged were actual or suspected enemy troop concentrations.

 k. In the Leyte operation, because of the plentiful supply of field artillery, few terrestrial fire missions were fired by antiaircraft units. However, from 21 to 24 Oct 1944, the 502d AAA Gun Bn fired 1,775 rounds in support of the 7th Div. Targets were reported as troop

---

[1] See Chap 5, Sect VI.

concentrations, road junctions, tank concentrations, enemy command posts, and supply areas; reports from liaison planes indicated that the fire was effective. In one case the all-night fire of this battalion was helpful in breaking up what appeared to be a major counter-attack before it could be launched.

l. By the time of the Luzon invasion the infantry and artillery commanders were becoming more aware of the particular advantages antiaircraft weapons had as a result of their flat trajectories and their accuracy at even extreme ranges. As a result, increasing use was made of these weapons in a ground role. In addition a critical shortage of field artillery ammunition existed while large quantities of 90-mm ammunition were available. The antiaircraft artillery therefore fired many missions which would normally have been given to the field artillery.

m. As this use increased the other arms developed great confidence in the accuracy of antiaircraft artillery ground fire. In a mission of the 163d AAA Gun Bn on 30 Apr 1945 a 90-mm gun was called on by the infantry to fire on an enemy mortar position which had been approached by friendly infantry on two sides to within a distance of only 50 yards. The mission was accomplished and the mortar was destroyed with one round squarely on the target.

n. On 14 Feb 1945 the 518th AAA Gun Bn was attached to the 517th FA Bn for target assignment and observation purposes in positions northeast of Manila. Firing was conducted for eight days from these positions. Field artillery observers reported that the many missions assigned were completed with excellent results. Throughout the nights harassing missions were fired, and some counter-battery fire was received, but no casualties were sustained. By 25 Feb the battalion had moved forward to new positions and all registration fire was complete. The unit continued in its field artillery role until 11 Mar when it was returned to its primary mission, the antiaircraft defense of Clark Field.

o. The 161st AAA Gun Bn had a detachment in action in the Balete Pass area from 4 Apr 1945 to 21 May 1945. In this series of missions 64 caves, 42 pillboxes, 13 buildings, 16 guns, and 92 vehicles were destroyed. Twenty-six of the enemy were killed, one tank was probably destroyed, and 19 harassing missions were fired. The large number of caves destroyed testifies to the effectiveness of the antiaircraft gun in an infantry support role in mountainous terrain. Between 16 Apr and 4 May, Btries B and C were in position at Laguna de Bay for shore protection and ground support, where they sank two boats and fired 64 harassing missions. From 6 May to 27 June these same batteries were in position at Ipo Dam in a ground support role, destroying seven caves, one pillbox, and one building, killing 91 Japanese, and firing 274 harassing missions. In the meantime, Btry D had been in action at the

Marikina watershed reservation from 21 Apr to 22 June. In the course of their terrestrial firing they destroyed 31 caves and four buildings, killed two Japanese, and fired 95 harassing missions. Btry A, after the action at Balete Pass, moved up the Cagayan Valley during the period 9 July to 4 Aug. While supporting the 37th Div they killed 20 Japanese, destroyed one gun, and fired 29 harassing missions.

p. The 163d AAA Gun Bn, which at Hollandia had been among the first 90-mm organizations to act in a ground support role, again had an opportunity for terrestrial fire in the Luzon Campaign. On 10 Apr 1945, Btries A and B were attached to the 544th FA to support the 33d Div in their drive on Baguio. In this action, many caves were closed, trucks destroyed, and enemy troops dispersed. After the capture of Baguio, Btry A went into position on a mountain top and continued firing as field artillery for five weeks. During this period 20 caves, two trucks, three bridges, and 22 houses were destroyed, and 21 troop concentrations, six road junctions and gun positions, two roadblocks, five command posts, and two pillboxes were taken under fire. Eighty-three percent of the firing was done using height-finder observation; in the remaining missions, observation was furnished by liaison planes or forward observers.

q. The 739th AAA Gun Bn was attached to the 40th Div on 17 Apr 1945, and went into position at Guimbolan, Negros, P. I. At one time there were eight guns from this battalion in the front line firing as direct-support weapons. Often this fire was placed only 50 to 100 yards in front of the advancing infantry. A large number of dugouts, pillboxes, machine and antiaircraft guns were credited to these guns. A total of 12,500 rounds of 90-mm ammunition was expended in the ground missions fired.

r. Btry C was the only unit of the 166th AAA Gun Bn to undertake a field artillery mission in the Zamboanga operation. On 12 Mar an enemy emplacement was neutralized at a range of 3,500 yards. The battery attempted to register on other targets at greater range but was unsuccessful due to the difficulty of observing bursts in heavily wooded terrain without smoke shells.

s. The 496th AAA Gun Bn undertook its first terrestrial mission in the Sansapor area of New Guinea on 25 Feb 1945, when it fired on an enemy troop concentration in the Wesan River Valley at a range of 12,000 yards. Observers were sent down the coast in a landing craft and reported 80% coverage of the area with the 211 rounds fired. On 11 May Btry C was attached to the 983d FA Bn and occupied position for terrestrial firing near Matina airdrome on Mindanao. The fire was controlled by the field artillery battalion using liaison planes and forward observers. The guns were set up in a triangle formation with one gun in the center so that three guns could fire on any target. From 11 May to 24 May the battery fired on enemy supply dumps, installations, entrenchments, pillboxes, towns, gun positions, ferries, and troop concentrations. On 24 May the battery moved to Libby airdrome and continued their support of the 983d FA Bn, firing upon similar varieties of targets. On 5 June the battery again moved, this time to the vicinity of Tugbok, where an observation post was set up on the radar mount to adjust fire for the battery and for the 982d FA Bn. On the night of 9 June the radar indicated a target estimated as two vehicles on a road in enemy territory. Fire was adjusted by the radar spotting the bursts, and the target disappeared from the scopes. This was repeated on 11 June when an estimated four more enemy vehicles were destroyed. From this time until the road was captured, no more enemy activities were detected at night. This was an excellent illustration of the effective use of the radar-gun team in terrestrial fire.

t. No ground support missions were fired by the gun battalion on Iwo Jima since to clear the mask on any target on the island the elevation was too high to bring the range within island limits. However, several terrestrial missions were fired from Iwo Jima against Kama and Kingoku Rocks lying off shore a distance of 3500 yards. The first of these missions was on 28 Feb 1945, when both time fuzed and point detonating shells were used. A second mission was fired on 2 Mar and another on 7 Mar when evidence of enemy activity again appeared. On 12 Mar a detachment of Marines landed on the two rocks and found them abandoned by the enemy.

u. On 19 Apr 1945, Btry C, 507th AAA Gun Bn was attached to XI Corps for field artillery missions. The battery went into position near Payatas, Luzon, to support the 6th Div in its assault on Mt. Pacawagon, which was about 6500 yards from the position. A fire direction center was set up by the battery directly under the division artillery. The battery was registered by a field artillery liaison plane on 20 Apr and for the next four nights harassing fire was conducted on eight different points on the mountain. The fire was coordinated with five field artillery battalions, all firing on assigned areas of the mountain.

v. The 734th AAA Gun Bn was attached to the 43d Div on 4 Apr 1945. On that date Btry C's guns were emplaced in the Laguna de Bay area for the purpose of reinforcing the 192d FA Bn. Missions were assigned by the field artillery fire direction center. The battery fired a total of 561 rounds of 90-mm ammunition from this position. Btry D also fired 265 rounds in support of the 103d FA Bn in this same area. Btries A and B were emplaced together near Laguna de Bay on 9 Apr. They were directly under the command of XI Corps, and the battalion operations section operated the fire direction center. Targets taken under fire included enemy bivouac areas, convoys, pillboxes, caves, and hill positions. A total of 2,608 rounds were fired on these missions.

w. The 746th AAA Gun Bn landed on Cebu on 8 Apr 1945. The sole mission of the battalion in this operation was the support of the infantry with terrestrial fire. The battalion was put under the tactical control of the Americal Div Arty and on 9 Apr it was emplaced as a unit in an area selected by them. In view of the unlikelihood of air attacks or counter-battery fire, this mass formation was justified as an infiltration defense measure; also, it facilitated the firing of battalion concentrations. Generally, targets were assigned by the artillery fire direction center and fires observed by field artillery observers. Some missions were of a direct fire nature at short ranges and were observed through the telescopic sights directly, or with a BC scope. Between 9 and 18 Apr the missions were primarily of the direct fire type, but after the 18th the enemy had been pushed back and the missions become generally long range interdiction, harassing, neutralization, and concentration fires. On 28 Apr the battalion completed the terrestrial fire phase of the operation. During this phase 8,261 rounds of 90-mm ammunition were expended. Results of this fire were difficult to assess or record due to the long ranges and the fact that the field artillery engaged the same targets. However, it is definite that caves were closed, concrete fortifications were destroyed, and supply dumps were damaged or destroyed by the 90-mm guns.

  x. In the Okinawa operation the 502d AAA Gun Bn again fired field artillery fire, this time in support of XXIV Corps Artillery. Btries B and C fired 10,902 rounds of such fire in 104 missions and at 1,131 different targets. Inasmuch as practically all missions were of a harassing nature and not observed, the accuracy and results were not definitely determined but subsequent inspection of the target area confirmed the effectiveness of the 90-mm gun in this role.

  y. Btries A and D of the 504th AAA Gun Bn also fired some terrestrial missions in the Okinawa operation. Registration was conducted by the radar-liaison plane team. One battery worked with the 7th Div Arty and one with the 96th Div Arty. The two batteries fired a total of 626 missions expending 9,053 rounds of AP and 2,076 rounds of point detonating HE ammunition. The first mission fired by this battalion was against the Japanese Army Headquarters in Shuri. Btry A fired 200 rounds at this target three days after the operation began.

  z. On 11 and 12 Aug 1945 the 513th AAA Gun Bn conducted terrestrial fire missions with the 120-mm gun to determine its effectiveness in such a role. The tests were conducted on the 11th AB Div Arty range near Batangas, Luzon, P.I. It was concluded that this gun could be successfully employed in ground support missions.

Section III

Off-Shore Defense

112. __General__. It was normal in all Pacific areas for antiaircraft units to be charged with the ground and seaward defense of their immediate positions. In the Pacific Ocean area the garrison forces of the captured islands frequently consisted almost entirely of antiaircraft troops However, the Antiaircraft Artillery Commander was seldom charged with the full responsibility for the off-shore defense of an occupied area. An exception to this was made in late Nov 1944 when intelligence reports indicated enemy plans for a combined air, parachute and water-borne attack on Morotai, in the Netherlands East Indies.

113. __Morotai__. a. The distribution of antiaircraft weapons was particularly favorable for a defense of this nature. Thirty-six automatic weapons sections, each with a 40-mm gun and quadruple cal .50 machine-gun mount, were spaced about one-third of a mile apart along the coast line. Twelve searchlights, of which six were equipped with radars and each of which was provided with a cal .50 machine gun, augmented the defenses. In addition five gun batteries added 90-mm guns, radars, and more cal .50 machine guns to the seaward defense. On a small island off the west shore another gun battery and two searchlights provided defense outside the anchorage. A communication system and an intelligence system, composed principally of seaward warning radars, was in operation. The whole-hearted support of the field artillery was insured, as earlier work by the antiaircraft units in support of the field artillery batteries had laid a basis of cooperation and understanding.

b. When Hq. 214th AAA Group was given the added responsibility of the off-shore defense by the Task Force Commander, an underground operations center was immediately constructed. This housed the necessary long and short range plotting boards, a radio for communication with the field artillery fire direction center and another for the special net of antiaircraft units given off-shore defense missions, the telephone switchboard, the monitoring connection on to the group antiaircraft tactical net, and the operating personnel. Taking advantage of the protection afforded by underground locations, provision was also made for the speedy transfer of all Antiaircraft Artillery Operations Center (AAOC) communications into this shelter in case conditions forced abandonment of the unprotected fighter sector building.

c. The organization and operation of the Off-Shore Defense Center

(OSDC) was made the particular concern of the group executive officer.

    d. The responsibility of the Antiaircraft Artillery Commander was only for "off-shore" defense. In the event the enemy reached the shore the antiaircraft artillery was to continue action against the enemy still waterborne and defend its own installations.

    e. The general assignment of weapons to off-shore defense required that all 90-mm gun batteries, and all automatic weapons within 500 yards of the shore line, be prepared to deliver fire on any hostile surface craft that came within range. Gun batteries, when designated for such a mission, came under the direct control of the OSDC. Automatic weapons battalion commanders were made responsible for close-in defense against hostile surface craft. The searchlight battalion commander designated one searchlight, in close proximity to each 90-mm gun battery on the shore line, to pass to the direct control of the OSDC at the time the 90-mm gun battery to which it was attached was given the primary mission of engaging surface craft. Subsequently, a searchlight was stationed at each gun battery along the shore and provision made for its remote control by the gun radar against air or waterborne targets. Illumination desired by either automatic weapons or field artillery was to be requested through the OSDC.

    f. All antiaircraft observers, both visual and radar, reported movements of surface craft to the AAOC over the usual channels until the observer's unit came under the control of the OSDC, when the reports were transmitted direct. Any report of questionable movement of surface craft was relayed to the OSDC by the AAOC on duty and thereafter the AAOC tactical net was monitored at the OSDC.

    g. A daily report of scheduled movements of friendly craft, received from the Port Director, was posted at all times in the OSDC and the AAOC. Movements of unidentified surface craft well beyond the range of 90-mm guns were reported to the PT base and fighter sector controller. Except when urgent identification was necessary, surface craft were not illuminated prior to a check with the Port Director and the Naval PT Base for identification.

    h. A liaison officer was furnished by division artillery headquarters, whose principal duty was the passing of instructions and information to the Field Artillery Fire Direction Center.

    i. Inasmuch as it was expected that there would be an air alert whenever a waterborne attack developed the use of the antiaircraft tactical nets for off-shore defense purposes was unsound. In the event of a waterborne attack it was provided that the administrative lines to the units in the off-shore defense be immediately cleared and reserved. In addition, a separate radio channel was allotted for communication with the antiaircraft artillery units in the off-shore defense.

j. The Antiaircraft Artillery Commander was responsible for the off-shore defense from 1 Dec 1944 to 5 Apr 1945. No enemy attacks developed but enough alerts were called as a result of unidentified craft approaching the shore to test the intelligence and control system and to indicate its fundamental soundness.

k. Another instance of a similar placing of full responsibility for off-shore defense on the Antiaircraft Artillery Commander occurred at Ie Shima in May 1945 when the Commanding Officer of the 136th AAA Group was designated Seaward Defense Commander.

Section IV

Infantry Action

114. <u>General</u>. The campaigns in the Pacific theater were characterized by small areas of operations, by the absence of what in other theaters have been known as "rear areas", and by enemy infiltration tactics. In this theater, all areas have been, for the most part, combat areas and as a result, most combat units, regardless of their primary duties, have become involved in infantry action to a greater or lesser degree. Antiaircraft units were not excepted from this general rule. These infantry combat actions generally may be classed as either minor patrol actions and perimeter defense activities involved in carrying out local security measures, or general infantry action where the entire battalion or a large proportion thereof was involved in a planned operation. Action of the latter type was sometimes due to the lack of hostile air reaction or to a situation becoming so desperate that the antiaircraft artillery was needed to assist and reinforce the available infantry.

115. <u>Bougainville</u>. It was in this latter type of action that the first use was made of antiaircraft artillery as infantry. In Mar 1944 the situation on Bougainville was critical, with the enemy mounting heavy counter-attacks against our limited perimeter. Personnel from the 251st AAA Group[1] were therefor organized into the 251st Provisional Infantry Battalion to occupy defensive positions along the perimeter, which they held for three weeks.

116. <u>Wakde</u>. Again at Wakde, in May 1944, constant enemy pressure was being exerted against the perimeter defenses around the American positions on Arara Island. On 27 May Btry A, 166th AAA Gun Bn manned these defenses and successfully turned back a series of infiltration attacks which took place until the arrival of infantry elements from the 6th Div on 13 Jun. Later in the summer the gun battalion provided a small detachment to guard a radio station on Jarseen Island, 30 miles east of Wakde. In the course of security patrol actions near the installation, 16 Japanese were killed.

117. <u>Cebu</u>. On Cebu Island both the antiaircraft automatic weapons and gun battalions had primary artillery ground support missions. These were completed on 28 Apr 1945, and the personnel of the 746th AAA Gun Bn,

---

[1] 746th AAA Gun Bn, 199th and 951st AAA AW Bns, and 373d AAA SL Bn.

on that date, relieved infantry units northeast of Cebu City from their perimeter defense, conducted extensive patrols, and manned road blocks. On 10 May a Provisional Infantry Battalion was formed with personnel from Hq and Btries A, and B of the 478th AAA AW Bn and Btries A, B, and D of the 745th AAA Gun Bn. This provisional battalion maintained a perimeter defense organized around 22 strong points dominating the Sogod-Tabuelan road. From each position offensive combat patrols were sent daily into enemy areas, which resulted in killing 13 of the enemy. The mission was completed on 7 Jun 1945.

118. **Mindanao.** a. Antiaircraft units were used as infantry on a large scale in the Mindanao operation. There had been no enemy air action, and after being relieved of their primary mission, and storing their equipment, the following units were formed into a provisional antiaircraft group, under Hq, 487th AAA AW Bn, for use as infantry.

   487th AAA AW Bn (less Btry D)
   383d AAA AW Bn
   496th AAA Gun Bn (less Btry C)
   Btry B, 166th AAA Gun Bn
   Btry B, 222d AAA SL Bn

The group was attached to the 106th Div (PA) on 1 June.

   b. The mission of the group was to defend the main lines of communication in the Parang-Cotabato-Digos area. It accomplished this mission by vigorous daily patrolling. Although the activities of the group were hampered by a lack of machine guns, mortars, automatic rifles and sufficient tommy guns the patrols killed fifty of the enemy during June.

   c. By 1 Jul the 383d AAA AW Bn (-Btry D) and Btry B of the 166th AAA Gun Bn had been detached from the group for other assignments. The remaining units were then attached to the 24th Div. Part of the group continued to guard lines of communication while the remainder was organized into a task force with an offensive mission of pushing down to the Sarnagani Bay area from the north to help round up the 1100 enemy troops in the area.

   d. In an action on 4 Jul a patrol of two officers and five enlisted men from Btry B, 496th AAA Gun Bn and six enlisted men from the Philippine Army, ambushed a column of 90 Japanese south of Marbel. After the head of the column had proceeded 40 yards beyond the point of the ambush the patrol opened fire. One Filipino remained behind and saw the enemy remove 40 dead from the trail.

   e. Leaving a road block guard at Tupi the main body of the task force continued to Korondal on 14 Jul. During the period 16 Jul - 2 Aug mopping up operations and patrols over the assigned area accounted for

52 enemy dead. In the entire series of operations during Jun, Jul and Aug the antiaircraft units were responsible for killing 132 of the enemy and capturing 49. Our casualties were four killed, and five wounded in action. The Hq, 487th AAA AW Bn not only had tactical responsibility for the operation, but also arranged for the supply of 1200 antiaircraft and 3000 Philippine troops during the period, moving 754 tons of ammunition and operating six LCM's with antiaircraft crews.

119. Luzon. a. On 15 Mar the 382d AAA AW Bn was attached to XIV Corps. During Apr and May the battalion was used primarily to furnish ground defense around towns in the Batangas - Lipa area against enemy infiltration attacks. In 60 ground contacts with the enemy 78 Japanese were killed, six wounded and seven captured.

b. The rapid advance in Luzon which by-passed many areas not cleared of the enemy made it necessary for antiaircraft troops to engage in many minor combat actions while securing the areas around their tactical positions. For example, the 951st AAA AW Bn engaged in many small actions in the period from Jan to May 1945.

c. In Jan Btry B fired on an enemy column which dispersed. A Filipino collaborationist was captured by Btry D and handed over to the guerrillas. Patrols of Japanese were occasionally discovered, and a series of minor actions took place in which from one to eight enemy soldiers were killed. Small skirmishes, ambushes, and raids on houses in outlying areas concealing enemy soldiers continued until the end of May.

120. Okinawa. Here again the antiaircraft artillery was used as infantry in the later stages of the action. In May the 870th AAA AW Bn relieved a battalion of the 237th Inf at Kerama Retto when the 44th AAA Group took over command of those islands. Btries A and B were assigned to Takashiki Shima, and Btries C and D to Zamami Shima with the mission of eliminating the remnants of the enemy from the area. Combat patrols from the antiaircraft units were aided by psychological warfare teams. Up until the end of the war the 870th succeeded in evacuating several hundred civilians, killed approximately 150 of the enemy, and captured 100.

Section V

Special Searchlight Operations

121. <u>Battlefield Illumination</u>. a. The activity of antiaircraft searchlight battalions in the Pacific theater, like those of the firing battalions, was not limited to antiaircraft missions. Searchlights played a part in the ground fighting notably in the field of battlefield illumination.

b. The first use of the searchlight in this role in the southern Pacific was at Bougainville in Mar 1944 when the enemy made repeated heavy attacks on the perimeter defenses. During this period the 373d AAA SL Bn used its searchlights nightly to illuminate the front lines. The indirect method of illumination, wherein the beam was spread and reflected from low clouds, created an excellent moonlight effect. Infantry commanders were able to call for illumination of specific areas and have their request fulfilled within three minutes. Immeasurable assistance was rendered to the infantry in repelling the enemy's fanatical night attacks.

c. In the Admiralty Islands in Oct 1944 the 237th AAA SL Bn conducted interesting experiments using polished aluminum reflectors made from the bomb-bay doors of wrecked airplanes as a substitute for clouds. The light was set at 90° elevation and the aluminum surface placed above it at a 45° angle. The light thus reflected made a man visible at 1500 feet and at that distance covered an area 300 feet wide.

d. The most extensive use of the searchlight in the ground support role in the Southwest Pacific Area was by the 227th AAA SL Bn in the Luzon Campaign. Btry A was attached to the 43d Div to provide battlefield illumination in the Ipo Dam action. On 8 May 1945 eight lights were emplaced 2500 to 4000 yards from the Japanese positions. Each light was well defiladed and reveted. When the lights went into action the infantry reported them a definite aid, even though there were only scattered clouds to reflect the light. Initially the lights were traversed from side to side but later a steady beam was used. The beams were from five to seven degrees wide and ultimately sixteen lights were in use.

e. The lights were used from dusk until dawn and the initial plan called for general illumination of the area; later, specific sections were lighted according to the wishes of the infantry battalions. On the very nights the Japanese would usually choose for an attack, dark nights with an overcast sky, the lights worked at their best. On one occasion when the ceiling was high a plane spread smoke as an experimental substitute. The result was fair, but not as effective as a good cloud ceiling. Special missions were undertaken to cover our own troop movements, to give security to pinned-down patrols, to prevent surprise attacks by the enemy, to repulse "Banzai" charges, to stop infiltration, and to permit night evacuation of wounded.

f. The infantry officers, in praising the new tactics, declared that much better control of their men at night was possible. However, the most beneficial effect was on the morale of the men, which skyrocketed when they were no longer under the constant threat of an unseen infiltration after nightfall, or of being shot by mistake by friendly troops. Artificial moonlight relieved the constant watchfulness and nervousness after dark which was a source of considerable psychoneurosis. A night infiltration attack was now "like hunting coons on a moonlight night", as one infantry platoon sergeant put it.

g. During and after the use of the lights all prisoners of war taken in the area were questioned as to their opinions of the operation. Of the first 27 interrogated, sixteen stated definitely that the searchlights hindered the Japanese movements at night and eight more thought the movements of our forces against them were facilitated by the lights.

122. **Cooperation with the Air Force**. a. **Beacons and runway markers** repeatedly aided combat airplanes in their movements. Almost from the beginning of the war the assignment of certain lights for airdrome beacons and runway markers was common. For example in Feb 1943 the searchlights of the 214th CA (AA) (later the 250th AAA SL Bn) were used to assist in bomber landings on Guadalcanal. Later in 1944 the 222d AAA SL Bn performed frequent missions for the planes using the air fields at Sansapor and Noemfoor.

b. **Artificial horizon** was a technique of great assistance to the bombers of the Thirteenth Air Force. This method was adopted to assist the heavily loaded B-24's to get safely away on their missions. A number of heavy bombers had been lost because their pilots, unable to clearly distinguish the horizon while taking off at night, dipped a wing into the sea or into some land obstruction. Searchlights, located 1000 and 2000 yards from the ends of the runways and off to the side, laid their beams horizontally at 90° angles to the runway, making a clear artificial horizon for the pilot to level on. Bomber losses on take-off in the Thirteenth Air Force from then on were practically eliminated.

123. **Shore Illumination from Surface Craft**. On 18 Apr 1944 Btry C of the 227th AAA SL Bn experimented with a light mounted on a patrol torpedo boat which moved parallel to the shore line about two and one-half miles off-shore while two other PT boats cruised 300 yards offshore, one on each side of the beam. The light was controlled by radio

instruction from one of the inshore boats. In an actual patrol one enemy truck was located moving along the shore and was destroyed. The bobbing of the boat made control of the light difficult and at times threatened to illuminate the inshore craft. It was concluded that with the addition of a gyroscopic stabilizer this type of operation would be very successful, and that if two searchlight equipped boats were used the shore shadows could be eliminated and the inshore boats could stay in the V of the lights with little danger of being illuminated.

124. <u>Illumination for Construction</u>. On numerous occasions searchlight battalions in combat locations were used to provide illumination for construction projects, enabling the engineers to work 24 hours a day. The 237th AAA SL Bn thus illuminated the Mokerang Airstrip at Los Negros in Apr 1944. The unit tied mattress covers across the light to eliminate the glare. The 373d AAA SL Bn served the same function at the Lingayen airstrip in Jan 1945 and the 227th AAA SL Bn assisted the 43d Div in the construction of their base camp on Luzon in a similar manner.

Section VI

Non-Combat Functions

125. **General.** The war in the Pacific, more than any prior conflict, was a war of logistics. Never have supply lines been longer, and never was a greater volume of supplies necessary than in these operations. The supply routes shifted constantly with the tactical situation, and bases had to be cut out of jungle or coral, then later rolled up; supplies of all sorts had to be reloaded and reshipped. Such a situation created a permanent shortage of service personnel. Antiaircraft units which were manning tactical positions around the bases where the frequency and intensity of enemy air raids had diminished, were logical sources of additional manpower for the service functions. There were also many units concentrated in rear areas, engaged in training, recuperation, staging, or reorganization that were sources for extra service personnel. Finschhafen in 1944 and 1945 provides an example of this use of antiaircraft troops.

126. **Dock Details.** Throughout the war more antiaircraft personnel were used for dock work than for any other single non-antiaircraft duty. Although antiaircraft commanders frequently found it difficult to preserve the identity and integrity of their units, only rarely did the service functions performed by their men prevent the efficient performance of their primary mission. In Apr 1945 at Malabang, north of Cotabato in Mindanao, Btry B, 166th AAA Gun Bn, had such a large number of men on dock details that the battery was unable to man its positions during a red alert. The battery was immediately relieved of its dock duties.

127. **Military Police.** Another important service role filled by antiaircraft troops was military police duty. In mid-1942 the 197th and 208th CA (AA) pioneered in military police duty when carefully selected details reinforced the base military police detachment at Townsville during a troublesome period. In other crowded rear bases and staging areas antiaircraft troops functioned notably well as military police. In the forward areas, especially in the Philippines, details from antiaircraft units in tactical positions freed the assault forces from military police duty pending the arrival of regular detachments and made it possible for the infantry units to use their full complement for mopping-up operations.

128. **Other Service Functions.** a. There were a host of other missions repeatedly undertaken and successfully performed. In Australia, early in 1942, antiaircraft personnel manned and protected boats carrying

supplies to the meager garrisons at small settlements on the northwest coast of the continent between Fremantle and Darwin, at a time when the location of the enemy forces was most uncertain and his airplanes ranged unopposed over the northern coast.

    b. At Nadzab in 1944 positions were needed for the emplacements of the 161st AAA Gun Bn on the opposite side of the Erap River from the airstrips and other installations. The engineers were unable, due to their other commitments, to build the necessary bridge. Its construction was completed by antiaircraft troops and thus opened up an area that was subsequently used extensively by the Air Force.

    c. The following are some of the miscellaneous service functions credited to antiaircraft units:

AGENCIES	DUTIES
Base Quartermaster	Operation of bakery Operation of Ice Plant Warehouse attendants, clerks, and trucking of materiel
Base Engineers	Hauling and rolling logs, and stacking lumber at saw mill Providing illumination for air strip construction Salvage of unused buildings
Base Ordnance	Breaking down ammunition Rebuilding and rearranging ammunition dump Repair and reclamation of vehicles Loading, reloading, and stacking of bombs
Base Medical Service	Construction of hospitals
Base Special Service	Providing illumination for athletics and entertainment functions
Base Chemical Warfare	Warehouse Details
Base Transportation Corps	Transportation of 1st Philippine Regiment by truck (Ormoc - Dulag, Leyte) General Trucking and hauling runs
Base Post Office	Mail handling

AGENCIES	DUTIES
Base Post Exchange	Merchandising
Railway Department	Railway police
Base Personnel Division	Establishment and operation of casual camp and rotation detachments
	Operation of Ground Forces transient camps
Port Command	Operation of refrigeration barge
	Administrative work in Pier Superintendent's office

129. <u>Manus Island</u>. a. In general, service functions were performed under the immediate supervision of an established service agency. The operation of the base supply installations at Manus Island, Admiralties group, in 1945, is a notable instance of a whole supply base directly under the control of an antiaircraft unit. In at least one other instance the responsibility of closing a base was put on an AAA Group headquarters. The problems that arise in such a situation are illustrated by the story of the Manus Base.

b. The supply installations at Manus were operated originally by the Sixth Army, and later by the Eighth Army. Upon the departure of the latter from Manus Island, on 11 Apr 1945, the senior United States Army commander was designated Commanding Officer, United States Forces, and as such was responsible for the operation of the base and all services involved.

c. The senior officer present at that time was the Commanding Officer, 77th AAA Group. Attached to the Group were about 3,060 Coast Artillery personnel. In addition, approximately 2,050 personnel of a Postal Unit, a Station Hospital, the Air Transport Command, and other Air Corps organizations were present. On 8 May all Army units on Manus and adjacent islands were attached to the 77th AAA Group for supply and at the same time the Commander, 7th Fleet, was charged with the responsibility of furnishing with rations and supplies, common to both Army and Navy, all Army units at Manus. Supplies peculiar to the Army were made a responsibility of the Commanding General, USASOS, who in turn designated USASOS Base F, at Finschhafen, New Guinea, as the supply base for the Admiralties.

d. The initial difficulties experienced were due to the lack of specific procedures for requisitioning replacement items and prescribing authorized levels of supply, and a shortage of automotive parts, but these were cleared up shortly. The general condition of the supply point was found to be below standard in many respects, particularly the condition of some of the dumps. The destruction of approximately 400 tons of spoiled rations, and the sorting and disposition of excessive quantities of clothing, left behind by the departing units, was a major task.

    e. Supplies for some units arrived long after their departure. As of 31 Mar 1945, 1,041 tons of all types of such material had arrived, causing considerable waste of shipping space and unnecessary handling of supplies.

    f. The Group Commander concentrated every effort toward improving the condition of supply dumps and warehousing facilities. Six officers and 200 enlisted men were detailed on a permanent basis for the sole purpose of manning the supply point. These men had to be drawn from units required in the antiaircraft defense of the island, already understrength in personnel. All items in stock were serviced, sorted and cleaned, new inventories were taken and accurately tabulated, and an office accounting system was installed.

    g. The details of re-supply, maintenance and repair of equipment and supplies at Manus were gradually worked out after visits by staff officers of higher headquarters and conferences with representatives of USASOS, Base F. Special arrangements, such as for the shipment and return, by air, of shoe repair and the air delivery of critical spare parts, were made.

        Section   I   General

        Section   II   Organization

        Section   III   Training

        Section   IV   Supply

Section I

General

130. <u>General</u>. a. At the beginning of the war the United States Army forces in the Pacific east of the Philippines were concentrated in the Hawaiian Islands and under the control of the Hawaiian Department. There was no joint command with the United States Navy, which controlled its own forces through the Commander-in-Chief, Pacific Fleet. The lack of coordination evidenced at the time of the Pearl Harbor disaster and the knowledge that amphibious operations would be necessary for effective attack on the Japanese holdings dictated that joint operational commands be set up for the war in the Pacific.

b. A directive of the Joint Chiefs of Staff on 30 Mar 1942 divided the entire Pacific area, excluding Alaska, and China-Burma-India, into three areas, the Southeast Pacific, Pacific Ocean Area, and the Southwest Pacific Area. Only the latter two were concerned directly with operations against the Japanese. The Pacific Ocean Area was subdivided into the North, South, and Central Pacific. The Commander-in-Chief, Pacific Ocean Area, was to exercise control over the North and Central Pacific and was to appoint the Commander, South Pacific Area, who, acting under his authorizations, would control its joint forces. The Commander-in-Chief, Southwest Pacific Area, was to be a United States Army officer, by agreement with the Australian, British, and Dutch governments.

c. In carrying out these decisions Admiral Chester W. Nimitz, U.S.N., was appointed Commander-in-Chief, Pacific Ocean Area, and in turn named Vice-Admiral Robert L. Ghormely, U.S.N., as Commander of the South Pacific Area, while General Douglas MacArthur, U.S.A., was designated as Commander-in-Chief, Southwest Pacific Area.

d. The approximately four year campaign in the Pacific uncovered many problems in administration, training, and supply that had no precedents for their solution. By 17 Mar 1942, when General MacArthur arrived in Australia from the Philippines, Malaya and Singapore had fallen, Burma had been invaded, and Borneo, Timor, Celebes, New Britain, New Ireland, Sumatra, and Ambon had been occupied. An attack on Java was imminent. Darwin had been eliminated as a useable port. The Japanese were threatening Port Moresby, New Caledonia, and the Fiji Islands. They had decisive air superiority and control of the seas north of New Guinea and New Hebrides. Australia and New Zealand seemed their next objective.

e. While the Army and Navy in general continued to handle their own supply problems, different concepts of command, organization, and training were evident in the three areas and had some effect on the tactical use and day by day activities of the antiaircraft units which were serving in all combat zones.

  f. As has been indicated in the report on the Philippine Defense Campaign, little of the equipment of the antiaircraft units engaged there was of late design, although the troops used it to good advantage. Its loss in the course of the campaign and the surrender was therefor not serious.

  g. The organizations which came to the South and Southwest Pacific Areas early in 1942 were likewise equipped with much obsolescent armament, notably the 3-inch guns with M-4 directors, and 37-mm guns with the central tracer fire-control system, although there were only a very few of the latter weapons. The SCR-268 radar, on which both guns and searchlights relied for target location, although also out of date, was the only radar then in quantity production. However, the other items of organizational equipment and the individual equipment were standard.

  h. The problem of replacement of obsolete items and supply of new materiel over communications lines up to 9,000 miles in length and threatened by the enemy's naval and air forces, introduced innumerable difficulties. That our antiaircraft units never suffered severe supply shortages is a great credit to the supply services and to the Navy.

  i. The problems of rehabilitation, refitting, and refresher training in the Pacific Ocean Area were simplified by the quantity of shipping in the control of the Navy, which made it possible to replace assault units with less experienced ones, whereas in the Southwest Pacific Area there was usually not enough shipping at hand even to take forward all the units needed for combat.

  j. The following sections detail the solutions of the administration, training, and supply problems in the Pacific Ocean, South Pacific, and Southwest Pacific Areas, and, where pertinent, the circumstances which led to the course taken.

Section II

Organization

131. **General**. The general organization in the various combat areas of the Pacific is described in the following paragraphs. Most operations, including the first landings on Japanese-held territory on Guadalcanal and Papua, were conducted by balanced task forces that included air, land, and sea components. The strategic planning, to include the mission of each task force, and its general composition was done by either the Commander-in-Chief, Pacific Ocean Area, or the Commander-in-Chief, Southwest Pacific Area. The details were worked out by the subordinate units concerned. In each operation two fundamental principles of organization were carried out to the maximum, cooperation between army and navy, and unity of command.

132. **Pacific Ocean Area**. a. As set up in Mar 1942, the Pacific Ocean Area was commanded by Admiral Chester Nimitz and subdivided into three smaller areas, the North, South and Central Pacific areas. Direct control was maintained over the first two subdivisions by the Commander-in-Chief, Pacific Ocean Area. As far as antiaircraft operations are concerned, only the Pacific Ocean Area and its chief subordinate command, the Central Pacific Area, with Admiral Spruance as a commander, are involved.

b. With its headquarters in Hawaii, United States Army Forces, Pacific Ocean Area, commanded all army troops in the area.

c. The administration and training of all antiaircraft units in Hawaii, which comprised the staging area for operations in the central and western Pacific, were carried on by the Hawaiian Antiaircraft Command.

d. Operations in the Gilberts and the western Carolines were carried out by task forces organized and planned by the Commander-in-Chief, Pacific Ocean Area, the planning being coordinated with United States Army Forces, Pacific Ocean Area.

e. For the operation in the Marshalls, Commander-in-Chief, Pacific Ocean Area, submitted an outline plan with a directive to the Commanding General, United States Army Forces, Central Pacific Area. Overall command was assigned to the V Amphibious Corps and Task Force 52 and planning was coordinated among all the above mentioned headquarters.

f. The operation against the Mariannas was conducted under the Commander-in-Chief, Pacific Ocean Area, with planning coordinated with Headquarters, United States Army Forces, Central Pacific Area. The command of the operation itself was assigned to Task Force 51.

g. For the Leyte operations, carried out by General MacArthur's command, some troops came from the Pacific Ocean Area, including the XXIV Corps and the 7th and 96th Infantry Divisions. The antiaircraft artillery used to support these units also came from Pacific Ocean Area.

h. Although on 6 Apr 1945, United States Army Forces, Pacific, was set up under General MacArthur, the troops in the Ryukyus operations remained under Admiral Nimitz' command since the planning, training and assault phases of the operation had already been carried out by the latter's headquarters. The Commanding General, Tenth Army, who was also expeditionary force commander, was responsible through Admiral Turner, in charge of the entire operation, to Admiral Nimitz. All antiaircraft artillery in the Ryukyus was commanded by the Commanding General, Tenth Army Antiaircraft Artillery, who was also the Antiaircraft Officer on the Army special staff. The units that had staged in the Hawaiian Islands were commanded by the 53d AAA Brigade which took over control of all antiaircraft units on the island of Okinawa on 20 Apr 1945. (L / 17).

133. <u>South Pacific Area</u>. a. To conform to the subdivision of the area of the Pacific, the United States Army Forces in the South Pacific (USAFISPA) was established to include all Army troops in that area. Its headquarters was opened at Auckland, New Zealand, with an advance echelon at Noumea, New Caledonia. Major General Millard F. Harmon was the first commander.

b. No special antiaircraft command channels were set up initially, but the Commanding Officer, 70th CA (AA), which was defending harbor and airdrome installations in New Caledonia, served as advisor to the Commanding General on antiaircraft matters.

c. Early in Oct 1942 an Antiaircraft Section was organized in the Headquarters, USAFISPA, on the arrival of additional personnel for the purpose.

d. In Jan 1943, when the 214th CA (AA) went to Guadalcanal to relieve the Marine Defense Battalion at Henderson Field, it was relieved from the direct command of USAFISPA and was attached to the Americal Division which had replaced the Marine assault forces on the island. Later, when XIV Corps arrived at Guadalcanal, the regiment came under the regional antiaircraft command, set up under the directives of the Commander, South Pacific Area. Upon its move to Guadalcanal in July 1943 the 70th CA (AA) also came under this command.

e. Late in Oct 1943 Hq 68th AAA Brigade assumed the responsibilities of the XIV Corps Antiaircraft Command and controlled all the Army antiaircraft units in the Solomons. The groups in the New Hebrides and New Caledonia continued under their respective Island Commands in accordance with the South Pacific directives, without any intermediate antiaircraft command.

f. On 15 Jun 1944 the South Pacific Area ceased to function as a tactical command. The bulk of the antiaircraft artillery were on that date transferred to the command of the Southwest Pacific Area, and the remainder, progressively as they were moved, or staged for moving, to the western area were similarly transferred. At the time there were one brigade and ten group headquarters, twelve gun battalions, ten automatic weapons battalions, six searchlight battalions, one separate searchlight battery, and one operations detachment on the antiaircraft troops list, all of which in time were reassigned to the 14th Antiaircraft Command in the Southwest Pacific Area.

134. <u>The Southwest Pacific Area</u>. a. On 26 Jul 1941 the War Department had constituted the United States Army Forces of the Far East (USAFFE) whose headquarters were established in Manila with Gen. Douglas MacArthur commanding.

b. A convoy departed Honolulu on 21 Nov 1941 with troops and supplies intended for the Philippines. It was still at sea on 7 Dec. It was then designated a task force, ordered to proceed to Australia, and arrived at Brisbane on 22 Dec, where it was designated United States Forces in Australia (USFIA). The designation was changed on 5 Jan 1942 to United States Army Forces in Australia (USAFIA), and its headquarters was moved to Melbourne. All United States Army troops, including antiaircraft units, as they thereafter arrived in Australia were assigned to USAFIA for administration and supply.

c. General MacArthur arrived in Australia on 17 Mar, still designated as Commanding General, USAFFE. On 18 Apr he was designated Supreme Commander, Southwest Pacific Area (SWPA). General Headquarters, Southwest Pacific Area (GHQ, SWPA), was established in Melbourne. In the meantime, orders had been issued on 22 Mar transferring all personnel of USAFFE, except those in the Philippines, to USAFIA.

d. The directive from the Joint Chiefs of Staff setting up the Pacific Ocean Area and Southwest Pacific Area Commands stated that the Joint Chiefs of Staff would exercise jurisdiction over all matters pertaining to operational strategy. The United States Chief of Staff, General Marshall, would act as the executive to issue instructions to General MacArthur, whose command consisted of:

Commander-in-Chief, SWPA

Allied Land Forces:	Allied Air Forces:	Allied Naval Forces:
General Sir Thomas Blamey	Lieutenant General G. H. Brett	Vice Admiral H. F. Leary

USFIP:	USAFIA:
Lieutenant General Jonathan Wainwright	Major General J. F. Bannes

    e. The 41st Div, 147th FA, and 2d Bn, 148th FA, were assigned to Allied Land Forces for operational control. Other United States Army Forces remained under USAFIA. USFIP became inactive with the surrender of Corregidor.

    f. On 20 Jul 1942, USAFIA was discontinued and the United States Army Services of Supply (USASOS) was organized by GO No 17, GHQ, SWPA to continue its functions.

    g. The Fifth Air Force under Major General George C. Kenney was constituted on 3 Sept 1942 by GO No 28, GHQ, SWPA, and assigned for operational control to the Commander, Allied Air Forces.

    h. The Sixth Army was activated on 16 Feb 1943 with General Walter Krueger (then Lieutenant General) commanding.

    i. USAFFE, which had been inactive after the arrival of General MacArthur in Australia, was reconstituted on 26 Feb 1943 and all units of the United States Army in the Southwest Pacific Area were assigned to it.

USAFFE

Sixth Army	Fifth Air Force	USASOS	USFIP

    j. As operations in the theater increased in scope and intensity the need for an antiaircraft headquarters to formulate and coordinate administration, training, and supply policies for all antiaircraft artillery in the Southwest Pacific Area was recognized and the 14th AA Command was activated on 15 Nov 1943 by GO No 73, USAFFE, and assigned to USAFFE. All antiaircraft units in the Southwest Pacific Area were at the same time assigned to the new command.

USAFFE

Sixth Army	Fifth Air Force	USASOS	14th AA Command	USFIP

k. The Far Eastern Air Forces (FEAF) was activated on 2 Aug 1944 from personnel assigned to a provisional organization constituted 15 Jun 1944. The Eighth Army was activated on 7 Sept 1944.

```
                              USAFFE
                             /
Sixth Army    Eighth Army    FEAF    14th AA Command    USASOS
```

l. This organization continued until 6 Apr 1945 when the United States Army Forces Pacific (AFPAC) was organized. As constituted, it was to consist of all army forces assigned to USAFFE and United States Army Forces, Pacific Ocean Area. Orders making the various assignments of units were issued at intervals. USASOS was discontinued 19 Jun 1945 and United States Army Forces, Western Pacific (AFWESPAC) was organized 19 Jun 1945.

```
                                AFPAC
                               /
AFWESPAC   Sixth    Eighth   FEAF   Army Forces POA   Hawaiian
           Army     Army                              Department
```
All non-tactical army commands including the 14th AA Command

m. Army Forces Middle Pacific (AFMIDPAC) was constituted by GO No 13, AFPAC, 20 Jun 1945, effective 1 Jul 1945. The new command was to take over the forces and installations under the control of the Army Forces, Pacific Ocean Area and of the Hawaiian Department. All United States Army forces in the Pacific were then under one command.

n. The organization on V-J Day was as follows:

```
                              AFPAC
                             /
AFWESPAC      Sixth      Eighth     AFMIDPAC        FEAF
              Army       Army
```

o. The antiaircraft units that arrived in the theater prior to 20 Jul 1942 were assigned to USAFIA. They were further assigned to an antiaircraft brigade for tactical control and the brigade in turn to the Allied Air Force for operational control. From 20 Jul 1942 to 16 Feb 1943, the units were assigned to USASOS with the tactical and operational assignments being unchanged. When the Sixth Army was activated on 16 Feb 1943 the antiaircraft units were assigned to it but the operational control remained with the Air Forces. On its activation on 15 Nov 1943, all antiaircraft artillery units were assigned to the 14th AA Command.

p. The Command, which was a non-tactical organization, was responsible for the training, technical supply, and combat availability of the units. Antiaircraft requirements for specific operations were determined at GHQ and the 14th AA Command furnished the required number of each type of unit. Units were attached to task forces for specific operations, and on completion of the mission, the units reverted to 14th AA Command control. Responsibility for training and technical supply remained with the Command even after units were committed.

Section III

Training

135. **General.** a. The combat operations in the Pacific were complicated by a training problem of considerable magnitude. The rapid advance of Japanese forces threatened the vital bases of Allied strength in Australia and made it necessary to engage the enemy before the Allied forces were fully prepared. American antiaircraft units were rushed to the combat zone before their training had been completed, and continued to train while in tactical position.

b. To a large degree training remained a vital consideration throughout the war. For antiaircraft units this training was complicated by several factors. First, the scattered locations of the units over vast areas, in Australia, New Guinea, and the far flung islands of the Central, South, and Southwest Pacific made centralized control of training difficult if not impossible. Secondly, the constant introduction of new materiel and the development of new operational techniques made retraining of experienced personnel a constant necessity. The conditions imposed by an amphibious war fought in tropical jungles necessitated types of training not included in training programs conducted in the United States.

136. **Training Prior to 15 Nov 1943.** a. (1) **40-mm Gun Training** was one of the first training problems to arise when the American built Bofors were received in the theater. At this time, by necessity, training was conducted mainly in tactical positions, and on the individual initiative of the local commander. The only coordination above the brigade level in the Southwest Pacific was through the Antiaircraft Officer, GHQ, and his office did not have the staff to provide either inspectors or instructors. In early July the 40th CA Brigade (AA) was advised that the new guns would arrive in a very short time and that the brigade should arrange for instruction in the use of the gun. The Brigade Commander assigned the task to the Commanding Officer of the 208th CA (AA) whose organization was in tactical position in Townsville. The loan of two Australian Bofors was secured for instructional purposes. No copies of the training manual for the American gun had been received in the theater nor did any manuals accompany the guns, so copies of the Australian drill manual were also procured. Fortunately, an officer recently arrived from the United States had in his possession an ordnance instruction manual on the weapon. With the above material as a basis, personnel of the 208th regiment prepared a manual to use as a guide in the school to be established. A drill was devised pat-

terned on the Australian drill but modified to meet the requirements of the American gun. A course of instruction using the question and answer method was prepared and simplified drawings of the main parts of the gun and their functions were made and photostated. The whole was incorporated in a training publication which was issued to each officer and enlisted man attending the school.

(2) Several sessions of the school were held, each session of ten days duration. Selected officers and all chiefs of section of the units scheduled to receive the new guns attended. Fortunately, just prior to the scheduled opening of the school, the first American Bofors arrived and the students were able to work with these guns from the beginning. The school was very successful and the attending personnel returned to their organizations qualified as instructors and supplied with an adequate training manual.

(3) In the Hawaiian Islands the Hawaiian AAA Command had been conducting intensive training programs for all the antiaircraft units under its control. The training and tactical control of units was grouped according to their principal weapons. The 70th AAA Brigade was in charge of automatic weapons units, which fired extensively against sleeve and drone (OQ2A) targets and trained intensively in the operation of the M-5 director.

b. 90-mm gun training also became a necessity in 1942. The first units in Australia, New Caledonia, the Fijis, and the Society Islands had arrived equipped with the three-inch gun.

(1) The first 90-mm guns arrived in Australia late in Nov 1942. Most of them were unloaded at Townsville and were taken in charge by the 25th Ord Co which was the base organization handling antiaircraft repairs at the time. The G-3, USASOS, recommended against the use of the guns until special training, including firing at towed targets, had been given to the batteries receiving them. Accordingly, a directive was issued for the organization of training teams to give this instruction. The 40th and 41st CA Brigades (AA) immediately began preparations for the instruction of their assigned units.

(2) Mechanics from both the 197th and 208th regiments worked on the guns in the shops in Townsville as the 25th Ord Co mechanics cleaned and checked them. One gun and its fire-control equipment was temporarily turned over to the Hq, 208th CA (AA). A team of enlisted men selected largely from the headquarters of the regiment and under the leadership of officers of the gun battalion, 94th CA (AA), who had used the 90-mm gun in the United States, familiarized themselves with the equipment and its use insofar as was practicable. Both brigades organized records sections and computing sections for the planned target practices. The records section of the 40th AAA Brigade was composed of personnel of the headquarters of the 40th AAA Brigade and the

208th CA (AA). The 197th CA (AA) contributed to the records section of the other brigade.

(3) The 41st AAA Brigade selected a firing point on the shore about 25 miles north of Townsville, the nearest place with a suitable field of fire. It was intended that units of the other brigade would fire from their tactical positions. No guns were issued to any organization until late in Feb of 1943 when two batteries were shipped to Port Moresby for Btries A and B of the 208th CA (AA) and guns were issued to units of the 94th CA (AA) then in Townsville. Unfortunately, no tow target planes were available so target practice could not be fired. The guns were used in combat in New Guinea after training given in some instances by the training teams of the brigades and in others by the units themselves, and with only test and calibration firing.

(4) Early in 1943 the 70th CA (AA) began to receive 90-mm materiel, including the M-7 director. By 15 Mar four batteries were equipped with the new 90-mm guns and the training of the regiment was directed toward familiarization of the personnel in the use of the new equipment. The regiment also trained Marine crews for three 90-mm gun batteries, Naval Construction crews for one battery, and conducted a gunnery school for six weeks for their officers.

(5) In Mar 1943, the Navy made a VJ towing squadron available, and target ammunition was released by USAFISPA. All gun batteries were enabled to fire target practice, some for the first time.

(6) Meanwhile on Oahu the 53d AAA Brigade supervised the training of all gun battalions occupying tactical positions on the island. This training included instruction and practice in firing at radio-controlled targets (PQ8A) with night firing at illuminated targets, firing with pre-cut fuzes at low flying incoming targets, direct fire at naval and mechanized targets, and terrestrial fire with field artillery adjustment and fire direction center control, using forward observers.

c. <u>Target Recognition</u> was featured in the training in all areas of the Pacific. Programs were set up by the Hawaiian AAA Command for units under its control; units in the South Pacific engaged in such training. In Dec 1942 a school for training in target recognition and identification of aircraft was established by the 41st CA Brigade (AA) at Townsville, Australia. This school was attended not only by American and Australian antiaircraft personnel but also by Army Air Force pilots and civilian defense workers. Eventually, this school supplied most of the instructional personnel and initial equipment for the 14th AA Command target recognition school which was established subsequently at Finschhafen, New Guinea.

d. <u>Officer Candidate Schools</u> were established in the Fijis and Australia. The school in the Fijis was organized in Aug 1942, and included facilities for training antiaircraft officers. In Dec another officer candidate school for the Southwest Pacific theater was established near Brisbane.

(1) The antiaircraft section of the OCS was staffed by three officers sent from the Antiaircraft School at Camp Davis, N.C. and four ordnance enlisted instructors from the Ordnance School at Aberdeen.

(2) The first three classes received a three month course consisting of approximately five weeks of basic instruction given applicants for all branches, followed by seven weeks of advanced instruction during which each man specialized in his particular field. This method was necessary because 11 branches were represented in the school. The first class opened on 4 Jan 1943 with approximately 50 students in the antiaircraft section. During this first class two 90-mm guns with associated M-7 directors and M-2 height finders were secured. In addition, four 40-mm guns, one Cal .50 machine gun, one Sperry and one General Electric searchlight were added to the antiaircraft materiel.

(3) At this time both 90-mm and 40-mm materiel were new to the theater, and the school thus not only provided replacement officers but also qualified instructional personnel to assist in training units in the use of the new equipment.

(4) Theoretical instruction was reduced to a minimum and emphasis placed upon operation of equipment. The absence of school troops and the small number of qualified personnel in the vicinity made it necessary for the students to perform most of the maintenance for the school materiel.

(5) The staff of the antiaircraft section spent a considerable portion of their time in research and study in order to keep abreast of the rapid development of antiaircraft artillery. The three, and later four-month interval between classes gave opportunity for a complete revision in the program of instruction for each succeeding class. As a result, the section was able to provide qualified technical advice and information to the AA office, GHQ, and to the AA Section, Sixth Army, on various problems submitted by them.

(6) One interesting feature of the course arose as the result of the lack of any suitable antiaircraft firing range facilities in the vicinity of the Officer Candidate School area. At the termination of the classroom instruction, the entire class was moved by convoy to a firing range on the coast approximately 55 miles from the school. There a complete camp was established and antiaircraft firing instruction conducted for a period from a week to ten days. This gave the firing portion of the course the nature of a field problem, considerably improving the practical value of the course.

(7) Altogether eight classes were graduated between the start of the school and its termination 15 Jun 1945. A total of 3,763 second lieutenants was commissioned by the school out of the 5,946 enrolled. The percentage graduated was 63.3. The percentage of antiaircraft personnel graduated was 63.5.

e. <u>Antiaircraft Training Centers</u> gradually were developed as the numbers of troops in the theater increased. In Apr 1943 the 41st CA Brigade (AA) established a training center at Townsville to receive newly arriving troops and to indoctrinate them into the peculiarities of the theater. At its peak facilities were available for some 12,000 troops. The training center at Townsville continued in operation until May 1944 when antiaircraft units from the United States were no longer landing in Australia. Units in Hawaii were receiving special training in tropical amphibious warfare and in many cases spent a week at the Unit Jungle Training Center on Oahu.

137. <u>Training Subsequent to 15 Nov 1943</u>. a. <u>Training Centers</u> were established on a more organized and centralized basis during the latter period of the war.

(1) The Hawaiian AAA Command continued to conduct its training under centralized control. Although training centers were not available, training to include firing was conducted by battalions, under brigade or group supervision. During 1944 and 1945 emphasis was placed upon training units for specific operations, emphasizing ship to shore movements, and loading and landing for amphibious operations. Additional practice in terrestrial firing of both guns and automatic weapons was stressed as the reports from the combat fronts indicated the increasing importance of antiaircraft artillery in its supporting roles.

(2) Battalions scheduled for movement to combat areas were assigned special Transport Quartermaster Teams including antiaircraft personnel trained in the Army Port and Service Command School. A series of semi-weekly exercises using targets of opportunity, and, less frequently, planes making simulated attacks in specified areas, was conducted to train personnel in AAOR and AAAIS techniques.

(3) Carefully prepared special training was carried out for the units preparing for the Leyte and Ryukyus operations. Gun battalions designated for Leyte engaged in a special 22-week training program conducted by the Hawaiian AAA Command. Trial shot problems were fired from the same lot numbers as those to be taken on the operation, to determine proper muzzle velocities.

(4) For the Ryukyus operation the special training of the units to be committed was conducted by the 53d AAA Brigade from 2 Dec 1944 to 17 Feb 1945 and thereafter by the 43d and 44th AAA Groups. This training included special instruction in the use of new equipment

such as the N-2 gates for the SCR-584, and D-7 bull-dozer equipment, the firing of VT-fuzed ammunition, and practical amphibious operations at Maui.

(5) In early 1944 the 117th AAA Group assisted in antiaircraft training on Guadalcanal for all units located there. Training stressed gun and searchlight drill and jungle tactics. In Mar the 68th AAA Brigade organized an AAA Combat Training Center at Guadalcanal where specialized instruction in gun, automatic weapons, and searchlight materiel was given. Instructors were obtained from various units on a temporary duty basis, and from the United States. The school troops were provided from the Hq and Hq Btry, 70th AAA Group. Two OQ2A detachments were assigned to the school and a firing point constructed. Later, a battery of 90-mm guns, a platoon of automatic weapons, and a platoon of searchlights, all from the 117th AAA Group, were attached to the school.

(6) Rocket projectors were used and a Navy utility squadron furnished the tow target missions. The student body increased until each course was operating two sections, with students coming from all units in the area from New Zealand to Bougainville. The school was continued until 18 Jun 1944 when it was closed by USAFISPA when that command's tactical responsibilities ceased.

(7) In the Southwest Pacific, in Nov 1943, all antiaircraft units in the area were assigned to the 14th AA Command, to be attached to various task forces for operations, and to the air force and service commands for guarding airstrips and base installations. This centralized the responsibility for training that had in the past been so widely decentralized. The Command continued the operation of the 41st CA Brigade training center and opened a new and larger one at Finschhafen on 1 Jul 1944. Prior to the closing of this latter training center on 26 Jun 1945, one brigade, 11 groups, and 42 battalions, a total of 32,683 troops, had been trained there. A smaller training center was opened at Milne Bay on 1 Dec 1944 for units stationed at Milne Bay which were prevented from coming to the Finschhafen center by lack of shipping. One searchlight battalion, one automatic weapons battalion, and one seacoast battalion were trained at the Milne Bay training center before its closing on 8 Jan 1945.

(8) Concurrent with the movement of the 14th AA Command to Manila in June 1945 the training center at Finschhafen was closed and a training center was established at San Marcelino, near Subic Bay, on Luzon. It was planned to have facilities for the simultaneous training of from three to five battalions but, due to the cessation of hostilities, the training center was not used except as a transient camp for antiaircraft troops arriving on Luzon.

(9) After the close of the Philippine campaign, in addition

to the training centers operated directly by the 14th AA Command, centers were operated by the 68th AAA Brigade at Luna, La Union on Luzon; by the 32d AAA Brigade on Leyte; and by the 33d AAA Group at Zamboanga, Mindanao.

(10) For organizations committed to the invasion of Japan, the operation of these training centers provided refresher instruction that was as complete as could be desired. Aerial targets- towed, radio-controlled, and rockets- were available. Small arms and grenade ranges and facilities for short and long range field artillery firing insured all-around instruction. The arrival of VJ-day curtailed the intensive training programs at all centers.

b. <u>Specialist Schools</u> were established extensively and used to meet specific shortages or inadequacies of trained specialists.

(1) The elaborate training facilities in Hawaii provided complete training for radar operators, communications personnel, and other specialists.

(2) In the South Pacific, a special radar school was set up on Guadalcanal by USAFISPA, under supervision of the Hq, 68th AAA Brigade, to give training in operation and maintenance of SCR-584's to officers and enlisted men from all South Pacific gun battalions.

(3) The 475th AAA AW Bn conducted a special school on Guadalcanal in the operation and maintenance of the air-transportable 40-mm gun, on the loading of transport planes, on parachute techniques, and on the use of Weiss sights. Arrangements were made with the 13th Bomber Command Training Center for tracking missions. The Radio-Controlled Target Detachment flew OQ-type missions for automatic weapons and conducted a school in OQ-type flying and maintenance for selected officers and men from units in the South Pacific area.

(4) In the Southwest Pacific Area the training center at Finschhafen either operated or made available to antiaircraft units the following schools: radar, target recognition, communications, chemical warfare, cooks' and bakers', tractor mechanics, M-3 oil gear, and bomb reconnaissance and disposal. The target recognition school was the clearing house for target recognition training throughout the Command. Not only did it train officers and enlisted men in the techniques of instruction and the use of recognition training aids, but it also acted as a distribution center for recognition training facilities and aids. The radar school gave refresher courses for radar officers, courses in radar technique for gun battery range officers, courses for radar repairmen and refresher training for operators. These last courses were given especially for units being re-equipped with more modern types of radar.

c. __Instruction teams__ were extensively used because the scarcity of shipping prevented the return of units to the training center for periodic refresher training needed by units in tactical position.

(1) When information was received from the War Department that instruction teams were being formed at the Antiaircraft School and would be available on request, teams were requested at once and in the early summer of 1944 two SCR-584 teams and one IFF team arrived. Four gun teams were requested and arrived in Oct 1944. These teams not only gave on-site instruction to units in tactical positions but also were used at the training center. Standardized instruction was given on the latest antiaircraft techniques and firing procedures.

(2) The results achieved with the gun teams brought about an additional request for four automatic weapons and one searchlight team. While awaiting their arrival, two provisional automatic weapons and one provisional searchlight team were organized from personnel in the theater. Two automatic weapons teams arrived from Finschhafen in Jan 1945 and two more automatic weapons and one searchlight team followed in Feb. A VT fuze instruction team arrived in May and an AAIS-AAOR team was organized shortly thereafter. The results obtained by the teams proved the need for continuation of this type of instruction for the duration of the war. The 14th AA Command requested and received approval for T/O additions which permitted the formal organization on 13 Jun 1945 of the AA Technical Instruction Team Detachment, composed of instruction teams, the G-3 research section, the radio-controlled aerial target detachment and a firing point records section.

(3) During the period of their use, the gun instruction teams instructed 23 gun battalions and the automatic weapons teams 27 automatic weapons battalions, as well as the machine gunners of three gun battalions, six searchlight battalions, and five machine gun batteries. The searchlight teams instructed seven battalions, the VT fuze teams 15 and the communication teams seven battalions.

d. __Training Literature__ published within the theater was of especial importance due to the failure to receive promptly or inadequate quantities of War Department publications. New equipment, even of such technical nature as radars and directors, was often received months before the pertinent WD manuals could be made available. Soon after the activation of the 14th AA Command ineffectual attempts were made to secure manuals direct from the Adjutent General for direct distribution. Attempts to obtain advance copies met with better success and frequently these early manuals were mimeographed and sent to the units. In addition to the reproduction of WD publications, 14th AA Command training bulletins, training circulars, technical bulletins, information bulletins, and training center memos were published. These were all published in conformance with standard practices and every effort was made to keep them up to date through constant revision.

Section IV

Supply

138. __General__. a. The problems of supply for antiaircraft units in the Pacific War were, for the most part, no different from those that faced every combat unit in the theater. Food, clothing, vehicles, and small arms and ammunition were obtained through the normal supply channels. The long supply lines, the climate, the effects of sea and jungle, all made supply one of the prime determining factors for operations in the Pacific.

b. In this section only those aspects of supply peculiar to antiaircraft units will be considered. Antiaircraft supply problems were intensified by the complexity and variety of antiaircraft materiel, which included machine guns, 37-mm and 40-mm automatic weapons, 90-mm guns, directors, height-finders, sound locators, radars and searchlights. In addition technological advances were so outstandingly rapid, that by the close of the war, almost all items of antiaircraft materiel used in 1942 had been rendered obsolete. The replacement of this obsolete equipment with new items of equipment and the provision of adequate maintenance and repair facilities constituted the principal supply problems that were peculiar to antiaircraft units.

c. Since the detailed aspects of antiaircraft supply were to a large degree similar in all parts of the Pacific, and since the operations in the Southwest Pacific illustrate all the complexities of antiaircraft supply, the supply situation in that area will be treated more fully than that in the Pacific Ocean and the South Pacific areas.

139. __Pacific Ocean Area__. a. In every Pacific operation the supply and maintenance of antiaircraft units with the complex variety and large quantities of materiel and supplies was conditioned by the tremendous distances between the zone of the interior and the combat areas, the constant shortage of shipping, and the ravages of a climate that made maintenance of all equipment a constant problem. The rapidity with which new antiaircraft weapons and fire-control equipment were developed, followed closely by their emergence from the production line, put additional strains on the transportation means that were available.

b. The fact that Hawaii was the staging center for most of the Pacific Ocean area operations in the Gilberts, the Marshalls, the Mariannas, the Carolines and the Ryukyus enabled some centralization of policy, and permitted the use, in each successive operation, of new methods based upon the lessons learned in the operations that had gone on before.

c. Supply problems for units in the Hawaiian Islands were similar to those in the zone of the interior. The distance from the San Francisco Port of Embarkation was no greater than that from east to west within the continental limits of the United States and the supply route was relatively safe from enemy naval activity.

d. One advantage in the Pacific Ocean area was the complete dependence upon water transportation. The problem of moving supplies by land as in Australia or by air as in New Guinea, did not exist. The problems of loading and unloading equipment thus became one of the paramount factors in supply.

e. In the Gilbert Islands operations, it was found that too many vehicles and too much heavy transportation equipment was taken by antiaircraft units, inasmuch as mobility was not essential on these small islands. The confusion so difficult to avoid in landing operations was present to a considerable degree. Unfortunately, the use of a Regulating Point was abandoned and equipment became badly mixed up. It was recognized that a liaison officer from the unit was needed to see that equipment was put ashore in proper order.

f. The same difficulties were experienced in the Marshall Islands operations and at that time it was decided that in preparation for future operations, each battalion should send one officer and two enlisted men to Transport Quartermaster School for training. Another result of the Marshall operations was a decision to provide each antiaircraft battery with its own tractor and bulldozer for the immediate primary objective of preparing field fortifications.

g. Several innovations therefore were used in the Mariannas operations. Larger amounts of antiaircraft artillery were needed for both the assault of Saipan and Guam in Jun 1944, and the subsequent garrisoning of those strategic bases. The units were equipped prior to leaving Oahu with 90-mm and 40-mm guns, and M-3 cal .50 machine-gun mounts. The automatic weapons batteries were each equipped with one M-16 multiple gun motor carriage whose mobility and fire power proved very effective. It was decided to maintain a pool of them for future operations. The gun battalions were each equipped with two D-8 tractor-dozers for use in unloading, moving into position and establishing revetments.

h. Each antiaircraft headquarters down to and including sections were furnished SCR-300 radios which proved exceedingly satisfactory.

i. Ammunition supply provided for the antiaircraft assault units carrying ten units of fire, and units assigned to the garrison carrying five. Resupply averaging ten units was held in floating reserve at

-181-

Kwajalein subject to call.

j. Again at Saipan the landing of materiel proved to be a problem not yet successfully mastered. The tactical situation did not permit the beaching of LST's and on D ≠ 2 (17 Jun 1944) it was decided to tranship 90-mm guns, M-16 multiple motor carriages and fire-control equipment on LCM's. One director was drowned out in unloading and consequently this method of transhipment was abandoned. On the next day the LST's were beached and the unloading of equipment over pontons into shallow water showed that the M-4 tractors could perform satisfactorily in as much as four feet of water.

k. Due to landing difficulties no gun battery was equipped completely until D ≠ 14. Equipment was unloaded haphazardly on all beaches and the segregation of antiaircraft equipment proved to be a tremendous job.

l. At Angaur in the Carolines, in Sept 1944, the shortage of shipping made it necessary to reduce the number of units of fire originally planned (five), and to eliminate some of the M-51 multiple machine gun carriages in the assault echelon. The landing was made in a very efficient manner. The Transport Quartermaster carried out his unloading plan without confusion. Some difficulties were encountered due to unbanded boxes and crates. Some radio failures probably were due to insufficient maintenance as a result of inaccessability of equipment aboard ship.

m. The Ryukyus was not only the last but by far the largest operation in which MIDPAC units participated. All of the assault antiaircraft units mounting from Oahu were completely equipped with all of their T/E and special equipment. All of the special equipment had been checked by Hq Tenth Army. The release of the 53d AAA Brigade from the Hawaiian AAA Command made it necessary for the brigade to assume many supply functions previously performed by the Command, namely to procure and distribute major ordnance items through the Ordnance Officer, CPBC and Tenth Army, and to procure certain critical items of engineer and signal supply from CPBC.

n. Here, again the specially trained Transportation Quartermaster teams performed effectively. Materiel losses due to stevedoring and pilferage were held to a minimum. All assault equipment was completely waterproofed. Shore party personnel and engineer units assisted materially in providing shore transportation and in preparing fortifications. This partially compensated for the antiaircraft units having been forced, as a result of insufficient tonnage allocations, to leave a large portion of their general purpose vehicles for later shipment. The inability to operate engines in power plants and motor vehicles aboard ship during the long trip necessitated some third echelon repairs on arrival. Antiaircraft equipment had been provided with distinctive unit markings which greatly increased the ease of separating it on the beaches and in the supply dumps.

o. Several difficulties were found in connection with radar maintenance. Most radars had not been properly moisture and fungi proofed which caused considerable difficulty. As a result of the unloading priorities which had been established spare radar units were not available until L / 30. Critical shortages developed early. Signal radar maintenance teams were attached to assault units and did excellent work when they arrived in time.

p. Although in general the supply and maintenance was adequate in the Ryukyus certain minor difficulties arose. Some vital parts were damaged during transit and in unloading. There were acute shortages of cleaning and preserving materials, sandbags and some spare parts. The opinion was expressed that certain special items of equipment should be provided for use in the Pacific where units were to be in position for long periods of time. Ice machines, lumber, screening, electric generators, and water trailers were either not supplied or not available in sufficient quantity.

140. South Pacific Area. a. The antiaircraft operations in the South Pacific area were limited in scope and therefor did not involve as many and as complex supply problems as those that arose in the Pacific Ocean and the Southwest Pacific areas. The only two combat operations in the area that involved antiaircraft artillery to any considerable degree were those at Guadalcanal and in the Northern Solomons.

b. The only supply problem that was solved in a manner unique to this area was the use by the army units of antiaircraft materiel belonging to Marine units. On Guadalcanal, for example, gun batteries of the 70th CA (AA) took over the 90-mm guns used by the 3d Marine Defense Battalion. Such cooperation between Naval, Marine and Army units was a common solution to the shortage of equipment that constituted a major supply problem in the theater during the earlier phases of the war.

141. Southwest Pacific Area. a. All of the supply difficulties reported in other areas were present in increased degrees in the Southwest Pacific area. The supply lines were longer and more hazardous. The tactical defense of Australia in the first half of 1942 and its later use as a base added long and difficult land supply lines. The operations in Australia and Papua in 1942 and 1943, the landings along New Guinea in 1943 and 1944, from Woodlark to Morotai, and the capture of the Philippines were operations that involved every conceivable problem in antiaircraft logistics, and were dependent upon land, water and air transport of all kinds.

b. **Australia.** (1) The scarcity of materiel in the United States, the long supply lines to the theater, and the shortage of shipping created acute supply problems in 1942. The first shipments of American-made 40-mm guns reached Australia in Aug 1942 and the 90-mm guns and M-7 directors that replaced the original 3-inch gun equipment arrived in Nov. Further delays in re-equipping the units scattered in northern Australia and New Guinea were caused principally by the scarcity of water transportation.

(2) To meet the general supply situation, Australian supplies were acquired whenever suitable. However, the antiaircraft tactical positions were mostly along the northernmost fringe of Australia and the principal manufacturing and shipping centers were hundreds of miles southward. Transportation thus became an acute problem. The overland rail route presented difficulties because of the unloading and reloading required at several state border lines where the railway gauges changed. Nevertheless, the Australian railroads carried much American tonnage throughout the war.

(3) A test motor convoy was run from Brisbane to Townsville by the 208th CA (AA) on its arrival in Mar 1942. The very poor road conditions and the absence of repair facilities proved the impracticability of long distance overland truck transportation. In addition there were no through roads north of Cairns.

(4) A constantly increasing quantity of light-weight non-bulky supplies and emergency items was carried northward in commercial transport airplanes converted for the purpose, and later by our troop carrier squadrons.

(5) For at least a year the shipping situation from the United States to and within the Southwest Pacific was desperate. For this reason such antiaircraft equipment as was actually in Australia had to be treated with great care, and maintenance of materiel was highly stressed both in the course of normal activities and in training schools on old as well as new equipment.

(6) The antiaircraft supply and maintenance problems with chemical, quartermaster, and medical items were common to all arms and services. The Signal Corps, Engineer Corps, and Ordnance Department furnished the antiaircraft artillery with its major armament and technical equipment. Adequacy of the supply and maintenance of this materiel was a major problem that existed, though in diminishing degree, throughout the war.

(7) The amount of special antiaircraft equipment reaching Australia in 1942 and early 1943 was so small that the Antiaircraft Officer, GHQ, was able to supervise its distribution and maintenance directly

through the supplying branches. However, as new antiaircraft equipment continued to be produced in increasing quantities, the arrival of this equipment at widely scattered ports of destination in the theater, and its distribution to the similarly scattered units, became a major problem which was not solved satisfactorily until the 14th AA Command was activated in Nov 1943. As an aid in solving this problem, special staff officers from the technical supply branches were made part of the G-4 Section of the Command, where their technical knowledge was utilized to assist in coordination between the sources of supply and the using units.

(8) The shortages of some special tools and spare parts for 40-mm and 90-mm guns were never alleviated. The deficiencies arose when new weapons arrived without these articles, as well as from a result of combat and normal wear and tear. In only a few cases could they be made up by use of components of obsolete or excess equipment.

c. (1) The Antiaircraft Supply Liaison System was developed in Oct 1943 in order to provide central control and to expedite the flow of materiel to the using troops when it finally began to arrive in quantity. The Antiaircraft Officer, GHQ, appointed antiaircraft liaison officers at Oro Bay and Milne Bay, who were to report directly to his office all determinable information on antiaircraft materiel entering, leaving, or stored at those two bases.

(2) Two factors made necessary this close supervision of antiaircraft materiel within the theater. First, all movements of bulky or heavy equipment from the United States were necessarily made by water shipment, and due to limited shipping, cargoes were discharged at those bases that were most convenient for the maximum utilization of the vessel, regardless of whether this was the original shipping destination or not. Secondly, inability of supply service personnel to identify a considerable portion of the antiaircraft materiel as such, resulted in much critical equipment being lost or mislaid at the ports. Some equipment was issued to rear-area units when it was urgently required by organizations in forward areas.

(3) Upon activation of the 14th AA Command one of its first projects was to expand the liaison system and to submit to USASOS a plan for the continued operation of the system as a recognized activity. The original proposal as tentatively approved contemplated the segregated storage of all antiaircraft materiel in a separate area at each base and supply point. These assembly areas were to be operated by the liaison officers, using troops drawn from antiaircraft units in the vicinity.

(4) With the increased amount of equipment arriving in the theater and the expansion of storage and cargo receiving facilities by bases, it became apparent that segregated storage of antiaircraft

materiel was neither feasible nor necessary. Since the Command lacked the organization and the personnel to operate supply depots, that part of the plan was therefore abandoned and all equipment was received, stored, and issued by the appropriate services.

(5) The liaison officers were retained, however, and at all important bases they traced antiaircraft equipment by searching docks, depots, dumps, beaches, and by checking the cargo manifests of all incoming and outgoing vessels. They were able to locate and identify much critically needed equipment long before it would have been reported through normal USASOS channels.

(6) By means of prompt reports the liaison officers kept the Command informed of the stock status and arrival and shipment of critical antiaircraft items at their bases. On numerous occasions a liaison officer's records proved to be more accurate than the base's stock records. As a result USASOS, or one of the intermediate supply control sections, frequently issued releases on controlled items at the request of the Command even though base depot reports did not yet show the equipment to be on hand.

(7) By direct communication between liaison officers and by information distributed by the Command, all liaison officers were kept informed of the general status of issue and shipment of antiaircraft materiel.

(8) The contact maintained by the antiaircraft liaison officers with GHQ Regulating Officers was invaluable. With one liaison officer at the receiving port securing high shipping priority by personal contact with the regulating officer, and another expediting shipment from the originating base, shipments were often quickly effected, and equipment which might otherwise have reached a port after the departure of the unit for which it was destined, arrived in time for issue. Personal contact by the liaison officer with the supply agency concerned, the Air Transport Command, and the GHQ Regulating Officers, was able to accomplish many emergency air shipments of critically needed parts. At the close of the war these representatives were operating in all major AFWESPAC (formerly USASOS) bases in the theater.

d. (1) <u>Maintenance of equipment</u> was a problem complicated during the first part of the war by three factors:

    (a) The paucity of spare parts, which was aggravated by the difficulties of transportation and the consequent desire of units, particularly at outlying stations, to keep large stocks on hand;

    (b) the deterioration introduced by the heat and humidity of the tropics;

(c) the shortage of skilled maintenance personnel and the difficulties of getting them to outlying stations.

(2) The first factor was eventually fairly well overcome by establishing central depots. The third factor was solved temporarily by organizing maintenance teams from base maintenance personnel, which teams accompanied the early task forces to the more distant points. Subsequently, trained maintenance teams were brought from the US in sufficient numbers to permit attachment to committed antiaircraft forces. The remaining factor, traceable to tropical conditions, was more difficult to overcome. Gradual progress was made by prompt dissemination of helpful information to using units, daily operation of electrical equipment to keep it dry, and eventually by the receipt and application of tropic-proofing materials.

(3) In instances when units received new equipment with which they were unfamiliar, senior commanders in the field usually arranged to give selected personnel instruction in the care and use of the new equipment before it was issued, either by sending them to a special school or by sending maintenance or special instruction teams to the troops.

(4) After the establishment of the 14th AA Command it was able to secure additional maintenance teams for the theater, and to organize instruction teams and training centers, as is more fully described in Sect III above. Personnel of the signal corps, radar, engineer, and ordnance special staff sections of the Command made frequent visits to units in the field and staging areas, and made available to them much late technical data and information.

(5) Even though new and modified equipment of a highly technical nature was being made available to a large number of units in ever increasing tempo, by the close of the war the maintenance program had proved more than capable of handling the many tasks confronting it.

e. (1) <u>Engineer searchlight maintenance</u> during the early months of the war was complicated by the scarcity of trained personnel. The limited number available were kept at the base depots where all third, fourth, and fifth echelon maintenance was performed. As the area of combat expanded, units at a distance from a depot were required to perform their own third and fourth echelon maintenance. Later, the three searchlight battalions then in the theater contributed skilled mechanics to help establish a searchlight depot in New Guinea. Maintenance teams were formed at about the same time. In Oct 1944, 13 searchlight maintenance teams were attached or assigned to the 14th AA Command and employed under the supervision of the Engineer Officer.

(2) When a searchlight battery was detailed for battlefield illumination, or when it operated separately from its parent

battalion, a maintenance team was attached to it. A team was attached to each searchlight battalion or part thereof committed to an operation. When the unit had completed its mission or was in a static position, the team was released for another operation.

(3) These teams were highly mobile, carried a supply of spare parts to augment that carried by the units, and were especially valuable on amphibious operations for the quick repair of damaged equipment. Their prompt and technically accurate reports of materiel failures or deficiencies also facilitated the issuance of modification work orders.

(4) A number of modification projects were initiated, notably:

    (a) shortening of the extended-hand-control to three feet so as to make its use possible where the searchlight was sited on a mound or very high ground;

    (b) the installation of two waterproof snap switches on the 1942 Sperry searchlight to make the light rotate automatically when used as an airstrip beacon; and

    (c) modification of the searchlight trailer to enable it to carry the complete equipment of a searchlight section.

(5) Experiments in air transportation of the equipment of a searchlight section[1] were so satisfactory that in Jan 1945 orders were placed for modification kits to make all searchlights air-transportable. The first shipment of the kits arrived in Leyte shortly before the end of hostilities.

(6) In order to speed up the movement of searchlight sections during a landing operation, a special theater authorization was obtained for the equipping of each searchlight in a semi-mobile unit with a trailer. In addition, special authorization was obtained for one spare searchlight unit, complete with power plant, per battery, to prevent a gap in the searchlight defense while a damaged searchlight was being replaced or repaired.

f. (1) Ordnance maintenance problems were handled in 1942 by the 25th Ord Med Maint Co which came to Australia with the first antiaircraft troops. Detachments from the company were sent to Fremantle, Darwin, and Townsville with the antiaircraft units sent initially to those widely scattered places. Subsequently the company was based at Townsville; from here teams were sent with the antiaircraft batteries

---

[1] See Sec IV A.

that went on to the more forward locations. As many as seven such detachments were out at times. Although the shortage of spare parts presented a serious obstacle, this was overcome to a large extent by the use of good maintenance technique, efficient machine work, and improvisation.

(2) Although the company's personnel were not acquainted with either the Bofors or the 90-mm gun, their technical knowledge and ability was such that by the time they had serviced the newly-arrived weapons they were entirely competent to care for them. In early 1943 their base of operations was moved to Port Moresby to meet the needs of the increasing number of antiaircraft units in New Guinea.

(3) In Nov 1943, the 267th Ord Maint Co (AA), with its newer and more complete shop equipment, arrived in the Southwest Pacific Area. The number of these antiaircraft maintenance companies in the theater increased until in Mar of 1944 there were a total of five, which was scarcely adequate for the work to be done. However, in Oct of 1944 the 3073d Ordnance Service Composite Company arrived in Finschhafen, New Guinea, to ease the situation. This company consisted of eight teams, each of which included personnel and equipment sufficient to provide ordnance maintenance for three battalions of antiaircraft artillery during an invasion and for several weeks following the initial assault.

(4) All antiaircraft ordnance maintenance organizations were assigned to USASOS (later AFWESPAC) and attached to the Army responsible for task force operations. The teams often were re-attached directly to the senior antiaircraft headquarters in the operation, a plan which proved most effective. Regardless of attachment they remained available to any antiaircraft unit requiring their services until the operation was advanced sufficiently so that the normal base service installations could be established.

(5) Ordnance maintenance difficulties arose at Nadzab, Morotai, and Noemfoor as a result of the withdrawal by the Sixth and Eighth Armies of their ordnance maintenance companies while the antiaircraft units remained in position, attached to the Far East Air Force. The air force ordnance maintenance units had neither the trained personnel nor the parts and equipment to handle this added responsibility. As a result of these experiences effort was made to have the AA Ordnance Maintenance Companies assigned to the 14th AA Command, which could then insure that the necessary maintenance personnel were always provided.

(6) Seventy-two percent of the ordnance antiaircraft modification work orders had been completed in the Southwest Pacific area by the close of the war. In certain cases, modification work order kits were handled by the supplying agencies in the same manner as other major items of antiaircraft equipment, and antiaircraft personnel in the units made the changes. This procedure was followed in the installation of the M3 oil gears and M7A1 computing sights on the 40-mm guns, the voltage

regulators on gun generators, and the M9A1 director conversion kits.

(7) From the early days in Australia, equipment modifications, based on battle and field experience, were proposed by the antiaircraft units in the field, and later by members of the ordnance section of the 14th AA Command. These were subjected further to technical experimentation on the part of antiaircraft and ordnance specialists. The more important modifications resulting from this system were the installation of the M33 multiple machine gun mount on LCM's and of the 40-mm gun on the half track carriage M3, and the development of a terrestial fire-sighting system for the motor carriage M16.

(8) The extremely close liaison between the antiaircraft units in the field and ordnance research laboratories of the War Department was notable, and after the formation of the ordnance section of the 14th AA Command, that headquarters acted as the focal point from which the Ordnance Department antiaircraft experts operated.

(9) Newly developed ordnance items of major importance were supplied to the units as rapidly as production and shipping permitted. Ordnance teams were often, by request, made available on temporary duty to accompany the new equipment into the field, where they instructed the using personnel in its proper operation and maintenance.

(10) Ammunition supply difficulties were more a matter of quality than of quantity, and were traceable largely to inadequate storage facilities under tropical conditions. In the early war years, the shortage of service personnel hindered the erection of well-planned ammunition dumps, and much deterioration of containers and rounds occurred from the effects of tropical sun, rain, and humidity. Unfortunately, little effort was made at any of the storage points to observe lot numbers, either in storing, or, more important, in loading out for task forces. A check made at Cape Gloucester in Jun 1944 revealed over three dozen different lot numbers in three units of fire in one gun battery, with not over 75 rounds of any one lot.

(11) Initially, Australian or British ammunition was used by American 40-mm automatic weapons units in the Southwest Pacific. However, when American ammunition became available in quantity, British ammunition was used only for training purposes, or in emergencies.

(12) There was never a general antiaircraft ammunition shortage in the theater, although there were a few instances of local shortages. Under these circumstances resupply was quickly effected by air shipment from the nearest stocks.

(13) Toward the end of the war, when antiaircraft artillery was called upon to engage in terrestrial firing in support of the infantry, 90-mm smoke shells seldom were available; more of this type of

shell could have been used advantageously. The war ended before this deficiency was made up.

(14) The proximity type fuze reached the theater in 1944 but in very limited quantities only. By the time its issue could even approach being general, Japanese air activity was at an end. For additional information on the use of the VT fuze see Chap 2, Sec VIII and XII.

g. (1) Radar supply and maintenance of antiaircraft radar, at the beginning of hostilities, was the responsibility of the Base Signal Office. However, as the radar problem mushroomed into large proprotions, special radar sections were set up within the Signal Corps to handle radar equipment exclusively.

(2) As technical improvements were made based on laboratory experimentation in the United States and practical experiences in the field, the types of radar in the hands of combat units became outdated by newer models. This introduced a continuous problem of resupply and changing maintenance technique, in addition to the training and operating problem.

(3) The variations between the A, B, and C models of the SCR-268 were not sufficient to create a problem for the searchlight batteries, but when the gun batteries were issued the SCR-584 to replace the SCR-268 special instruction in operation and maintenance was a necessity. In Jul 1945, when the AN/TPL-1 became available for searchlight use, a special training program was necessary. The war ended before the antiaircraft searchlight units had been supplied completely with this latest model. Only 31 sets were shipped to the theater prior to Japan's defeat.

(4) A radar section was formed as part of the special staff of the 14th AA Command. This section supervised special radar instruction and by inspections kept informed on the state of training of radar crews and the condition of equipment in the various units. It made recommendations as to the allocation of new type equipment to antiaircraft units. Upon the issue of the new radar to a unit, technical teams, whenever possible, were sent to instruct the using personnel on its proper operation and maintenance.

(5) At the beginning of the war signal radar maintenance units were scarce, and thus practically all repair work above second echelon was performed by technicians of USASOS at its major bases. Later, however, as the number of maintenance units increased, they were attached directly to the antiaircraft units in order to provide immediate service for critical equipment. Seven were available to the 14th AA Command in Jul 1945.

(6) Frequent inspections of the radar in the hands of units were made by radar personnel and where maintenance performances were not up to the standards, instruction teams were sent to provide the needed instruction.

(7) By the war's end maintenance units and special radar instruction teams were present in sufficient quantity for all antiaircraft units staging in Luzon for the invasion of Japan.

(8) A radar school was opened at Finschhafen, New Guinea, in 1944. In addition to the training of operators, training was given also in maintenance and repairs of radar and associated IFF equipment.

(9) As a result of the maintenance problems arising from the climatic conditions of the jungles, a project was initiated in mid-1944 to tropic-proof antiaircraft radar. Due to an initial delay in securing the required materials the program did not get underway for about three months, but once started, all radar equipment was successfully tropic-proofed in about two months.

(10) War Department modification work orders for radars presented little difficulty since few were forthcoming in the early stages of the war, and later on there were signal radar maintenance units, experienced technicians within the antiaircraft artillery, and civilian research experts available to carry out the work. In fact, many modifications peculiar to the theater were proposed by the 14th AA Command and later published in a series of emergency modification work orders authorized by the Commanding General, USAFFE. In addition, civilian specialists from the radar laboratories in the United States proved especially helpful on all technical radar problems and were able to introduce several beneficial modifications while working in conjunction with the Army specialists.

(11) Shortage of suitable storage and transportation facilities for radar supplies of units in amphibious operations led to a re-distribution in 1945 of K-60 van trucks no longer needed as elements of SCR-268-B sets. Some were issued to gun battalions for transportation of M9 directors and tools, test equipment, and spare parts for the SCR-584. Searchlight battalions being re-equipped with the AN/TPL-1 radar were allowed K-60 trucks to provide both transportation and housing for tools and AN/TPL-1 spare parts and test equipment. These were special authorizations for equipment in excess of T/O & E, approved by the Theater Commander.

5. RESEARCH and DEVELOPMENT

Section   I   General

Section   II   Air Transportation of Antiaircraft Artillery

Section   III   Flakintel

Section   IV   Searchlight-Fighter Team

Section   V   Evasive Action Studies

Section   VI   Ground Target Location and Survey by Gun
                    Radar-Liaison Plane Team

Section   VII   Moving Target Indicator

Section   VIII   Radar Mortar Location

Section I

General

142. __General__. a. The special conditions encountered in the Pacific war, the long lines of communication to the mainland, and the resulting time lags, were responsible for much pioneering work being done in the theater in the improvement of antiaircraft equipment and the development or improvement of techniques for its use. Technical and tactical questions were continually arising because of the unique features of tropical terrain and weather, and the characteristics peculiar to the enemy, that had to be solved with minimum delay. In many instances the delay between the posing of a problem in the Pacific, and the delivery of corrective materials or instructions as the result of research on it in the United States would have meant loss of life and have hampered our operations against the enemy.

b. Research in the theater permitted quick checking, under combat conditions, of a hypothesis or a conclusion and permitted prompt action to be taken. Many modifications of equipment were undertaken and proved in combat, based upon the initiative of units in the field, despite the handicap of inefficient and inadequate fabrication and testing equipment.

c. In some instances research on special problems was carried on concurrently in all theaters. Among such problems may be listed Flakintel; target location and survey by radar tracking of liaison planes; and the use of radar for mortar location. Variations in procedures within the different theaters occurred, due to the special terrain conditions, and to the tactics, technique, and weapons employed by the enemy.

d. The fighter-searchlight team procedure developed at Orlando, Florida had to be altered to suit the particular terrain conditions in the tropical islands of the Pacific. Because of the peculiar flying tactics of the Japanese Air Force, independent study of their evasive action was necessary.

e. During the early defense of Australia and New Guinea and the offensive operations that followed, there was great need for air transportation of antiaircraft artillery. The strategy of island hopping and jumping far forward to establish air bases at points not connected by land or sea routes required quick transport of antiaircraft defenders for these bases.

f. The moving target indicator, a radical modification to the radar set SCR-584, was developed and constructed in the United States, then sent to Oahu and Luzon for testing, where it arrived too late for combat tests. This device, to distinguish moving from stationary targets, would undoubtedly have improved search technique considerably, as Japanese low-flying aircraft, by taking advantage of strong fixed echoes and heavy ground "clutter" on radar scopes, quite often came into close range undetected.

g. The first experiments in the use of radar for mortar location were conducted in the European Theater of Operations and in the United States; information on this technique was late in arriving in the Pacific. To continue the testing of mortar detection by radar, an automatic plotter was needed. Six units were designed and constructed in the SWPA at least two months before the first IBM plotter arrived. Training in the use of the equipment was begun immediately, under antiaircraft supervision; however, the war ended before combat tests could be made.

h. The history of the major research problems is described briefly in the following pages, with references being made to pertinent detailed reports.

i. Countless improvements and "gadgets" were developed by the men in combat positions to make their fire more effective, their equipment more efficient, and their positions safer. Among these were the water chest hangers, ammunition feed, bolt retracting lever and handlebar devices developed for the water cooled machine gun on the M-2 mount; the several types of ammunition racks and azimuth and elevation scales for the 40-mm guns; and the cable and accessory racks for searchlights and guns. No attempt is made to describe these in detail.

Section II

Air Transportation of Antiaircraft Artillery

143. <u>Automatic Weapons</u>. a. The need for air transportation for antiaircraft troops came sharply to the attention of our commanders in Australia in Mar 1942, when it was decided to move some newly arrived antiaircraft units into Darwin. Japanese air activity had caused the diversion of the convoy originally destined for that point, and antiaircraft defenses were badly needed for the airdromes from which the few allied fighter planes in that area were operating. The air forces supplied airplanes of all sizes and descriptions, from huge flying boats to small two-passenger planes, whatever could carry a man or two, and antiaircraft equipment. Within 26 days the 102d CA Bn (AA), then armed only with cal .50 machine guns, was transported in 124[1] plane loads to the northern Australian port, the first mass movement of troops by air in the Southwest Pacific[2].

b. When the planning for advances against the Japanese on the north shore of New Guinea indicated the need for fighter airdromes in the mountains south of the coast line, the nature of the antiaircraft defenses which could be established for these airdromes became a matter of considerable concern. As a result, a study was initiated at Port Moresby early in 1943 to determine the feasibility of air transportation of the 40-mm gun. After study and experiments, a satisfactory procedure was developed in Feb 1943 and adopted as the standard for the 40th AAA Brigade, which then controlled all American antiaircraft artillery in New Guinea.[3]

c. The SOP thus developed was used by all automatic weapons units as a basis for the air loading practice that was held during that period. It involved very little dismantling of the gun and required two C-47 transport planes per gun section for the transportation of the materiel, ammunition, and crew. With a trained crew a gun could be unloaded from a plane and put into position ready for action within 20 minutes.

---

[1] See History of 102d CA Bn (AA).

[2] See Report of Air Movement, 15 Apr 1942 - 102d CA Bn (AA).

[3] See History of 101st AAA AW Bn.

d. Inasmuch as the plywood ramps furnished for the C-47 transport were not strong enough to carry the weight of the guns, the antiaircraft troops devised a ramp made from metal run-way stripping and piping, suitably welded. Subsequently, this type of ramp was adopted by the Air Forces for loading all sorts of heavy equipment and could be found at practically every airdrome in New Guinea.

e. The first actual use of the procedure for air shipment of 40-mm guns was the movement of elements of Btry C of the 211th AAA AW Bn on 29 Jul 1943 to Tsili-Tsili.[1] This operation was so successful that it served as a standard for all later air moves of antiaircraft artillery. On 28 Oct 1943 this battery moved again by air from Tsili-Tsili to Nadzab. All automatic weapons units of the 40th AAA Brigade were thereafter instructed in air loading, including actual loading of gun sections on transport planes loaned for the purpose, or on mockups made at the several locations.

f. In Apr and May of 1944 the 101st AAA AW Bn experimented with loading an M-45 quadruple machine gun mount on a C-47 transport. The experiment worked out satisfactorily with no modification of the mounts or the ramp. In Oct the 102d AAA AW Bn A/T experimented with a new mount for the M-45 which was air loaded successfully on a C-47 transport using the standard ramp.[2]

g. In Jul of 1944 both the 101st[3] and the 102d[4] Battalions received the airborne 40-mm gun, M-5 mount. Both units conducted separate experiments on the loading, and worked out SOP's. Since no training literature was received with the equipment, it was necessary for the using units to solve the problem of loading.

h. On 6 Oct 1944 experimental loading of a 40-mm gun, M-5 mount, on a Glider, CG 13 was conducted.[5] This was found to be a relatively simple problem, the gun being loaded directly from a $2\frac{1}{2}$-ton truck. No glider moves were made, however.

i. With the increased use of the C-46 transport plane it was apparent that it might be used by antiaircraft artillery to transport

---

[1] See Report on Airborne Operations of the 211th AAA AW Bn - 20 Nov 1945.

[2] Letter, 102d AAA AW Bn A/T, "Report on Mounting the M-45 on Two Wheel Trailer".

[3] See "Air Movement Logistics, C-47, 1 Feb 1945, 101st AAA AW Bn."

[4] See Letter, Hq, 102d AAA AW Bn, 21 Jun 1944, "Movement Report".

[5] See History of 102d CA Bn (AA).

their equipment. On 9 May 1945 an experimental loading of a 40-mm gun, air-transportable, on a C-46 transport plane was made. The door of a C-46 being approximately seven feet six inches from the ground, the gun was loaded directly from the bed of a 2½-ton truck. Inasmuch as there were no suitable C-46 ramps available, standard C-47 ramps were used for the loading. In addition to the gun, a ¼-ton truck was loaded into the transport. There was sufficient room in the cargo space to secure both the gun and vehicle at the proper tie-down stations. A straight-type ramp of shorter length was constructed that worked more efficiently with the C-46 than the available C-47 ramps.

144. **Guns**. Since the 40-mm guns flown into inland airfields lacked the range to reach the enemy at medium altitudes it was desirable to move in larger armament if practicable. In May and Jun of 1943, at Port Moresby, a 3-inch gun on M2A2 mount was dismantled and loaded, less bogies, into two C-47 transports.[1] However, since the 90-mm guns had become standard equipment in the theater the same battery, after its move to Dobodura, made a careful study of that weapon and in Nov 1943 published a complete SOP for the air movement of a 90-mm battery with associated equipment and necessary personnel, ammunition and supplies. It was found that the 90-mm gun could be loaded more easily than the 3-inch gun. The SOP included shipment of the SCR-268 radar which was in use by the gun batteries at that time. The radar was never actually dismantled and loaded, as the procedure involved cutting the antenna into two parts and dismantling the platform. It was planned to transport an entire gun battery in 54 loads[2], with no plane carrying more than 5,000 pounds. The development of the C-46 would have made the 90-mm gun even more air-transportable. However, no 90-mm guns were flown in this theater.

145. **Searchlights**. a. Antiaircraft personnel experimented with loading 60-inch searchlights into a C-47 transport and worked out a procedure therefor in Dec 1943. Several units conducted individual and simultaneous tests and arrived at similar procedures.[3]

---

[1] See History of 745th AAA Gun Bn.

[2] See "Standard Operating Procedure for Airborne Movement of 90-mm Gun", 745th CA Bn (AA Gun).

[3] See Letter, Btry B, 250th AAA SL Bn, 6 Nov 1944, "Report on Air Transport of Standard 60" Searchlight".

b. Experiments were conducted by several units on the air loading of vehicles. Loading of "jeeps" and trailers was a routine matter but heavier vehicles were needed. As early as Nov 1943 searchlight units stripped and loaded a weapons carrier in a C-47. Another unit devised and used a loading plan for a 2½-ton truck which included the disassembling and cutting of the frame.[1]

---

[1] See Letter, 102d AAA AW Bn A/T, 28 Oct 1944, "Recommendation to Include Trucks, 2½-ton, six by six, cargo, in Air Echelon of T/O & E's 44-225S, 44-226S, and 44-227S".

Section III

Flakintel

146. a. Flakintel was the name given to the organization and procedure set up to advise Allied Air Force units concerning the Japanese antiaircraft fire which could be placed in the several likely avenues of aerial approach. Its purpose was to determine the least costly direction of approach and departure of our planes to the objective, based on the type of attack planned.

b. The first action towards supplying this information appears to have been taken in Townsville, Queensland, in Sept 1942. Officers of the American antiaircraft defenses, after discussing with the Commanding General, V Bomber Command, the effects of the enemy antiaircraft fire at Rabaul, undertook a study of these defenses in order to recommend routes of approach and retirement for varied bombing altitudes. This study resulted in the presentation in early Oct of a chart showing the zones and weights of antiaircraft fire over the target area and recommending routes and altitudes for high, medium, and low-level bombing. In the meantime, to provide more material for this work, Air Force observers had been directed to pay careful attention to the types and origin of antiaircraft fire received and to report this information through intelligence channels.

c. These initial studies created a great deal of interest and are believed to have been instrumental in bringing about a change in bombing tactics. Two antiaircraft officers, made available by the AAO, GHQ, were assigned to carry the study further, working in close cooperation with V Bomber Command Headquarters. As the progress of the war permitted the capture of Japanese antiaircraft weapons and various enemy documents on the use of the equipment, these officers accumulated a continually increasing supply of information. Their research led to the publication of a Flakintel SOP, analyzing in detail the Japanese antiaircraft artillery, and containing detailed information on the location of enemy antiaircraft installations in the vicinity of existing targets.[1]

---

[1] Flakintel Instructions, Hq Allied Air Forces, APO 925, 1 Sept 1943.
Flakintel Instructions, No.2, Analytical Study of Japanese Antiaircraft Artillery.
Flakintel Instructions, No.3, Area Reports.

d. In Mar 1943 an antiaircraft officer was placed upon temporary duty with V Bomber Command, and through the interest of the Commanding General thereof, Flakintel was incorporated as an integral part of air intelligence. Photo interpretation and target information sections of the Allied Air Forces lent their assistance in locating and identifying enemy defense installations. Collation maps, pin-pointing enemy antiaircraft defenses, were published and distributed to all groups and squadrons, and planned evasive action prior to and after the bombing run was introduced as a means of reducing the effectiveness of the hostile antiaircraft fire.

e. In the latter part of 1943 officers, on detached service from antiaircraft units in the field, were given a thorough course of Flakintel instruction before being attached to bombardment groups and higher air force headquarters. Publication of a Flakintel Bulletin[1] was initiated, in order to keep these advisers up to date. In May 1944 a Flakintel sub-section was established in the 14th AA Command. The number of Flakintel personnel was expanded through the assignment of additional officers to obtain the necessary strength to serve the growing air forces in the theater.

f. In May 1944 the Flakintel Analysis system was introduced, thus providing a mathematical method of determining the relative effectiveness of the various enemy antiaircraft defenses. In Aug 1944 the Flakintel Handbook was published.[2] This was a combination of the three previous Flakintel Manuals, and consolidated the accumulated intelligence of the Japanese antiaircraft artillery. In Mar 1945 two sections of the handbook were revised, to give the latest information on radio detection and on the 120-mm dual purpose gun, type 10. On 16 Jul 1945 Far East Air Forces absorbed all Flakintel functions, and all attached Falkintel personnel were assigned to that command.

g. The services of the Flakintel officers were used in planning operations down to the mission planning level of the air forces. They furnished advice as to the safest courses in and out of target areas, the evasive action to be taken, and routes to and from the target. They also attended the questioning sessions at the conclusion of air missions in order to secure the latest information of enemy flak for use in their own analysis as well as for use by the Flakintel office in its studies and publications. Flakintel officers accompanied the assault waves when landings in new territory were made, to secure the latest information on enemy materiel and to insure its prompt dissemination.

---

[1] *Flakintel Bulletin Number 1*, Hq Allied Air Forces, APO 925, Dec 1943

[2] *Flakintel Handbook*, Hq Allied Air Forces, APO 925, 1 Aug 1944.

h. Close liaison was maintained with the intelligence section of GHQ. Intercepted information collated by this section was correlated with photographic interpretations made by Flakintel. Complete and up-to-date enemy detection coverages were maintained by Flakintel so that air crews could be briefed on the best routes to avoid, or to delay detection.

Section IV

Searchlight-Fighter Team

147. General. a. The use of dayfighters at night inside the defended area as a supplement to, instead of as a substitute for, antiaircraft defense was a development worked out jointly by the antiaircraft artillery and the Air Forces in the Pacific.

b. From Port Moresby through the Solomons to Luzon the impassable terrain outside the occupied areas and the closeness of the perimeters to the defended areas precluded the use of the normal fighter-searchlight technique. Even the use of radar-equipped night fighters, which began to arrive in the theater in quantity late in 1944, did not solve the night air defense problem. Eventually, the close-in defense of an area at night was left to antiaircraft artillery.

148. Guadalcanal. At Guadalcanal in 1943 the effective work of the searchlights in illuminating high-flying raiders brought out the possibilities of the use of P-38 fighters against the illuminated targets after the guns had completed their firing. A technique was worked out which, in tests, resulted in the destruction of five enemy twin-engined bombers on a single night before cessation of attacks cut short the experiment at that place.

149. Morotai. a. In Nov 1944 when the basing of the 13th Air Force in the congested Morotai area made imperative the use of every possible means of air defense the antiaircraft commander renewed his suggestion made shortly after the landing that the overhead fighter plan be used. Discussion with the antiaircraft officer and the A-3 of the Air Force and pilots of the 148th Nightfighter Squadron led to experiments and the development of the procedures described below.

b. The plan was based on and subject to all implications of the premises that (1) the Morotai airdrome area presented a very compact and highly vulnerable target; (2) the defending antiaircraft artillery was efficient and available in adequate quantity; (3) the antiaircraft artillery could deliver more fire power under favorable or adverse conditions than any available night fighter action could deliver under the most favorable conditions of chase; and (4) therefore close-in fighter action must not interfere with the normal fire action of the antiaircraft artillery up to the point where the enemy passed his bomb release line and theoretically could do no more harm on that run.

c. It was also recognized that friendly planes in the vicinity of the enemy, or between him and the antiaircraft positions, seriously affected the efficiency of antiaircraft gun fire; also that antiaircraft fire discipline permitted the observance of a ceiling for fire which could be changed at will; and that the fire could be terminated at a certain time or line, and would not endanger friendly planes if they utilized properly operating radar identification equipment, kept out of prescribed areas, and did not attack until released to do so.

d. The first tests, using a P-61 night fighter as the patrol, proved that that plane did not have either the flexibility, speed, or rate of climb for the job. In the second test several P-38 fighters were used. The night of their first trial run produced an actual enemy raid during which one enemy plane was shot down by the fighter. During a period of five nights one P-38 shot down three enemy craft and probably destroyed two others out of a total of eight targets attacked. Mechanical troubles with the fighters, unfavorable weather conditions, and finally relief of the night-fighter squadron combined to eliminate this method of defense for several weeks until, just before Christmas, an Australian nightfighter squadron equipped with Spitfires assumed the mission. Their first opportunity was a complete success, the enemy bomber being shot down in flames on the Spitfire's second pass.

e. The only other opportunity the Spitfires had for attack was several nights later, on a brilliant moonlight night when the searchlight beams were invisible to the pilot. Being at greater altitude, he was unable to locate the enemy by the light reflection on its underside, and so lost his chance.

f. The operating procedure used at Morotai required the maintenance of a patrol by a high performance fighter at high altitude <u>over</u> the defended area during all the hours of possible attack when weather conditions were practicable for searchlight illumination and fighter attack. American pilots preferred to use a single fighter; the antiaircraft artillery favored that number as it simplified the problem of keeping track of the friend in the air. The Australian squadron preferred to operate with a team of two planes.

g. Whenever the patrol was in the air a ceiling for antiaircraft gun fire, at or near the maximum altitude at which enemy attack was expected (20,000 feet was normal at Morotai), was announced. The patrol operated at least 1,000 feet above this ceiling, flying courses which kept him directly overhead or to that side of the defended area opposite the expected direction of attack. The selection of the patrol area was dependent to some extent upon the brilliancy of the moonlight, as it affected the pilot's ability to keep close station.

h. The patrol and the antiaircraft artillery were alerted upon the detection of an approaching enemy, the pilot was given the direction of approach and, as soon as it was determined, the altitude. The patrol then moved out of the gun defended area and climbed to a superior altitude. If the enemy approached at an altitude above the established gunfire ceiling the controller authorized a new ceiling above the enemy and reported it to the patrolling pilot who immediately climbed above it.

i. The guns engaged the approaching enemy in normal manner, with searchlight illumination withheld until the first bursts appeared. If the plane was then illuminated, gunfire on it would be ceased by battery commander's order when the enemy either dropped his bombs, turned away from the defended area, or reached its edge. Either the battalion or the group commander could order the cessation of fire on an illuminated target by a single code word in case the battery commander failed to halt fire when it appeared desirable.

j. When the fighter pilot observed the illuminated target he would take position across the defended area from it and report his readiness to attack, but would not attack until released. The AAOO would notify the controller when the enemy plane was illuminated, when fire on it had ceased (determined by reports from the fire units and from observers at Group Headquarters) and when the fighter could safely be released to attack. The searchlights had standing orders to carry to the limit in these cases, using lights ahead of the enemy as long as practicable.

k. Once released to attack the fighter was free to go anywhere in pursuit of the illuminated plane except that he should not go below 10,000 feet altitude within the automatic weapons defended area. Fire units were prohibited from opening fire on a target in the general sector of the enemy once the fighter had been released to attack.

l. In case of multiple plane attacks the same procedure was followed except that the fighter was not released to attack an illuminated enemy if another was approaching from the direction the first was going, or if for any other reason fire on the second plane would endanger the attacking fighter. This procedure proved practical in actual raids, due to efficient AAAIS and observers' reports from the Group Headquarters OP.

m. The Spitfires, due to a small oxygen capacity, could not operate for long periods at altitudes where oxygen was needed, so for them the gunfire ceiling was set at 10,000 feet until an attack warning was received, when it was immediately lifted and the fighters climbed above it.

Section V

Study Of Evasive Action

150. a. In order to overcome a noticeable tendency in antiaircraft gun firing for the bursts to lag behind the targets, an intensive study to analyze the evasive tactics used by the enemy was initiated in Oct 1944, under the supervision of the 14th AA Command. The heavy enemy air action at Leyte had indicated that evasive action was resorted to immediately after the first bursts appeared. This evasive action followed a pattern. To obtain the necessary statistical information and to formulate procedures for increasing the accuracy of fire under these conditions an Evasive Action Research team was organized.

b. This team began operation on Leyte in Nov 1944. Data on 40 raids was recorded by 16-mm cameras and special recording devices designed and constructed by the team. Calculations of the courses showed that acceleration of Japanese aircraft after the opening of antiaircraft fire caused burst lags of approximately 40 yards on the later bursts. To compensate for this sudden acceleration the M-9 director was modified to permit introduction of a percentage prediction spot. This modification was installed on a limited number of directors.

c. Plans were made for continuing the study begun at Leyte to cover future operations. The Evasive Action Research Team was increased to enable the section to gather more data. New recording equipment was designed and built. The team landed at Lingayen Gulf on Luzon in Jan 1945 but the absence of enemy air activity precluded obtaining additional data.

d. The team arrived at Manila in May, where statistics from the Leyte courses were reanalyzed and a standard procedure for the analysis of data was developed.[1] Another modification to the M-9 director to compute for random evasive action of targets was designed.[2]

---

[1] Report: Standard Operating Procedure of Calculation and Analysis of Evasive Action Data, Hq 14th AA Command, undated.

[2] Report: Modification of M-9 Director to give Prediction on Curved Courses of Enemy Targets, Hq 14th AA Command, 3 Sept 1945.

e. In order to test theoretically the effectiveness of the modifications, six evasive action courses of the enemy were chosen at random from the recorded courses actually flown at Leyte. The amount of deviation of the burst from the target due to evasive action was computed for straight line prediction, X-Y sweep and X-Y-H (helical) sweep. The result of the computations indicated that if X-Y sweep and helical sweep had been used during those six courses the probabilities of obtaining hits would have been 118% to 308% greater than by straight line prediction.

f. Early in Nov 1944, at Morotai, a separate study was made of the evasive action tactics of Japanese aircraft.[1] Analysis was made of data which had been recorded during a considerable number of raids prior to the start of the study. No consistency in type of evasive action taken could be determined although most frequently there was a sharp dive, usually with increased power and with a turn to either side, occasionally varied by a straight ahead, wavy course directly across the defended area.

g. In an effort to determine the effectiveness of different type spot connections, a B-25 was used to make test runs following courses patterned after the observed enemy courses. During the test, careful plots were made of the various time-positions of the target (determined by radar), and of the projected points of burst, based upon firing data in which spot corrections had been placed as the battery simulated action. Unfortunately, only one test was made, however this test did corroborate observations that effective fire would have been delivered against the target plane well in advance of the bomb release line while the plane was still flying on a straight course.

h. Other organizations in combat positions experimented with various spot corrections, with varying success, in an effort to deliver more effective fire against the enemy during evasive action.

---

[1] Report: Evasive Action studies at Morotai, CO, 214th AAA Group, 6 Nov 1945.

Section VI

Ground Target Location and Survey

By Gun Radar - Liaison Plane Team

151. a. The use of antiaircraft artillery in a terrestrial role in support of the field artillery at Morotai, Netherlands East Indies, in Nov 1944 prompted a study of the use of the gun radar, SCR-584, as a means of quickly and accurately locating ground targets for the fire of antiaircraft guns. The plan called for the use of a field artillery liaison plane as a radar target to locate targets on the ground for artillery fire.

b. For the first experiment a radio SCR-610 was placed at the radar to communicate directly with the liaison plane. The plane was sent on a "target hunting" mission, flying at a low altitude over thick rain forest north of the Morotai location. Upon sighting a target the observer in the plane transmitted a warning on the radio and, as he approached the target, called for radar position readings by calling, "Ready, ready, ready, take," the "ready's" at about five second intervals, the "take" when the plane was directly over the target. At the word "take" the range to the target plane was read at the radar and azimuth and angle of elevation at the director. Azimuth was applied directly to the guns, using the azimuth clock, and the range, quickly converted to angle of elevation by use of firing tables, was applied with the gunners quadrant and almost immediately a round (PD fuze) was on the way. Single shots fired at three different targets fell close enough for fire for effect to be opened without further adjustment. In the case of the fourth, at extreme range, the initial round was spotted as 200 yards left and 100 yards over. Adjustment was made and the second round was a direct hit.

c. The results of the initial experiment were so successful that further trials were made to determine the suitability of this method for locating targets for the field artillery weapons. Readings from the radar were plotted on a map in the fire direction center of the antiaircraft battalion, and the coordinates of the target relayed to the field artillery battalion. Results of the field artillery firing, using this procedure, were also highly satisfactory.

d. In order to reduce the time for field artillery survey, a test was made using the SCR-584's and liaison plane for locating prominent points in the area outside the perimeter of Morotai which had not been previously mapped. The results of this mission are best told in the words of the field artillery battalion's report on the subject.[1]

e. (1) "A test survey was conducted by the 116th FA Bn in conjunction with the 528th AAA Gun Bn under actual combat conditions. The area surveyed was the complete zone of action of the 116th FA Bn in direct support of the 155th Inf. Although only one radar is necessary, two SCR-584 radars, 6,140 yards apart, were used for a double check. Readings were made at precisely the same moment but entirely independent of each other and polar plots of the data were made separately but on the same chart. Both stations were tied into the battalion orienting line by ground survey. After the necessary prearrangements were made the whole survey was completed in one hour and forty-five minutes flying time. Thirty-eight points were accurately located, none of which were shown on existing maps. Of these points, the battalion had previously adjusted on five, the others were road or trail crossings and junctions, stream forks, prominent trees, small clearing or other prominent features for future use as check points or reference points for the air observer.

(2) In the Battalion Fire Direction Center plotting was done simultaneously with the survey. Being on a common radio channel it was an easy matter to get the target description and the radar readings as they were made. The HCO handled them as replots and by the time the plane landed the points had all been plotted.

(3) It is interesting to note the time factors involved. This survey was made in one hour and forty-five minutes. By conservative estimate the same survey, if allowed by the enemy, would involve several months work by all of the survey personnel of a light battalion. Of course, a carefully conducted shot-in survey would have accomplished the same results, but would involve a much longer period of time and a considerable expenditure of ammunition.

(4) A check on the accuracy of the survey and a comparison of radar data to fired-in data proved more than satisfactory. A check between the relationship of the radar plot and the fire-in plot revealed that had radar been used for initial data, effective fire could have been placed on the target without adjustment. As for the other points of the survey, the fact that each point was polar plotted first with the data from one radar and then with the data of the other and that the two points with but two exceptions fell within a hundred yard circle seems to be conclusive proof of their accuracy."

---

[1] Narrative Report of Experiments AA Radar with Field Artillery Plane AARO 413.68 116th FA Bn made to CG, 14th AA Command 9 Dec 1944.

f. Realizing that there might be real danger to the plane and its pilot if he were to fly over all targets just above the tree-top height, or that he might give away to the enemy the fact that his position was located, experiments were made to determine the efficiency of checking positions with the plane flying several thousand feet above the target. As it was appreciated that the pilot's ability to determine when he was directly over the target would be very much less accurate under those circumstances, the pilot was directed to fly across the target at least three times from different directions, in each case reporting when he thought he was directly over the target. The same method of announcing positions was used as in the low flying case.

g. Two methods of recording positions were used in these experiments. In one method, readings were taken by single radar at a time indicated by the pilot. In the other method, two radars tracked the plane and both made records at approximately ten second intervals without command; the intersection of the plotted courses located the target. With either method the reading, corrected to horizontal range by application of the observed angle of elevation, was plotted. If an exact point was not located by the plotted "takes" or by the intersection of plotted courses, the center of the resulting small enclosed area was taken for the target point.

h. The question whether the use of slant range for the firing range would introduce serious range error was answered by the field artillery with a table which showed that in tracking a plane at 1000 and 2000 feet altitude, and at ranges out to 7000 yards, the difference between slant and the horizontal range varied from only eight to 73 yards, which could ordinarily be overlooked in field artillery firing. In cases when the plane had to fly at altitudes beyond 2,000 feet, particularly at short horizontal ranges, the correction could be made quickly by applying the angle of elevation and slant range to a graph to obtain the horizontal range. In tests conducted on ten different targets at varying ranges, it was determined by the study of the data obtained that an air observer could get a quick and accurate initial round without reference to a map of any sort.

i. Based on the results obtained in the field artillery survey, additional tests were conducted in surveying-in the elements of the antiaircraft defense. The liaison plane made six runs over two gun batteries, each gun battery radar reading on the plane while over the other battery. The gun director scope of the latter battery was placed at maximum elevation to check the position of the plane at the moment of reading. Variations in readings from one radar did not exceed one mil in azimuth and ten yards in range on four of the six readings by that radar. The data at the other radar showed a wider deviation, apparently due to the liaison plane being forced to make very sharp turns after crossing the battery. Traffic from a nearby airstrip was the cause and the result was a tendency to start the turn before actually crossing the battery. Using the mean of the more accurate set of readings, a trial shot problem was fired by each battery, with results considered excellent. A ground survey was run to compare the data and determine the accuracy of the radar plane method. The resulting error was found to be so small that it might have arisen in either method of surveying.

    j. Following distribution of reports on these tests gun battalions throughout the theater familiarized themselves with the procedure as rapidly as the necessary liaison planes could be arranged for, and the method received practical use on Okinawa.

Section VII

Moving Target Indicator

152. a. Following the design of the "Moving Target Indicator" modification to the SCR-584, and preliminary tests in the United States, the components of this equipment were shipped to Oahu in Jun 1945, with experts and trained personnel to continue experimentation.

b. After successful tests, in which the Hawaiian AA Command and the Navy participated, the equipment and personnel were sent to Luzon, where provision was made, in Aug, for additional tests at the AA Training Center at San Marcelino. Tests and experiments were continued by the Research Committee of the 14th AA Command.[1]

c. The results of the tests at Luzon bore out, in general, the conclusions reached at Oahu. In one respect, however, the modified MTI equipment exceeded its original expectations. The standard MTI equipment set-up affected only the PPI, and not the auto-track circuits of the SCR-584; the set could not track a target any better than a standard SCR-584 when ground clutter was present. However, one set was modified at San Marcelino so that the MTI equipment affected all circuits (PPI, range and auto track) of the SCR-584 with the result that the set would not only detect targets in bad ground clutter, but would automatically track them through the clutter as well.

d. Standard procedures for operation, alignment, and maintenance of the MTI equipment were laid down, in preparation for use of the equipment in the invasion of Japan. The termination of the war in Aug removed the need for the equipment, although the experiments and tests continued into the fall of 1945. In general, the objective of moving target indication was achieved.

---

[1] Training Circular Number 19 Employment of SCR-584 for the Detection of Ground Targets Hq 14th AA Command 19 Oct 1945.

Section VIII

Radar Mortar Location

153. a. Detailed information of the work done in the European Theater of Operations and the United States on the location of mortar positions by radar reached the Pacific theater in Apr 1945. During that month Btries A and B, 163d AAA Gun Bn were engaged in supporting the 33d Div's drive into Baguio. European reports stressed the efficiency of the SCR-584 in locating enemy mortars and artillery pieces by the tracking and plotting of their projectile's trajectory. Btry A was directed to bring its radar forward up the Villa Verde Trail. Considerable difficulty was experienced in moving the radar along the narrow, muddy, hairpin trail. The final location employed, while the best available, was hampered by fixed echoes, by too close proximity to the enemy lines, and by the enemy shelling, intermittent during the day and constant at night. Nevertheless the radar did succeed in locating one enemy gun and narrowed the many suspected sectors of fire to three.[1]

b. After this combat test, a coordinated program of research and development was started in May. The G-3 Research Section, 14th AA Command, undertook the project of studying radar mortar location and developing accessories and techniques suitable for use with the available radar equipment. The immediate objective was to facilitate the training of selected antiaircraft artillery units in this work.

c. Although experiments had been made with various radar sets and methods, effort was concentrated on modifying the SCR-584. Experiments indicated that automatic plotting methods of recording data gave the greatest accuracy in determining the mortar location. Several automatic plotters were developed and gave good results. The Evasive Action Research Team designed and constructed six mortar-shell trajectory plotting boards. These were field tested and with a few modifications were found to give results comparable to the IBM Plotter which was shipped to the theater at the conclusion of the war.

d. Early in July the Sixth Army, preparing for operations in Japan, requested that a radar mortar location detachment be attached to it for operations during the projected offensive. A detachment was organized, equipped, and trained at the Antiaircraft Training Center at

---

[1] Unit History 163d AAA Gun Bn.

San Marcelino, Luzon. Standard operating procedures were developed, automatic plotters were constructed, and the results in tests were regarded, in general, as highly satisfactory. However, the termination of the war with Japan ended the requirement for the detachment and precluded service use of the equipment and methods.

6. STATISTICAL Summaries

Section I
Section II

Section I

Operations

154. <u>General</u>. a. The following paragraphs consist of charts, tables, and graphs that present the available data on antiaircraft operations. They have been compiled from unit histories, after-action reports, and daily combat operation reports. In many cases the hazards of combat caused the loss of important files and records. Most of the figures given for the Philippine Defense Campaign have been prepared from diaries written by participants during internment as prisoners of war, since the original records were destroyed on Bataan and Corregidor. Where figures from various sources have not agreed, a careful attempt has been made to evaluate all possible relevant information to determine relative credibility.

b. The figures for planes destroyed, probably destroyed, and damaged are based upon official credits given by proper authorized sources and not upon claims however valid they may seem. Consequently, it is felt that the total results of antiaircraft fire as given are conservative and represent a minimum figure.

155. <u>Effect of Antiaircraft Fire on Planes Engaged</u>.

EFFECT OF AA FIRE ON PLANES ENGAGED

Campaign	Destroyed, Probably Destroyed & Damaged
PHILIPPINE DEFENSE	12%
CENTRAL PACIFIC	4%
EAST INDIES	13%
PAPUA	8%
GUADALCANAL	35%
NEW GUINEA	11%
NORTHERN SOLOMONS	19%
EASTERN MANDATES	33%
BISMARCK ARCHIPELAGO	6%
WESTERN PACIFIC	38%
SOUTHERN PHILIPPINES	34%
LUZON	32%
RYUKYUS	69%

156. Antiaircraft Artillery Action by Campaigns.

CAMPAIGNS	NUMBER PLANES	ENEMY TYPE OF FIGHTER	ENEMY TYPE OF BOMBER	TARGET UNKNOWN	AIR ALT. OF ATTACK (THOUSANDS OF FT.) 0-3	3-10	10-20	20-UP	UNKNOWN	FIRE HELD	A.A.A. TARGETS DAY	NIGHT	ENGAGED SEEN	UNSEEN	ACTION RESULTS DEST.	PROB.	DAMAGED
1. Philippine Defense Total	2076	unk	1620	unk	unk	200	350	1008	518	-	1960	116	-	-	173	21	66
2. Central Pacific																	
Pearl Harbor	53	7	21	No Data	Data	41	0	0	2	1	9	44	-	-	2	0	0
Makin				25	10										0	2	0
3. East Indies																	
Darwin	238	91	147	0	18	0	0	220	0	-	0	18	18	0	2	1	0
Port Moresby	506	160	113	233	47	0	173	53	233	191	65	0	65	0	10	0	0
Horn Island	16	0	16	0	0	0	0	16	0	-	16	0	16	0	0	0	0
Total	760	251	276	233	65	0	173	289	233	191	81	18	99	0	12	1	0
4. Papuan																	
Townsville	4	0	4	0	0	0	0	0	4	0	0	4	4	0	0	0	0
Darwin	155	32	107	16	1	2	6	142	4	-	-	-	-	1	0	0	0
Port Moresby	181	37	35	109	47	0	18	7	109	unk	42	11	53	1	5	5	0
Milne Bay	69	23	46	0	44	0	0	0	25	unk	44	0	44	0	3	1	3
Merauke	21	1	20	0	1	10	0	10	0	0	11	0	11	0	0	0	0
Dobadura	*22	17	5	unk	22	0	0	0	0	0	22	0	22	0	0	0	0
Popondetta	37	17	20	0	0	0	35	2	0	0	0	0	0	0	0	0	0
Oro Bay	8	0	8	0	0	8	0	0	0	0	8	0	8	0	0	0	0
Total	497	127	245	125	115	20	59	161	142	0	127	15	142	0	8	1	3
5. Guadalcanal																	
Guadalcanal	220	0	95	125	9	0	17	65	129	120	3	73	5	71	14	8	6
New Hebrides	10	1	2	7	0	0	1	0	9	2	0	5	0	5	0	0	0
Total	230	1	97	132	9	0	18	65	138	122	3	78	5	76	14	8	6
6. New Guinea																	
Port Moresby	145	76	12	57	13	0	16	44	72	unk	14	38	22	30	4	0	0
Milne Bay	76	30	46	0	0	3	76	0	0	0	76	0	76	0	0	0	0
Oro Bay	250	73	107	70	40	12	136	1	61	0	38	151	154	35	7	0	0
Dobadura	97	17	19	61	4	22	0	18	53	1	22	31	22	31	1	1	1
Bulolo-Wau	40	11	29	0	2	33	0	0	0	0	40	0	40	0	0	0	0
Goodenough	32	0	2	30	0	0	4	0	28	0	0	32	4	28	0	0	0
Kiriwina	44	0	32	12	0	6	16	21	1	1	0	43	0	43	1	1	1
Woodlark	1	0	1	0	1	0	0	0	0	0	0	0	0	0	0	0	0
Morobe	7	4	3	0	0	2	4	0	1	1	0	2	0	2	0	0	0
Nassau Bay	1	0	1	0	0	1	0	0	0	0	1	0	1	0	0	0	0
Lae	34	6	12	16	1	0	27	6	0	0	18	0	18	0	0	0	0
Merauke	16	0	0	16	0	0	0	0	16	10	16	0	16	0	0	0	0

- 217 -

CAMPAIGNS	NUMBER PLANES	ENEMY TYPE OF TARGET			AIR ATTACKS ALT OF ATTACK (THOUSANDS OF FT)					FIRE HELD	A.A. TARGETS ENGAGED				ACTION RESULTS		
		FIGHTER	BOMBER	UNKNOWN	0-3	3-10	10-20	20-UP	UNKNOWN		DAY	NIGHT	SEEN	UNSEEN	DEST.	PROB.	DAMAGED
Finschhafen	32	7	17	8	3	5	15	0	9	1	6	0	6	1	0	0	0
Tambu Bay	8	0	2	6	0	0	4	0	2	1	0	2	2	0	3	0	0
Garoke (Bena Bena)	24	6	18	0	24	0	0	0	0	1	0	0	0	0	0	0	0
Tsili Tsili	37	26	11	0	6	31	0	0	0	0	37	0	37	0	0	0	0
Nadzab	48	9	20	19	9	0	7	29	3	1	0	7	7	0	0	2	0
Gusap	66	30	13	23	15	28	0	0	23	3	33	0	33	0	0	2	1
Saidor	52	13	25	14	4	32	5	0	11	3	17	29	17	29	0	0	0
Hollandia	5	0	5	0	1	1	0	0	0	3	0	5	2	3	0	0	0
Aitape	1	0	1	0	0	0	0	0	0	0	0	0	0	0	0	1	0
Wakde	16	0	11	5	3	6	2	0	2	2	0	11	4	10	0	7	0
Biak	124	45	44	35	45	18	17	3	32	2	45	51	42	54	24	7	10
Noemfoor	13	1	9	3	4	6	1	12	2	2	0	13	3	10	2	1	1
Sansapor	23	4	15	4	0	12	2	0	9	6	0	23	1	23	3	0	0
Morotai	179	37	107	35	55	17	63	42	2	13	24	141	56	109	17	7	12
Total	1371	396	561	414	234	238	396	176	327	45	388	584	567	405	62	22	25
7. Northern Solomons																	
Russell Islands	1	0	1	0	0	0	1	0	0	0	0	1	0	1	1	0	0
New Georgia Group	28	7	21	0	2	2	6	18	0	7	0	21	0	21	2	2	0
Treasury Islands	145	0	0	145	0	0	0	0	145	unk	0	77	77	0	8	4	0
Bougainville	37	7	11	19	2	11	0	0	24	4	19	18	19	18	4½	4	1
Total	*211	14	33	164	4	13	7	18	169	11	19	117	96	40	15½	10	1
8. Eastern Mandates																	
Eniwetok Total	9	0	8	1	0	0	1	0	8	-	0	3	3	0	0	1	0
9. Bismarck Archipelago																	
Arawe	214	65	12	137	6	14	3	0	191	-	110	49	112	47	7	2	0
Cape Gloucester		Unknown	Unknown			Unknown						Unknown			Unknown		
Admiralty Islands	9	4	3	2	6	0	1	0	2	0	2	5	5	2	0	1	0
Green Island	11	0	0	11	4	0	0	0	7	0	0	4	0	4	0	0	0
Total	234	69	15	150	16	14	4	0	200	0	112	58	117	53	7	3	0
10. Western Pacific																	
Saipan	79	37	22	20	25	0	28	19	7	0	27	52	26	53	27	1	1
Angaur	4	0	0	4	2	0	0	2	0	0	0	4	0	4	0	0	0
Iwo Jima	12	0	4	8	3	0	3	1	5	0	0	12	3	9	2	2	1
Total	95	37	26	32	30	0	31	22	12	0	27	68	29	66	29	3	2
11. Southern Philippines																	
Leyte – Samar	1278	374	242	662	406	286	133	81	372	52	908	318	414	812	251	113	151

- 218 -

		ENEMY AIR ATTACKS								A.A.A. ACTION							
	NUMBER PLANES	TYPE OF PLANES		TARGET		ALT. OF ATTACK (THOUSANDS OF FT)					FIRE HELD	TARGETS		ENGAGED		RESULTS		
		FIGHTER	BOMBER	UNKNOWN	0-3	3-10	10-20	20-UP	UNKNOWN			DAY	NIGHT	SEEN	UNSEEN	DEST.	PROB.	DAMAGED
Mindoro	145	40	94	11	44	33	0	0	68	11	23	111	20	114	55½	4	15
Palawan	5	1	3	1	2	3	0	0	0	0	0	0	3	0	0	0	0
Zamboanga	2	1	0	1	1	0	0	0	1	0	1	0	1	0	0	0	1
Panay	1	No Action			1	No Action				No Action	Action				0	0	0
Cebu - Negros	1	1	0	0	1	0	0	0	0	0	0	0	0	0	0	0	0
Total	1431	417	339	675	454	322	133	81	441	63	932	432	438	926	306½	117	167
12. Luzon Total	31	9	15	7	11	16	0	0	4	3	16	15	16	15	6	0	4
13. Ryukyus																	
Okinawa	344	30	56	258	43	42	34	20	205	45	20	143	20	143	78	18	34
Ie Shima	*153	9	8	136	17	20	17	6	93	7	24	122	24	122	50	5	28
Total	497	39	64	394	60	62	51	26	298	52	44	265	44	265	128	23	62
Grand Total	7495	1367	3320	2352*	1008*	926	1223	1846	2492	488	3718	1813	1556	1846	921	212	336
							*A		Incomplete Data Morotai		Add credit to Fighter St. Team				4	2	0
							*B		Cape Gloucester		No Data Available						

Total Attacks 7495

Not Engaged
  Out of Range 744
  Hold Fire 488
  Unknown Reasons 732
    1964

Engaged 5531

Results:
  Planes Destroyed 921
  Planes Prob. Dest. 212
  Planes Damaged 336
    1469

157. Antiaircraft Action by Units.

UNIT	ENEMY AIR ATTACKS			ALT. OF ATTACK (THOUSANDS OF FT.)						FIRE HELD	A.A.A. TARGETS			ENGAGED		ACTION RESULTS		
	NUMBER PLANES	TYPE OF FIGHTER	BOMBER	UNKNOWN	0-3	3-10	10-20	20-UP	UNKNOWN		DAY	NIGHT	SEEN	UNSEEN	DEST.	PROB.	DAMAGED
70th AAA Gun Bn																	
Guadalcanal	45	2	13	30	3	0	4	4	34	10	0	34	0	34	0	0	0
New Georgia	28	7	21	0	1	2	6	19	0	7	0	21	0	21	1	1	0
Bougainville	26	0	24	2	0	3	6	4	13	5	12	3	3	12	3½	4	1
Luzon	22	4	15	3	5	16	0	0	1	0	5	17	2	20	0	0	0
	121	13	73	35	9	21	16	27	48	22	17	75	5	87	4½	5	1
76th AAA Gun Bn																	
New Georgia	9	0	9	0	0	0	0	9	0	0	0	8	0	8	0	0	0
Espiritu Santo	10	1	2	7	0	0	1	0	9	2	0	5	0	5	0	0	0
Admiralty Island	2	0	2	0	0	0	0	0	2	0	0	0	0	0	0	0	0
	21	1	13	7	0	0	1	9	11	2	0	13	0	13	0	0	0
777th AAA Gun Bn																	
Espiritu Santo	2	0	0	2	0	0	0	0	2	0	0	0	0	0	0	0	0
New Georgia	6	0	0	6	0	0	0	0	6	0	0	5	0	5	1	1	0
	8	0	0	8	0	0	0	0	8	0	0	5	0	5	1	1	0
93d AAA Gun Bn																	
Apamama Atoll		No	Action														
Ie Shima	138	10	6	121	0	0	0	0	138	---	Engaged		138		36 1/3	4	26
	138	10	6	121	0	0	0	0	138	---					36 1/3	4	26
98th AAA Gun Bn																	
Eniwetok	9	1	8	0	2	0	0	0	7	0	0	2	0	2	0	1	0
Makin	53	7	21	25	0	44	7	0	2	1	9	43	4	48	0	2	0
Okinawa	18	0	0	18	0	0	0	0	18	---	Engaged		18		0	0	1
	80	8	29	43	2	44	7	0	27	1	27	45	4	50	0	3	1
100th AAA Gun Bn																	
Finschhafen		No	Action														
161st AAA Gun Bn																	
Nadzab		No	Action														
Luzon	17	4	5	8	5	2	10	0	0	0	0	17	0	17	1½	0	1
	17	4	5	8	5	2	10	0	0	0	0	17	0	17	1½	0	1

UNIT	NUMBER PLANES	TYPE OF			ALT. OF ATTACK (THOUSANDS OF FT)					FIRE HELD	TARGETS ENGAGED				RESULTS		
		FIGHTER	BOMBER	UNKNOWN	0-3	3-10	10-20	20-UP	UNKNOWN		DAY	NIGHT	SEEN	UNSEEN	DEST.	PROB.	DAMAGED
163d AAA Gun Bn																	
Goodenough	28	0	0	28	0	0	0	0	28	0	0	28	0	28	0	0	0
Woodlark				No Action													
Hollandia	5	0	5	0	2	1	0	0	2	0	0	4	0	4	0	0	0
	33	0	5	28	2	1	0	0	30	0	0	32	0	32	0	0	0
164th AAA Gun Bn																	
Russell Island	1	0	1	0	0	0	1	0	0	0	0	1	0	1	1	0	0
165th AAA Gun Bn																	
Biak	124	45	44	35	45	18	17	12	32	2	45	51	61	35	7	3	3
Hollandia	3	0	3	0	1	2	0	0	0	0	0	3	0	3	0	0	0
	127	45	47	35	46	20	17	12	32	2	45	54	61	38	7	3	3
166th AAA Gun Bn																	
Finschhafen				No Action													
Hollandia	5	0	5	0	0	2	0	0	3	0	0	4	0	4	0	0	0
Wakde	16	0	11	5	3	6	2	3	2	2	0	14	4	10	0	1	0
Leyte	9	6	3	0	4	5	0	0	0	0	5	4	3	6	2	0	0
Mindoro	145	40	94	11	44	33	42	0	26	11	23	111	32	102	26	2	5
Palawan	5	1	3	1	2	5	0	0	0	0	0	1	0	1	0	0	0
Malabang				No Action													
Zamboanga	2	1	0	1	1	0	0	0	1	0	1	0	1	0	0	0	1½
	182	48	116	18	54	49	44	3	32	13	29	134	40	123	28	3	5½
168th AAA Gun Bn																	
Admiralty Islands	7	4	3	0	6	0	1	0	0	0	1	2	3	0	0	0	0
Leyte	511	83	77	351	143	182	143	39	4	8	180	323	183	320	28½	4	4
	518	87	80	351	149	182	144	39	4	8	181	325	186	320	28½	4	4
496th AAA Gun Bn																	
Sansapor	23	4	15	4	3	12	2	0	6	6	0	17	0	17	3	0	1
497th AAA Gun Bn																	
Guadalcanal				No Action													

UNIT	ENEMY AIR ATTACKS									A.A.A.					ACTION RESULTS		
	NUMBER PLANES	TYPE OF PLANES FIGHTER	TYPE OF PLANES BOMBER	TARGET UNKNOWN	ALT. OF ATTACK (THOUSANDS OF FT.) 0-3	3-10	10-20	20-UP	UNKNOWN	FIRE HELD	TARGETS DAY	TARGETS NIGHT	ENGAGED SEEN	ENGAGED UNSEEN	DEST.	PROB.	DAMAGED
501st AAA Gun Bn Saipan	67	29	18	20	25	0	19	16	7	0	27	40	26	41	2 1/3	0	0
502d AAA Gun Bn Leyte	428	65	41	322	61	26	180	10	151	18	39	369	108	300	36½	26	14
Okinawa	200	3	1	196	0	0	0	0	200	---	Engaged		186		8½	1	3
	628	68	42	518	61	26	180	10	351	18					45	27	17
503d AAA Gun Bn Okinawa	14	0	2	12	3	0	4	2	5	0	0	14	0	14	2	0	0
504th AAA Gun Bn Leyte	184	56	15	113	18	64	38	15	49	0	56	128	15	169	14	20	9
Okinawa	172	0	0	172	0	86	0	0	86	0	4	168	18	154	13½	5	3
	356	56	15	285	18	150	38	15	135	0	60	296	33	323	27½	25	12
505th AAA Gun Bn Kerama Retto	3	0	0	3	0	0	0	0	3	0	0	3	0	3	1	0	1
506th AAA Gun Bn Two Jima	12	7	5	0	3	0	0	5	4	0	0	7	0	7	1	2	0
507th AAA Gun Bn Luzon				No Action													
508th AAA Gun Bn Luzon	2	0	0	2	0	0	0	0	2	2	0	0	0	0	0	0	0
510th AAA Gun Bn Samar				No Action													
518th AAA Gun Bn Luzon				No Action													

UNIT	NUMBER OF PLANES	ENEMY TYPE FIGHTER	ENEMY TYPE BOMBER	TARGET UNKNOWN	AIR ATTACKS ALT OF ATTACK (THOUSANDS OF FT.) 0-3	3-10	10-20	20-UP	UNKNOWN	FIRE HELD	TARGETS DAY	TARGETS NIGHT	A.A.A. ENGAGED SEEN	NUMBER	ACTION RESULTS DEST.	PROB.	DAMAGED
528th AAA Gun Bn																	
Guadalcanal	218	8	110	100	2	0	11	53	152	109	3	73	5	71	11	8	6
Morotai	139	38	96	5	24	19	61	22	13	13	16	67	20	60	3	1	3¾
	357	46	206	105	26	9	72	75	165	122	19	140	25	131	14	9	9¾
734th AAA Gun Bn																	
Luzon			No	Action													
736th AAA Gun Bn																	
Treasury Island	145	0	0	145	0	0	0	0	145	-	0	77	-	-	7	3	0
737th AAA Gun Bn																	
Emirau			No	Action													
Luzon			No	Action													
738th AAA Gun Bn																	
Saipan	67	29	18	20	25	0	19	16	7	0	-	-	-	-	3 1/3	0	0
741st AAA Gun Bn																	
Milne Bay			No	Action								Unknown					
Kiriwina	44	0	32	12	0	6	16	21	1	-					0	0	0
Arawe	145	65	12	68	30	0	48	0	67	-	30	48	30	48	1	0	0
	189	65	44	80	30	6	64	21	68	-	-	-	-	-	1	0	0
742d AAA Gun Bn																	
Espiritu Santo			No	Action													
Cape Gloucester			No	Action													
743d AAA Gun Bn																	
Kiriwina	44	0	32	12	0	6	16	21	1	0	1	43	1	43	0	1	0
Port Moresby	145	76	12	57	13	0	16	44	72	-	12	22	14	20	2	0	0
	52	13	25	14	4	32	5	0	11	3	17	29	17	29	0	0	0
Saidor	241	89	69	83	17	38	37	65	84	3	30	94	32	92	2	1	0

- 223 -

UNIT	ENEMY AIR ATTACKS							FIRE HELD	A.A.A. TARGETS		ENGAGED		ACTION RESULTS		
	NUMBER PLANES	TYPE OF FIGHTER	TYPE OF BOMBER	TARGET UNKNOWN	ALT. OF ATTACK (THOUSANDS OF FT.) 0-3	3-10	10-20	20-UP	UNKNOWN		DAY	NIGHT	SEEN	UNSEEN	DEST.	PROB.	DAMAGED

UNIT	PLANES	FIGHTER	BOMBER	UNKNOWN	0-3	3-10	10-20	20-UP	UNKNOWN	FIRE HELD	DAY	NIGHT	SEEN	UNSEEN	DEST.	PROB.	DAMAGED
744th AAA Gun Bn																	
Freemantle				No Action													
Townsville				No Action													
Cape York				No Action													
Milne Bay				No Action													
Finschhafen	23	12	11	0	6	10	0	0	7	0	0	23	0	23	0	0	0
Nadzab				No Action													
Morotai	126	12	31	83	24	17	38	36	11	13	8	105	30	83	5	2	3
	149	24	42	83	30	27	38	36	18	13	8	128	30	106	5	2	3
745th AAA Gun Bn																	
Townsville	4	0	4	0	0	0	4	0	0	1	0	1	1	0	0	0	0
Port Moresby	118	78	40	0	0	0	10	107	1	-	14	38	22	30	2	0	0
Dobodura	31	0	24	7	0	0	10	21	0	0	0	31	0	31	1	0	1
Oro Bay	233	73	107	53	70	40	12	2	109	-	35	140	138	37	2	0	0
Noemfoor	10	1	9	0	2	6	0	0	2	0	0	10	0	10	1	0	0
	396	152	184	60	72	46	36	130	112	1	49	220	161	108	6	0	1
746th AAA Gun Bn																	
Fiji Islands				No Action													
Bougainville	37	7	11	19	0	11	0	0	26	3	19	18	19	18	0	0	0
Cebu	1	1	0	0	1	0	0	0	0	0	0	0	0	0	0	0	0
751st AAA Gun Bn																	
Guam				No Action													
Saipan	79	37	22	20	25	0	28	19	7	0	27	52	26	53	5	1	0
Ulithi				No Action													
752d AAA Gun Bn																	
Iwo Jima (120mm)	12	0	7	5	3	0	0	5	4	0	0	5	0	5	0	0	0
753d AAA Gun Bn																	
Kwajalein				No Action													
Apamama				No Action													

UNIT	ENEMY AIR ATTACKS								A.A.A. ACTION						
	NUMBER OF PLANES			TYPE OF TARGET UNKNOWN	ALT. OF ATTACK (THOUSANDS OF FT.)				FIRE HELD	TARGETS ENGAGED			RESULTS		
	FIGHTER	BOMBER			0-3	3-10	10-20	20-UP	UNKNOWN		DAY	NIGHT	SEEN	UNSEEN	DEST.	PROB.	DAMAGED
940th AAA Gun Bn Okinawa			No Action													
947th AAA Gun Bn Iwo Jima	12	0	7	5	3	0	0	5	4		Unknown				0	0	0
948th AAA Gun Bn Ie Shima			Unknown			No Data									2	1	1
967th AAA Gun Bn Guadalcanal			No Action														
Green Island	0	0	0	9	1	0	0	0	8	0	0	2	0	2	0	0	0
Leyte	9		No Action														
Marines (Okinawa)																	
16th AAA Bn			No Data												11	4½	13½
2d AAA Bn			No Data												9	2½	6½
8th AAA Bn			No Data												7	1	2
5th AAA Bn			No Data												1	0	0
Undetermined Credits			No Information														
Okinawa	-	-	-	-	-	-	-	-	-	-	-	-	-	-	2	1	0
Saipan	-	-	-	-	-	-	-	-	-	-	-	-	-	-	12	0	1
	-	-	-	-	-	-	-	-	-	-	-	-	-	-	14	1	1
55th CA (AA) (155-mm) Pearl Harbor			Unknown												2	0	0
200th CA (AA) Luzon			Unknown												51	2	0
515th CA (AA) Luzon			Unknown												35	0	0
Harbor Defenses – Manila	59th CA (HD)		60th CA (AA)					91st CA (PS)			Unknown				87	19	66

- 225 -

UNIT	ENEMY AIR ATTACKS									A.A.A. ACTION						
	NUMBER PLANES	TYPE OF PLANES			ALT. OF ATTACK (THOUSANDS OF FT.)					FIRE HELD	TARGETS		ENGAGED		RESULTS	
		FIGHTER	BOMBER	UNKNOWN	0-3	3-10	10-20	20-UP	UNKNOWN		DAY	NIGHT	SEEN	UNSEEN	DEST.	PROB.	DAMAGED

UNIT	NUMBER PLANES	FIGHTER	BOMBER	UNKNOWN	0-3	3-10	10-20	20-UP	UNKNOWN	FIRE HELD	DAY	NIGHT	SEEN	UNSEEN	DEST.	PROB.	DAMAGED
7th AAA AW Bn																	
Guam				No Action													
Leyte	90	76	13	1	90	0	0	0	0	2	89	1	90	0	9	1	20
Kerama Retto				No Action													
Ie Shima	138	10	7	121	0	0	0	0	138		Engaged		138		9 1/3	0	1
	228	86	20	122	90	0	0	0	138						18 1/3	1	21
101st AAA AW Bn																	
Port Moresby	475	276	162	37	101	0	10	104	260	-	107	0	107	0	15	0	0
Milne Bay	63	27	25	11	36	2	0	25	0	0	38	0	38	0	2	1	3
Nadzab	7	7	0	0	7	0	0	0	0	0	6	1	7	0	0	0	0
Luzon			No Data														
	545	310	187	48	144	2	10	129	260	0	151	1	152	0	17	1	3
102d AAA AW Bn																	
Darwin	434	125	309	0	4	2	60	368	0	0	0	18	18	0	2	1	0
Lae	34	6	12	16	1	0	18	0	15	10	18	0	18	0	0	0	0
Oro Bay	14	0	14	0	14	0	0	0	0	0	14	0	14	0	3	0	0
Nadzab	3	3	0	0	3	0	0	0	0	0	3	0	3	0	0	0	0
Finschhafen	19	7	12	0	3	5	10	0	1	-	3	0	3	0	0	0	0
Gusap	64	26	38	0	8	32	14	0	10	0	45	0	45	0	0	0	1
Leyte	63	10	35	18	63	0	0	0	0	4	13	50	63	0	4	5	5
Mindoro	63	14	44	5	37	13	0	0	13	3	16	44	51	9	4½	0	3
Luzon			No Action														
	694	191	464	39	133	52	102	368	39	17	112	112	215	9	13½	6	9
104th AAA AW Bn																	
Horn Island	16	0	16	0	0	0	0	16	0	0	0	0	0	0	0	0	0
Merauke	30	1	28	1	1	10	0	19	0	0	11	0	11	0	0	0	0
Milne Bay	183	105	75	3	44	0	76	0	63	0	120	0	120	0	3	0	0
Goodenough Island	32	0	2	30	0	0	4	0	28	0	120	32	4	28	1	0	0
Dobodura	31	0	24	7	0	0	10	21	0	0	Unknown				0	0	0
Hollandia	4	0	4	0	2	1	0	0	1	0	0	4	4	0	0	0	0
	296	106	149	41	47	11	90	56	92	0	131	36	139	28	1	0	0

UNIT	ENEMY AIR ATTACKS								FIRE HELD	A.A.A. ACTION				RESULTS		
	NUMBER PLANES	TYPE OF FIGHTER	TYPE OF BOMBER	TARGET UNKNOWN	ALT. OF ATTACK (THOUSANDS OF FT) 0-3	3-10	10-20	20-UP	UNKNOWN		TARGETS DAY	ENGAGED NIGHT	SEEN	UNSEEN	DEST.	PROB.	DAMAGED
---	---	---	---	---	---	---	---	---	---	---	---	---	---	---	---	---	---
198th AAA AW Bn																	
Sansapor	23	4	4	15	3	12	2	0	6	6	0	15	15	0	0	0	0
Luzon	16	8	2	6	4	1	0	0	11	0	3	13	12	4	2½	0	1
	39	12	6	21	7	13	2	0	17	6	3	28	27	4	2½	0	1
199th AAA AW Bn																	
Guadalcanal			No Action														
Bougainville	26	0	24	2	0	3	6	4	13	-	12	3	-	6	1	0	0
Leyte			No Action														
202d AAA AW Bn																	
Wakde	16	0	12	4	1	6	0	0	9	2	0	14	4	10	0	0	0
Leyte	6	6	0	0	6	0	0	0	0	0	4	2	6	0	1	0	0
Mindoro	145	40	94	11	44	33	0	0	68	11	23	105	110	18	25	2	7
Zamboanga	1	1	0	0	1	0	0	0	0	0	1	0	1	0	0	0	1½
Tawi Tawi			No Action														
	168	47	106	15	52	39	0	0	77	13	28	121	121	28	26	2	7½
205th AAA AW Bn																	
Fiji Islands			No Action														
Mindoro			No Action														
206th AAA AW Bn																	
Saipan	18	7	9	2	15	0	0	0	3	0	Engaged		18		1	0	0
Iwo Jima	12	2	5	5	3	0	0	5	4	0	Engaged		7		0	0	0
	30	9	14	7	18	0	0	5	7	0	-	-	25	-	1	0	0
207th AAA AW Bn																	
Milne Bay			No Action														
Hollandia			No Action														
208th AAA AW Bn																	
Milne Bay			No Action														

UNIT	ENEMY AIR ATTACKS									A.A. ACTION							
	NUMBER OF PLANES	TYPE FIGHTER	TYPE BOMBER	TARGET UNKNOWN	ALT. OF ATTACK (THOUSANDS OF FT.) 0-3	3-10	10-20	20-UP	UNKNOWN	FIRE HELD	TARGETS DAY	TARGETS NIGHT	ENGAGED SEEN	UNSEEN	RESULTS DEST.	PROB.	DAMAGED
209th AAA AW Bn																	
Goodenough Island	32	0	2	30	0	0	4	0	28	0	0	32	4	28	0	0	0
Kiriwine Island	14	0	0	14	2	0	0	0	12	0	Unknown		1	0	0	0	0
Nassau Bay	1	0	1	0	0	1	0	0	0	0	1	0	1	0	1	0	0
Morobe	7	0	2	5	0	2	4	0	1	1	1	2	2	0	0	0	0
Tambu Bay	8	0	6	2	3	2	3	0	0	0	8	0	8	0	3	0	0
Saidor	12	0	12	0	4	7	0	0	1	0	16	9	9	0	0	2	0
Luzon	16	1	11	4	11	5	0	0	0	0	0	0	16	0	0	0	1
	90	1	34	55	20	17	11	0	42	1	25	43	40	28	4	2	1
210th AAA AW Bn																	
Freemantle				No Action													
Townsville				No Action													
Cape York				No Action													
Milne Bay				No Data													
Bena - Bena				No Data													
Nadzab	6	6	0	0	6	0	0	0	0	0	6	0	6	0	0	0	0
Port Moresby	430	120	51	259	357	46	0	4	23	36	264	130	356	38	28¾	12	24
	436	126	51	259	363	46	0	4	23	36	270	130	362	38	28¾	12	24
211th AAA AW Bn																	
Townsville				No Action													
Port Moresby				No Data													
Oro Bay				No Data													
Milne Bay				No Data													
Dobodura				No Data													
Rorona				No Data													
Tsili Tsili				No Data													
Bena - Bena	24	6	18	0	24	0	0	0	0	0	Engaged		24	-	2	0	0
Nadzab			No	Data													
Admiralties	6	0	2	4	0	0	3	2	6	0	1	4	5	0	0	1	0
Leyte	301	173	89	39	222	74	3	2	0	0	200	101	288	13	40 3/4	26	28
	331	179	109	43	246	74	3	2	6	0	201	105	317	13	42 3/4	28	28

UNIT	ENEMY AIR ATTACKS								FIRE HELD	A.A.A. TARGETS			ENGAGED		ACTION RESULTS		
	NUMBER PLANES	TYPE BOMBER	TYPE FIGHTER	TARGET UNKNOWN	ALT. OF ATTACK (THOUSANDS OF FT) 0-3	3-10	10-20	20-UP	UNKNOWN		DAY	NIGHT	SEEN	UNSEEN	DEST.	PROB.	DAMAGED
383d AAA AW Bn																	
Aitape	1	1	0	0	1	0	0	0	0	0	Did Not Engage				0	0	0
Morotai	39	13	3	23	11	9	0	0	19	1	18	20	28	10	5	0	¼
Cotabato			No Action														
	40	14	3	23	12	9	0	0	19	1	18	20	28	10	5	0	¼
388th AAA AW Bn																	
Ie Shima	117	0	0	117	0	0	0	0	117		Engaged		117		2 1/3	0	0
389th AAA AW Bn																	
Morotai	34	14	16	4	20	14	0	0	0	5	6	23	29	0	2	2	1½
466th AAA AW Bn																	
New Hebrides				No Action													
Cape Gloucester				No Data													
469th AAA AW Bn																	
Oro Bay				No Action													
Cape Gloucester	4	0	3	1	1	2	0	0	1	0	0	4	4	0	0	0	0
Hollandia	137	99	29	9	137	0	0	0	0	0	99	38	137	0	16½	2	11
Leyte	4	2	1	1	4	0	0	0	0	0	2	2	4	0	1	0	0
Luzon	145	101	33	11	142	2	0	0	1	0	101	44	145	0	17½	2	11
470th AAA AW Bn																	
Milne Bay				No Action													
Woodlark	1	0	1	0	1	0	0	0	0	0	0	0	0	0	0	0	0
Arawe	18	5	3	10	3	8	7	0	0	0	6	9	8	7	6	2	0
Luzon	4	1	0	3	4	0	0	0	0	0	2	2	4	0	0	0	0
Panay			No Action														
	23	6	4	13	8	8	7	0	0	0	8	11	12	7	6	2	0
471st AAA AW Bn																	
Society Island			No Action														
Tulagi			No Action														
Emirau Island			No Action														
Luzon	5	1	0	4	3	0	0	2	0	0	0	5	5	0	0	0	0

UNIT	ENEMY AIR ATTACKS								FIRE HELD	A.A.A. ACTION						
	NUMBER TYPE OF PLANES			TARGET ALT. OF ATTACK (THOUSANDS OF FT.)						TARGETS ENGAGED				RESULTS		
	FIGHTER	BOMBER	UNKNOWN	0-3	3-10	10-20	20-UP	UNKNOWN		DAY	NIGHT	SEEN	UNSEEN	DEST.	PROB.	DAMAGED
472d AAA AW Bn Nadzab Luzon		No Action														
		No Action														
475th AAA AW Bn Guadalcanal		No Data														
476th AAA AW Bn Biak	45	44	35	18	17	12	32	2	0	58	66	102	22	16	2	7
Palawan	1	3	1	2	3	0	0	0	0	0	1	1	0	0	0	0
	46	47	36	20	20	12	32	2	0	58	67	103	22	16	2	7
124																
5																
129																
477th AAA AW Bn Dobodura		No Action														
Oro Bay		No Action														
478th AAA AW Bn Finschhafen		No Action														
Samar		No Action														
Cebu		No Action														
483d AAA AW Bn Angaur	0	0	4	2	0	0	2	0	0	0	4	0	4	0	0	0
Iwo Jima	0	4	8	3	0	3	1	5	0	0	12	9	3	1	0	1
4																
12	0	4	12	5	0	3	3	5	0	0	16	9	7	1	0	1
16																
485th AAA AW Bn Leyte	34	42	217	64	15	0	2	212	12	58	223	278	3	31	10	14
Okinawa	30	56	258	43	42	34	20	205		Unknown				13½	3	1
293																
344	64	98	475	107	57	34	22	417						44½	13	15
637																
487th AAA AW Bn Noemfor	1	8	0	2	6	0	0	1	2	0	5	5	0	1	1	0
Mindoro		No Action														
9																
779th AAA AW Bn Okinawa	0	0	32	1	0	0	0	31	0	0	1	1	0	0	0	0
32																

UNIT	ENEMY AIR ATTACKS								FIRE HELD	A.A.A. TARGETS		ENGAGED		ACTION RESULTS		
	NUMBER PLANES	TYPE OF FIGHTER	BOMBER	TARGET UNKNOWN	ALT. OF ATTACK (THOUSANDS OF FT) 0-3	3-10	10-20	20-UP	UNKNOWN		DAY	NIGHT	SEEN	UNSEEN	DEST.	PROB.	DAMAGED
785th AAA AW Bn Morotai	46	16	28	2	28	6	12	0	0	8	5	33	35	3	2	2	4¼
807th AAA AW Bn Saipan				No Action													
834th AAA AW Bn Okinawa	108	0	0	108	0	0	0	0	108		Unknown				0	0	0
861st AAA AW Bn Okinawa	344	30	56	258	43	42	34	20	205		Unknown		6	0	3½	0	2
Leyte	6	5	0	1	6	0	0	0	0	0	6	0			1	0	0
	350	35	56	259	49	42	34	20	205						4½	0	2
864th AAA AW Bn Saipan	67	29	15	23	25	0	19	16	7	0	Unknown				2 1/3	0	0
865th AAA AW Bn Saipan	19	11	8	0	11	0	0	0	8	0	Unknown				1	0	0
866th AAA AW Bn Leyte	165	52	1	112	41	22	1	0	101	0	46	119	162	3	35	7	21
Okinawa	109	0	0	109	0	0	0	0	109		Unknown				2	0	0
	274	52	1	221	41	22	1	0	210						37	7	21
867th AAA AW Bn Eniwetok	8	1	2	5	1	0	0	7	0	0	0	1	1	0	0	0	0
Saipan	18	7	8	3	13	0	0	0	5		Unknown				0	0	0
	26	8	10	8	14	0	0	7	5						0	0	0
868th AAA AW Bn Guam			No Action														
869th AAA AW Bn Apamama			No Action														

- 231 -

UNIT	ENEMY AIR ATTACKS									FIRE HELD	A.A.A. ACTION						
	NUMBER PLANES	TYPE OF PLANES			TARGET ALT. OF ATTACK (THOUSANDS OF FT)						TARGETS ENGAGED				RESULTS		
		FIGHTER	BOMBER	UNKNOWN	0-5	5-10	10-20	20-UP	UNKNOWN		DAY	NIGHT	SEEN	UNSEEN	DEST.	PROB.	DAMAGED
870th AAA AW Bn																	
Okinawa				No Action													
925th AAA AW Bn																	
New Caledonia	40	0	0	40	0	2	0	0	40		Unknown				0	0	0
New Georgia	28	7	21	0	2	6	18	0			Unknown				0	0	0
Green Island				No Action													
Leyte	68	7	21	40	2	6	18	40			0		0		0	0	0
933d AAA AW Bn																	
New Hebrides	9	0	3	6	1	1	7	0	0	4	–	–	–		0	0	0
Russell Islands	1	0	1	0	0	0	1	0	0	0	0	0	0	0	0	0	0
Admiralty Islands				No Action													
	10	0	4	6	1	1	8	0	0	4	0	0	0	0	0	0	0
945th AAA AW Bn																	
Society Island				No Action													
New Hebrides				No Action													
Treasury Island	40	0	0	40	0	0	0	0	40	–	0	26	20	0	1	1	0
948th AAA AW Bn																	
Ie Shima				No Data													
950th AAA AW Bn																	
Guadalcanal	218	0	10	208	10	0	14	40	154	120	2	8	10	0	3	0	0
Luzon	2	0	2	0	2	0	0	0	0	0	0	2	–	–	0	0	0
	220	0	12	208	12	0	14	40	154	120	2	10	10	0	3	0	0
951st AAA AW Bn																	
Fiji Island				No Action													
Bougainville				No Data													
Luzon	7	3	4	0	5	2	0	0	0	0	6	1	4	–	1	0	1

UNIT	NUMBER PLANES	TYPE FIGHTER	TYPE BOMBER	TARGET UNKNOWN	ALT. OF ATTACK (THOUSANDS OF FT) 0-3	3-10	10-20	20-UP	UNKNOWN	FIRE HELD	TARGETS DAY	TARGETS NIGHT	ENGAGED SEEN	ENGAGED UNSEEN	DEST.	PROB.	DAMAGED
662d MG Btry Gusap	9	8	1	0	9	0	0	0	0	0	8	0	8	0	0	0	0
663d MG Btry Gusap	8	7	1	0	8	0	0	0	0	0	7	0	7	0	0	0	0
664th MG Btry Finschhafen	No Data																
665th MG Btry Nadzab	No Data																
670th MG Btry Nadzab	No Data																
671st MG Btry Gusap	3	3	0	0	3	0	0	0	0	0	3	0	3	0	0	0	0
672d MG Btry Gusap	1	0	1	0	1	0	0	0	0	0	0	0	0	0	0	0	0
673d MG Btry Hollandia				No Data													
Admiralties				No Data													
Leyte				No Data													
Mindoro				No Data													
674th MG Btry Biak	46	15	8	23	19	1	0	0	26	0	18	28	41	5	0	0	0
Sansapor	23	4	15	4	3	12	2	0	6	6	0	15	15	0	0	0	0
	69	19	23	27	22	13	2	0	32	6	18	43	56	5	0	0	0
675th MG Btry Biak	37	28	4	5	19	2	0	0	16	0	29	8	34	3	1	2	0
Sansapor	23	4	15	4	3	12	2	0	6	6	0	15	15	0	0	0	0
	60	32	19	9	22	14	2	0	22	6	29	23	49	3	1	2	0

UNIT	NUMBER PLANES	TYPE FIGHTER	TYPE BOMBER	TARGET UNKNOWN	ALT. OF ATTACK (THOUSANDS OF FT.) 0-3	3-10	10-20	20-UP	UNKNOWN	FIRE HELD	TARGETS DAY	NIGHT	ENGAGED SEEN	UNSEEN	DEST.	PROB.	DAMAGED
707th MG Btry																	
Dobadura	53	17	5	31	22	0	0	0	31	0	22	0	22	0	0	0	0
Wanigela				No Action													
Nadzab	5	5	0	0	5	0	0	0	0	0	5	0	5	0	0	1	0
Noemfor				No Action													
Luzon				No Action													
	58	22	5	31	27	0	0	0	31	0	27	0	27	0	0	1	0
708th MG Btry																	
Townsville	4	0	4	0	0	0	4	0	0	0	0	0	0	0	0	0	0
Popondetta	37	17	20	0	0	0	0	37	0	0	0	0	0	0	0	0	0
Bulolo	40	11	29	0	2	38	0	0	0	0	40	0	40	0	0	0	0
Nadzab	45	9	30	6	5	3	8	29	0	0	5	0	5	0	0	1	1
Noemfor	7	1	6	0	0	6	0	0	1	0	0	1	1	0	0	0	0
Luzon			No Action														
	133	38	89	6	7	47	12	66	1	0	45	1	46	0	0	1	0
709th MG Btry																	
Dobadura	82	0	0	82	0	0	0	0	82	0	Unknown		0	0	0	0	0
Tsili Tsili	37	31	6	0	37	0	0	0	0	0	3	0	3	0	0	0	0
Gusap	66	0	0	66	0	0	0	0	66	0	Unknown				0	0	0
Milne Bay	80	43	36	1	0	0	0	0	80	-	-	-	-	-	0	0	0
	265	74	42	149	37	0	0	0	228						0	0	0
230th AAA SL Bn																	
Leyte	39	16	6	23	11	0	0	0	28	1	2	36	14	24	4½	0	1
237th AAA SL Bn																	
Leyte	149	61	76	12	54	46	27	19	3	4	23	122	44	101	2	0	1
294th AAA SL Bn																	
Okinawa	28*	0	28	0	0	0	28	0	0	0	0	28	0	28	1	0	0
* Incomplete																	

158. Relative Standing from Combat Records of AAA Units

AAA Unit	Plane Attacks	Destroyed	Results of Fire Probably Destroyed	Damaged
502d AAA Gun Bn	628	45	27	17
485th AAA AW Bn	637	44 ½	13	15
211th AAA AW Bn	331	42 3/4	28	28
866th AAA AW Bn	274	37	7	21
93d AAA Gun Bn	138	36 1/3	4	26
168th AAA Gun Bn	518	28 ½	4	4
210th AAA AW Bn	436	28 ¼	12	24
166th AAA Gun Bn	182	28	3	5 ½
504th AAA Gun Bn	356	27 ½	25	12
202d AAA AW Bn	168	26	2	7 ½
7th AAA AW Bn	228	18 1/3	1	21
469th AAA AW Bn	145	17 ½	2	11
101st AAA AW Bn	545	17	1	3
476th AAA AW Bn	124	16	2	7
528th AAA Gun Bn	357	14	9	9 ¼
102d AAA AW Bn	694	13 ½	6	9
165th AAA Gun Bn	124	7	3	3
736th AAA Gun Bn	145	7	3	0
470th AAA AW Bn	23	6	2	0
745th AAA Gun Bn	396	6	0	1
744th AAA Gun Bn	149	5	2	3
751st AAA Gun Bn	79	5	1	0
383d AAA AW Bn	40	5	0	¼
70th AAA Gun Bn	121	4 ½	5	1
861st AAA AW Bn	350	4 ½	0	2
230th AAA SL Bn	39*	4 ½	0	1
209th AAA AW Bn	90	4	2	1
738th AAA Gun Bn	67	3 1/3	0	0
496th AAA Gun Bn	23	3	0	1
950th AAA AW Bn	220	3	0	0
198th AAA AW Bn	39	2 ½	0	1
388th AAA AW Bn	117	2 1/3	0	0
864th AAA AW Bn	67	2 1/3	0	0
501st AAA Gun Bn	67	2 1/3	0	0
785th AAA AW Bn	46	2	2	4 ¼
389th AAA AW Bn	34	2	2	1 ¼
948th AAA Gun Bn	UNK	2	1	1
743d AAA Gun Bn	241	2	1	0
237th AAA SL Bn	149	2	0	1
503d AAA Gun Bn	UNK	2	0	0
161st AAA Gun Bn	17	1 ½	0	1
506th AAA Gun Bn	12	1	2	0

675th AAA MG Btry	60	1	2	0
487th AAA AW Bn	9	1	1	0
945th AAA AW Bn	40	1	1	0
77th AAA Gun Bn	8	1	1	0
505th AAA Gun Bn	3	1	0	1
483d AAA AW Bn	16	1	0	1
951st AAA AW Bn	7	1	0	1
104th AAA AW Bn	296	1	0	0
199th AAA AW Bn	26	1	0	0
206th AAA AW Bn	30	1	0	0
865th AAA AW Bn	19	1	0	0
164th AAA AW Bn	1	1	0	0
741st AAA Gun Bn	189	1	0	0
294th AAA SL Bn	28*	1	0	0
98th AAA Gun Bn	80	0	3	1
707th AAA MG Btry	58	0	1	0
708th AAA MG Btry	133	0	1	0
		546	182	247
Marine credits		28	8	22
Undetermined credits		14	1	1
Philippine Defense Campaign				
200th CA (AA)		51	2	0
515th CA (AA)		35	0	0
Harbor Defenses of Manila				
59th CA (HD))				
60th CA (AA) (		87	19	66
91st CA (PS))				
Pearl Harbor				
55th CA (155-mm)		2	0	0
		921	212	336

* Incomplete Data

159.   a. AMMUNITION EXPENDITURES

Location of Operation	Number of Attacks	Rounds Fired			Results of Fire							Rounds Fired Per Plane Dest-Prob Dest-Dam			Percentage of Planes Dest, Prob Dest & Dam
		90-mm	40-mm	cal .50	90-mm			40-mm				90-mm	40-mm		
					Dest	Prob	Dam	Dest	Prob	Dam					
BIAK	124	5806	5622	227612	7	3	3	16	4	7*		446	208		33%
MOROTAI	179	8515	6836	110268	8	3	6	9	4	6		501	365		20%
LEYTE	1278	28283	47825	731709	81	50	27	166½	63	123**		179	136		40%
MINDORO	145	6161	10165	158797	26	2	5	29½	2	10		185	245		53%
LUZON	31	2245	2100	75969	1½	0	1	4½	0	3		898	280		32%
OKINAWA	344	21674	9188	149112	40	14	21	32	3	12***		282	195		32%
IE SHIMA	153	8437	2139	43241	38	5	27	12	0	1		121	157		54%
TOTALS	2254	81121	83875	1496708	201½	77	90	269½	76	162		219	165		38%

* Does not incl 1 Dest - 2 Prob dest by MG Btry
** Does not incl 3 Dest - 1 Dam by SL Bn MG's
*** Does not incl 4 Dest - 1 Dam by SL Bn MG's
     2 Dest - 1 Prob Dest - Undetermined

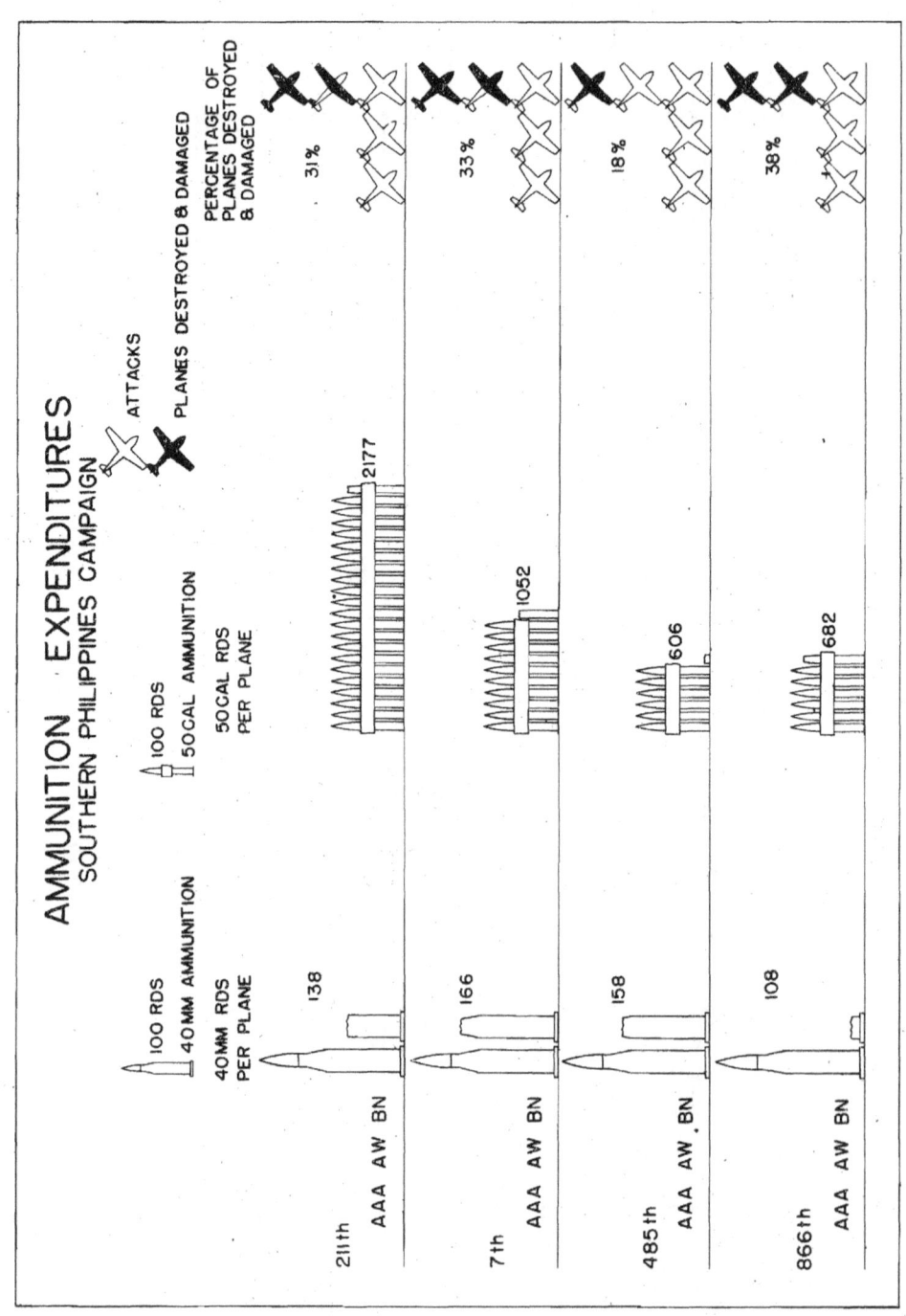

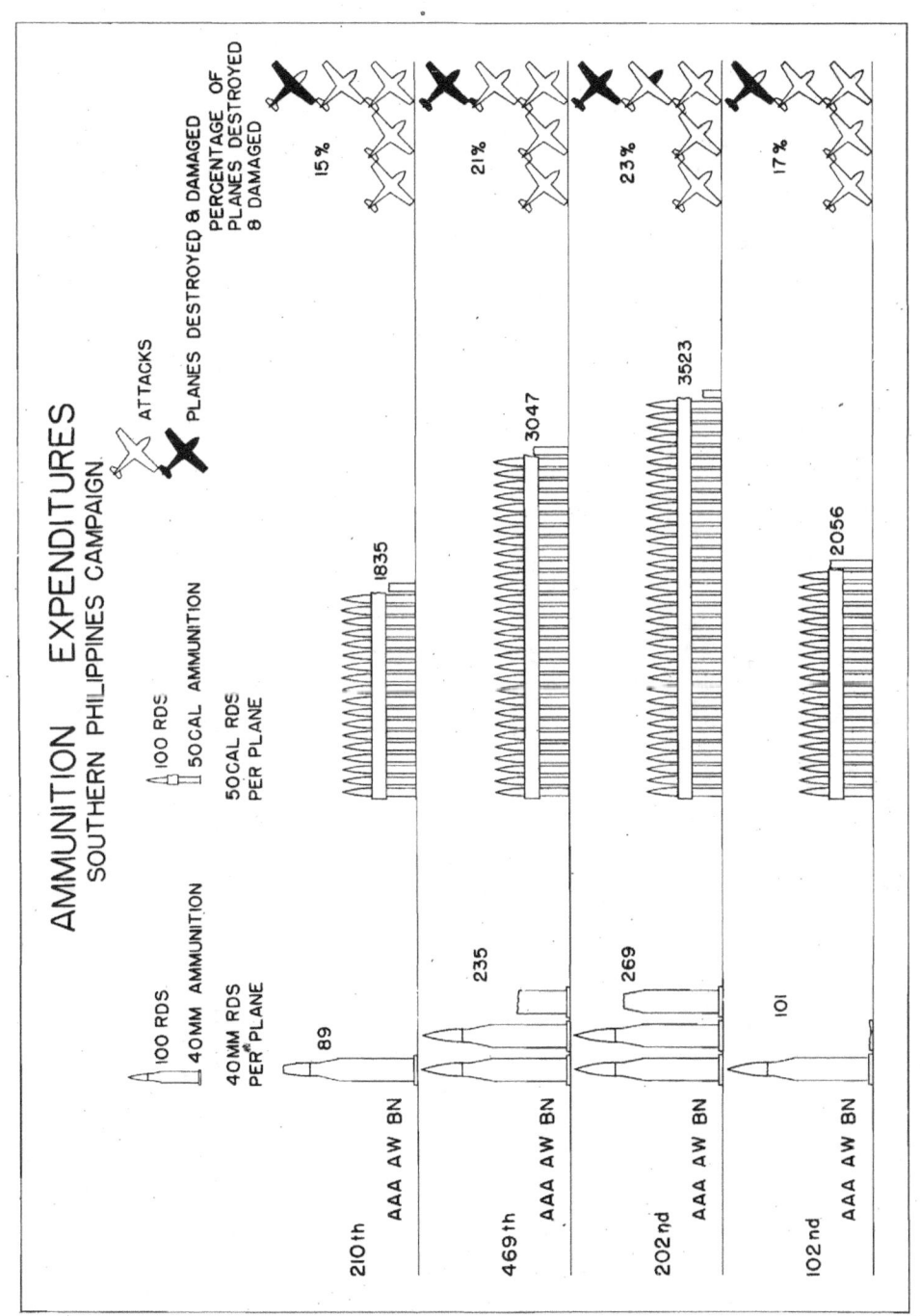

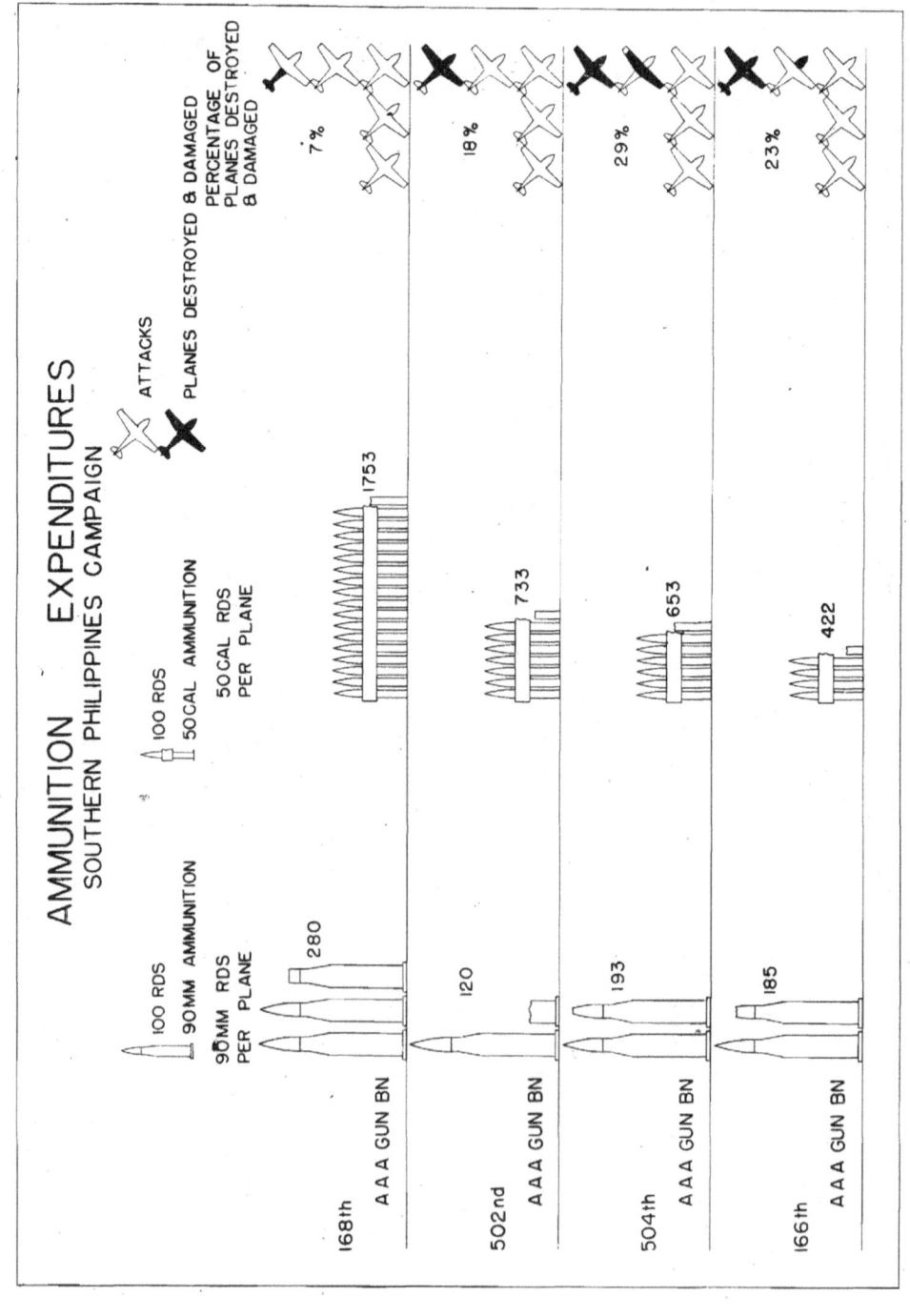

160.

TOTAL PACIFIC OPERATIONS

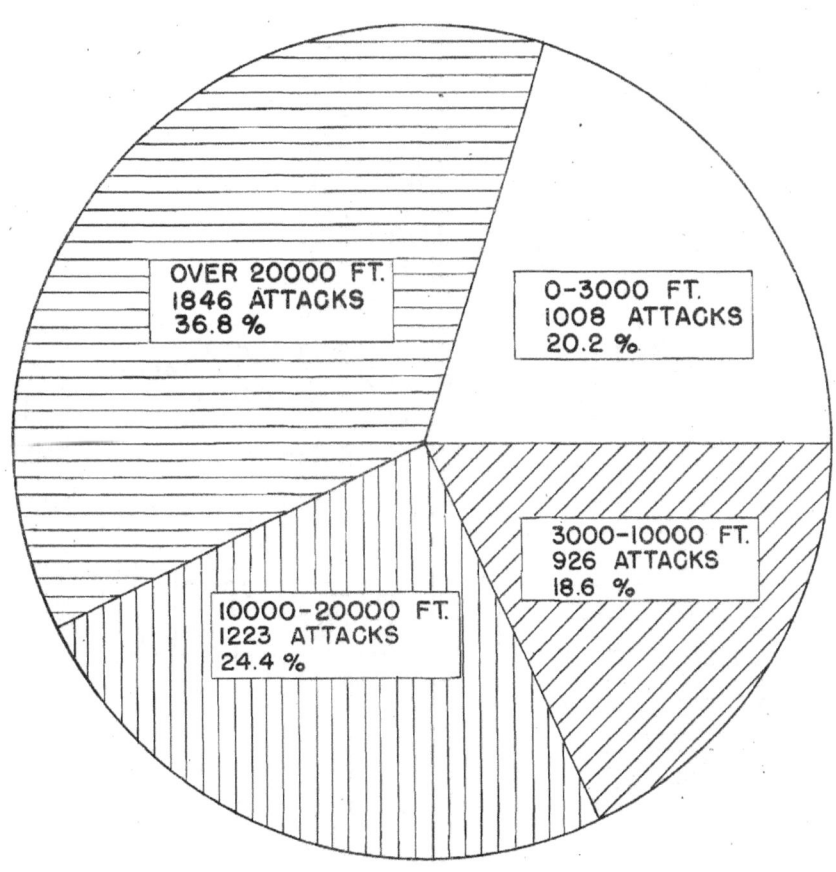

ANTIAIRCRAFT TARGETS ENGAGED

ALTITUDE OF ATTACKS
(TOTAL KNOWN ALTITUDE ATTACKS 5003)

- 241 -

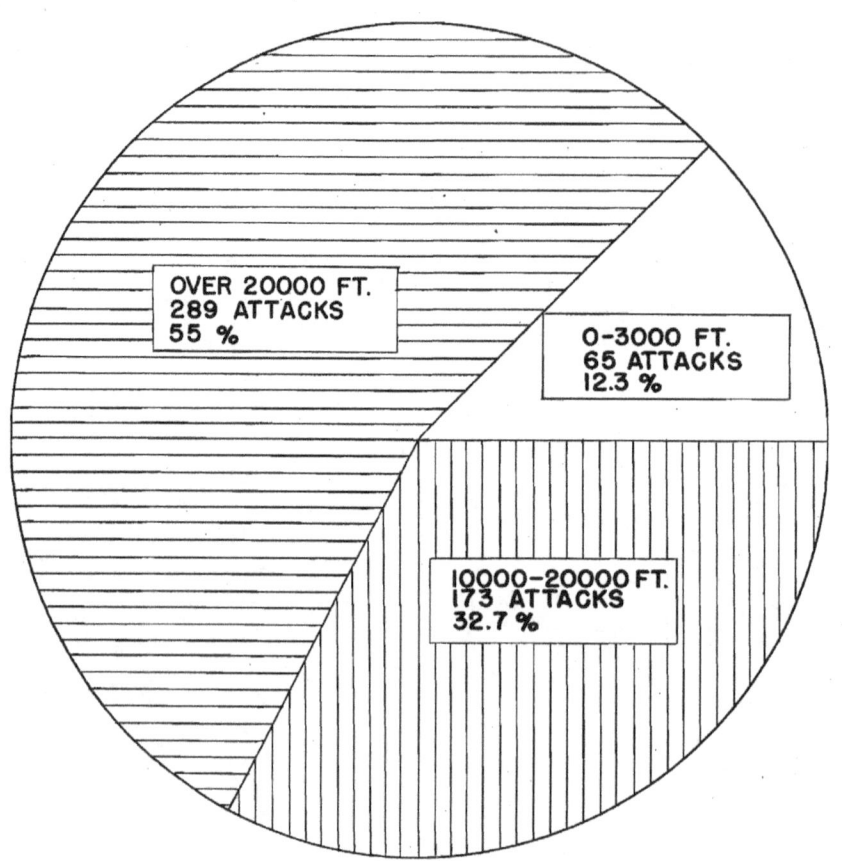

PAPUAN CAMPAIGN

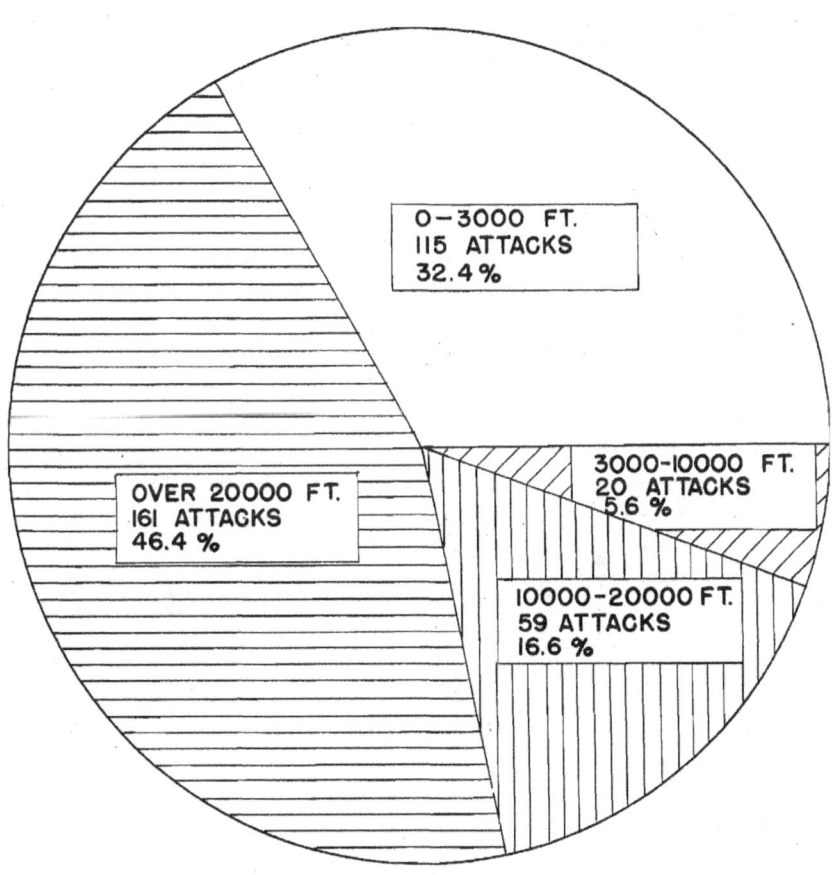

ANTIAIRCRAFT TARGETS ENGAGED

ALTITUDE OF ATTACKS
(TOTAL KNOWN ALTITUDE ATTACKS 355)

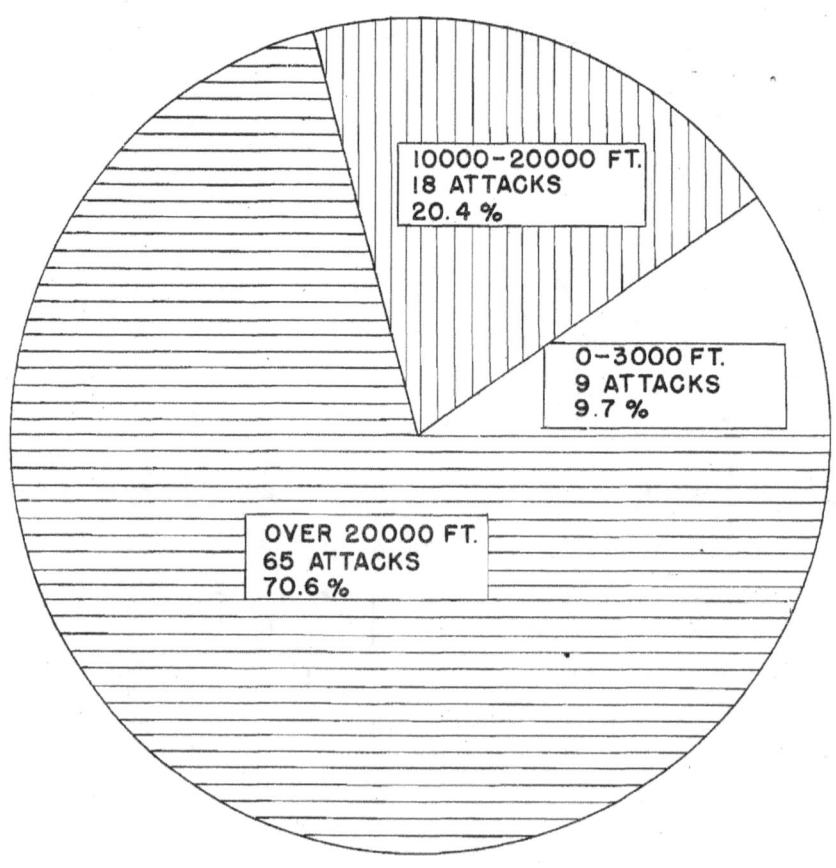

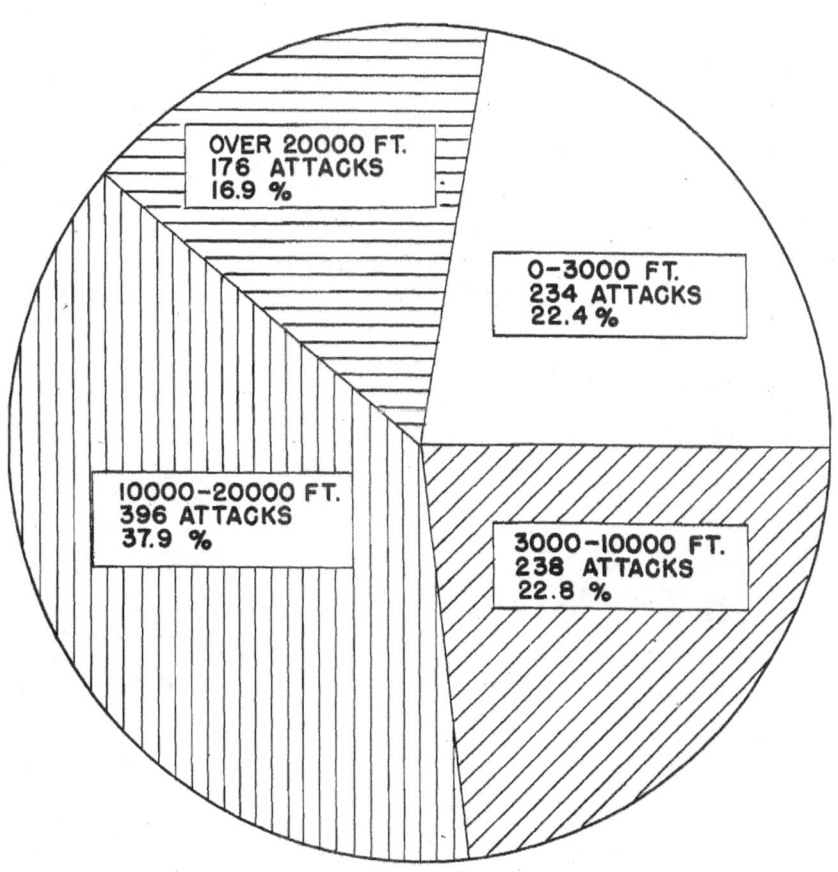

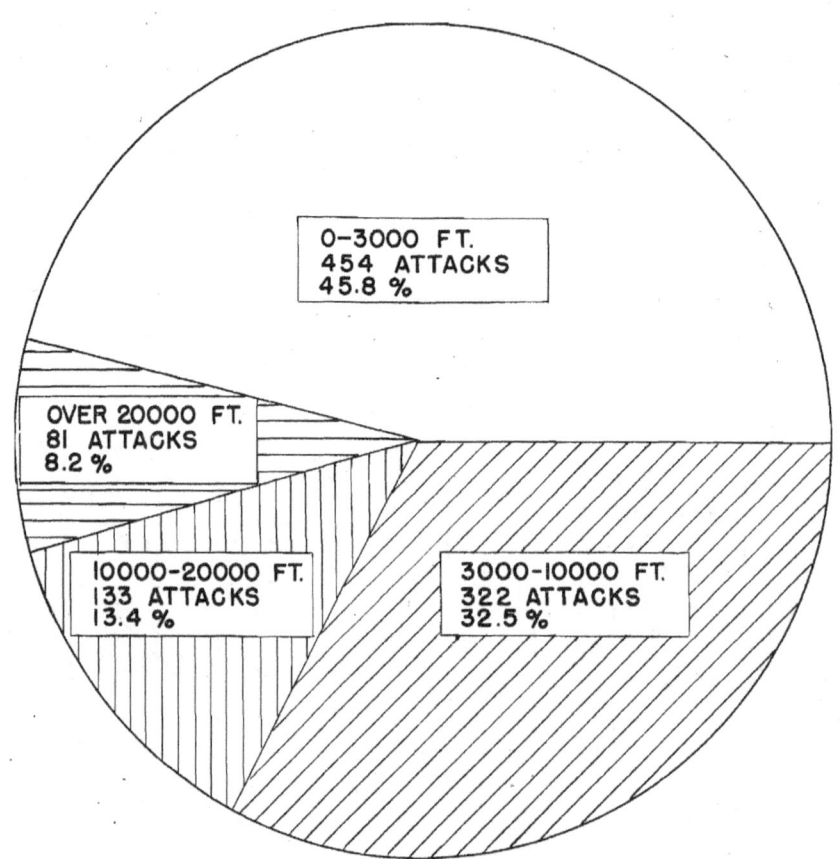

SOUTHERN PHILIPPINE CAMPAIGN

NIGHT 31.7% | DAY 68.3%

ANTIAIRCRAFT TARGETS ENGAGED

0-3000 FT.
454 ATTACKS
45.8 %

OVER 20000 FT.
81 ATTACKS
8.2 %

10000-20000 FT.
133 ATTACKS
13.4 %

3000-10000 FT.
322 ATTACKS
32.5 %

ALTITUDE OF ATTACKS
(TOTAL KNOWN ALTITUDE ATTACKS 990)

RYUKYUS CAMPAIGN

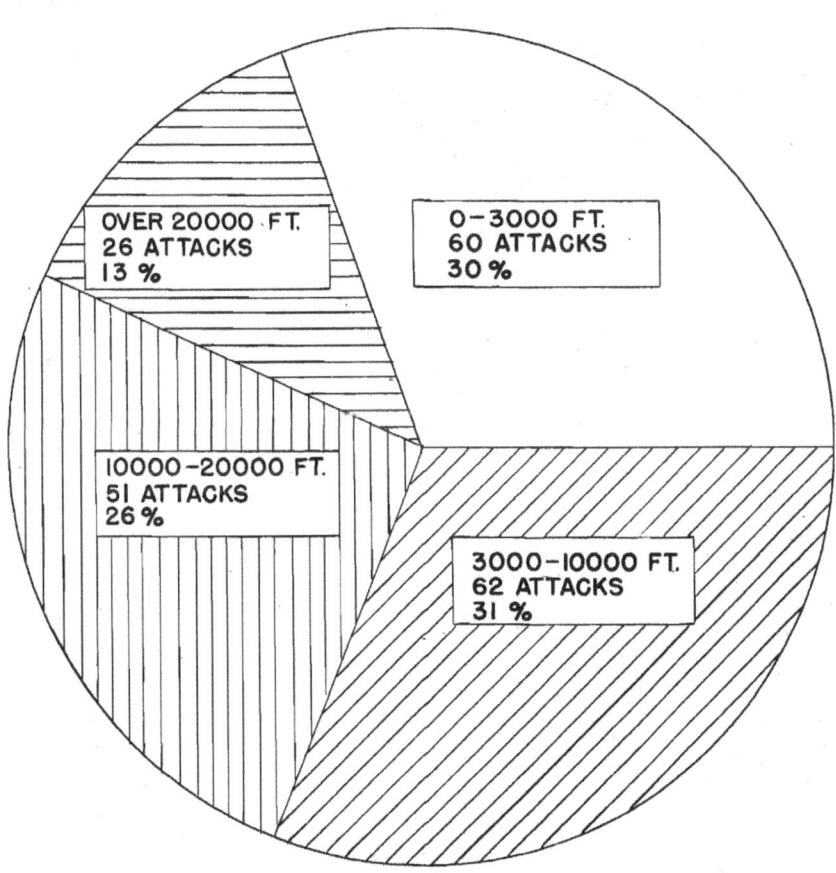

ANTIAIRCRAFT TARGETS ENGAGED

NIGHT 86%   DAY 14%

ALTITUDE OF ATTACKS
(TOTAL KNOWN ALTITUDE ATTACKS 199)

- OVER 20000 FT. — 26 ATTACKS — 13%
- 0–3000 FT. — 60 ATTACKS — 30%
- 10000–20000 FT. — 51 ATTACKS — 26%
- 3000–10000 FT. — 62 ATTACKS — 31%

161. **Terrestrial Fire Missions.**

   a. Gun Battalions.

Targets or Fire Missions

Unit	Place	Rounds Fired	Caves	Pill-boxes	Tanks	Guns	Trucks	Buildings	Boats	Troops	Supply Dumps	Bridges	Others
161 Gun	Balete Pass		69	42	1	16	2	13					271
	Marikina Watershed		31					4					85
	Laguna de Bay								2				64
	Ipo Dam		7	1				1					274
	Cagayan Valley					1							49
163 Gun	Hollandia	445											
	Luzon	2793											3
	Baguio	2457	17	2		7	2	29		37		3	
165 Gun	Biak	197			1	1							
166 Gun	Wakde			X		X		X		X			X
	Zamboanga					1							
168 Gun	Los Negros					X							
496 Gun	New Guinea	211											1
	Mindanao	3936	X	X	X	X	X	X	X	X	X		X
502 Gun	Leyte	1775			X					X	X		X
	Okinawa							X		X	X		X
504 Gun	Okinawa	11120						X		X	X		X
506 Gun	Iwo Jima												X
507 Gun	Luzon	1206											8

- 248 -

a. Gun Battalions (cont'd)

Targets or Fire Missions

Unit	Place	Rounds Fired	Caves	Pill-boxes	Tanks	Guns	Trucks	Build-ings	Boats	Troops	Supply Dumps	Bridges	Others
518 Gun	Luzon												X
734 Gun	Laguna de Bay	3434	X	X			X			X	X		X
739 Gun	Negros	12500	X	X	X	X		X		X	X		X
741 Gun	Arawe N.B.	42									2		
751 Gun	Saipan	1380				X				X			X

b. AAA AW Battalions

Unit	Place	Rounds Fired 40-mm	Rounds Fired .50 cal	Caves	Pillboxes	Targets or Fire Missions Tanks	Guns	Buildings	Troops	Others
198 AW	Luzon	10913	133660	X	X		X	X	X	X
209 AW	New Guinea	2443	19300						X	X
	Luzon	4370	452915		28	2	13			
210 AW	Luzon		X	X	X				X	X
469 AW	Luzon	2040	6300	X	X		X		X	X
470 AW	Negros	13662	407895	35	7		19	5		
476 AW	Biak		X	X						
478 AW	Cebu	X		7	19		25		12	
487 AW	Mindanao	3911		5	9		1	42		
864 AW	Saipan	X		X						
925 AW	Leyte	3743		X	X		X	X	X	
950 AW	Corregidor	88							1	

ANNEX A

REORGANIZATIONS AND REDESIGNATIONS OF

ANTIAIRCRAFT ARTILLERY ORGANIZATIONS

    1. General. Antiaircraft artillery organizations in the Pacific areas were reorganized and redesignated progressively, but actually belatedly, as new Tables of Organization were adopted by the War Department. The delays were the result of late receipt of the tables in the distant theaters, passage of time necessary to secure theater and War Department authorization, and finally the time necessary to effect such changes in organizations scattered over wide areas, many in tactical positions.

    The following pages detail the changes in organization and designation referred to in the text of this report.

    2. Reorganization and Redesignations in the Southwest Pacific Area.

        A.   Reorganizations and Redesignations of 13 August 1942.

            (1) Directive - GHQ, SWPA Ltr, AG 322.011, 1 August 1943.
Pursuant to the above directive units were reorganized to conform with Tables of Organization 4-111, 1 April 1942. The Second Battalion of the 94th CA Regiment (AA) was deactivated to provide personnel and equipment for the new batteries of the three CA Regiments (AA) in the SWPA.

Old Designation	New Designation
Hq 94th CA (AA)	Same
Hq 1st Bn, 94th CA (AA)	Same
Btry A, Hq and 2 Plats	Btry I, 94th CA (AA)
1 Plat	Btry K, 94th CA (AA)
Btrys B, C, D	Same
Hq 2d Bn, 94th CA (AA)	Split between Hq 3d Bn and 94th, 197th, and 208th Regts
Btry E, 2 Plats & 2/3 Hq	Btry K, 197th CA (AA)
1 Plat & 1/3 Hq	Btry K, 208th CA (AA)
Btry F	Btry A, 208th CA (AA)
Btry G	Btry A, 197th CA (AA)
Btry H	Btry A, 94th CA (AA)
Hq 3d Bn, 94th CA (AA)	Hq 2d Bn, 94th CA (AA)
Btrys I - K - L - M	Btrys E - F - G - H 94th CA (AA)
Btry A, 197th CA (AA)	Btry I and 1 plat of Btry K 197th CA (AA)
Btry A, 208th CA (AA)	Btry I and 1 plat of Btry K 208th CA (AA)

(2) **Reorganization of 13 August 1942.**

Unit	T/O Applicable
40th CA Brig (AA)	4-10-1, 1 Apr 1942
41st CA Brig (AA)	Ch 1, 21 Apr 1942
101st CA Bn (AA)	4-195, 1 Apr 1942
102d CA Bn (AA)	" " " " "
104th CA Bn (AA)	" " " " "

B. **Reorganizations of 15 May 1943.**

Old Designation	New Designation	T/O Applicable
Hq & Hq Btry, 94th CA (AA)	Hq & Hq Btry, 94th AAA Gp	44-12 (14 Apr 1943)
1st Bn, 94th CA (AA)	743d CA Bn (AA)	4-175 (1 Apr 1942)
2d Bn 94th CA (AA)	209th CA Bn (AA)	4-195 (1 Apr 1942)
		Ch 1 & 2
3d Bn, 94th CA (AA)	236th AAA SL Bn	44-135 (27 Feb 1943)
Hq & Hq Btry, 197th CA (AA)	Hq & Hq Btry, 208th AAA Gp	44-12 (14 Apr 1943)
1st Bn, 197th CA (AA)	744th CA Bn (AA)	4-175 (1 Apr 1942)
2d Bn, 197th CA (AA)	210th CA Bn (AA)	4-195 (1 Apr 1942)
		Ch 1 & 2
3d Bn, 197th CA (AA)	237th AAA SL Bn	44-135 (27 Feb 1943)
Hq & Hq Btry, 208th CA (AA)	Hq & Hq Btry, 208th AAA Gp	44-12 (14 Apr 1943)
1st Bn, 208th CA (AA)	745th CA Bn (AA)	4-175 (1 Apr 1942)
2d Bn, 208th CA (AA)	210th CA Bn (AA)	4-195 (1 Apr 1942)
		Ch 1 & 2
3d Bn, 208th CA (AA)	238th AAA SL Bn	44-135 (27 Feb 1943)

C. **Redesignation of 1 December 1943.**

Directive - General Order #3, 14th AA Command 1 December 1943.

Old Designation	New Designation	T/O Applicable
Btry A, 228th AAA SL Bn	Btry C, 236th AAA SL Bn	
Btry B, " " " "	Btry C, 237th AAA SL Bn	
Btry C, " " " "	Btry C, 238th AAA SL Bn	
707th CA Btry (AA)	707th MG Btry A/B (AA)	4-278 (5 Sep 1942)
708th " " "	708th " " " "	" " " " "
709th " " "	709th " " " "	" " " " "
Band 197th CA Regt (AA)	281st AGF Band	
Band 208th CA Regt	280th AGF Band	

D. **Reorganization and Redesignation of 5 June 1944.**

(1) Directive - Pursuant to General Order #31, 14th AA Command, 5 June 1944, all units carrying Coast Artillery (AA) designation were redesignated AAA units.

(2) Directive - General Order #31, 14th AA Command, 5 June 1944.

Old Designation	New Designation	T/O Applicable
707th MG Btry A/B (AA)	707th AAA MG Btry	44-217 (20 Aug 1943)
708th " " " "	708th " " "	" " " " "
709th " " " "	709th " " "	" " " " "

E. **Reorganization and Redesignation of Antiaircraft Units to Air Transportable and Self - Propelled, 15 September 1944.**

Directive - General Order #54, 14th AA Command, 31 August 1944.

Unit	T/O Applicable
101st AAA AW Bn A/T	44-225 S (9 May 1944)
102d " " " "	" " " " " "
209th " " " S/P	44-75, (19 April 1944)

F. **Reorganization and Redesignation of Antiaircraft Units to Mobile T/O's, 25 April 1945.**

Directive - General Order #33, 14th AA Command, 10 April 1945.

Unit	T/O Applicable
104th AAA AW Bn (Mobile)	44-25 (22 Apr 1944) Ch 1, 2, 3
210th " " " "	" " " " " " " " "
211th " " " "	" " " " " " " " "
743d AAA Gun Bn (Mobile Type A)	44-15 (17 Nov 1944)
744th " " " " " "	" " " " "
745th " " " " " "	" " " " "

3. **Reorganizations and Redesignations In USAFISPA.**

A. **Reorganization of November - December 1942.**

(1) Directive - General Order #31, U.S. Forces in Fiji (1 Nov 1942).

Unit	T/O Applicable
251st CA (AA)	4-111 (1 Apr 1942)

(2) Directive - Hq, USAFISPA Ltr, AGO-322, 13 December 1942.

Unit	T/O Applicable
70th CA (AA)	4-111 (1 Apr 1942).

(3) Directive - WD radiogram 251,712, (Dec 1942) and COMGENSOPAC radiogram 270,200, Dec 1942.

Unit	T/O Applicable
198th CA (AA)	4-111 (1 Apr 1942)

B. **Reorganization of 1 November 1943.**

Directive - General Order #306, Hq. USAFISPA, 18 Oct 1943.

Old Designation	New Designation	T/O Applicable
Hq & Hq Btry, 76th CA (AA)	Hq & Hq Btry, 76th AAA Gp	44-12 (14 Apr 1943)
1st Bn, 76th CA (AA)	76th AAA Gun Bn	44-115 (18 Mar 1943)
2d Bn, 76th CA (AA)	933d AAA Gun Bn	44-125 (27 Feb 1943)
3d Bn, 76th CA (AA)	374th AAA SL Bn	44-135 (27 Feb 1943)
Hq & Hq Btry, 77th CA (AA)	Hq & Hq Btry, 77th AAA Gp	44-12 (14 Apr 1943)
1st Bn, 77th CA (AA)	77th AAA Gun Bn	44-115 (18 Mar 1943)
2d Bn, 77th CA (AA)	938th AAA AW Bn	44-125 (27 Feb 1943)
Btry I	Btry A, 374th AAA SL Bn	44-138 (27 Feb 1943)

C. **Reorganizations of 10 November 1943.**

Directive - General Order #339, Hq., USAFISPA, 27 October 1943.

Old Designation	New Designation	T/O Applicable
Hq & Hq Btry, 214th CA (AA)	Hq & Hq Btry, 214th AAA Gp	44-12 (14 Apr 1943)
1st Bn, 214th CA (AA)	528th AAA Gun Bn	44-115 (18 Mar 1943)
2d Bn, 214th CA (AA)	950th AAA AW Bn	44-125 (27 Feb 1943)
3d Bn, 214th CA (AA)	250th AAA SL Bn	44-135 (27 Feb 1943)
Hq & Hq Btry, 70th CA (AA)	Hq & Hq Btry, 70th AAA Gp	44-12 (14 Apr 1943)
1st Bn, 70th CA (AA)	70th AAA Gun Bn	44-115 (18 Mar 1943)
2d Bn, 70th CA (AA) (less Btry H)*	925th AAA AW Bn (less Btry D)**	44-125 (27 Feb 1943)
Btry I, 70th CA (AA)	725th AAA SL Btry (Sep)	44-138 (27 Feb 1943)
Btry K, 70th CA (AA)	Btry C, 250th AAA SL Bn	44-138 (27 Feb 1943)

* Battery H had been converted to a 90-mm Battery in June 1943, and became Battery D, 967th AAA Gun Battalion on 10 November 1943.

** Battery D, 925th AAA AW Battalion was activated and cadred by personnel from Batteries A, B, & C.

D. **Reorganizations on 1 March 1944.**

Directive - General Order #224, Hq., USAFISPA, 10 Feb 1944.

Old Designation	New Designation	T/O Applicable
Hq, 198th CA (AA)	Hq, 198th AAA Gp	44-12 (10 Nov 1943)
1st Bn, 198th CA (AA)	736th AAA Gun Bn	44-115 (16 Nov 1943)
2d Bn, 198th CA (AA)	945th AAA AW Bn	44-125 (30 Sep 1943)
3d Bn, 198th CA (AA)	373d AAA SL Bn	44-135 (28 Dec 1943)
Hq, 251st CA (AA)	Hq, 251st AAA Gp	44-12 (10 Nov 1943)
1st Bn, 251st CA (AA)	746th AAA Gun Bn	44-115 (16 Nov 1943)
2d Bn, 251st CA (AA)	951st AAA AW Bn	44-125 (30 Sep 1943)
3d Bn, 251st CA (AA)	disbanded (all personnel to 373d AAA SL Bn)	

4. **Reorganization and Redesignation of Units in POA and MIDPAC.**

A. **Reorganization of February - July 1944 in POA and MIDPAC.**

(1) Directive - WD ltr, AG 320.2 (31 Jul 43) PE-A-M-C, 20 August 43, subj: "Utilization of Personnel".

Unit	General Order	Date	T/O&E Applicable
868th AAA AW Bn	233 HCPA	30 Jul 44	44-125 (19 Apr 44)
206th AAA AW Bn	223 HCPA	16 Jul 44	44-125 (19 Apr 44)
864th " " "	" "	" " "	" " " "
865th " " "	" "	" " "	" " " "
867th " " "	" "	" " "	" " " "
501st AAA Gun Bn	" "	" " "	44-115 (26 Apr 44)
504th " " "	" "	" " "	" " " "
751st " " "	" "	" " "	" " " "
139th AAA Gp, Hq & Hq Btry	222 HCPA	16 Jul 44	44-12 (10 Nov 43)
93d AAA Gun Bn	205 HCPA	28 Jun 44	44-115 (26 Apr 44)
96th " " "	" "	" " "	" " " "
97th " " "	" "	" " "	" " " "
98th " " "	" "	" " "	" " " "
503d " " "	" "	" " "	" " " "
506th " " "	" "	" " "	" " " "
750th " " "	" "	" " "	" " " "
752d " " "	" "	" " "	" " " "
753d " " "	" "	" " "	" " " "
754th " " "	" "	" " "	" " " "
755th " " "	" "	" " "	" " " "
771st " " "	" "	" " "	" " " "
947th " " "	" "	" " "	" " " "

Unit	General Order	Date	T/O&E Applicable
483d AAA AW Bn	205 HCPA	28 Jun 44	44-125 (19 Apr 44)
811th " " "	" "	" " "	" " " " "
869th " " "	" "	" " "	" " " " "
870th " " "	" "	" " "	" " " " "
304th AAA Gun Bn	202 HCPA	25 Jun 44	44-115 (26 Apr 44)
7th AAA AW Bn	" "	" " "	44-115 (19 Apr 44)
504th AAA Gun Bn	132 HCPA	9 May 44	44-115 (16 Nov 43)
502nd AAA Gun Bn	111 HCPA	20 Apr 44	44-115 (16 Nov 43)
503rd " " "	" "	" " "	" " " " "
738th " " "	" "	" " "	" " " " "
750th " " "	" "	" " "	" " " " "
751st " " "	" "	" " "	" " " " "
752nd " " "	" "	" " "	" " " " "
753rd " " "	" "	" " "	" " " " "
754th " " "	" "	" " "	" " " " "
755th " " "	" "	" " "	" " " " "
771st " " "	" "	" " "	" " " " "
Hq & Hq Btry, 429th AAA Bn (Comp)	" "	" " "	44-116 (16 Nov 43)
Btry A, 429th AAA Bn (Comp)	" "	" " "	44-117 (16 Nov 43)
Btry B, 429th AAA Bn (Comp)	" "	" " "	" " " " "
Med Det, 429th AAA Bn (Comp)	" "	" " "	44-115 (16 Nov 43)
64th AAA Gun Bn	97 HCPA	13 Apr 44	44-115 (16 Nov 43)
93rd " " "	" "	" " "	" " " " "
96th " " "	" "	" " "	" " " " "
97th " " "	" "	" " "	" " " " "
98th " " "	" "	" " "	" " " " "
369th " " "	" "	" " "	" " " " "
501st " " "	" "	" " "	" " " " "
485th AAA AW Bn	" "	" " "	44-125 (30 Sep 43)
230th AAA SL Bn	" "	" " "	44-135 (28 Dec 43)
294th " " "	" "	" " "	" " " " "
295th " " "	" "	" " "	" " " " "
296th " " "	" "	" " "	" " " " "
325th " " "	" "	" " "	" " " " "
726th AAA SL Btry (Sep)	" "	" " "	44-138 (28 Dec 43)
716th " " "	" "	" " "	" " " " "
			(Col 8)
Hq & Hq Btry, 139th AAA Gp	67 HCPA	6 Mar 44	44-12 (10 Nov 43)
206th AAA AW Bn	" "	" " "	44-125 (30 Sep 43)
861st " " "	" "	" " "	" " " " "
864th " " "	" "	" " "	" " " " "

Unit	General Order	Date	T/O&E Applicable
865th AAA AW Bn	67 HCPA	6 Mar 44	44-125 (30 Sep 43)
866th " " "	" "	" " "	" " " " "
867th " " "	" "	" " "	" " " " "
868th " " "	" "	" " "	" " " " "
869th " " "	" "	" " "	" " " " "
870th " " "	" "	" " "	" " " " "
Hq & Hq Btry, 97th AAA Gp	53 HCPA	22 Feb 44	44-12 (10 Nov 43)
" " " " , 98th " "	" "	" " "	" " " " "
" " " " , 136th " "	" "	" " "	" " " " "
" " " " , 137th " "	" "	" " "	" " " " "
" " " " , 138th " "	" "	" " "	" " " " "
" " " " , 369th " "	" "	" " "	" " " " "

(2) Directive - WD ltr, AG 320.2 (1-15-42) MR-M-C, January 19 1942, subj: "Constitution, Activation and Movement of CA (AA) Units", and WD radiogram, June 29, 1942, the units listed below were redesignated.

Old Designation	New Designation	General Order	Date
1st Plat, Btry E, 94th CA (AA)(SM)	1st Plat, Btry A, 428th Sep CA Bn, (AA)(Comp)	113 HHD	30 Jun 42
3d Plat, Btry E, 94th CA (AA)(SM)	1st Plat, Btry A, 429th CA Bn, (AA)(Comp)	" "	" " "
Btry B, 95th CA (AA)(SM)	Btry B, 429th CA Bn (AA)(Comp)	" "	" " "
Btry C, 95th CA (AA)(SM)	Btry B, 429th Sep CA Bn (AA)(Comp)	" "	" " "
Btry A, 105th Sep CA Bn (AA)	Btry C, 428th Sep CA Bn (AA)(Comp)	" "	" " "
Btry B, 105th Sep CA Bn (AA)	Btry C, 429th Sep CA Bn (AA)(Comp)	" "	" " "

B. **Activations in POA and MIDPAC.**

(1) Directive - WD ltr, AG 322 (11 May 44) OB-I-GNGCT-M, 13 May 1944, subj: "Constitution, Activation and Disbandment of CA Units".

Unit	General Order	Date	T/O&E Applicable	Source of Personnel
Hq & Hq Btry, 86th AAA Gp	158 HCPA	26 May 44	44-12 (10 Nov 43)	428th CA Regt
947th AAA Gun Bn (SM)	" "	" " "	44-115 (16 Nov 43)	(AA)(Comp)
948th AAA Gun Bn (SM)	" "	" " "	" " " " "	and
811th AAA AW Bn (SM)	" "	" " "	44-125 (30 Sep 43)	429th AAA Bn,
162d AAA Opns Det	" "	" " "	44-7 (28 Feb 44)	SM (Comp)
163d AAA Opns Det	" "	" " "	" " " " "	

(2) Directive - WD ltr, AG 322 (15 Oct 43) OB-I-GNGCT-M, 16 October 1943, subj: "Activation and Inactivation of Certain CA Units".

Unit	General Order	Date	T/O&E Applicable	Source of Personnel
861st AAA AW Bn	169 HCPA	5 Nov 43	44-125 (27 Feb 43)	305th CA
Med Det, 861st AAA AW Bn	" "	" " "	44-125M (27 Feb 43)	Barrage
Hq & Hq Btry, 861st AAA AW Bn	" "	" " "	44-126 (27 Feb 43)	Balloon Bn
Four (4) AW Btrys	" "	" " "	44-127 (27 Feb 43)	

(3) Directive - WD ltr, AG 320.2 (1-15-42) MR-M-C, January 19 1942, subj: "Constitution, Activation and Movement of CA (AA) Units", and WD radiogram, June 29, 1942.

Unit	General Order	Date	T/O&E Applicable	Source of Personnel
428th Sep CA Bn (AA)(Comp)	113 HHD	30 Jun 42		
1st Plat Btry A (SL)			4-18	1st Plat. Btry E, 94th CA (AA)(SM)
Btry B (Gun)			4-17	Btry A, 105th Sep CA Bn(AA)
Btry C (37mm Gun)			4-28	Btry B, 95th CA(AA)(SM)
429th Sep CA Bn (AA)(Comp)	113 HHD	30 Jun 42		
1st Plat Btry A (SL)			4-18	3d Plat, Btry E, 94th CA (AA)(SM)
Btry B (Gun)			4-17	Btry B, 105th Sep CA Bn(AA)
Btry C (37mm Gun)			4-28	Btry C, 95th CA(AA)(SM)

(4) Directive - WD ltr, SPAG 320.2 (3-19-42) MR-M-GN, March 24 1942, subj: "Constitution and Activation of Units, Hawaiian Department".

Unit	General Order	Date	T/O&E Applicable	Source of Personnel
710th CA Btry (Gun)(AA)(SM)	84 HHD	18 May 42	4-17)	Hawaiian Antiaircraft Artillery Command
711th " " " " "	" " "	" " "	" ")	
712th " " " " "	" " "	" " "	" ")	
713th " " " " "	" " "	" " "	" ")	
714th " " " " "	" " "	" " "	" ")	
715th " " " " "	" " "	" " "	" ")	

(5) Directive - WD ltr, AG 320.2 (3-2-42) MR-M-G, subj: "Reorganization of CA, Hawaiian Department", March 6, 1942.

Unit	General Order	Date	T/O&E Applicable	Source of Personnel
Hq & Hq Btry, Hawn AAA Comd	38 HHD	16 Mar 42	4-222	Hawaiian Antiaircraft Artillery Command

C. **Inactivations in POA and MIDPAC.**

Directive - WD ltr, AG 320.2 (1-15-42) MR-M-C, January ?. 1942, subj: "Constitution, Activation and Movemer ʳ CA (AA) Units", and WD radiogram, June 29, 1942, t⸱   .t listed below was inactivated.

Unit	General Order	Date
1st Bn, 95th CA (AA) (SM)	113 HHD	30 Jun 42

D. **Disbandment of Units in POA and MIDPAC.**

Directive - WD ltr, AG 322 (11 May 44) OB-I-GNGCT-M, 13 May 1944, subj: "Constitution, Activation, and Disbandment of CA Units", the units listed below were disbanded.

Unit	General Order	Date
428th CA Regt (AA) (Comp)	158 HCPA	26 May 44
429th AAA Bn, (SM) (Comp)	" "	" " "

E. **Reorganization Of the Hawaiian Antiaircraft Artillery Command.**

(1) Directive - WD ltr, AG 322 (1 August 43) OB-IGNGCT-M, 4 Nov 43, subj: "Reorganization of the Hawaiian Antiaircraft Artillery Command", and WD radiogram, 8370, 2 Dec 43, the following units are redesignated, reorganized, disbanded, or activated, effective 12 December.

Old Designation	New Designation	T/O&E Applicable	
Hq & Hq Btry, HAAC	Hq & Hq Btry, AAA Comd (HAW)	44-1-38	(4 Nov 43)
Intell Btry, 53d CAB	53d AAA Intellignece Btry	44-147S	
Hq & Hq Btry, 53d CAB	Hq & Hq Btry, 53d AAA Brig	44-10-1	(29 Mar 43)
Hq & Hq Btry, 64th CA (AA)	Hq & Hq Btry, 136th AAA Gp	44-12	(14 Apr 43)
Band, 64th CA (AA)	264th Army Band	4-111	(1 Nov 40)
Hq & Hq Btry, 1st Bn, 64th CA (AA)	Hq & Hq Btry, 64th AAA Gun Bn	44-116 44-115-M	(18 Mar 43) (18 Mar 43)

Old Designation	New Designation	T/O&E Applicable	
Btry H, 64th CA (AA)	Btry A, 64th AAA Gun Bn SM)		
Btry B, 64th CA (AA)	Btry B, 64th AAA Gun Bn SM)	44-117	(18 Mar 43)
Btry G, 64th CA (AA)	Btry C, 64th AAA Gun Bn SM)		
Btry D, 64th CA (AA)	Btry D, 64th AAA Gun Bn SM)		
Hq & Hq Btry, 2d Bn, 64th CA (AA)	Hq & Hq Btry, 750th AAA Gun Bn	44-116 44-115-M	(18 Mar 43) (18 Mar 43)
Hq & Hq Btry, 2d Bn, 98th CA (AA)	Hq & Hq Btry, 755th AAA Gun Bn	44-116 44-115-M	(18 Mar 43) (18 Mar 43)
Btry F, 98th CA (AA)	Btry A, 755th AAA Gun Bn SM)		
Btry G, 98th CA (AA)	Btry B, 755th AAA Gun Bn SM)		
Btry H, 98th CA (AA)	Btry C, 755th AAA Gun Bn SM)		
712th CA Btry (AA)	Btry D, 755th AAA Gun Bn SM)	44-117	(18 Mar 43)
Btry F, 93d CA (AA)	Btry A, 751st AAA Gun Bn SM)		
Btry H, 93d CA (AA)	Btry B, 751st AAA Gun Bn SM)		
Btry C, 64th CA (AA)	Btry C, 751st AAA Gun Bn SM)		
Btry F, 64th CA (AA)	Btry D, 751st AAA Gun Bn SM)		
Hq & Hq Btry, 97th CA (AA)	Hq & Hq Btry, 97th AAA Gp	44-12	(14 Apr 43)
Band, 97th CA (AA)	297th Army Band	4-111	(1 Nov 40)
Hq & Hq Btry, 1st Bn, 97th CA (AA)	Hq & Hq Btry, 97th AAA Gun Bn	44-116 44-115-M	(18 Mar 43) (18 Mar 43)
Btry F, 97th CA (AA)	Btry A, 97th AAA Gun Bn SM)		
Btry B, 97th CA (AA)	Btry B, 97th AAA Gun Bn SM)	44-117	(18 Mar 43)
Btry C, 97th CA (AA)	Btry C, 97th AAA Gun Bn SM)		
710th CA Btry (Gun)(AA)(SM)	Btry D, 97th AAA Gun Bn SM)		
Hq & Hq Btry, 2d Bn, 97th CA (AA)	Hq & Hq Btry, 754th AAA Gun Bn	44-116 44-115-M	(18 Mar 43) (18 Mar 43)
711th CA Btry (AA)(SM)	Btry A, 754th AAA Gun Bn SM)		
714th CA Btry (AA)(SM)	Btry B, 754th AAA Gun Bn SM)		
Btry G, 97th CA (AA)	Btry C, 754th AAA Gun Bn SM)		
Btry D, 97th CA (AA)	Btry D, 754th AAA Gun Bn SM)	44-117	(18 Mar 43)
Btry G, 93d CA (AA)	Btry A, 93d AAA Gun Bn SM)		
Btry B, 93d CA (AA)	Btry B, 93d AAA Gun Bn SM)		
Btry C, 98th CA (AA)	Btry C, 93d AAA Gun Bn SM)		
713th CA Btry (AA)(SM)	Btry D, 93d AAA Gun Bn SM)		
Hq & Hq Btry, 95th CA (AA)	Hq & Hq Btry, 138th AAA Gp	44-12	(14 Apr 43)
Hq & Hq Btry, 1st Bn, 369th CA (AA)	Hq & Hq Btry, 369th AAA Gun Bn	44-116 44-115-M	(18 Mar 43) (18 Mar 43)

Old Designation	New Designation	T/O&E Applicable	
Btry B, 369th CA (AA) Btry C, 369th CA (AA) Btry D, 369th CA (AA)	Btry B, 369th AAA Gun Bn SM) Btry C, 369th AAA Gun Bn SM) Btry D, 369th AAA Gun Bn SM)	44-117	(18 Mar 43)
Hq & Hq Btry, 1st Bn, 98th CA (AA)	Hq & Hq Btry, 98th AAA Gun Bn	44-116 44-115-M	(18 Mar 43) (18 Mar 43)
Btry D, 93d CA (AA) Btry B, 98th CA (AA) Btry C, 93d CA (AA) Btry D, 98th CA (AA)	Btry A, 98th AAA Gun Bn SM) Btry B, 98th AAA Gun Bn SM) Btry C, 98th AAA Gun Bn SM) Btry D, 98th AAA Gun Bn SM)	44-117	(18 Mar 43)
Hq & Hq Btry, 2d Bn, 95th CA (AA)	Hq & Hq Btry, 752d AAA Gun Bn	44-116 44-115-M	(18 Mar 43) (18 Mar 43)
Btry H, 97th CA (AA) Btry F, 95th CA (AA) Btry G, 95th CA (AA) Btry H, 95th CA (AA)	Btry A, 752d AAA Gun Bn SM) Btry B, 752d AAA Gun Bn SM) Btry C, 752d AAA Gun Bn SM) Btry D, 752d AAA Gun Bn SM)	44-117	(18 Mar 43)
Hq & Hq Btry, 369th CA (AA)	Hq & Hq Btry, 369th AAA Gp	44-12	(14 Apr 43)
Band, 369th CA (AA)	299th Army Band	4-111	(1 Nov 40)
Hq & Hq Btry, 2d Bn, 369th CA (AA)	Hq & Hq Btry, 870th AAA AW Bn	44-126 44-125-M	(27 Feb 43) (27 Feb 43)
Btry E, 369th CA (AA) Btry F, 369th CA (AA) Btry G, 369th CA (AA) Btry H, 369th CA (AA)	Btry A, 870th AAA AW Bn) Btry B, 870th AAA AW Bn) Btry C, 870th AAA AW Bn) Btry D, 870th AAA AW Bn)	44-127	(27 Feb 43)
Hq & Hq Btry, 3d Bn, 64th CA (AA)	Hq & Hq Btry, 864th AAA AW Bn	44-126 44-125-M	(27 Feb 43) (27 Feb 43)
Btry I, 64th CA (AA) Btry K, 64th CA (AA) Btry L, 64th CA (AA) Btry M, 64th CA (AA)	Btry A, 864th AAA AW Bn) Btry B, 864th AAA AW Bn) Btry C, 864th AAA AW Bn) Btry D, 864th AAA AW Bn)	44-127	(27 Feb 43)
Hq & Hq Btry, 3d Bn, 97th CA (AA)	Hq & Hq Btry, 868th AAA AW Bn	44-126 44-125-M	(27 Feb 43) (27 Feb 43)
Btry I, 97th CA (AA) Btry K, 97th CA (AA) Btry L, 97th CA (AA) Btry M, 97th CA (AA)	Btry A, 868th AAA AW Bn) Btry B, 868th AAA AW Bn) Btry C, 868th AAA AW Bn) Btry D, 868th AAA AW Bn)	44-127	(27 Feb 43)

Old Designation	New Designation	T/O&E Applicable	
Hq & Hq Btry, 93d CA (AA)	Hq & Hq Btry, 137th AAA Gp	44-12	(14 Apr 43)
Band, 93d CA (AA)	293d Army Band	4-111	(1 Nov 40)
Hq & Hq Btry, 3d Bn, 93d CA (AA)	Hq & Hq Btry, 865th AAA AW Bn	44-126 44-125-M	(27 Feb 43) (27 Feb 43)
Btry I, 93d CA (AA) Btry K, 93d CA (AA) Btry L, 93d CA (AA) Btry M, 93d CA (AA)	Btry A, 865th AAA AW Bn) Btry B, 865th AAA AW Bn) Btry C, 865th AAA AW Bn) Btry D, 865th AAA AW Bn)	44-127	(27 Feb 43)
Hq & Hq Btry, 3d Bn, 98th CA (AA)	Hq & Hq Btry 869th AAA AW Bn	44-126 44-125-M	(27 Feb 43) (27 Feb 43)
Btry I, 98th CA (AA) Btry K, 98th CA (AA) Btry L, 98th CA (AA) Btry M, 98th CA (AA)	Btry A, 869th AAA AW Bn) Btry B, 869th AAA AW Bn) Btry C, 869th AAA AW Bn) Btry D, 869th AAA AW Bn)	44-127	(27 Feb 43)
Hq & Hq Btry, 3d Bn, 95th CA (AA)	Hq & Hq Btry, 866th AAA AW Bn	44-126 44-125-M	(27 Feb 43) (27 Feb 43)
Btry I, 95th CA (AA) Btry K, 95th CA (AA) Btry L, 95th CA (AA) Btry M, 95th CA (AA)	Btry A, 866th AAA AW Bn) Btry B, 866th AAA AW Bn) Btry C, 866th AAA AW Bn) Btry D, 866th AAA AW Bn)	44-127	(27 Feb 43)
Hq & Hq Btry, 98th CA (AA)	Hq & Hq Btry 98th AAA Gp	44-12	(14 Apr 43)
Hq & Hq Btry, 1st Bn, 93d CA (AA)	Hq & Hq Btry 294th AAA SL Bn	44-136 44-135-M	(27 Feb 43) (27 Feb 43)
Btry A, 98th CA (AA) Btry E, 93d CA (AA) Btry A, 93d CA (AA)	Btry A, 294th AAA SL Bn) Btry B, 294th AAA SL Bn) Btry C, 294th AAA SL Bn)	44-138	(27 Feb 43)
Hq & Hq Btry, 2d Bn, 93d CA (AA)	Hq & Hq Btry, 295th AAA SL Bn	44-136 44-135-M	(27 Feb 43) (27 Feb 43)
Btry A, 64th CA (AA) Btry A, 97th CA (AA) Btry E, 64th CA (AA) Btry A, 96th CA (AA) Btry E, 96th CA (AA) Btry E, 95th CA (AA)	Btry A, 295th AAA SL Bn) Btry B, 295th AAA SL Bn) Btry C, 295th AAA SL Bn) Btry A, 296th AAA SL Bn) Btry B, 296th AAA SL Bn) Btry C, 296th AAA SL Bn)	44-138	(27 Feb 43)

Old Designation	New Designation	T/O&E Applicable	
Btry A, 369th CA (AA)	726th AAA SL Btry, Sep	44-138	(27 Feb 43)
Hq & Hq Btry, 96th CA (AA)	Hq & Hq Btry, 139th AAA Gp	44-12	(14 Apr 43)
Band, 96th CA (AA)	296th Army Band	4-111	(1 Nov 40)
Hq & Hq Btry, 1st Bn, 96th CA (AA)	Hq & Hq Btry, 96th AAA Gun Bn	44-116 44-115-M	(18 Mar 43) (18 Mar 43)
Btry B, 96th CA (AA) Btry C, 96th CA (AA) Btry D, 96th CA (AA)	Btry B, 96th AAA Gun Bn SM) Btry C, 96th AAA Gun Bn SM) Btry D, 96th AAA Gun Bn SM)	44-117	(18 Mar 43)
Hq & Hq Btry, 2d Bn, 96th CA (AA)	Hq & Hq Btry, 753d AAA Gun Bn	44-116 44-115-M	(18 Mar 43) (18 Mar 43)
Btry F, 96th CA (AA) Btry G, 96th CA (AA) Btry H, 96th CA (AA)	Btry A, 753d AAA Gun Bn SM) Btry B, 753d AAA Gun Bn SM) Btry C, 753d AAA Gun Bn SM)	44-117	(18 Mar 43)
Hq & Hq Btry, 3d Bn, 96th CA (AA)	Hq & Hq Btry, 867th AAA AW Bn	44-126 44-125-M	(27 Feb 43) (27 Feb 43)
Btry I, 96th CA (AA) Btry K, 96th CA (AA) Btry L, 96th CA (AA) Btry M, 96th CA (AA)	Btry A, 867th AAA AW Bn) Btry B, 867th AAA AW Bn) Btry C, 867th AAA AW Bn) Btry D, 867th AAA AW Bn)	44-127	(27 Feb 43)
AA Det, Btry A 16th CA(HD) AA Det, Btry E 55th CA(HD) AA Det, Btry C 16th CA(HD) AA Det, Btry F 55th CA(HD)	Btry A, 750th AAA Gun Bn SM Btry B, 750th AAA Gun Bn SM Btry C, 750th AAA Gun Bn SM Btry D, 750th AAA Gun Bn SM		

(2) Units to be Activated.

Unit	T/O&E Applicable	
Hq & Hq Btry, 751st AAA Gun Bn	44-116 44-115-M	(18 Mar 43) (18 Mar 43)
Hq & Hq Btry, 93d AAA Gun Bn	44-116 44-115-M	(18 Mar 43) (18 Mar 43)
Btry A, 369th AAA Gun Bn, SM	44-117	(18 Mar 43)
Hq & Hq Btry, 70th AAA Brig	44-10-1	(29 Mar 43)
Hq & Hq Btry, 296th AAA SL Bn	44-136 44-135-M	(27 Feb 43) (27 Feb 43)

Unit	T/O&E Applicable
Btry A, 96th AAA Gun Bn, SM) Btry D, 753d AAA Gun Bn, SM)	44-117 (18 Mar 43)
Btry A, 750th AAA Gun Bn, SM) Btry B, 750th AAA Gun Bn, SM) Btry C, 750th AAA Gun Bn, SM) Btry D, 750th AAA Gun Bn, SM)	44-117 (18 Mar 43)

    (3) <u>Disbanded</u>.

      (a) Concurrently with the action outlined above, the 715th Coast Artillery Btry (Gun) (AA) (SM) will be disbanded. Personnel and equipment will be absorbed by <u>units</u> activated above.

      (b) Concurrently with the reorganization and redesignation of the active elements of the 95th, 97th and 98th Coast Artillery Regiments (AA), as set forth above, these regiments (less redesignated elements) are disbanded.

ANNEX B

UNIT COMMENDATIONS

AND CITATIONS

UNIT COMMENDATIONS

The following is a list of the commendations and citations received by antiaircraft units for combat operations in the Pacific area as reported in unit histories made available to this Board:

1. <u>Antiaircraft Groups</u>:

<u>33d AAA Group</u> - a. Commendation from Commanding Officer, 86th Fighter Wing for splendid cooperation in the installation and operation of air defenses at Sansapor in October 1944.

b. Commendation from Commanding General, Sixth Infantry Division for destruction of a single enemy reconnaissance plane at Sansapor, 30 December 1944.

<u>94th AAA Group</u> - a. Commendation from Commanding General, 24th Division Artillery for adjusting and delivering effective fire on terrestrial targets at Hollandia, 4 May 1944.

b. Commendations from Commanding General, Eighth Army, and from Commanding General, Western Visayan Task Force for superior antiaircraft performance at Mindoro, 11 January 1945.

c. Presidential Unit Citation for participation in the Papuan Campaign (War Department General Order #21, 6 May 1943) awarded to Batteries D, G, and Detachment of Battery K of the 94th Coast Artillery (AA).

<u>97th AAA Group</u> - Commendation from Commanding General, 14th Antiaircraft Command for operations and performance on Leyte endorsed by Commanding General, Tenth Army, and Commanding General XXIV Corps, 20 February 1944.

<u>116th AAA Group</u> - Commendation from Commanding General, Kiriwina Task Force for operations on Kiriwina Island, March 1944.

<u>136th AAA Group</u> - Commendation from Commanding General, Tenth Army AAA, for operations in the Ryukyus, 24 - 25 May 1945.

<u>197th AAA Group</u> - Commendation from Commander, United States Naval Forces, SWPA for efficient installation of antiaircraft defenses in the Perth-Fremantle area, 1 April 1942. (Unit then 197th Coast Artillery (AA).

<u>198th AAA Group</u> - Commendation for exceptionally meritorious conduct during the battle of Falamai Peninsula (Treasury Islands), 27 October 1943.

208th AAA Group - Presidential Unit citation fro participation in the Papuan campaign. Section IV, War Department General Order #21, 6 May 1943.

214th AAA Group - a. Commendation from Commanding General, USAFISPA, 12 June 1943 for development and execution of searchlight-night fighter technique used at Guadalcanal.

b. Commendation from Commanding General, XI Corps for superior performance of duty at Morotai, N.E.I., 8 November 1944.

251st AAA Group - a. Commendation from Headquarters, Artillery Group at Bougainville for perimeter defense and close fire support, 19 April 1944.

b. Commendation from Commanding Officer, 145th Infantry for occupying defensive positions and conducting patrols on Bougainville in April 1944.

2. AAA Automatic Weapons Battalions

7th AAA AW Battalion - a. Commendation from Commanding General, Army Garrison Force, APO 245 for defense against low-level enemy bombers and Kamekazi planes at Ie Shima, 10 August 1945.

b. Included in commendation of 97th AAA Group by Commanding General, 14th Antiaircraft Command, noted above.

c. Commendation from Commanding Officer, 420th Field Artillery Group for 2d Platoon, Battery B for automatic weapons protection on Ie Shima in repelling an amphibious landing, 9 April 1945.

d. Commendation from Commanding General, Tenth Army AAA for operations on Ie Shima, 24 - 25 May 1945.

101st AAA AW Battalion - Presidential Unit Citation for participation in Papuan campaign. Section III, War Department General Order #21, 6 May 1943.

102d AAA AW Battalion - Commendation from Commanding General, Eighth Army and Commanding General, Visayan Task Force to Batteries B and C for superior antiaircraft defense in Mindanao, 11 January 1945.

104th AAA AW Battalion - Presidential Unit Citation to Battery C for participation in Papuan campaign. Section IV, War Department General Order #21, 6 May 1943.

198th AAA AW Battalion - a. Commendation from Commanding Officer, 152d Infantry to 2d Platoon Battery B for close support of attacking infantry on Luzon, 27 May 1945.

b. Commendation from Commanding General, 43d Division Artillery to Battery D for artillery support from exposed positions on Luzon. 26 May 1945.

209th AAA AW Battalion - Presidential Unit Citation to Battery C for participation in Papuan Campaign. Section IV, War Department General Order #21. 6 May 1943.

210th AAA AW Battalion - Commendation from Commanding General, 158th Regimental Combat Team for artillery support missions and patrolling activity at Legaspi, Luzon. 25 May 1945.

211th AAA AW Battalion - a. Presidential Unit Citation for Papuan campaign, Section IV, War Department General Order #21. 6 May 1943.

b. Letter from Commander-in-Chief, SWPA and Commanding General, Sixth Army regarding Leyte operations. "This is superior shooting." November 1944.

c. Included in commendation from Commanding General, XI Corps to 214th Group at Morotai. 8 November 1944.

383d AAA AW Battalion - Commendation from Commanding General XI Corps for D-Day performance at Morotai against the enemy. 17 October 1944.

389th AAA AW Battalion - a. Included in commendation from Commanding General, XI Corps to 214th AAA Group at Morotai, 8 November 1944.

b. Commendation from Commanding General, 41st Infantry Division for operations at Biak. 26 August 1944.

c. Presidential Unit Citation for antiaircraft performance at Biak. War Department General Order #45, 12 June 1945.

478th AAA AW Battalion - Commendation from Commanding General, Americal Division for terrestrial fire and maintenance of road blocks and strong points on Cebu. April - June 1945.

785th AAA AW Battalion - a. Commendation to Battery B from Commanding General, XI Corps for manning positions without cover at Morotai. 8 January 1945.

b. Included in commendation from Commanding General, XI Corps to 214th AAA Group at Morotai. 8 November 1944.

870th AAA AW Battalion - Commendation from Commanding General, Tenth Army AAA for successful operation in the attack and capture of a hill above Tokashiki, Okinawa. 26 June 1945.

945th AAA AW Battalion - Commendation from Commanding Officer, 198th CA (AA) to Battery C (then Battery G of the 198th CA (AA)) for defense against enemy attacks in November 1943 on Sterling Island in the Northern Solomons. 8 January 1944.

3. <u>AAA Gun Battalions</u>

   <u>64th AAA Gun Battalion</u> - Commendation from Commanding General, Island Command, Guam for patrolling and mopping up of enemy troops on Guam, (351 Japanese killed and 26 captured), 14 May 1945.

   <u>93d AAA Gun Battalion</u> - Commendations from CINCPOA, Commanding General, Tenth Army AA, Commanding General, ISCOM and Commanding General 136th AAA Group for action on Okinawa on night of 24 - 25 May. ($15\frac{1}{2}$ planes destroyed in one night's action).

   <u>161st AAA Gun Battalion</u> - a. Commendation from Commanding General, 25th Infantry Division to Battery A for fire support at Balete Pass, 11 June 1945.

   b. Commendation from Commanding Officer, 152d Infantry to Battery D for fire support at Woodpecker Ridge, 17 June 1945.

   c. Commendation to Batteries B and C, 161st AAA Gun Battalion for operations at Ipo Dam, from Commanding General 43d Division Artillery, 25 May 1945.

   <u>163d AAA Gun Battalion</u> - Commendation from Commanding General, 24th Division Artillery for terrestrial fire on targets at Hollandia airdrome. 4 May 1944.

   <u>164th AAA Gun Battalion</u> - Commendation from Commanding Officer Base F for participation in harbor defenses at Finschhafen, 13 April 1945.

   <u>166th AAA Gun Battalion</u> - a. Commendation from Commanding General, Eighth Army for antiaircraft performance in Western Visayan Task Force, 11 January 1944.

   b. Commendation to Battery B from Commanding General, X Corps for infantry operation on Mindinao. January 1945.

   <u>496th AAA Gun Battalion</u> - Commendation from the Commanding Officer CTG 78.5 for shooting down lone observation plane at Sansapor. 30 December 1944.

   <u>503d AAA Gun Battalion</u> - Commendation from Commanding General, 53d AAA Brigade for shooting down last two planes destroyed in the war (6 August 1945 on Okinawa).

   <u>504th AAA Gun Battalion</u> - Commendations from Commanding General, XXIV Corps Artillery, Commanding General, 7th Division Artillery, and Commanding Officer, 31st FA Battalion for night harrassing fires on Okinawa. April and June 1945.

   <u>518th AAA Gun Battalion</u> - a. Commendations from Commanding General, XIV Corps Artillery for ground fire missions on Luzon. 8 March 1945.

b. Commendation from Commanding General, 46th Division Artillery to Battery A for terrestrial fire in mountains northwest of Fort Stotsenburg. 27 March 1945.

743d AAA Gun Battalion - Presidential Unit Citation to Battery D for participation in Papuan campaign. Section IV War Department General Order #21, 5 May 1943.

744th AAA Gun Battalion - Included in commendation from Commanding General, XI Corps to 214th AAA Group at Morotai. 8 November 1944.

745th AAA Gun Battalion - Presidential Unit Citation for Papuan campaign. Section IV War Department General Order #21. 6 May 1943.

771st AAA Gun Battalion - Commendation from Commanding General, Island Command, Guam for patrolling and mopping up of enemy troops on Guam (140 Japanese killed and 8 captured), 14 May 1945.

4. AAA Searchlight Battalions

222d AAA Searchlight Battalion - a. Commendation from Commanding Officer, 86th Fighter Wing for operations at Sansapor (33d AAA Group). October 1944.

b. Commendation from Commanding General, XIII Bomber Command for lighting friendly planes into landing strips at Noemfoor. 24 October 1944.

227th AAA Searchlight Battalion - Commendation to Battery A and Det. Battery C from Commanding General, 43d Infantry Division for battlefield illumination in Ipo Dam area. 26 June 1945.

236th AAA Searchlight Battalion - a. Presidential Unit Citation to a Detachment, Battery B for participation in Papuan campaign. Section IV War Department General Order #21.

b. Commendation to Battery A in letter to Commanding General, 32d AAA Brigade from Commanding Officer, No. 71 Wing Hq., RAAF, for assisting return of planes to strips on Goodenough Island. 4 December 1943.

237th AAA Searchlight Battalion - Commendation from Commanding General, Eighth Army for antiaircraft operation in Western Visayan Task Force. 11 January 1945.

250th AAA Searchlight Battalion - a. Commendation from Commanding Officer, Base F, USASOS for providing radar surveillance and searchlight illumination of targets in the harbor defenses of Finschhafen. 13 April 1945.

b. Commendation from Comairsols for fighter - searchlight coordination at Guadalcanal (13 May 1945).

c. A further commendation from Comairsols for assisting in the destruction of two enemy planes by night fighters on 6 October 1943.

d. Commendation from Commanding General, USAFISPA for the same.

<u>373d AAA Searchlight Battalion</u> - Commendations from Commanding General, 37th Infantry Division, Commanding General, Hq Artillery Group, Bougainville, and Commanding Officer, 145th Infantry for battlefield illumination in perimeter defense at Bougainville on 8 March 1944.

5. <u>Other Units</u>

<u>707th Machine Gun Battery</u> - Presidential Unit Citation for Papuan campaign. Section IV War Department General Order #21. 6 May 1943.

<u>708th Machine Gun Battery</u> - a. Presidential Unit Citation for Papuan campaign. Section IV War Department General Order #21. 6 May 1943.

b. Commendation from Commanding General, SWPA, and Commanding General, Sixth Army for operations at Noemfoor - 7 July 1944.

<u>709th Machine Gun Battery</u> - Presidential Unit Citation for Papuan campaign. Section IV War Department General Order #21. 6 May 1943.

<u>145th Operations Detachment</u> - Commendation from Commanding Officer 35th AAA Group for work with Harbor Defenses at Finschhafen. 13 April 1945.

<u>158th AAA Operations Detachment</u> - Commendation from Commanding Officer, Base F, USASOS and Commanding Officer, 141st Coast Artillery Group for work with Harbor Defenses at Finschhafen. 24 January 1945.

ANNEX C

GEOGRAPHICAL STATION LIST OF ANTIAIRCRAFT ARTILLERY UNITS

IN THE PACIFIC[1] 7 DECEMBER 1941 TO 15 AUGUST 1945

I

Philippine Islands
7 December 1941 - 6 May 1942

                From   To

1. Clark Field

    *200th CA (AA)

2. Manila Area

    *60th CA (AA)
    *515th CA (AA)
     (activated 8 Dec 1941)
    *Btries E and I, 59th CA (HD)[2]
    *Btries C and E, 91st CA (HD)[2]

II

Central Pacific

3. Oahu

    *Hq 53d AAA Brigade   7 Dec 1941
    *64th CA (AA)   7 Dec 1941
    *97th CA (AA)   7 Dec 1941
    *251st CA (AA)   7 Dec 1941
    *98th CA (AA)   7 Dec 1941
    *95th CA (AA) (less 1st Bn) 7 Dec 1941

---

[1] Asterisk indicates unit in tactical position

[2] Equipped with AA 3-inch guns

	From	To

4. Canton Island

   *1st Plat. Btry A (SL), Btries B (Gun) and C (AW), 428th Sep CA Bn (AA) (Comp)

5. Christmas Island

   *1st Plat, Btry A (SL), Btries B (Gun) and C (AW), 429th Sep CA Bn (AA) (Comp)

6. Tongareva

   *1st Plat, Btry Z (SL), Btry B (AW), 415th Sep CA Bn (AA) (Comp)

7. Baker Island

	From	To
*Btry F, 64th CA (AA)	1 Sept 1943	-[1]
*Btries K and M, 98th CA (AA)	1 Sept 1943	-
*One Plat of Btry A, 97th CA (AA)	1 Sept 1943	-

8. Makin Island

	From	To
*Btries K and L, 93d CA (AA)	20 Nov 1943	-
*1st Bn, 98th CA (AA)	21 Nov 1943	-

9. Apamama Atoll

	From	To
*Btry A, 93d AAA Gun Bn	13 Jan 1944	-
*One Plat of Btry B, 294th AAA SL Bn	13 Jan 1944	-
*Btry C, 753d AAA Gun Bn	13 Jan 1944	-
*Btry C, 869th AAA AW Bn	13 Jan 1944	-
*Hq, 296th AAA SL Bn	13 Jan 1944	-

III

Australia

10. Brisbane

[1] (-) indicates unit at given location on 15 Aug 1945.

	From	To
208th CA (AA)	9 Mar 1942	18 Mar 1942
Hq 40th AAA Brigade	28 Mar 1942	6 Jun 1942
94th CA (AA)	29 Mar 1942	1 Jun 1942
104th AAA AW Bn	30 Mar 1942	1 Jun 1942
102d AAA AW Bn	9 Mar 1942	13 Mar 1942
		17 Apr 1942
Hq 14th AA Command	15 Nov 1943	3 Jul 1944

11. Fremantle

*197th CA (AA)	23 Mar 1942	27 Jul 1942

12. Darwin

*102d AAA AW Bn	19 Mar 1942	5 Nov 1942
	1 May 1942	5 Nov 1942

13. Iron Range

*Hq 2d Bn, 197th CA (AA)	1 Oct 1942	25 May 1943
*Btries E and F, 197th CA (AA)	1 Oct 1942	25 May 1943
*Btry A, 197th CA (AA)	1 Oct 1942	25 May 1943
*Btry B, 197th CA (AA)	21 Nov 1942	25 May 1943
*Btry K, 197th CA (AA)	24 Aug 1942	25 May 1943

14. Cooktown

*Btry M, 94th CA (AA)	6 Dec 1942	19 Mar 1943
*Hq and Btry D, 104th AAA AW Bn	6 Jun 1942	13 Jul 1942
		14 Jul 1942

15. Horn Island

*Btries A and B, 104th AAA AW Bn	13 Jun 1942	1 Dec 1942
*Hq 104th AAA AW Bn	20 Jul 1942	1 Dec 1942
*Btry H, 94th CA (AA)	20 Sept 1942	1 Dec 1942
*One Plat of Btry A, 94th CA (AA)	20 Sept 1942	1 Dec 1942

16. Charters Towers

*Hq, 94th CA (AA)	5 Jun 1942	17 Sept 1942
*2d Bn, Btries G and H, 94th CA (AA)	5 Jun 1942	13 Aug 1942
		20 Jul 1943

	From	To

17. Mareeba

	From	To
*Hq, 1st Bn and Btries B and C, 94th CA (AA)	5 Jun 1942	14 Jun 1943
*Btries E and F, 94th CA (AA)	5 Jun 1942	25 May 1943
*Btry A, 94th CA (AA)	5 Jun 1942	13 Jul 1943

18. Reid River and Woodstock

	From	To
*Btries H and D, 94th CA (AA)	5 Jun 1942	18 Sept 1942
*Hq 2d Bn, 94th CA and Btries L and M	5 Jun 1942	6 Dec 1942
		4 Dec 1942
*One Plat, Btry A and one Plat, Btry E, 94th CA (AA)	5 Jun 1942	4 Dec 1942
		14 Jun 1943

19. Cairns

	From	To
*Hq 94th CA (AA)	2 Sept 1942	13 Jun 1943
*Hq 3d Bn, 94th CA (AA)	2 Sept 1942	13 Jun 1943

20. Townsville

	From	To
*208th CA (AA), Btries A,B,G,H, and I	18 Mar 1942	15 Oct 1942
*Btries C and E, 208th CA (AA)	18 Mar 1942	14 Dec 1942
*Hq 2d Bn and Btries D and F, 208th CA (AA)	18 Mar 1942	4 Jul 1943
*Hq 3d Bn, 208th CA (AA) and Btry K, 94th CA (AA)	18 Mar 1942	20 Aug 1943
*197th CA (AA)	9 Aug 1942	
*Hq, 2d Bn and Btries A, E, and F, 197th CA (AA)	9 Aug 1942	1 Oct 1942
*Btry I, 197th CA (AA)	9 Aug 1942	26 Oct 1942
*Btry B, 197th CA (AA)	9 Aug 1942	20 Nov 1942
*Hq and Btry G, 197th CA (AA)	9 Aug 1942	4 Jul 1943
*Btry A, 743d AAA Gun Bn and Btry K, 94th CA (AA)	3 Dec 1942	2 Jun 1943
*Btry K, 94th CA (AA)	3 Dec 1942	2 Jun 1943
*Btry H, 197th CA (AA)		6 Sept 1943
*Hq 3d Bn and Btries C, D, and K, 197th CA (AA) (1st Bn)		23 Sept 1943
*Hq and Btries A and B, 104th AAA AW Bn	3 Dec 1942	14 May 1943
		10 Aug 1943
*Hq 40th AAA Brigade	9 Jun 1942	10 Feb 1943

	From	To
*707th AAA MG Btry	21 Jun 1942	16 Sept 1942
*708th AAA MG Btry	24 Jun 1942	27 Sept 1942
*709th AAA MG Btry	27 Jun 1942	19 Aug 1942
*102d AAA AW Bn	17 Nov 1942	4 Jul 1943
662d AAA MG Btry	15 Aug 1943	3 Sept 1943
663d AAA MG Btry	15 Aug 1943	
664th AAA MG Btry	15 Aug 1943	
665th AAA MG Btry	15 Aug 1943	
Hq 3d AAA AB Bn	15 Aug 1943	7 Nov 1943
Hq 9th AAA AB Bn	15 Aug 1943	7 Nov 1943
670th AAA MG Btry	20 Aug 1943	7 Nov 1943
671st AAA MG Btry	20 Aug 1943	7 Nov 1943
672d AAA MG Btry	2 Sept 1943	7 Nov 1943
163d AAA Gun Bn	10 Sept 1943	7 Nov 1943
161st AAA Gun Bn	10 Sept 1943	7 Nov 1943
Hq 6th AAA Group	11 Sept 1943	28 Oct 1943
477th AAA AW Bn	11 Sept 1943	7 Jan 1944
472d AAA AW Bn	15 Sept 1943	24 Dec 1943
674th AAA MG Btry	16 Sept 1943	7 Nov 1943
208th AAA AW Bn	23 Sept 1943	28 Jan 1944
207th AAA AW Bn	30 Sept 1943	29 Nov 1943
675th AAA MG Btry	30 Sept 1943	6 Dec 1943
478th AAA AW Bn	22 Oct 1943	1 Feb 1944
168th AAA Gun Bn	12 Nov 1943	21 Feb 1944
166th AAA Gun Bn	12 Nov 1943	5 Feb 1944
Hq 120th AAA Group	26 Nov 1943	9 Mar 1944
350th AAA SL Bn	26 Nov 1943	10 Feb 1944
476th AAA AW Bn	28 Nov 1943	8 Apr 1944
383d AAA AW Bn	9 Dec 1943	10 Mar 1944
227th AAA SL Bn	11 Dec 1943	29 Mar 1944

21. Port Moresby

	From	To
*101st AAA AW Bn	3 May 1942	8 Dec 1943
*708th AAA MG Btry	27 Sept 1942	23 Oct 1942
*Hq 1st Bn, 208th CA (AA)	19 Oct 1942	13 Jul 1943
*Btry A, 1st Bn, 208th CA (AA)	19 Oct 1942	22 Jun 1943
*Btry B, 1st Bn, 208th CA (AA)	19 Oct 1942	23 Jul 1943
*Btry C, 1st Bn, 208th CA (AA)	18 Nov 1942	4 Jan 1943
*Btries D and G, 94th CA (AA)	4 Dec 1942	14 Apr 1943
*Hq, 40th AAA Brigade	14 Feb 1943	22 Mar 1943
*Btry C, 210th AAA AW Bn	7 Jul 1943	15 Sept 1943
*Btry D, 210th AAA AW Bn	15 Sept 1943	6 Dec 1943
*707th AAA MG Btry	1 Aug 1943	6 Sept 1943
662d AAA MG Btry	6 Sept 1943	16 Nov 1943
665th AAA MG Btry	6 Sept 1943	7 Dec 1943
Hq 3d AAA AB Bn	11 Nov 1943	15 Feb 1943
Hq 9th AAA AB Bn	11 Nov 1943	2 Dec 1943

	From	To
Hq 12th AAA AB Bn	11 Nov 1943	6 Dec 1943
672d AAA MG Btry	11 Nov 1943	3 Jan 1944
674th AAA MG Btry	11 Nov 1943	27 Mar 1944
675th AAA MG Btry	10 Dec 1943	28 Mar 1944

22. **Milne Bay**

	From	To
*Dec, 101st AAA AW Bn	25 Jun 1942	31 Oct 1942
*Btry C, 104th AAA AW Bn	30 Jul 1942	31 May 1943
*709th AAA MG Btry	19 Aug 1942	17 Jan 1943
*Btries A and B, 744th AAA Gun Bn	15 Mar 1943	15 Oct 1943
*Hq and Btries A and B, 210th AAA AW Bn	29 May 1943	23 Jun 1944
*Hq 94th AAA Group	17 Jun 1943	6 Aug 1943
*Btry D, 104th AAA AW Bn	28 Jul 1943	19 Oct 1943
*238th AAA SL Bn	23 Aug 1943	10 Sept 1943
*Btry A, 237th AAA SL Bn	29 May 1942	11 Oct 1943
*Hq 237th AAA SL Bn	27 Sept 1943	9 Nov 1943
*Btry B, 237th AAA SL Bn	27 Sept 1943	25 Dec 1943
*Btry C, 237th AAA SL Bn	1 Dec 1943	2 Mar 1944
*Hq, 32d AAA Brigade	14 Oct 1943	3 Nov 1943
*Btry D, 741st AAA Gun Bn	14 Oct 1943	8 Dec 1943
*Btry A, 741st AAA Gun Bn	14 Oct 1943	25 Jan 1944
*Btries B and C, 741st AAA Gun Bn	14 Oct 1943	15 Mar 1945
236th AAA SL Bn	30 Oct 1943	26 Nov 1943
Btries C and D, 470th AAA AW Bn	30 Oct 1943	26 Nov 1943
Hq, 6th AAA Group	1 Nov 1943	8 May 1944
Hq, 10th AAA Group	4 Nov 1943	23 Mar 1944
202d AAA AW Bn	1 Dec 1943	16 Mar 1945
*207th AAA AW Bn	3 Dec 1943	16 Mar 1945
Hq 15th AAA Group	14 Dec 1943	3 Mar 1944
229th AAA SL Bn	3 Jan 1944	12 Sept 1945
224th AAA SL Bn	29 Jan 1944	1 Jul 1945
*208th AAA AW Bn	1 Feb 1944	-
100th AAA Gun Bn	18 Feb 1944	4 Dec 1944
496th AAA Gun Bn	4 Apr 1944	30 Jun 1944
Hq 33d AAA Group	11 Apr 1944	20 Apr 1944

23. **Merauke**

	From	To
*Btry D, 104th AAA AW Bn	15 Aug 1942	22 Jul 1943

24. **Wanigela**

	From	To
*707th AAA MG Btry	6 Oct 1942	26 Nov 1942

		From	To

25. Borona

	From	To
*708th AAA MG Btry	26 Oct 1942	2 Dec 1942

26. Poppendetta

	From	To
*708th AAA MG Btry	2 Dec 1942	19 Feb 1943

27. Oro Bay

	From	To
*Hq, 211th AAA AW Bn	13 Jul 1943	16 Mar 1944
*Btry B, 236th AAA SL Bn	6 Jan 1943	8 Mar 1943
*Btry C, 102d AAA AW Bn	13 Jul 1943	18 Nov 1943
*Btry B, 477th AAA AW Bn	Feb 1944	Nov 1944
469th AAA AW Bn	2 Nov 1943	5 Jan 1944
Btry C, 745th AAA Gun Bn	6 Jan 1943	6 Jun 1943

28. Dobodura

	From	To
*707th AAA MG Btry	26 Nov 1942	1 Aug 1943
*709th AAA MG Btry	17 Jan 1943	18 Jun 1943
*Hq 15th AAA Group	4 Mar 1944	16 Mar 1944
*Btry C, 745th AAA Gun Bn	6 Jun 1943	17 Jun 1944
*Btry D, 745th AAA Gun Bn	1 Apr 1943	17 Jun 1944
*Btry A, 745th AAA Gun Bn	5 Jul 1943	29 Feb 1944
*Hq 745th AAA Gun Bn	13 Jul 1943	17 Jun 1944
*Btry B, 745th AAA Gun Bn	24 Jul 1943	17 Jun 1944
*Btry B, 236th AAA SL Bn	11 Jun 1943	1 Nov 1943
*Btry C, 104th AAA AW Bn	10 Jun 1943	3 Feb 1944
*208th AAA Group	9 Jul 1943	27 Apr 1944
*102d AAA AW Bn less Btry C	13 Jul 1943	14 Oct 1944
*Hq 197th AAA Group	13 Jul 1943	3 Nov 1943
*238th AAA SL Bn less Btries A and C	11 Sept 1943	30 Mar 1945
*477th AAA AW Bn less Btry B	11 Jan 1944	-

29. Bulolo

	From	To
*708th AAA MG Btry	19 Feb 1943	9 Jul 1943

30. Wau

	From	To
*Det, 708th AAA MG Btry	9 Jul 1943	15 Sept 1943

31. Goodenough Island

	From	To
*Btries A and B, 104th AAA AW Bn	28 Mar 1943	17 Apr 1944

	From	To
*Hq and Btry D, 104th AAA AW Bn	20 Oct 1943	17 Apr 1944
*Btry C, 104th AAA AW Bn	4 Feb 1944	5 Apr 1944
*Btry A, 236th AAA SL Bn	14 Jun 1943	5 Jan 1944
*94th AAA Group	6 Aug 1943	17 Apr 1944
*Hq 236th AAA SL Bn	6 Aug 1943	29 Oct 1943
*Hq 32d AAA Brigade	3 Nov 1943	21 Feb 1944
*Btries B and C, 163d AAA Gun Bn	15 Nov 1943	16 Apr 1944
*Hq and Btry A, 227th AAA SL Bn	5 Apr 1944	22 Apr 1944
*Btries A and D, 743d AAA Gun Bn	2 Jun 1943	13 Oct 1943
*Hq 209th AAA AW Bn	2 Jun 1943	13 Oct 1943

32. Kiriwina Island

	From	To
*Hq and Btries B and C, 743d AAA Gun Bn	30 Jun 1943	25 Dec 1943 14 Apr 1944
*Btry D, 741st AAA Gun Bn	8 Dec 1943	20 Sept 1944
*Hq 116th AAA Group	16 Dec 1943	2 Apr 1944
*236th AAA SL Bn less 1st Plat, Btry A	4 Jul 1943	20 Sept 1944
*Btries B and D, 209th AAA AW Bn	30 Jun 1943	25 Dec 1943
*Btry A, 209th AAA AW Bn	30 Jun 1943	30 Sept 1944
*Hq 209th AAA AW Bn	13 Oct 1943	30 Sept 1944
*Btry C, 209th AAA AW Bn	27 Nov 1943	30 Sept 1944

33. Woodlark Island

	From	To
*Btries A and D, 163d AAA Gun Bn	27 Nov 1943	14 Mar 1944
*1st Plat of Btry B, 236th AAA SL Bn	19 Nov 1943	2 Feb 1944
*Hq and Btries A and B, 470th AAA AW Bn	27 Nov 1943	14 Mar 1944

34. Morobe

	From	To
*Btry C, 209th AAA AW Bn	20 Apr 1943	27 Jun 1943

35. Nassau Bay

	From	To
*Btry C, 209th AAA AW Bn	3 Jul 1943	5 Aug 1943

	From	To

36. <u>Tambu Bay</u>

*Btry C, 209th AAA AW Bn	5 Aug 1943	14 Nov 1943

37. <u>Tsili-Tsili</u>

*709th AAA MG Btry	7 Jul 1943	23 Sept 1943
*Btry C, 211th AAA AW Bn	29 Jul 1943	28 Oct 1943

38. <u>Bena Bena (Garoka Field)</u>

Det C, 211th AAA AW Bn	12 June 1943	24 Jul 1943

39. <u>Nadzab</u>

*707th AAA MG Btry	6 Sept 1943	1 Jul 1944
*708th AAA MG Btry	15 Sept 1943	2 May 1944
Btry C, 210th AAA AW Bn	15 Sept 1943	23 Jun 1944
Btry D, 210th AAA AW Bn	15 Dec 1943	23 Jun 1944
Btries C and D, 744th AAA Gun Bn	10 Oct 1943	27 Jun 1944
*Hq 197th AAA Group	29 Sept 1943	13 Jul 1944
Hq 12th AAA AB Bn	6 Dec 1943	20 Jun 1944
665th AAA MG Btry	7 Dec 1943	9 Nov 1944
Det from Btry A, 237th AAA SL Bn	17 Dec 1943	8 Feb 1944
Btry B, 237th AAA SL Bn	30 Dec 1943	2 Oct 1944
101st AAA AW Bn	21 Dec 1943	12 Nov 1944
670th AAA MG Btry	26 Dec 1943	27 Oct 1944
472d AAA AW Bn	31 Dec 1943	12 Mar 1945
Btry C, 211th AAA AW Bn	28 Oct 1943	18 Jan 1944
161st AAA Gun Bn	14 Jan 1944	26 Dec 1944
350th AAA SL Bn	18 Feb 1944	22 Mar 1945
Hq 10th AAA Group	7 Mar 1944	5 Nov 1944
Hq 40th AAA Brigade	22 Mar 1944	7 Nov 1944
662d AAA MG Btry	10 Jun 1944	8 Nov 1944
671st AAA MG Btry	10 Jun 1944	27 Oct 1944
709th AAA MG Btry	10 Jun 1944	27 Oct 1944
Hq 3d AAA AB Bn	12 Jun 1944	11 Nov 1944
672d AAA MG Btry	22 Jul 1944	27 Oct 1944

40. <u>Lae</u>

*Btry D, 102d AAA AW Bn	19 Sept 1943	19 Nov 1943

41. <u>Kaiapit</u>

*709th AAA MG Btry	23 Sept 1943	12 Oct 1943

	From	To
42. Gusap		
*709th AAA MG Btry	12 Oct 1943	10 Jun 1944
*662d AAA MG Btry	16 Nov 1943	10 Jun 1944
*663d AAA MG Btry	16 Nov 1943	10 Jun 1944
*102d AAA AW Bn	19 Nov 1943	13 Jun 1944
*Hq 9th AAA AB Bn	2 Dec 1943	13 Jun 1944
*671st AAA MG Btry	15 Dec 1943	10 Jun 1944
*673d AAA MG Btry	3 Jan 1944	22 Jul 1944
*Hq 3d AAA AB Bn	15 Feb 1944	12 Jun 1944
43. Finschhafen		
*Btries A and B, 744th AAA Gun Bn	20 Oct 1943	5 Sept 1944
*Hq and Btry B, 102d AAA AW Bn	23 Oct 1943	16 Dec 1943
		20 Jan 1944
Hq 119th AAA Group	30 Oct 1943	27 Feb 1945
*Hq and Btry A, 237th AAA SL Bn	11 Nov 1943	4 Nov 1944
*664th AAA MG Btry	1 Dec 1943	5 Jun 1944
*478th AAA AW Bn	5 Feb 1944	12 Feb 1945
*166th AAA Gun Bn	5 Feb 1944	9 May 1944
Hq 32d AAA Brigade	24 Feb 1944	6 Apr 1944
*Hq, 120th AAA Group	20 Mar 1944	9 Dec 1944
165th AAA Gun Bn	20 Mar 1944	20 Apr 1944
674th AAA MG Btry	27 Mar 1944	18 Apr 1944
470th AAA AW Bn	27 Mar 1944	26 Dec 1944
Btries B and C, 237th AAA SL Bn	3 Apr 1944	20 Apr 1944
Hq 32d AAA Brigade	6 Apr 1944	1 Jul 1944
Hq 116th AAA Group	6 Apr 1944	20 Apr 1944
Hq 33d AAA Group	20 Apr 1944	28 Jul 1944
Btry A, 222d AAA SL Bn	22 Apr 1944	18 Jun 1944
Btry B, 222d AAA SL Bn	22 Apr 1944	14 Jul 1944
Hq and Btry C, 222d SL Bn	22 Apr 1944	9 Sept 1944
389th AAA AW Bn	1 May 1944	10 Sept 1945
487th AAA AW Bn	13 May 1944	8 Jun 1944
Hq 208th AAA Group	14 May 1944	25 May 1944
382d AAA AW Bn	15 May 1944	27 Feb 1945
785th AAA AW Bn	18 May 1944	11 Aug 1944
Hq 35th AAA Group	18 May 1944	16 Feb 1945
*102d AAA AW Bn	14 Jun 1944	12 Nov 1944
Hq 214th AAA Group	22 Jun 1944	2 Aug 1944
528th AAA Gun Bn	22 Jun 1944	5 Sept 1944
250th AAA SL Bn less Btry A	22 Jun 1944	9 Aug 1945
950th AAA AW Bn	23 Jun 1944	9 Dec 1944

	From	To
Hq 14th AA Command	3 Jul 1944	27 Jun 1945
Hq 25th AAA Group	3 Jul 1944	1 Oct 1944
508th AAA Gun Bn	12 Jul 1944	9 Dec 1944
Hq 197th AAA Group	18 Jul 1944	11 Sept 1944
510th AAA Gun Bn	22 Jul 1944	11 Sept 1944
507th AAA Gun Bn	12 Aug 1944	27 Feb 1945
Btries A and D, 741st AAA Gun Bn	20 Sept 1944	17 May 1945
Hq and Btries A and C, 209th AAA AW Bn	15 Oct 1944	13 Nov 1944
709th AAA MG Btry	3 Nov 1944	14 Aug 1945
670th AAA MG Btry	5 Nov 1944	14 Aug 1945
Hq 9th AAA AB Bn	8 Nov 1944	1 Aug 1945
672d AAA MG Btry	9 Nov 1944	13 Aug 1945
Hq 3d AAA AB Bn	11 Nov 1944	14 Aug 1945
671st AAA MG Btry	11 Nov 1944	13 Aug 1945
101st AAA AW Bn	12 Nov 1944	27 Feb 1945
395th AAA AW Bn	15 Nov 1944	15 Mar 1945
742d AAA Gun Bn	21 Nov 1944	4 Aug 1945
Hq 70th AAA Group	24 Nov 1944	30 Jun 1945
734th AAA Gun Bn	30 Nov 1944	13 Mar 1945
739th AAA Gun Bn	30 Nov 1944	20 Apr 1945
205th AAA AW Bn	1 Dec 1944	27 Feb 1945
233d AAA SL Bn	2 Dec 1944	7 Jul 1945
662d AAA MG Btry	6 Dec 1944	13 Aug 1945
Hq 102d AAA Brigade	6 Dec 1944	16 Feb 1945
Hq 6th AAA Group	6 Dec 1944	16 Feb 1945
466th AAA AW Bn	7 Dec 1944	
475th AAA AW Bn	15 Dec 1944	3 Jul 1945
497th AAA Gun Bn	16 Dec 1944	3 Jul 1945
117th AAA Group	17 Dec 1944	14 Aug 1945
76th AAA Group	2 Jan 1945	2 Aug 1945
164th AAA Gun Bn	2 Jan 1945	1 Aug 1945
945th AAA AW Bn	9 Feb 1945	7 Jul 1945
736th AAA Gun Bn	10 Feb 1945	30 Jun 1945
374th AAA SL Bn	6 May 1945	21 Jun 1945
Hq and Btries A and D, 743d AAA Gun Bn	12 May 1945	3 Jul 1945

44. **Saidor**

	From	To
*Btries B and D, 209th AAA AW Bn	1 Jan 1944	30 Nov 1944
*Hq and Btries A and D, 743d AAA Gun Bn	2 Jan 1944	10 May 1945
*2d Plat of Btry A, 236th AAA SL Bn	6 Jan 1944	30 Nov 1944

	From	To
45. Hollandia		
*Hq, 94th AAA Group	23 Apr 1944	15 Sept 1944
*Hq, 116th AAA Group	23 Apr 1944	30 Jun 1944
*165th AAA Gun Bn	23 Apr 1944	25 May 1944
*Hq and Btry A, 227th AAA SL Bn	23 Apr 1944	12 Mar 1945
*Btry B, 227th AAA SL Bn	23 Apr 1944	1 Jul 1945
*104th AAA AW Bn	1 May 1944	13 Jun 1945
*708th AAA MG Btry	2 May 1944	23 Jun 1944
*Btries B and C, 166th AAA Gun Bn	13 May 1944	7 Jul 1944
*163d AAA Gun Bn	13 May 1944	15 Mar 1945
210th AAA AW Bn	3 Jul 1944	17 Oct 1944
Hq, 32d AAA Brigade	4 Jul 1944	14 Oct 1944
Hq, 40th AAA Brigade	10 Nov 1944	5 Dec 1944
741st AAA Gun Bn	20 Mar 1945	
207th AAA AW Bn	23 Mar 1945	
46. Aitape		
*Btries B and C, 743d AAA Gun Bn	20 Apr 1944	1 Jun 1945
*383d AAA AW Bn	22 Apr 1944	2 Sept 1944
*Btry C, 227th AAA SL Bn	22 Apr 1944	10 Dec 1944
197th AAA Group	12 Sept 1944	26 Dec 1944
Hq and Btry C, 222d SL Bn	13 Sept 1944	26 Dec 1944
47. Wakde		
*Hq and Btries A and D, 166th AAA Gun Bn	17 May 1944	5 Nov 1944
*202d AAA AW Bn	21 May 1944	27 Sept 1944
*Btry B, 236th AAA SL Bn	20 May 1944	10 Oct 1944
48. Biak		
*165th AAA Gun Bn	27 May 1944	-
*476th AAA AW Bn	27 May 1944	2 Feb 1945
*674th AAA MG Btry	27 May 1944	14 Jul 1944
*675th AAA MG Btry	27 May 1944	14 Jul 1944
*Btry C, 236th AAA SL Bn	27 May 1944	10 Jul 1944
*Hq, 208th AAA Group	29 May 1944	-
745th AAA Gun Bn	21 Mar 1945	13 Jun 1945
Btry A, 223d AAA SL Bn	15 Mar 1945	-
Hq, 33d AAA Group	1 Apr 1945	13 Jul 1945
*675th AAA MG Btry	1 Apr 1945	31 Aug 1945

		From	To
49.	**Noemfoor**		
	*487th AAA AW Bn	22 Jun 1944	27 Mar 1945
	*Hq 116th AAA Group	2 Jul 1944	19 Mar 1945
	*745th AAA Gun Bn	2 Jul 1944	10 Mar 1945
	*708th AAA MG Btry	2 Jul 1944	31 Dec 1944
	*707th AAA MG Btry	2 Jul 1944	29 Dec 1944
	*Btry A, 222d AAA SL Bn	9 Jul 1944	15 Mar 1945
50.	**Sansapor**		
	*198th AAA AW Bn	31 Jul 1944	30 Dec 1944
	*496th AAA Gun Bn	30 Jul 1944	6 Apr 1945
	*Btry B, 496th AAA Gun Bn	30 Jul 1944	23 Apr 1945
	*Btry B, 222d AAA SL Bn	30 Jul 1944	5 Apr 1945
	674th AAA MG Btry	30 Jul 1944	5 Apr 1945
	*675th AAA MG Btry	30 Jul 1944	30 Mar 1945
51.	**Morotai**		
	*Hq 214th AAA Group	15 Sept 1944	
	*383d AAA AW Bn	15 Sept 1944	27 Apr 1945
	*389th AAA AW Bn	15 Sept 1944	13 Jul 1945
	*229th AAA SL Bn less Btry B	15 Sept 1944	7 Jul 1945
	*785th AAA AW Bn	15 Sept 1944	
	Hq 15th AAA Group	26 Sept 1944	19 Jun 1945
	*528th AAA Gun Bn	2 Oct 1944	28 Jul 1945
	496th AAA Gun Bn less Btry B	9 Apr 1945	30 Apr 1945

V

South Pacific

		From	To
52.	**New Zealand**		
	Hq 214th AAA Group	31 Dec 1943	10 Jun 1944
	950th AAA AW Bn	31 Dec 1943	10 Jun 1944
	250th AAA SL Bn	10 Jan 1944	10 Jun 1944
	528th AAA Gun Bn	10 Jan 1944	5 Jun 1944
53.	**New Caledonia**		
	*Hq 70th CA (AA)	12 Mar 1942	30 May 1943
	*1st Bn, 70th CA (AA)	12 Mar 1942	7 Jun 1943
	*2d Bn, 70th CA (AA)	12 Mar 1942	25 Jun 1943
	*3d Bn, 70th CA (AA)	12 Mar 1942	22 Dec 1943
	*Hq 214th CA (AA)	6 Nov 1942	25 Jan 1943
	*1st, 2d, and 3d Bns, 214th CA (AA)	6 Nov 1942	25 Jan 1943
	Hq 68th AAA Brigade	10 Aug 1943	6 Oct 1944
	Hq 117th AAA Group	3 Sept 1943	10 Dec 1943
	518th AAA Gun Bn	12 Nov 1943	30 Nov 1944

		From	To
54.	**Society Islands**		
	*1st and 2d Bns, 108th CA (AA)	17 Feb 1943	19 Feb 1943
	*Hq 198th CA (AA)	27 Feb 1942	19 Feb 1943
55.	**Fiji Island**		
	77th CA (AA)	16 May 1942	Apr 1943
	251st CA (AA)	31 May 1942	18 Nov 1943
56.	**Aitutataki Island**		
	*Det, Btry A (SL), Btry B (AW), 417th CA Bn (AA) (Comp)	Nov 1942	
57.	**Guadalcanal**		
	*Hq 214th CA (AA)	30 Jan 1943	26 Dec 1943
	*1st Bn, 214th CA (AA)	30 Jan 1943	4 Jan 1944
	*2d Bn, 214th CA (AA)	30 Jan 1943	26 Dec 1943
	*3d Bn, 214th CA (AA)	30 Jan 1943	26 Dec 1943
	*Hq 70th AAA Group	2 Jun 1943	14 Oct 1943
	*Hq and Btry D, 925th AAA AW Bn	11 Jun 1943	22 Nov 1943
	*471st AAA AW Bn	24 Aug 1943	30 Mar 1944
	*199th AAA AW Bn	21 Sept 1943	4 Jan 1944
	737th AAA Gun Bn	29 Sept 1943	4 Jan 1944
	*Hq 68th AAA Brigade	7 Oct 1943	15 Jun 1944
	*362d AAA SL Bn less Btry B	8 Oct 1943	12 Mar 1945
			20 Feb 1944
	*967th AAA Gun Bn	1 Nov 1943	12 Feb 1944
	*475th AAA AW Bn	3 Nov 1943	14 Dec 1944
	164th AAA Gun Bn	5 Nov 1943	29 Nov 1943
	Hq 14th AAA Group	7 Nov 1943	21 Mar 1944
	938th AAA AW Bn	20 Nov 1943	15 Feb 1943
	*Hq 117th AAA Group	15 Dec 1943	14 Dec 1944
	*497th AAA Gun Bn	12 Dec 1943	14 Dec 1944
	*356th AAA SL Bn	30 Dec 1943	14 Feb 1945
58.	**New Hebrides**		
	*76th CA (AA)	2 Sept 1942	7 Dec 1943
	*198th CA (AA)	27 Feb 1943	15 Oct 1943
	*77th CA (AA)	20 Apr 1943	20 Nov 1943
	*466th AAA AW Bn	16 Oct 1943	4 May 1944
	*742d AAA Gun Bn	16 Oct 1943	4 May 1944

VI

Northern Solomons

		From	To
59.	**Russell Island**		
	*70th AAA Gun Bn	15 Jun 1943	30 Jan 1943
	*Btry B, 362d AAA SL Bn	10 Oct 1943	10 May 1945
	*Hq, 13th AAA Group	6 Nov 1943	15 May 1944
	*164th AAA Gun Bn	29 Nov 1943	26 Dec 1944
	*933d AAA AW Bn	12 Dec 1943	3 Dec 1944
	*725th AAA SL Btry	31 Dec 1943	20 Mar 1944
	*Hq 76th AAA Group	10 Jun 1944	26 Dec 1944
60.	**New Georgia**		
	*70th AAA Gun Bn	30 Jun 1943	7 Nov 1943
	*Btry C, 250th AAA SL Bn	Jun 1943	
	*Btries A,B, and C, 925th AAA AW Bn	1 Jul 1943	16 May 1944
	*Hq 70th AAA Group	15 Oct 1943	17 Feb 1944
	*77th AAA Gun Bn	8 Dec 1943	4 Feb 1944
	*Btry A, 374th AAA SL Bn	8 Dec 1943	10 Jun 1944
	*Hq 77th AAA Group	14 Dec 1943	4 Jan 1945
61.	**Treasury Island**		
	198th CA (AA)	21 Oct 1943	7 Feb 1945
	*945th AAA AW Bn	21 Oct 1943	7 Feb 1945
	*736th AAA Gun Bn	27 Oct 1943	7 Feb 1945
	*Btry A, 373d AAA SL Bn	27 Dec 1943	17 Oct 1944
	Hq 198th AAA Group	6 Nov 1943	30 Sept 1944
62.	**Bougainville**		
	*Btry D, 70th AAA Gun Bn	8 Nov 1943	16 Dec 1944
	951st AAA AW Bn	4 Dec 1943	12 Dec 1944
	*251st CA (AA)	4 Dec 1943	16 Dec 1944
	*1st Bn, 251st CA (AA)	4 Dec 1943	20 Feb 1945
	*373d AAA SL Bn less Btry A	15 Dec 1943	16 Dec 1944
	*199th AAA AW Bn	15 Jan 1944	26 Feb 1945
	*Hq 68th AAA Brigade	15 Jul 1944	12 Dec 1944
	*70th AAA Gun Bn less Btry D	Jun 1944	Dec 1944
	Hq 198th AAA Group	30 Sept 1944	19 Feb 1945
	967th AAA Gun Bn		

VII

Eastern Mandates

		From	To

63. **Kwajalein Atoll**

	From	To
*Btries A and C, 98th AAA Gun Bn	31 Jan 1944	15 Feb
*Btry A, 867th AAA AW Bn	1 Feb 1944	
*96th AAA Gun Bn	4 Feb 1944	1 Oct 1944
*Hq 139th AAA Group	4 Feb 1944	20 Feb 1945
*Btry A less one Plat, 296th AAA SL Bn	4 Feb 1944	1 Oct 1944
*One Plat of Btry B, 230th AAA SL Bn	10 Apr 1944	12 Feb 1945

64. **Eniwetok Atoll**

	From	To
*Hq and Btry A, 867th AAA AW Bn	20 Feb 1944	-
*Btries A and C, 98th AAA Gun Bn	22 Feb 1944	-
*Two Plats of Btry A, 296th AAA SL Bn	22 Feb 1944	-
*Btry A, 96th AAA Gun Bn	25 Feb 1944	-

VIII

Bismarck Archipelago

65. **Arawe**

	From	To
*Btries C and D, 470th AAA AW Bn	15 Dec 1943	18 Mar 1944
*Hq 236th AAA SL Bn	16 Dec 1943	30 Apr 1945
*741st AAA Gun Bn	31 Jan 1944	20 Sept 1944
*Btry B, 236th AAA SL Bn	31 Jan 1944	30 Apr 1945

66. **Cape Gloucester**

	From	To
*469th AAA AW Bn	7 Jan 1944	13 Oct 1944
*Hq 6th AAA Group	11 May 1944	5 Dec 1944
*742d AAA Gun Bn	17 May 1944	19 Nov 1944
*466th AAA AW Bn	20 May 1944	6 Dec 1944
*Btry C, 238th AAA SL Bn	3 Aug 1944	11 Dec 1944

67. **Admiralty Islands**

	From	To
*Btry C, 168th AAA Gun Bn	2 Mar 1944	
*Btry A, 211th AAA AW Bn	2 Mar 1944	Oct 1944
*Btry B, 211th AAA AW Bn	9 Mar 1944	Oct 1944
*Hq and Btries A and D, 168th AAA Gun Bn	19 Mar 1944	5 Oct 1944

	From	To
*Hq 15th AAA Group	26 Mar 1944	15 Sept 1944
Hq and Btries C and D, 211th AAA AW Bn	26 Mar 1944	31 Mar 1944
237th AAA SL Bn	29 Mar 1944	1 Oct 1944
*673d AAA MG Btry	27 Mar 1944	3 Oct 1944
Hq 25th AAA Group	3 Oct 1944	19 Oct 1944
*933d AAA AW Bn	6 Dec 1944	
*70th AAA Gun Bn	21 Dec 1944	31 Dec 1944
*76th AAA Gun Bn	8 Jan 1945	
*77th AAA Gun Bn	8 Feb 1945	
*Hq 77th AAA Group	10 Feb 1945	

68. Green Island

	From	To
*967th AAA Gun Bn	15 Feb 1944	3 Oct 1944
*Btry A, 362d AAA SL Bn	25 Feb 1944	10 Mar 1945
*Hq 13th AAA Group	22 May 1944	1 Mar 1945
*925th AAA AW Bn	25 May 1944	1 Mar 1945
*Btry C, 374th AAA SL Bn	12 Jun 1944	1 Mar 1945

69. Emirau Island

	From	To
*737th AAA Gun Bn	25 Mar 1944	28 Apr 1945
*471st AAA AW Bn	25 Mar 1944	12 Dec 1944
*Hq 14th AAA Group	1 Apr 1944	12 Dec 1944
*725th AAA SL Btry	1 Apr 1944	28 Apr 1945

IX

Western Pacific

70. Saipan

	From	To
*Hq and Btries A and B, 751st AAA Gun Bn	17 Jun 1944	
*864th AAA AW Bn	17 Jun 1944	
*Hq 86th AAA Group	27 Jun 1944	
*Hq and Btries A and B, 206th AAA AW Bn	27 Jun 1944	9 Aug 1945
*Hq and Btries A and D, 865th AAA AW Bn	27 Jun 1944	
*Btries B and C, 867th AAA AW Bn	28 Jun 1944	15 Jul 1945
*501st AAA Gun Bn	28 Jun 1944	
*738th AAA Gun Bn	28 Jun 1944	
*Btry B, 296th AAA SL Bn	28 Jun 1944	
*Btry B less one Plat, 230th AAA SL Bn	28 Jun 1944	

	From	To
752d AAA AW Bn	27 Jan 1945	6 Apr 1945
*Hq 59th AAA Brigade	29 Jan 1945	
*Hq 69th AAA Group	15 Feb 1945	
865th AAA AW Bn	28 Feb 1945	
234th AAA Gun Bn	9 Jun 1945	

71. **Guam**

	From	To
*7th AAA AW Bn	24 Jul 1944	
*64th AAA Gun Bn	28 Jul 1944	
*Hq and Btries A and D, 868th AAA AW Bn	28 Jul 1944	
*771st AAA Gun Bn	10 Nov 1944	
*One Plat of Btry C, 294th AAA SL Bn	10 Nov 1944	

72. **Angaur**

	From	To
*483d AAA AW Bn	17 Sept 1944	20 Oct 1944

73. **Ulithi**

	From	To
*483d AAA AW Bn	20 Oct 1944	-
*Btries C and D, 751st AAA Gun Bn	23 Sept 1944	-
*Btry C, 230th AAA SL Bn	23 Sept 1944	-

74. **Iwo Jima**

	From	To
*506th AAA Gun Bn	25 Feb 1945	-
*483d AAA AW Bn	25 Feb 1945	-
*Hq 138th AAA Group	2 Mar 1945	-
*947th AAA Gun Bn	14 Mar 1945	-
*Btry C, 295th AAA SL Bn	14 Mar 1945	-
*752d AAA Gun Bn	30 Mar 1945	-
*Btries C and D, 206th AAA AW Bn		

75. **Leyte - Samar**

	From	To
*Hq 25th AAA Group	20 Oct 1944	-
*168th AAA Gun Bn	20 Oct 1944	-
*210th AAA AW Bn	20 Oct 1944	24 Jan 1945
*469th AAA AW Bn	20 Oct 1944	12 Jan 1945
*Btry C, 237th AAA SL Bn	20 Oct 1944	-
*502d AAA Gun Bn	20 Oct 1944	14 Mar 1945
*866th AAA AW Bn	20 Oct 1944	14 Mar 1945

	From	To
*211th AAA AW Bn	20 Oct 1944	13 Mar 1945
*504th AAA Gun Bn	21 Oct 1944	13 Mar 1945
*Hq 32d AAA Brigade	22 Oct 1944	-
*Btry A, 166th AAA Gun Bn	12 Nov 1944	25 Feb 1945
*Btries C and D and Hq 166th AAA Gun Bn	12 Nov 1944	8 Mar 1945
*Btry B, 166th AAA Gun Bn	12 Nov 1944	14 Apr 1945
*Btries A, C, and D, 202d AAA AW Bn	12 Nov 1944	28 Nov 1944
*Hq, 94th AAA Group	13 Nov 1944	28 Nov 1944
*Hq and Btry B, 202d AAA AW Bn	12 Nov 1944	18 Dec 1944
*Btry B, 237th AAA SL Bn	13 Nov 1944	16 Dec 1944
673d AAA MG Btry	13 Nov 1944	-
*Btries B and C, 102d AAA AW Bn	18 Nov 1944	24 Dec 1944
*Hq and Btries A and D, 102d AAA AW Bn	18 Nov 1944	8 Feb 1945
*7th AAA AW Bn	23 Nov 1944	8 Mar 1945
*Hq and Btry A, 237th AAA SL Bn	6 Dec 1944	-
*Hq 40th AAA Brigade	11 Dec 1944	3 Apr 1945
*510th AAA Gun Bn	11 Dec 1944	
*Hq 10th AAA Group	4 Jan 1945	2 Jul 1945
950th AAA AW Bn	7 Jan 1945	25 Jan 1945
Hq 120th AAA Group	11 Jan 1945	9 Apr 1945
513th AAA Gun Bn	31 Jan 1945	14 Mar 1945
*Hq 13th AAA Group	26 Feb 1945	-
*478th AAA AW Bn	28 Feb 1945	-
746th AAA Gun Bn	4 Mar 1945	7 Apr 1945
*236th AAA SL Bn	4 Mar 1945	-
*Hq 198th AAA Group	7 Mar 1945	-
*925th AAA AW Bn	7 Mar 1945	-
*967th AAA Gun Bn	10 Mar 1945	-
*199th AAA AW Bn	11 Mar 1945	-
*Hq 15th AAA Group	21 Jun 1945	-
Btry B, 227th AAA SL Bn	3 Jul 1945	-
945th AAA AW Bn	13 Jul 1945	-
528th AAA Gun Bn	2 Aug 1945	-

76. Mindoro

	From	To
*202d AAA AW Bn	15 Dec 1944	14 Mar 1945
*Btry B, 237th AAA SL Bn	16 Dec 1944	27 Feb 1945
*Hq 94th AAA Group	30 Dec 1944	
*Btries B and C, 102d AAA AW Bn	30 Dec 1944	
*Hq 102d AAA AW Bn	11 Feb 1945	

	From	To
*205th AAA AW Bn	17 Mar 1945	
*Hq 116th AAA Group	5 Apr 1945	17 Apr 1945
*487th AAA AW Bn	6 Apr 1945	

77. Palawan

	From	To
*Btry A, 166th AAA Gun Bn	25 Feb 1945	17 Jul 1945
*476th AAA AW Bn less Btries C and D	28 Feb 1945	16 Jul 1945
*Det of Btry D, 237th AAA SL Bn	1 Mar 1945	

78. Zamboanga

	From	To
*Hq and Btries C and D, 166th AAA Gun Bn	10 Mar 1945	17 Jul 1945
*202d AAA AW Bn	14 Mar 1945	-
*Btries A and B, 166th AAA Gun Bn	10 Mar 1945	-
476th AAA AW Bn	17 Jul 1945	-
Hq 33d AAA Group	17 Jul 1945	-

79. Mindanao

	From	To
*Det of Btry B, 237th AAA SL Bn	17 Apr 1945	-
*Hq 116th AAA Group	17 Apr 1945	-
*487th AAA AW Bn	17 Apr 1945	-
*Btry B, 166th AAA Gun Bn	17 Apr 1945	-
*496th AAA Gun Bn	3 May 1945	-
*383d AAA Gun Bn	3 May 1945	-
*Btry B, 222d AAA SL Bn	3 May 1945	-

80. Panay

	From	To
*470th AAA AW Bn	27 Mar 1945	21 Apr 1945
739th AAA Gun Bn	22 Jul 1945	
Btry A, 233d AAA SL Bn	23 Jul 1945	

81. Cebu

	From	To
*478th AAA AW Bn	26 Mar 1945	
*746th AAA Gun Bn	8 Apr 1945	

82. Negros

	From	To
*739th AAA Gun Bn	17 Apr 1945	22 Jul 1945
*Hq and Btries A and B, 470th AAA AW Bn	21 Apr 1945	22 Jul 1945

XI

Luzon

83. Luzon

Unit	Date	
*Hq 68th AAA Brigade	9 Jan 1945	-
*Hq 197th AAA Group	9 Jan 1945	-
*Hq 251st AAA Group	9 Jan 1945	-
*Hq 70th AAA Gun Bn	9 Jan 1945	-
*Hq 161st AAA Gun Bn	9 Jan 1945	-
*Hq 198th AAA AW Bn	9 Jan 1945	-
*209th AAA AW Bn	9 Jan 1945	-
*470th AAA AW Bn	9 Jan 1945	-
*951st AAA AW Bn	9 Jan 1945	-
*Hq and Btry C, 222d AAA SL Bn	9 Jan 1945	-
*373d AAA SL Bn	11 Jan 1945	-
*707th AAA MG Btry	11 Jan 1945	-
*708th AAA MG Btry	11 Jan 1945	-
*469th AAA AW Bn	16 Jan 1945	-
*518th AAA Gun Bn	25 Jan 1945	-
*Hq 14th AAA Group	25 Jan 1945	-
*471st AAA AW Bn	22 Jan 1945	-
*Btry C, 227th AAA SL Bn	29 Jan 1945	-
*950th AAA AW Bn	29 Jan 1945	-
*210th AAA AW Bn	29 Jan 1945	-
*508th AAA Gun Bn	9 Jan 1945	-
*Hq 120th AAA Group	29 Jan 1945	-
*382d AAA AW Bn	6 Feb 1945	-
*Btry A, 102d AAA AW Bn	6 Feb 1945	-
*382d AAA AW Bn	13 Feb 1945	-
*Hq 102d AAA Brigade	9 Mar 1945	-
*Hq 6th AAA Group	9 Mar 1945	-
*Hq 35th AAA Group	9 Mar 1945	-
*507th AAA Gun Bn	13 Mar 1945	-
*101st AAA AW Bn	14 Mar 1945	-
*Hq and Btry A, 227th AAA SL Bn	22 Mar 1945	-
*163d AAA Gun Bn	22 Mar 1945	-
*Hq 119th AAA Group	24 Mar 1945	-
*513th AAA Gun Bn	25 Mar 1945	-
*472d AAA AW Bn	27 Mar 1945	-
*734th AAA Gun Bn	31 Mar 1945	-
350th AAA SL Bn	7 Apr 1945	-
Hq, 40th AAA Brigade	9 Apr 1945	-
*362d AAA SL Bn	21 Apr 1945	-
737th AAA Gun Bn	12 May 1945	-
725th AAA SL Btry	12 May 1945	-

	From	To
104th AAA AW Bn*	22 Jun 1945	-
745th AAA Gun Bn	24 Jun 1945	-
Hq 14th AA Command	27 Jun 1945	-
743d AAA Gun Bn	14 Jul 1945	-
497th AAA Gun Bn	27 Jun 1945	-
736th AAA Gun Bn	15 Jul 1945	-
233d AAA SL Bn less Btry A	16 Jul 1945	-
389th AAA AW Bn	20 Jul 1945	-
229th AAA SL Bn	24 Jul 1945	-
742d AAA Gun Bn	11 Aug 1945	-
Hq 76th AAA Group	11 Aug 1945	-
Hq 117th AAA Group	11 Aug 1945	-
250th AAA SL Bn less Btry A	27 Aug 1945	-
709th AAA MG Btry	27 Aug 1945	-

XII

Ryukyus

84. **Ryukyus**

	From	To
861st AAA AW Bn	1 Apr 1945	-
485th AAA AW Bn	1 Apr 1945	-
502d AAA Gun Bn	2 Apr 1945	-
504th AAA Gun Bn	2 Apr 1945	-
Hq 97th AAA Group	3 Apr 1945	-
Hq and Btry A, 230th AAA SL Bn	3 Apr 1945	-
Btry A, 295th AAA SL Bn	3 Apr 1945	-
Btry C, 294th AAA SL Bn	3 Apr 1945	-
93d AAA Gun Bn	3 Apr 1945	-
7th AAA AW Bn	27 Mar 1945	-
866th AAA AW Bn	5 Apr 1945	-
Hq 53d AAA Brigade	8 Apr 1945	-
834th AAA AW Bn	27 Apr 1945	-
Hq 136th AAA Group	27 Apr 1945	-
Hq 137th AAA Group	3 May 1945	-
505th AAA Gun Bn	3 May 1945	-
870th AAA AW Bn	10 May 1945	-
388th AAA AW Bn	18 May 1945	-
948th AAA Gun Bn	2 Jun 1945	-
98th AAA Gun Bn	7 Jun 1945	-
Btry A, 250th AAA SL Bn	7 Jun 1945	-
Hq 44th AAA Group	8 Jun 1945	-
503d AAA Gun Bn	23 Jun 1945	-
Hq 43d AAA Group	5 Jul 1945	-
369th AAA Gun Bn	Jul 1945	-
514th AAA Gun Bn	Jul 1945	-
586th AAA AW Bn	Jul 1945	-

ANNEX D

ANTIAIRCRAFT ARTILLERY UNITS ENTITLED TO
BRONZE ARROWHEAD AWARD FOR
ASSAULT WAVES OF LANDING OPERATIONS

Operation	Period of Assault Phase	Units
ARAWE	15 Dec 43 – 0525 to 0900	Det Btrys C & D, 470th AAA AW Bn Hq, 236th AAA SL Bn
SAIDOR	2 Jan 44 – 0705 to 0900	Btrys B & D, 209th AAA AW Bn 743d AAA Gun Bn (less Btrys B & C)
GREEN ISLAND	15 Feb 44 – 0830 wave	Hq, 14th AAA Gp 967th AAA Gun Battalion (-Btrys C & D) Btry A, 362d AAA SL Bn
ADMIRALTY ISLANDS (LOS NEGROS)	28 Feb 44 – 0800 to 1015 29 Feb 0800 to 0900 2 Mar 0900 to 1200	Btry A, 211th AAA AW Bn Btry C, 168th AAA Gun Bn 673d AAA MG Btry
AITAPE	22 Apr 44 – 0715 to 1000 23 Apr 44 – 0700 wave	383d AAA AW Bn Btry C, 743d AAA Gun Bn
HOLLANDIA	22 Apr 44 – 0705 to 1200	Hq, 116th AAA Gp 469th AAA AW Bn 2 Sects, Btry B, 227th AAA SL Bn
TANAHMERAH BAY	22 Apr 44 – 0715 to 0815	Hq, 94th AAA Gp 104th AAA AW Bn (-Btry C) 163d AAA Gun Bn (-Btry A & D) Det, Hq, 227th AAA SL Bn Det, Btry A, 227th AAA SL Bn
ARARA (WAKDE)	17 May 44 – 0715 to 0900 18 May 1130 to 1400	Btrys B & C, 202d AAA AW Bn

Operation	Period of Assault Phase	Units
BIAK	27 May 44 - 0715 to 1500	Hq, 208th AAA Gp 476th AAA AW Bn (less Btry D & Med Det) Hq & Btry B, 165th AAA Gun Bn Det, Btry C, 236th AAA SL Bn 674th AAA MG Btry 675th AAA MG Btry
NOEMFOOR	2 July 44 - 0710 to 0950	Hq, 116th AAA Gp 487th AAA AW Bn 745th AAA Gun Bn (-Btrys A & C) 2 Sects, Btry A, 222d AAA SL Bn 707th & 708th AAA MG Btrys
MOROTAI	15 Sept 44 - 0830 to 1000	Det Hq, 214th AAA Gp 383d AAA AW Bn Btrys B & D, 744th AAA Gun Bn Det Hq, 744th AAA Gun Bn 229th AAA SL Bn (less Btry B)
LEYTE	20 Oct 44 - 1000 to 1600	Det, Hq, 32d AAA Brig Det, Hq, 25th AAA Gp 211th AAA AW Bn 469th AAA AW Bn 485th AAA AW Bn Det Hq, Btrys A & D, 168th AAA Gun Bn 502d AAA Gun Bn 504th AAA Gun Bn 1st Plat, Btry A, 230th AAA SL Bn Det, Btry C, 237th AAA SL Bn
PANOAN ISLAND	20 Oct 44 - 0900	Plat, Btry C, 210th AAA AW Bn
MONO ISLAND (TREASURY)	26 Oct 43 - 0900	198th AAA AW Bn
ORMOC	7 Dec 44 - 0707 wave	Det Hq, Btrys A & D, 7th AAA AW Bn

Operation	Period of Assault Phase	Units
MINDORO	15 Dec 44 - 0730 to 1051	Hq, 94th AAA Gp 166th AAA Gun Bn Btry B, 237th AAA SL Bn
LINGAYEN	9 Jan 45 - 0930 to 1700	Det Hq, 197th AAA Gp 198th AAA AW Bn 470th AAA AW Bn 70th AAA Gun Bn Det Hq, & Det Btry C, Med Det, 222d AAA SL Bn Det Hq, & Det Btrys A & B 373d AAA SL Bn 161st AAA Gun Bn 144th AAA Opns Det 951st AAA AW Bn
NASUGBU, LUZON	31 Jan 45 - 0815 wave	Det Hq & Btry A, 102d AAA Bn A/T 152d Abn AAA Bn (Organic unit 11th Abn Div)
BATAAN, LUZON	15 Feb 45 - 0930 wave	Btrys A & C, 950th AAA AW Bn
ZAMBOANGA	10 Mar 45 - 0930 to 1100	202d AAA AW Bn 166th AAA Gun Bn (-Btrys A & B) Btry B, 237th AAA SL Bn
CEBU	26 Mar 45 - 0830 to 1630	478th AAA AW Bn

Section II

Personnel

162. <u>General</u>. The following graphs and charts on personnel strength are based upon figures obtained from Machine Records Branch of the Office of the Adjutant General, War Department, and include all units in the Pacific. The casualty figures were obtained from the same sources and include not only those from antiaircraft units but also seacoast units. It is estimated that of the 6424 casualties incurred up to 1 Jun 1942, approximately 2950 were from seacoast units. Since the seacoast artillery casualties during the remainder of the war were neglibible, the final total of antiaircraft artillery casualties is estimated to be approximately 4900.

163. **Personnel Strength.**
   a. Pacific Theater.

AUTHORIZED AND ACTUAL AA PERSONNEL STRENGTH IN PACIFIC THEATER

T/O STRENGTH AA UNITS

ACTUAL STRENGTH

b. South Pacific.

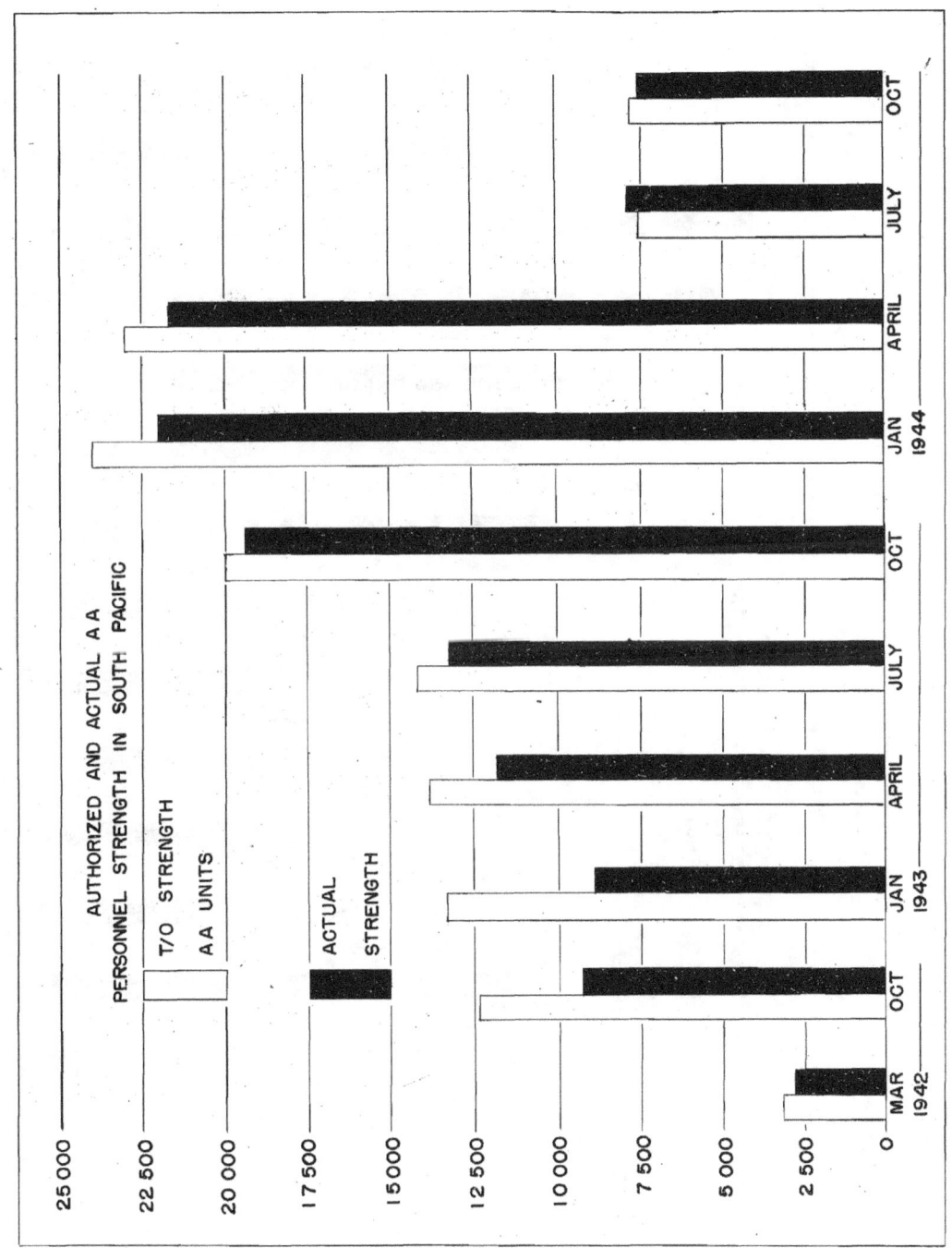

c. Middle Pacific.

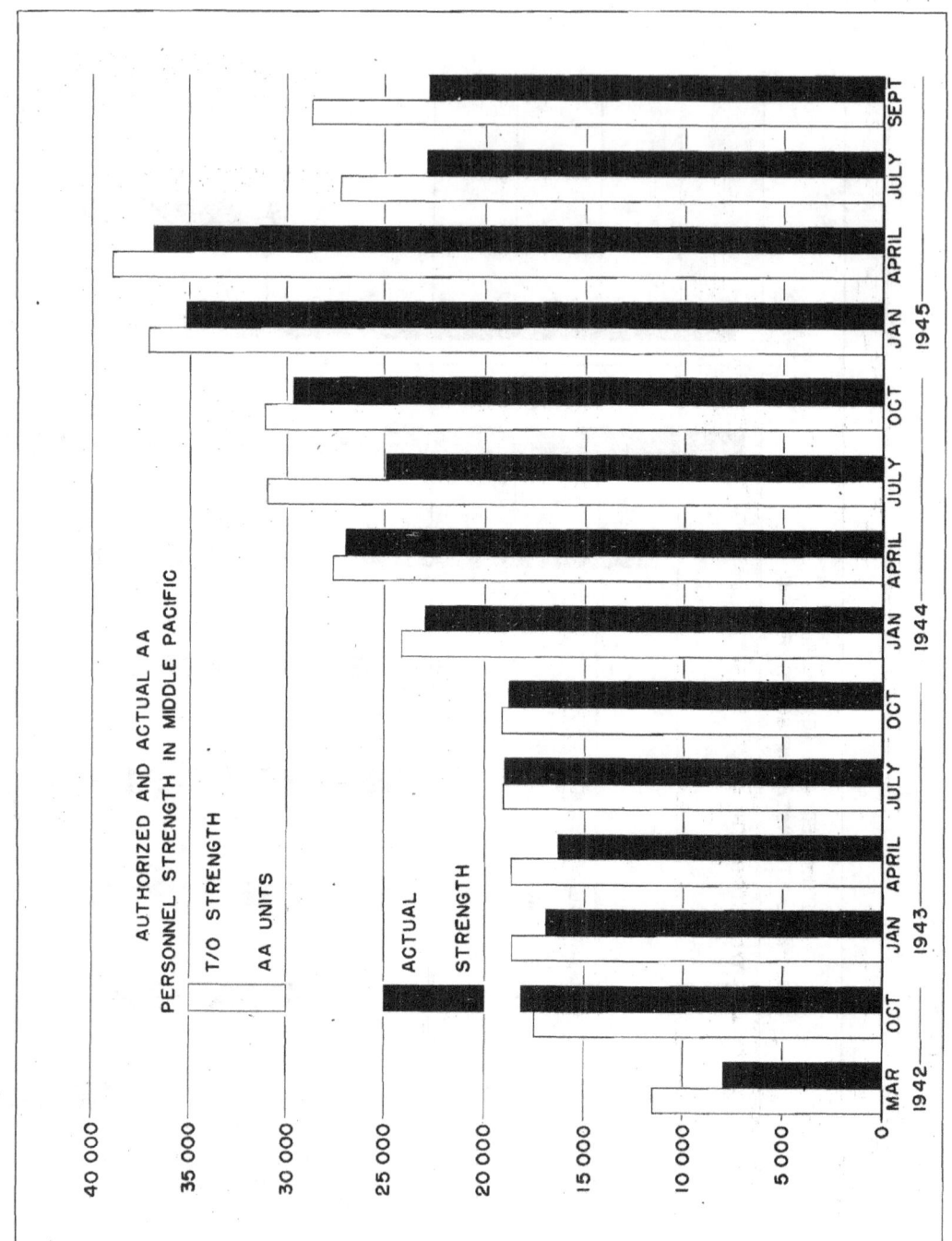

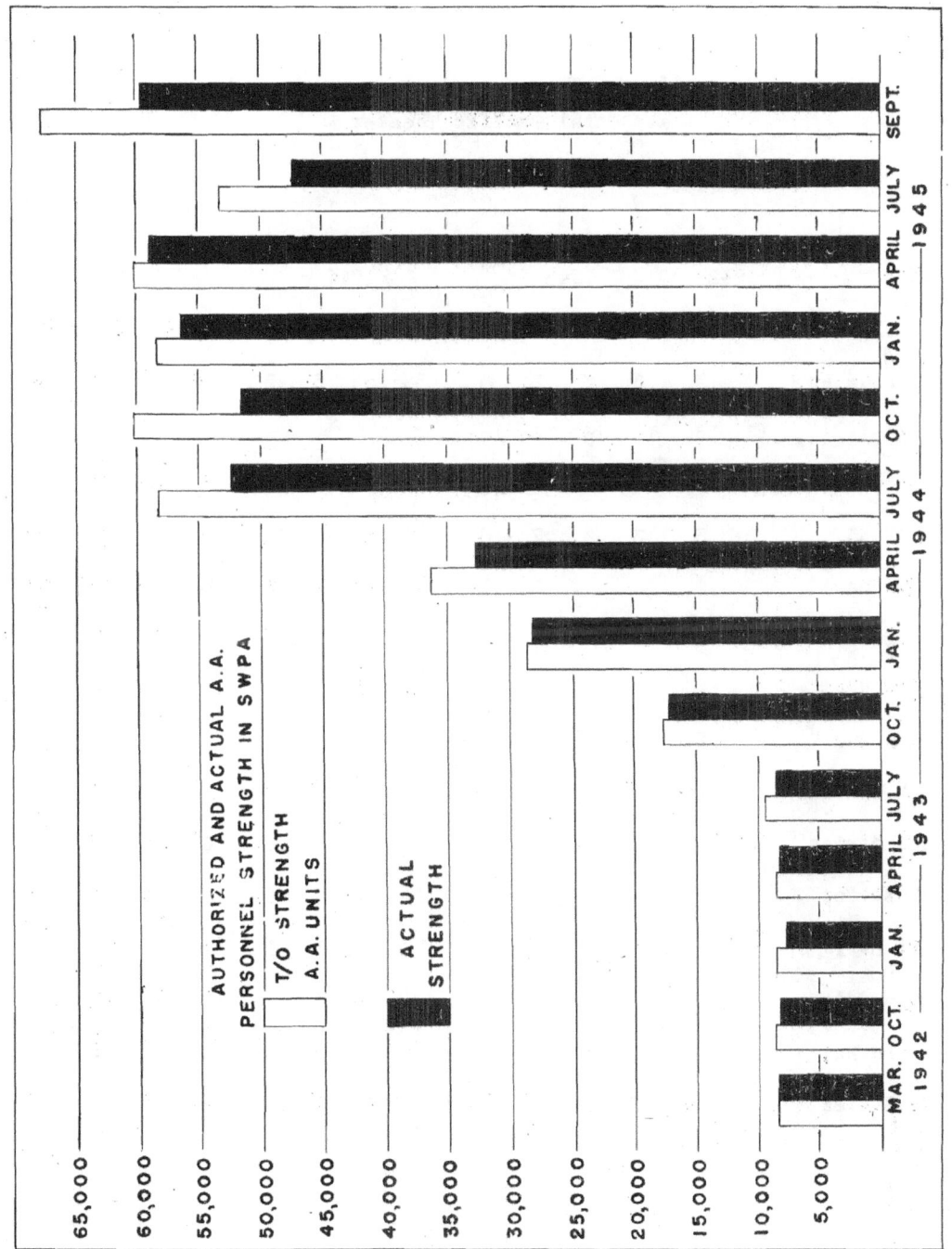

164. Units Present in Theater by Type

a. Total Pacific Theater

TYPE	1942 Mar	1942 Oct	1943 Jan	1943 Apr	1943 Jul	1943 Oct	1944 Jan	1944 Apr	1944 Jul	1944 Oct	1945 Jan	1945 Apr	1945 Jul	1945 Sept
Brigade Hq	3	3	3	3	3	5	5	5	5	5	8	8	8	8
Regts	13	16	16	16	13	13	2							
Group Hq					3	7	23	26	29	29	34	34	34	34
AW Bns	3	3	3	3	7	18	34	40	46	47	50	51	61	52
Gun Bns					3	11	36	42	45	51	53	43	53	54
SL Bns					3	5	15	19	19	20	19	16	15	15
Comp Regt					1	1	1	1						
Comp Bns		2	4	4	3	3	3	1						
Bar Bln Bns		1	1	1										
Gun Btries	6	6	6	6	6	6				6	6	6	6	6
SL Btries							3	3	3	4	5	4	4	4
Int Btry		1	1	1	1	1	1	1	1	1	1	1	1	1
Opns Dets								3	3	5	10	10	10	10
AB Bn Hq						3	3	3	2	2	2	2	2	
MG Btries		3	3	3	3	15	15	15	15	15	14	14	11	3

-256-

b. South Pacific Area

TYPE	1942		1943				1944			
	Mar	Oct	Jan	Apr	Jul	Oct	Jan	Apr	Jul	Oct
Brigade Hq						1	1	1	1	
Regts	2	6	6	6	6	6	2			
Group Hq						3	8	10	4	4
AW Bns					1	4	9	11	3	3
Gun Bns						3	11	13	4	4
SL Bns						2	5	6	3	3
SL Btries							1	1		
Opns Dets									1	
Comp Bns			2	2	2	2	2			

-257-

c. Middle Pacific Area

TYPE	1942 Mar	1942 Oct	1943 Jan	1943 Apr	1943 Jul	1943 Oct	1944 Jan	1944 Apr	1944 Jul	1944 Oct	1945 Jan	1945 Apr	1945 Jul	1945 Sept
Brigade Hq	1	1	1	1	1	1	2	2	2	2	4	4	3	3
Regts	5	7	7	7	7	7								
Group Hq							7	7	8	8	13	13	8	8
AW Bns						1	9	11	13	14	19	20	12	12
Gun Bns							16	18	21	24	24	15	18	16
SL Bns							4	5	5	5	5	5	3	3
Bar Bln Bns		1	1	1	1								1	1
Comp Regt				1	1	1	1							
Comp Bns		2	2	2	1	1	1	1						
Int Btry		1	1	1	1	1	1	1	1	1	1	1	1	1
Gun Btries		6	6	6	6	6				6	6	6	6	6
SL Btries								2	2	2	3	3	3	3	3
Opns Dets										3	2	2	2	1	1

d. Southwest Pacific Area

TYPE	1942		1943				1944				1945			
	Mar	Oct	Jan	Apr	Jul	Oct	Jan	Apr	Jul	Oct	Jan	Apr	Jul	Sept
Brigade Hq	2	2	2	2	2	3	2	2	2	3	4	4	5	5
Regts	6	3	3	3										
Group Hq					3	4	8	9	17	17	21	21	26	26
AW Bns	3	3	3	3	6	13	16	18	30	30	31	31	39	40
Gun Bns					3	8	9	11	22	23	29	28	35	38
SL Bns					3	3	6	8	11	12	14	11	12	12
SL Btries									1	1	2	1	1	1
Opns Dets										3	8	8	9	9
AB Bn Hq						3	3	3	2	2	2	2	2	
MG Btries		3	3	3	3	15	15	15	15	15	14	14	11	3

-259-

165. COAST ARTILLERY CORPS CASUALTIES IN THE PACIFIC

DATE OF CASUALTY	KILLED IN ACTION (1)	WOUNDED (OR INJURED) IN ACTION						CAPTURED OR INTERNED						MISSING IN ACTION				TOTAL (18)	GRAND TOTAL (19)
		Died of Wounds (2)	Returned to Duty (3)	Evacuated to U.S. (4)	Wounded (Missing in Action Status) (5)	Wounded (Current Status) (6)	TOTAL (7)	Died of Wounds (8)	Died of Other Causes (9)	Returned to Military Control (10)	Prisoners of War (11)	Interned (12)	TOTAL (13)	Declared Dead (14)	Determined Dead (15)	Returned to Duty (16)	Missing in Action (Current Status) (17)		
1941																			
December — Officers	1		0	0	0		0		0	0	0		0					0	1
December — Enlisted	33		22	8	4		34		1	2	2		3					3	70
1942																			
January — Officers	2	1	1		1		3		1	0	0		1			0		1	6
January — Enlisted	49	1	24		7		32		1	2	2		3			1		5	86
February — Officers	1		0		0		0		0	0	0		0					0	1
February — Enlisted	2		5		9		14		2	4	2		4					4	20
March — Officers	0		1	0	0		1		0	0	0		0					0	1
March — Enlisted	21		20	1	1		21		2	2	2		4					4	46
April — Officers	6	0	0	0	0		0		0	0	0		0					0	6
April — Enlisted	64	8	38	1	6		47		6	14	14		20				1	21	132
May — Officers	12	1	0	0	0		1	1	161	144			306	2	0	2	5	315	328
May — Enlisted	60	32	36	6	6		80	19	1,165	3,789			4,973	44	123	197	250	5,587	5,727
June — Officers							0						0					0	0
June — Enlisted				1			1		2				2					2	3
July — Officers							0			1			1					1	0
July — Enlisted				1			1		2				2			1		3	4
August — Officers	0						0			1			1					1	0
August — Enlisted	1						0		2				2					3	3
September — Officers	0		0				0						0					0	0
September — Enlisted	2		1				0		1				1					1	2
October — Officers				0			0						0					0	0
October — Enlisted				1			1						0					1	1
November — Officers	2		0				0						0					0	2
November — Enlisted	4		1				1						0					0	5
December — Officers	0						0						0					0	0
December — Enlisted				1			1		1				1					4	2

DATE OF CASUALTY	KILLED IN ACTION	WOUNDED (OR INJURED) IN ACTION						CAPTURED OR INTERNED				MISSING IN ACTION						GRAND TOTAL
		Died of Wounds	Returned to Duty	Evac- uated to U.S.	Wounded (Missing in Action Status)	Wounded (Current Status)	TOTAL	Died of Wounds	Died of Other Causes	Returned to Military Control	Prisoners of War	In- ternment	TOTAL	Declared Dead	Deter- mined Dead	Returned to Duty	Missing in Action (Current Status)	TOTAL
	(1)	(2)	(3)	(4)	(5)	(6)	(7)	(8)	(9)	(10)	(11)	(12)	(13)	(14)	(15)	(16)	(17)	(18)	(19)
1943																			
January Officers	0	0	0	0			0		0	0			0	0				0	0
Enlisted	0	1	4	3			8		1	1			2	1				3	11
February Officers	0		0	0			0		1				1					1	1
Enlisted	0		1	2			3		0				0					0	3
March Officers	0		0				0												0
Enlisted	9		7				7												18
April Officers	0		0				0		1	0			0	0				0	1
Enlisted	1		6				9		0	2			2	2				0	10
May Officers			0				0		1	0			1				6	6	6
Enlisted			1				1		15	1			16				54	70	71
June Officers	0		0				0		0							0		0	0
Enlisted	1		7				7		1							1		3	11
July Officers			0	0			0						0					0	0
Enlisted			5	3			8						1					1	9
August Officers	0	0	0	0			0												0
Enlisted	0	1	5	1			6												6
September Officers	0		0	0			0												0
Enlisted	1		1	1			2												3
October Officers	0		0	0			0												0
Enlisted	6		1	5			6												12
November Officers	0		1	1			2												2
Enlisted	3		4	0			4												7
December Officers	0		2	0			2												2
Enlisted	4		14	9			23												27

DATE OF CASUALTY	KILLED IN ACTION (1)	WOUNDED (OR INJURED) IN ACTION						CAPTURED OR INTERNED						MISSING IN ACTION					GRAND TOTAL (19)
		Died of Wounds (2)	Returned to Duty (3)	Evacuated to U.S. (4)	Wounded (Missing in Action Status) (5)	Wounded (Current Status) (6)	TOTAL (7)	Died of Wounds (8)	Died of Other Causes (9)	Returned to Military Control (10)	Prisoners of War (11)	Interned (12)	TOTAL (13)	Declared Dead (14)	Determined Dead (15)	Returned to Duty (16)	Missing in Action (Current Status) (17)	TOTAL (18)	
1944																			
January Officers	0	0	0	0	0		0												0
Enlisted	1	3	15	2	1		21												22
February Officers	1	0	1				1												2
Enlisted	1	1	2				3												4
March Officers	3	0	1	1			2												5
Enlisted	12	3	25	11	2		41												53
April Officers	0	0	0	0	0		0												0
Enlisted	10	1	19	2	1		23												33
May Officers	0	1	1	1	0	0	3		0	0			0					0	3
Enlisted	9	0	18	8	1	2	27		1	2			3					3	39
June Officers	1	0	1	0	0		1		0	0			0					0	2
Enlisted	6	3	11	9	2		25		1	1			2					2	31
July Officers	0	0	1	0	0	0	2		0	0			0					0	2
Enlisted	3	3	3	3	2	4	8		1	1			2					2	13
August Officers	0	0	0				0												0
Enlisted	3	1	10				15												18
September Officers	0	0	0			0	0												0
Enlisted	14	1	6			4	6												22
October Officers	0	0	4	3			7												7
Enlisted	16	6	57	27			90												106
November Officers	0	0	1	0		0	1												1
Enlisted	2	0	18	28		4	50												52
December Officers	3	0	4	1		1	7												10
Enlisted	21	1	55	39		4	109												130

DATE OF CASUALTY	KILLED IN ACTION	WOUNDED (OR INJURED) IN ACTION						CAPTURED OR INTERNED					MISSING IN ACTION						GRAND TOTAL
		Died of Wounds	Returned to Duty	Evacuated to U.S.	Wounded (Missing in Action Status)	Wounded (Current Status)	TOTAL	Died of Wounds	Died of Other Causes	Returned to Military Control	Prisoners of War	Interned	TOTAL	Declared Dead	Determined Dead	Returned to Duty	Missing in Action (Current Status)	TOTAL	
	(1)	(2)	(3)	(4)	(5)	(6)	(7)	(8)	(9)	(10)	(11)	(12)	(13)	(14)	(15)	(16)	(17)	(18)	(19)
1945																			
January Officers	0	0	1	2			3						0					0	3
Enlisted	4	1	13	3			17						1					1	22
February Officers	1	0	2	0		1	3		0	0			0					0	4
Enlisted	6	2	8	10		2	22		1	1			2					2	30
March Officers	0	0	0	0		0	0												0
Enlisted	9	1	13	11		1	26												35
April Officers	1	0	5	1		0	6												7
Enlisted	10	9	43	21		26	99										1	1	110
May Officers	0	0	3	1		1	5										2	2	7
Enlisted	5	5	23	7		6	41										1	1	47
June Officers	2	1	0	0		0	1												3
Enlisted	21	5	9	9		5	28												50
July Officers	0		0	0		0	0												0
Enlisted	1		5	6		3	14										1	1	15
August Officers		0	0	0		0	0												0
Enlisted		1	1	1		2	4												4
Date Unknown Officers	0	0		0	0	0	0		22	0			22			2	0	22	22
Enlisted	2	1		2	1	2	4		252	9			261			199	3	264	270
AGGREGATE																			
Officers	36	5	30	12	1	3	51	1	186	144			331	2	0	2	13	348	435
Enlisted	417	96	557	244	35	59	991	19	1,456	3,833			5,308	47	123	199	313	5,990	7,398
TOTAL	453	101	587	256	36	62	1,042	20	1,642	3,977			5,639	49	123	201	326	6,338	7,833

The Adjutant General's Office
Machine Records Branch
7 March 1946

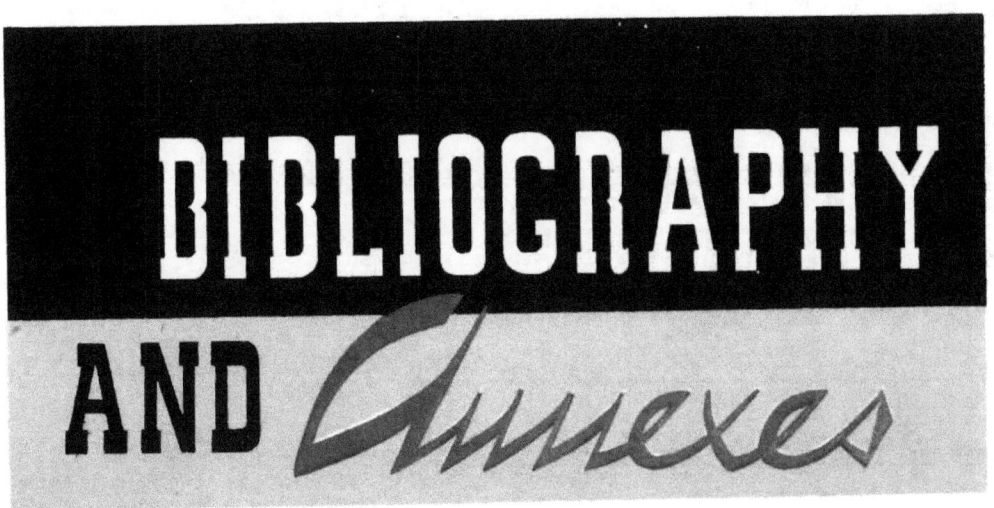

BIBLIOGRAPHY

<u>Report of Performance of Coast Artillery Personnel and Equipment in the Philippine Campaign</u> - General MacArthur, File AG 384.7, 27 May 1942.

<u>Memorandum to Ass't Chief of Staff, G-1, USAFFE</u> from Commanding General, Philippine Defense Command. 8 September 1941.

<u>Antiaircraft Artillery in the Philippines</u> - 20 September 1943 - Lt. Col. S. M. Mellnik, File 314.7, Military Intelligence Division, WDGS, Special Report Philippine Islands.

<u>Daily Action Reports</u> - File AAO, GHQ, SWPA.

<u>Chronological Reports of Raids</u> - G-3, 14th AA Command.

<u>Aircraft Destroyed</u> - File 370.2 AAO, GHQ, SWPA.

<u>Seacoast and Antiaircraft Artillery Operations in the Pacific Area During World War II</u> - Hq, MIDPAC. 20 Nov 1945.

<u>Antiaircraft Artillery Operations</u> - Sixth Army. January 1946.

<u>Antiaircraft Artillery Operations</u> - Eighty Army. 26 December 1944 to 4 July 1945.

<u>Tenth Army Antiaircraft Artillery Action Report of Operations in the Ryukyus Campaign</u>. 26 March to 30 June 1945.

Quarterly Report (s) of Antiaircraft Artillery Operations, 14th Antiaircraft Command. December 1943 to July 1945.

Report of Enemy Aircraft Destruction, 1 Sept 1944 to 31 Dec 1944, prepared by G-2, 14th Antiaircraft Command.

Analysis of Enemy Air Raids, 1 Jan 1945 to 24 Jan 1945, dtd, 25 Feb 1945, prepared by G-2, 14th Antiaircraft Command.

History of G-3 Section, 14th Antiaircraft Command.

History of G-4 Section, 14th Antiaircraft Command.

Report - Modification of M-9 Director to give Prediction on Curved Courses of Enemy Targets, Hq 14th Antiaircraft Command, 3 Sept 1945.

Employment of SCR 584 for the Detection of Ground Targets, Training Circular Number 19, Hq 14th Antiaircraft Command, 19 October 1945.

Report - Standard Operating Procedures of Calculations and Analysis of Evasive Action Data, Hq 14th Antiaircraft Command.

Combat Operations Reports - G-3, 14th Antiaircraft Command.

AAAIS and AAOR Report - G-2 Section, 14th Antiaircraft Command.

Flakintel Instructions, Hq Allied Air Forces, APO 925, 1 Sept 1943.

Flakintel Instructions No. 2, Analytical study of Japanese Antiaircraft Artillery.

Flakintel Instructions No. 3, Area Reports.

Flakintel Bulletin No. 1, Hq Allied Air Force, APO 925, December 1943.

Flakintel Handbook, 1 August 1944.

Reports of AA Observers on Task Force Operations, File AAO, GHQ, SWPA.

S-3 Reports, 32d Brigade.

Disassembly and Loading of 90-mm AA Gun for Shipment by Air in C-47 Aircraft, 40th CA Brigade.

Report After Action Against the Enemy, 53d Antiaircraft Artillery Brigade, Phase I, Nansei Shoto Operation, 8 September 1945.

Report of Enemy Aircraft Destroyed by AAA Fire in Leyte Operation. (Revised), 13 March 1945, 32d Brigade.

Historical Report of M-1 Operation, 68th AAA Brigade.

Morotai Combat File, 40th AAA Brigade.

History of 60th Coast Artillery (AA), File 500-5-1, Recovered Personnel Section, AFWESPAC.

History of 60th Coast Artillery (AA), File 500-5-3, Recovered Personnel Section, AFWESPAC.

History of Corregidor and Bataan - File 520-22, Recovered Personnel Section, AFWESPAC.

History of 200th Coast Artillery (AA) (including 515th Coast Artillery (AA)) File 500-4, Recovered Personnel Section, AFWESPAC.

Report - Evasive Action Studies at Morotai, Commanding Officer, 214th AAA Group, 6 November 1945.

The AAA Defense of Morotai, NEI, 214th AAA Group, 5 January 1945.

Combat Operations Report, 15 Sept 1945, Schouten Islands, 208th AAA Group.

SOP for Loading 40-mm Bofors in C-47 Transport, 745th AAA Gun Bn.

Report on Loading 40-mm Gun, Mount M-5 for Air Movement, 102d AAA AW Bn.

Final Combat Report (Biak), 165th AAA Gun Bn.

Report of Air Movement, 102d CA Bn (AA), 15 April 1942.

Report of Airborne Operations of the 211th AAA AW Bn, 20 Nov 1945.

Narrative Report of Experiments AA Radar with Field Artillery Plane - 116th Field Artillery made to Commanding General, 14th AA Command, 9 December 1944, File AARO 413.68.

Unit Histories of the 32d, 40th, 41st, 53d, 68th, and 102d AAA Brigades.

Unit Histories of the 6th, 10th, 13th, 14th, 15th, 25th, 33d, 35th, 43d, 44th, 70th, 76th, 77th, 94th, 97th, 116th, 117th, 119th, 120th, 136th, 197th, 198th, 208th, 214th, and 251st AAA Groups.

Unit Histories of the 7th, 101st, 102d, 104th, 198th, 199th, 202d, 205th, 207th, 208th, 209th, 210th, 211th, 382d, 383d, 389th, 395th, 466th, 469th, 470th, 471st, 472d, 475th, 476th, 477th, 478th, 487th, 586th, 779th, 785th, 834th, 861st, 866th, 870th, 925th, 933d, 938th, 945th, 950th, and 951st AAA AW Battalions.

Unit Histories of the 63d, 70th, 76th, 77th, 93d, 100th, 161st, 163d, 164th, 165th, 166th, 168th, 496th, 497th, 502d, 503d, 504th, 507th, 508th, 510th, 513th, 514th, 518th, 528th, 734th, 736th, 737th, 739th, 741st, 742d, 743d, 744th, 745th, 746th, 948th, and 967th AAA Gun Battalions.

Unit Histories of the 222d, 224th, 227th, 229th, 230th, 233d, 237th, Btry A 250th, 294th, 295th, 325th, 350th, 356th, 373d, 374th AAA SL Battalions and 725th AAA SL Btry (Sep).

Unit Histories of the 662d, 665th, 670th, 671st, 672d, 674th, 675th, 707th, 708th, and 709th AAA Machine Gun Batteries.

Unit Histories of the 3d and 9th AAA AB Battalions.

Unit Histories of the 143d, 144th, 145th, 146th, 156th, 158th, 159th, and 160th AAA Operations Detachments.

www.ingramcontent.com/pod-product-compliance
Lightning Source LLC
Chambersburg PA
CBHW060230240426
43671CB00016B/2900